STEPHEN DOUGLAS

The Last Years, 1857–1861

COURTESY CHICAGO HISTORICAL SOCIETY

One of Douglas' last photographs, probably May, 1861.

Stephen Douglas

The Last Years, 1857–1861

By Damon Wells

UNIVERSITY OF TEXAS PRESS, AUSTIN

International Standard Book Number 0-292-77635-7
Library of Congress Catalog Card Number 73-149020

Printed in the United States of America

First Paperback Printing, 1990

♾ The paper used in this publication meets the minimum requirements of American National Standard for Information Sciences—Permanence of Paper for Printed Library Materials, ANSI Z39.48-1984.

TO FRANK VANDIVER

CONTENTS

ILLUSTRATIONS

PREFACE

My interest in Stephen Douglas goes back to the evening in 1959 when I watched a Broadway dramatization of the Lincoln-Douglas Debates. The performance was entertaining enough, but I left the theater with the uneasy feeling that the playwright felt that in order to make Abraham Lincoln a hero, he had to make Stephen Douglas a villain.

American historiography has often suffered from the same assumption. There seemed to me to be serious discrepancies between the picture of Douglas that emerged from reading the text of the debates themselves and the much less favorable one gathered from a study of their commentators. Historians as a rule proved unusually harsh toward the man. I felt there was a need for a fresh and impartial look at the debates from Douglas' point of view.

I soon discovered that the story of the 1858 senatorial campaign in Illinois could not be properly told without an analysis of the principle of popular sovereignty, which was the key plank in the Douglas platform. In turn Douglas' defense of popular sovereignty could not be adequately understood without reference to his long quarrel with President James Buchanan over the interpretation and application of the principle. Thus the decision to begin this study with the year 1857.

At the suggestion of Professor Frank Vandiver I then decided to carry Douglas' story forward from the 1858 debates to the time of his death in 1861. I have never regretted that decision. The period 1857–1861 was not only the most crucial time in the career of Stephen Douglas, it was the most critical era in the history of the American nation. During these years Douglas had to choose between answering the urgent problems posed by sectionalism and slavery with new and imaginative solutions or clinging to stale outlooks and formulae, between being a positive force on the national scene or becoming a political anachronism. America too had important decisions to make. During the greater part of these years it could still choose between the adjustment of sectional differences and civil war.

This is basically a political biography. I have dealt with the details of Douglas' private and family life, and with his position on economic issues such as tariffs and public improvements, only insofar as they illuminate his response to the larger questions of slavery, sectionalism, secession, and civil war.

Chapter 1 is a brief summary of Douglas' life prior to 1857. Chapter 2 deals with the Buchanan-Douglas feud and is principally concerned with events from late 1857 to mid-1858. Chapter 3 is an analysis of the principle of popular sovereignty. Chapter 4 discusses the Lincoln-Douglas Debates and the Illinois senatorial election of November, 1858. Each of the next three chapters is concerned with one year in the life of Stephen Douglas. Each attempts to weave a study of his policy, strategy, and tactics around the central events or themes which characterized that year. Chapter 5 deals with the increasing difficulty Douglas encountered in 1859 in continuing to try to play the role of a national political figure in a sectional age. It focuses on the Dorr Letter, the *Harper's Magazine* article, the Ohio campaigns, and Douglas' reaction to John Brown's raid on Harpers Ferry. Chapter 6 discusses Douglas' position in the Democratic conventions at Charleston and Baltimore, and his campaign for the presidency in 1860. Chapter 7 begins with Douglas' return to Washington in December of 1860 following his defeat by Lincoln in the presidential race. It is concerned largely with Douglas' efforts to forestall secession and civil war, and concludes with his strong support of President Lincoln and the Union cause when all attempts at peace had failed. In Chapter 8 I have attempted to draw some conclusions from my study of Douglas.

I confess to being an admirer of Stephen Douglas; I trust that I have not become an apologist for him. While I have little sympathy for those historians who, like James Ford Rhodes, adopt an attitude of thinly disguised hostility toward Douglas, I cannot go to the other extreme and agree with George Fort Milton, who seems to feel that if left alone, Douglas could have almost singlehandedly prevented the Civil War. My estimate of Douglas lies somewhere in between, but I am not in agreement with those contemporary historians who seem to think that a fairer and more moderate assessment can be reached simply by endorsing apparently contradictory views of Douglas.

I have not sought to disregard Douglas' shortcomings, but I have tried to impose some pattern upon them and to discover why his career was a compound of resounding successes in the short run and heartbreaking failures over a longer period of time.

In the last analysis it seems to me that Douglas was for too long out of step with his times. His intense involvement with the American political scene—his great accomplishments in enacting the Compromises of 1850 and 1854, in the successful fight against Lecompton, and in the senatorial campaign of 1858—tended at times to disguise a growing and more fundamental alienation from the mainstream of American political life. By the time our study opens in 1857, that alienation had reached acute proportions. There was more motion than ever in Douglas' public life, but less positive action and lasting accomplishment.

In part, Douglas fell victim to his own virtues. He sought to be a nationalist in an age of sectionalism; he preached the value of compromise when most Americans suspected the notion.

In other respects, Douglas' political failures are less excusable. His refusal to condemn slavery publicly placed him at odds with the growing feeling of revulsion people in the North were coming to have toward the peculiar institution. His attempt to convert his attitude of professed amorality into a principle—popular sovereignty—found him dismissed by antislavery men as immoral and by proslavery men as unreliable. For too long, Douglas, professing to "care not" about the future of slavery, overlooked how much

Americans could care once their consciences had been aroused or their way of life supposedly threatened. He failed to win the great fight of his career, the presidential campaign of 1860, largely because he could satisfy neither the proponents nor the enemies of slavery.

Yet if Douglas was during the last years of his life in some respects a failure, he was not ultimately the tragic figure some historians have suggested. During the campaign of 1860 a profound change began to take place in Stephen Douglas. The old outmoded nationalism he had preached for so long began to give way to Unionism. The attack on Fort Sumter completed the transformation. It was not so much that in the end the statesman in Douglas vanquished Douglas-the-politician. That contest had always been heavily weighted in favor of the former. But for the first time in many years the whole of the statesman's policy was in tune with his age. The long, frustrating search for compromise was over. The need to appear to deny the interests of his own section in favor of appeasing the South and the tiresome espousal of a principle of dubious value could now be forgotten. In the support of President Lincoln and the defense of the Union, Douglas had found a policy worthy of his great talents.

D.W.

ACKNOWLEDGMENTS

I want to express my appreciation to the staff of the Fondren Library at Rice University for their unfailing co-operation in the research and preparation of this work. Particular thanks are due to Mrs. Marvine Brand, Mrs. Mary Holien, Mrs. Monika Orr, Miss Gylene Wilcox, Mr. James Dyson, Mr. James Mayfield, and Mr. Richard Perrine.

In Washington, the staff of the Readers, Manuscript, and Rare Book Divisions of the Library of Congress afforded much valuable assistance. Miss Mary Johnson and Mr. Karl Trever helped to unlock many of the treasures of the National Archives.

The staff of the American History Room of the New York Public Library provided me with much material not readily available elsewhere.

In Richmond, the librarians at the Virginia Historical Society and the Virginia State Library made my visit to their gracious old city not only delightful but productive.

Mr. J. Donald Thomas and his assistants at the Harper Library of the University of Chicago granted me access to the Douglas Papers and were unfailing in helping me wend my way through that massive collection.

At the Huntington Library, Miss Janet Hawkins and Mrs. Barbara Boucot went out of their way to be helpful.

Mr. Hugh G. Grubbs, County Clerk of Young County, Texas, went to considerable trouble in searching for the records of Douglas' landholdings during the early days of Texas. Mr. James R. Gough, Chief, Appellate Division, United States Attorney's Office,

Southern District of Texas, was of inestimable help in clearing up difficult points of constitutional and statute law relative to the President's power to suppress an insurrection in a state. My sincere thanks to both of these men.

During a delightful week that I had at the Huntington Library in the spring of 1967, Professor Allan Nevins spent many hours with me discussing my project. His helpfulness and encouragement have provided me with some very pleasant memories.

I would like to say a word of thanks to Professor R. John Rath, who, as Chairman of the Department of History at Rice University, guided my graduate work with unfailing interest and consideration.

Professor Joseph A. Ward, Jr., of the English Department at Rice read my manuscript and made many valuable suggestions that greatly improved the final version. In the History Department, Professor S. W. Higginbotham's careful and rigorous criticisms improved many parts of the study. The late Professor Andrew Forest Muir gave freely of his vast knowledge of historical style and technique in a spirit of helpfulness. I am deeply indebted to him.

Professor Frank E. Vandiver, my thesis director, was largely responsible for my undertaking the Ph.D. program at Rice and for encouraging me to stay with it. He went over my manuscript with painstaking care and offered many excellent suggestions for improving both style and content. Always his advice took the form of constructive criticism. For a Jefferson Davis scholar to be tolerant of a Douglas theme is asking a great deal; for him to be encouraging, as Professor Vandiver was, is surely magnanimity.

I want to add a final and very special word of appreciation to Mrs. Dan Deerman, who not only typed the manuscript, but made many helpful suggestions on points of style and grammar. My debt to her is a large one.

STEPHEN DOUGLAS

The Last Years, 1857–1861

1. The Return of a Champion

The little man pulled back the heavy red curtain and the pale first rays of dawn brought a faint glow of color to the green and mahogany and brass of the compartment. He took a towel and began to wipe away the moisture that had gathered on the glass and now he could see the waters of the lake, gray and heavy in the early light, stretching away toward the horizon. He knew that was Lake Erie out there and that the train had made good time in the night over the rails of the Michigan Southern, that Cleveland was far behind, and that he was now in the heart of his beloved Northwest.[1]

He took out one of the long Havana cigars he loved and examined it carefully.[2] In a little while the train would be coming into

[1] It was the morning of July 9, 1858. Douglas was coming from Clifton Springs in western New York state to Chicago. His route would have taken him over the rails of the New York and Erie Railroad as far as Buffalo, then via the Lake Shore Railroad to Cleveland, and finally over the Michigan Southern to Chicago. *Appleton's New and Complete United States Guide Book for Travellers* (New York, 1854). Douglas' journey largely followed the route taken today by the Penn Central from Buffalo to Chicago.

[2] For a study of some of Douglas' personal habits, see George Murray McConnel, "Recollections of Stephen A. Douglas," *Transactions of the Illinois*

Toledo and the lake would be left behind and in its place would be the rich dairy lands and orchards of Michigan and after that the green and yellow corn fields of Indiana and then, at the end of the line, Chicago, the restless, vibrant, hustling young giant of a city he had helped to build.[3] The little man lit the cigar, drew deeply upon it, and watched the heavy smoke rise toward the ceiling of the compartment. Stephen Douglas was coming home.

It had been a good trip. He had been to visit his mother in upstate New York[4] and must have been glad to exchange the frenzied, overcharged atmosphere of Washington for the rural calm of Ontario County. He had always loved the Capital with its ceaseless activity and challenge, but the Congress that had just ended had been the most bitter and exhausting he had known, and he did not want another like it soon.[5] He must have desired a long vacation or at least a few weeks of leisure in Washington, but in the end he had made a frenzied departure from the Capital only a few days after adjournment and had left behind a great deal of unfinished business.[6] Even on the way up from Washington he had to pause in New York City for a few days to mend political fences and to visit with supporters like Fernando Wood, who lent him $40,000 to finance his upcoming campaign.[7] Rest seemed to be for

State Historical Society for 1900, p. 48; Frank E. Stevens, "Life of Stephen Arnold Douglas," *Journal of the Illinois State Historical Society* 16, nos. 3–4 (October 1923 and January 1924): 350.

3 Douglas was one of the major landowners in Chicago during its early years. Robert W. Johannsen, ed., *The Letters of Stephen A. Douglas*, pp. 259, 337, 338. He was instrumental in making the city a great rail terminus; ibid., pp. 197, 221–226, and 244–245. In 1856 Douglas donated the land for the new University of Chicago; ibid., pp. 389–390, 390n. From 1849 onward Chicago was Douglas' home town.

4 Sarah Fiske Douglas, Stephen Douglas' mother, following the death of her first husband, Dr. Stephen Douglas, married Gehazi Granger and left the old Douglas homestead in Brandon, Vermont, to live in Clifton Springs, New York.

5 The 1st session of the 35th Congress had adjourned on June 14, 1858. A brief special session of the Senate was called on the fifteenth and adjourned on the sixteenth. *Cong. Globe*, 35th Cong., 1st sess., pp. 3051 and 3061.

6 Johannsen, ed., *Letters of Douglas*, p. 422.

7 Roy F. Nichols, *The Disruption of American Democracy*, p. 218; Johannsen, ed., *Letters of Douglas*, p. 422. Douglas was facing a campaign for re-election to the United States Senate from Illinois.

other people that summer. While most of his Senate colleagues were now returning to a few quiet months at their homes or to the welcome change of a law office in some great city, Stephen A. Douglas that July morning of 1858 was going back to Illinois to face the greatest challenge of his life.

It was not a new story. In more than twenty years of public life he had allowed himself only one real respite from his political labors. That had been in 1853 when he went to Europe after the death of his first wife.[8] Even if his overcrowded life had permitted more free moments, he probably would not have used them. Leisure was alien to the restless United States Senator from Illinois, who seemed to draw his strength from action and achievement. There would be no rest until the long campaign for re-election was over and the people of Illinois had returned their verdict in November. The next best thing was a long train journey like this one with its many hours of enforced idleness, the ever-changing panorama outside the compartment window, and the ceaseless motion that touched something deep and fundamental inside the little man.

He had come this way many times before. The first time there had been no railroad and he had traveled by foot and stagecoach, by flatboat and paddlewheeler, from his childhood home in Brandon, Vermont, right down to the waters of the Mississippi.[9] That had been in 1833 when he was twenty years old. He stayed in St. Louis for a few weeks, but before the year was out he recrossed the great river into Illinois, stopped briefly at Jacksonville, and finally settled in the little town of Winchester. He arrived with fifty cents in his pocket.[10] Douglas taught school to make ends meet that first cold winter on the prairie, "having during the whole time a goodly number of scholars, and giving as I believe general satisfaction to both scholars and parents."[11] But the young man grew

[8] George Fort Milton, *The Eve of Conflict*, p. 33; Johannsen, ed., *Letters of Douglas*, p. 267.

[9] Johannsen, ed., *Letters of Douglas*, pp. 59–62, 324, 444–445.

[10] Ibid., pp. 60–62.

[11] Ibid., p. 62.

restless with the coming of spring, and by April he had closed his school and returned to Jacksonville. There he passed his bar examination and opened a law office. Although he was still not yet twenty-one, his practice flourished, and he earned the approval of older people like Justice Samuel Lockwood of the Illinois Supreme Court.[12] But the courtroom, like the classroom, could not hold the energetic, ambitious young man from the East, and he soon turned to the rough-and-tumble world of frontier politics.

The Northwesterners liked the little Vermonter with the mass of black hair, the high, fine forehead, and the gray eyes that seemed to be charged with boundless energy and love of life. They accepted his outspoken bluntness and his rough good-natured ways that usually stopped short of vulgarity. Many years later Douglas eulogized a Senate colleague as "bold, manly and unequivocal."[13] Those were the qualities in a man Douglas prized above all others, and they were the ones that counted for most with the people of Illinois. Douglas returned the admiration his new neighbors felt for him, and he had been in Illinois only a few weeks when he wrote his family: "I have become a Western man, have imbibed Western feelings, principles, and interests and have selected Illinois as the favorite place of my adoption, without any desire of returning to the land of my fathers except as a visitor."[14]

He was like a diamond, this man Douglas: small and hard and rare. There was nothing simple about him: his personality was many faceted, but all its complexities lay on the surface. He was not shallow, but he had the kind of depth that could be fathomed at a glance, and those whom he met soon felt they knew and understood him.

Stephen Douglas had about him none of the snobbishness the Westerners had come to associate with newly arrived Yankees. He would drink his new neighbors' corn liquor and eat their heavy

[12] Ibid., pp. 63, 445.

[13] *Cong. Globe*, 35th Cong., 2nd sess., p. 407.

[14] Johannsen, ed., *Letters of Douglas*, p. 3.

frontier fare,[15] and most of all he would talk to them. He was a born orator. With his deep resonant voice and the ready flow of words from a quick, clear mind, it was said that he "swayed the tides of public opinion as vassals to his will."[16]

The great gift of empathy with his audience—the priceless ability to give expression to what his listeners felt in their hearts—made him a natural leader of men.[17] During the seven years following his arrival in Illinois, the young Jacksonian pushed and fought and argued his way to the offices of state's attorney, member of the state legislature, register of the Federal Land Office, and secretary of state. In February of 1841 he was chosen justice of the Illinois Supreme Court at age twenty-seven.[18]

Full-grown now, Douglas stood barely five feet tall and weighed just over a hundred pounds. He had more than his share of self-confidence, and at times the cocksure attitude with which he greeted any challenge was mistaken for arrogance. He had an outsized ambition, and like many physically small persons he would occasionally go to ridiculous lengths to prove himself. He was a born fighter. He never ran from any encounter no matter how unpromising, and he often seemed to seek out trouble on his own. For Stephen Douglas, politics was merely a genteel extension of a frontier boxing match on a Saturday afternoon; the long story of his public life frequently resembled an essay in political pugilism.[19] He won most of his bouts. With his agile mind and powerful oratory he would vanquish almost any of his opponents, although he might not always convince them. Douglas was bold and aggressive, but there was nothing really foolhardy about the man. He had

[15] Gerald M. Capers, *Stephen A. Douglas: Defender of the Union*, p. 13; Stevens, "Life of Douglas," p. 299.

[16] *Cong. Globe*, 37th Cong., 1st sess., p. 36.

[17] Ibid., pp. 27, 29, 36.

[18] Johannsen, ed., *Letters of Douglas*, p. 445.

[19] See for example the account of Douglas' first campaign for a seat in Congress in 1838, Stevens, "Life of Douglas," pp. 315–320; and the story of his attack on the Illinois Supreme Court, ibid., pp. 335–336. *Cong. Globe*, 37th Cong., 1st sess., pp. 28–29, 35, contains comments on Douglas' political style.

more than a little of the gambler in him, but rarely took unnecessary risks. His was the true kind of courage—the kind that comes ultimately from wisdom rather than from reckless abandon.[20]

Stephen Douglas made many opponents during his rapid rise through the ranks of Illinois politics, but few real enemies. Nor did any scandal ever mar his public life. Most people soon forgot an occasional excess of bumptiousness or lack of subtlety on his part and recalled instead his courage and the sense of power he conveyed to those around him.[21] Harriet Beecher Stowe remembered best his animation.[22] He had not been in the West many months before his Illinois neighbors affectionately dubbed him the Little Giant; the title stayed with him for the rest of his life.[23]

The people of the new Fifth District of Illinois sent Stephen Douglas to Congress in 1843.[24] Three years later he was elected United States Senator.[25] The Little Giant would probably have made it to the upper house earlier, but he had been under the minimum age of thirty prescribed by the Constitution.[26]

From the time he first came to Congress, Douglas' story was America's story. He was involved in almost every major piece of legislation and every important policy decision from the annexa-

[20] *Cong. Globe*, 37th Cong., 1st sess., pp. 27–28, 30–31, 33–34, 36–38; Stevens, "Life of Douglas," pp. 312–313.

[21] See for example Lyman Trumbull's eulogy of Douglas, *Cong. Globe*, 37th Cong., 1st sess., p. 27. Douglas himself was not one to harbor a grudge for very long; ibid., p. 33.

[22] Robert Taft, "The Appearance and Personality of Stephen A. Douglas," *Kansas Historical Quarterly* 21 (spring 1954): 11.

[23] Stevens ("Life of Douglas," p. 285) thinks the sobriquet Little Giant was first applied to Douglas after a speech at Jacksonville, Illinois, in March, 1834.

[24] It was an off-year election to fill the seat in the district created in March, 1843, by the state legislature in accordance with the reapportionment dictated by the 1840 census. Douglas took his seat in Congress December, 1843. He was re-elected to the House in 1844 and again in 1846, but resigned his seat in April, 1847, because he had been elected to the Senate.

[25] Douglas was elected Senator by the Illinois Legislature December 13, 1846. In accordance with the custom of the times, he did not take his seat in the Senate until December of the following year at the first session of the new Congress.

[26] Milton, *Eve of Conflict*, p. 26.

tion of Texas onward. As chairman of the House and Senate Committees on Territories[27] he was responsible for the organization of a dozen territories and the admission of as many states. He saw America double in size and reach from the Atlantic to the Pacific.

With his rough common sense, his relentless search for practical solutions, and his great gift for improvisation, Douglas seemed to embody everything that was good in the American spirit at mid-century. His youth and rapid political rise symbolized the American ideal of the self-made man.[28]

He personified America in its high national period. He had been born during the first full year of the War of 1812 and had reached his majority when Andrew Jackson lived in the White House. He understood an age characterized by a vigorous, self-assertive policy abroad and by the restless, pushing growth of the country at home —an age when all problems, no matter how serious, could be sublimated into the overriding purpose of expanding and enriching the national domain.

He was above all a nationalist,[29] and his nationalism was essentially materialistic. The physical growth of the country and the building of railroads and dams, the improvement of rivers and harbors—these were the things that interested Stephen Douglas. The ideological cement of the Union he would leave to the dreamers. His mind was clever and imaginative, but not particularly creative. It gave off sparks of brilliance in an endless stream, but produced little that was really new. Douglas was quick to seize upon the ideas of others and adapt them to the needs of the moment, but he rarely created any really new ideas of his own. The Little Giant's dynamic political style was at bottom somewhat deceptive. His energetic approach to national problems often disguised the fact that he reacted to situations more than he produced them or even determined their broad outlines.[30]

27 Douglas was made the first chairman of the newly created Senate Committee on Territories when the 30th Congress organized in December, 1847. He had been chairman of the House Committee on Territories since 1845.

28 *Cong. Globe*, 37th Cong., 1st sess., pp. 29, 30, 37.

29 Ibid., p. 29.

30 Ibid.,

The intense pragmatism of the man and his gift for improvisation and political maneuver made him a natural agent of compromise. He was the moving force behind the settlement of 1850 and the author of the Kansas-Nebraska Act four years later. Perhaps the eager and frenetic way in which Douglas threw himself into shaping these compromises, his endless search for final solutions to the problem of slavery in the territories, and his blatant disregard for moral principles and for the long-range consequences of his actions were signs of political immaturity.[31] Yet his approach merely reflected the spirit of an earlier age that did not look upon a compromise as the embodiment of a moral and ethical creed. The America of the high national period did not treat compromise as an end in itself, but merely as a means incidental to getting on with the overriding task of nation-building. Perhaps that is why Douglas' legislation of 1850 and 1854 in the end largely failed to solve the terrible problems posed by the continued existence of slavery in America.

Even before 1850—probably about the time of the end of the Mexican war—a slow but profound change had begun to take place in the fundamental nature of American politics. For many years thereafter, Douglas' flexibility, which he prized above almost all political virtues, and his intense involvement on the national scene tended to hide a growing lack of understanding of his changing times. But by 1857 there was serious doubt that Douglas could adapt to the new age and continue to mesh his great energy and talent with the political environment around him. The Little Giant must have been uncomfortably aware that the old ingredients of the formula for his astounding political success were breaking down.

No longer was simple national expansion by itself enough to override all the divisive problems that threatened the country. With America now reaching to the shores of the Pacific, there was little

[31] For Douglas' role in the legislation of 1850 and 1854 see Holman Hamilton, *Prologue to Conflict*, pp. 133–150; Allan Nevins, *Ordeal of the Union*, I, 303–305, 313, 341–344; James C. Malin, *The Nebraska Question, 1852–1854*, pp. 438–448; Nevins, *Ordeal of the Union*, II, 80–121, 130–145.

more land to acquire, and the bothersome slavery question was making it difficult for America to digest the territory it already had. In the age Douglas knew best the sheer momentum of national expansion had dominated domestic politics; now the traditional situation seemed on the verge of reversing itself. The old predominant loyalties to the Union were breaking down, and in their place there appeared the new and pernicious forces of sectionalism. The pragmatic approach to politics was giving way now to an obsession with abstractions—rigid and exclusive principles clothed in the language of the moral imperative, which Douglas had always considered the peculiar preserve of philosophers and saints. Stephen Douglas had consistently treated politics as a game where the stakes were often high, but never really considered matters of life or death by those who played the game best. Yet the new breed of politicians—the Charles Sumners and the Salmon Chases, the William Lowndes Yanceys and the Louis T. Wigfalls—had other ideas. They played by different rules and with deadly seriousness.

And there were more apparent changes, too. In his early years on Capitol Hill Douglas could always count on the backing of a united party that dominated American political life and on the goodwill, or at least the tacit acquiescence, of a series of amiable Presidents. But by the beginning of 1857 things were different. There was severe disagreement among the Democrats over slavery, and their frantic efforts at preserving party unity were watched from the political wings by the new and aggressive Republican party with ill-disguised pleasure.

And down the hill at the White House, where Douglas had for so long been an honored guest, courted and admired by James Polk and Zachary Taylor, by Millard Fillmore and Franklin Pierce, the old warmth and cordiality had turned first to suspicion, then hostility, and finally to cold and measured hatred.

2. Douglas and Goliath

James Buchanan was a good man and a bad President. He had more than his share of charm, and some of the sketches of this courtly, rather fussy, old bachelor are among the most delightful in American history: James Buchanan, as squire of Wheatland, receiving his friends in its comfortable surroundings, and dispensing his sound, if somewhat ponderous, political wisdom as freely as he did the excellent Madeira from his ample cellars;[1] James Buchanan, as American minister to England, politely but firmly refusing to don court dress for a reception at Buckingham Palace;[2] James Buchanan, entertaining the visiting Prince of Wales with a cruise down the Potomac to Mount Vernon.[3] In the words of a sympathetic biographer: "He exemplified in his private conduct simplicity of manners, unfailing courtesy, and a kindly consideration for others. Although proud of his own attainments, he remained familiar and unaffected in his relations with others;

[1] Philip S. Klein, *President James Buchanan*, pp. 210–211.

[2] Ibid., p. 228. Buchanan was minister to England under President Franklin Pierce from 1853 to 1856.

[3] Ibid., p. 350.

treating his barber, his gardener and his poor relatives with no less regard and attention than he gave to people of eminence."[4]

Nor was Buchanan lacking in the talents of a public servant. With his penchant for legalistic, if rather tortuous, reasoning and a better-than-average flair for administrative routine, he would have made an excellent county judge, a good mayor, and a fair governor.

He made one of our worst Presidents. The story of his years in office is one of almost unrelieved failure. His inflexibility, coupled with his lack of courage and imagination, helped to split the Democratic party and to destroy it as a national institution. The Democrats would not elect another President for twenty-eight years. He did nothing to solve the terrible problems posed by slavery in America; what is worse, he did not really try. Faced with secession, he refused to take the forceful steps necessary to preserve the Union until time had run out.

He was the wrong man for the times. Had he served in a gentler age, had the decisions he was required to make been less crucial for the very existence of the nation, James Buchanan might today be remembered with that curious indulgence that America reserves for its less-than-successful Presidents: with tolerance, as in the instance of John Quincy Adams, or with more humor than censure, after the example of Warren Harding. But when the country needed a President of heroic strength, Buchanan could demonstrate only weakness. In the place of decision, he offered vacillation. Instead of leading, he was led by the stronger personalities that surrounded him. He was a poor actor and clever men soon detected the chinks in his armor. Thomas Hart Benton commented, "It is too true, he is not a firm, decided man—he is too apt to be swayed by others."[5] Commenting on one of Buchanan's frequent absences from Washington, Secretary of War John Floyd compared a cabinet meeting to "the play of Hamlet with the part of Hamlet left out."[6] If

[4] Ibid., p. 428.

[5] William N. Chambers, *Old Bullion Benton*, p. 429.

[6] George D. Harmon, "President James Buchanan's Betrayal of Governor Robert J. Walker of Kansas," *Aspects of Slavery and Expansion*, Lehigh University Publications, vol. III, no. 7, p. 17.

Buchanan's inveterate weakness exasperated Benton and Floyd, it caused Alexander Stephens to distrust him.[7] Andrew Jackson and James K. Polk had detected flaws in Buchanan's character at an even earlier date.[8]

Effective power in the Buchanan administration soon passed into the hands of a Directory composed largely of Southerners or Southern sympathizers.[9] On those few occasions when Buchanan attempted to lead the country on a course opposed by the Directory, the President usually came off second best. His plans for tariff revision and a Pacific railroad remained only a dream. For the most part, however, Buchanan offered little in the way of a positive program, and reserved his rare moments of forceful decision for veto messages: the Morrill land grant college proposal and the homestead bill both received the presidential quietus.[10] When neither inaction nor negative action would suffice, Buchanan would retreat. He would withdraw steadily into his political lair until he could go no farther. Then he would suddenly turn on his enemies, real or imagined, with a fury and vindictiveness that sometimes seemed to border on the absurd. This happened only twice in Buchanan's four years in office. The last time was his commendable, if long overdue, purge of the Southerners who had dominated both him and his cabinet; the first instance occurred when Buchanan

[7] Alexander H. Stephens, *A Constitutional View of the Late War between the States*, II, 150, 152.

[8] Milo M. Quaife, ed., *The Diary of James K. Polk*, II (entry for September 1, 1846), pp. 107–111; George Fort Milton, "Stephen A. Douglas' Efforts for Peace," *Journal of Southern History* 1 (August 1935): 267.

[9] Key figures in the Directory were Jacob Thompson of Mississippi, secretary of the interior; Jeremiah Black of Pennsylvania, attorney general; and the most powerful of all, Howell Cobb of Georgia, secretary of the treasury. Thomas W. Thomas wrote Alexander Stephens that Cobb "is the President as much as if he had been sworn in." Ulrich B. Phillips, ed., *The Correspondence of Robert Toombs, Alexander H. Stephens, and Howell Cobb, Annual Report of the American Historical Association for 1911*, II, 452. Although not in the cabinet, John Slidell should also be considered a part of the Directory.

[10] The land grant college proposal was vetoed February 24, 1859; the homestead bill, June 22, 1860. For the presidential veto messages see James D. Richardson, ed., *Messages and Papers of the Presidents*, V, 543–550, 608–614.

supported the Lecompton Constitution for Kansas and set out to break anyone bold enough to resist him.[11]

A brief look at Buchanan's career might suggest that he was motivated largely by a deep-seated conservatism, an aversion to agitation, and a conscious and sincere attachment to the status quo. But a closer scrutiny of the man suggests that the roots of his political behavior were emotional rather than philosophical, and that the dominant emotion was fear. Buchanan was apparently frightened during much of his public life. Martin Van Buren was among the first to detect the timorous streak in Buchanan's character, and he shared his discovery with Andrew Jackson some thirty years before Buchanan became President.[12]

Yet it is to James Buchanan's lasting credit that he seemed to have at least a partial understanding of his lack of capacity for dealing with the problems of the presidency. When he faced an unpleasant situation, his first response was often to deny that any problem existed. Should the difficulty persist, he would then recognize it only to deny that he had any power to deal with it. His favorite rationalization was the danger of too much executive power.[13] Although the need for action was clear, Buchanan would disclaim responsibility and hand the problem either to the Supreme Court, as he did in the Dred Scott case, or to Congress, as was done during the early days of the secession crisis. When he could neither ignore a problem nor pass the responsibility for solving it on to someone else, Buchanan had yet another recourse: he would announce that the problem was solving itself.[14] This kind of approach might in less critical times have been called sophisticated, but when

[11] For Buchanan's almost irrational reaction to the Lecompton struggle see the *New York Times*, February 1, 1858.

[12] Klein, *President James Buchanan*, p. 59. For other evidence of Buchanan's essentially timorous character see Sara Agnes Pryor, *Reminiscences of Peace and War*, p. 110; Allan Nevins, *The Emergence of Lincoln*, I, 63–67; Jefferson Davis, *The Rise and Fall of the Confederate Government*, I, 265–266; Quaife, ed., *Diary of Polk*, I, 102, 244; II, 107–111.

[13] Richardson, ed., *Messages and Papers of Presidents*, V, 431, 635, 662.

[14] Ibid., pp. 432, 553–555, 637.

applied to the series of crises which confronted America in the late 1850's, it seemed closer to escapism than to sophistication.

Long before James Buchanan took the oath of office, there began brewing on the plains of Kansas a political storm that could not forever be ignored nor easily disposed of. Whether the Kansas problem could have been solved at all remains an open question among historians; that it could have been solved by James Buchanan's meager talents does not.

Kansas today has a gentle appearance. In the winter the snow can come down from Canada onto the plains with alarming suddenness, and there are times in the summer when the heat seems to hang on remorselessly, but for the most part Kansas gives the casual visitor an impression of a tranquil and prosperous land.

But the calm is deceptive. In the summer the Kansas plains are wracked by thunderstorms, and in the late spring and early fall the vast flatness is the breeding ground of tornadoes. It is said that in these seasons the Kansas farmer lives with one eye on his plow and the other on the horizon.

The people are somehow different, too. Living in the geographical center of America, they are often dismissed by Sunday supplement writers as the most average of average Americans. But look closer. The people of Kansas today appear to be more serious than most Americans. They laugh less easily. The land and its people seem never to have quite recovered from the trauma that marked their early history.

First explored by Coronado in 1541, the major part of what is now Kansas passed into American hands at the time of the Louisiana Purchase. Along with the Territory of Nebraska, Congress in 1854 created the Kansas Territory, which comprised most of the present state of Kansas together with a quarter of what is today Colorado. But Congress acted hastily. In 1853 the entire Kansas-Nebraska area had almost no permanent white residents.[15] The creation of the two new territories helped to attract settlers from

[15] Washington *Daily National Intelligencer*, November 16, 1854.

the older sections intent on finding a new and better life. But the abrogation of the Missouri Compromise by the Kansas-Nebraska Act meant that when they got to their new home they would quarrel. For with all of its faults, the Missouri Compromise had for a third of a century furnished a workable solution to the terrible question of slavery in the territories. Suddenly, in 1854, that compromise was gone. Kansas soon became something more than another outlet for the surging tide of immigration from the older areas. It became a symbol of the whole future of slavery in America and the battleground where an ideological struggle was to be fought out in a brutally realistic form. Southern slaveowners, particularly those from Missouri, began to move in large numbers into the new territory, and in March, 1855, they captured control of the territorial legislature. Free-soilers and abolitionists did not sit idly by. Wave after wave of Northerners, many with the help of the New England Emigrant Aid Society, began to flood into the Kansas Territory. James H. Lane and Charles Robinson led the antislavery forces in the establishment of a free-soil government at Topeka. David Atchison and his lieutenants meanwhile claimed that their openly proslavery legislature at Shawnee Mission alone could speak for Kansas. A frightened President Franklin Pierce seemed to agree.[16]

Violence was not long in coming. Arms flowed into Kansas from both North and South. A free-soiler never ventured far from home without the company of his "Beecher's Bible." In February, 1856, Governor Wilson Shannon called for federal troops to maintain order. On May 21 proslavery forces sacked the free-soil center of Lawrence and two days later a fanatical fifty-six–year–old New Yorker named John Brown murdered five unarmed Southerners near Pottawatomie.

Armed bands now roamed Kansas at will. The little law and order that had once existed there was gone. Violence increased with the summer heat and reached its climax in August with the

[16] Richardson, ed., *Messages and Papers of Presidents*, V, 352–360, for Pierce's January 24, 1856, message to Congress on matters in Kansas.

siege of Fort Titus. Kansas had become the site of one of the first of the modern guerrilla wars.

President-elect James Buchanan disliked trouble and detested violence. He no doubt hoped that the storm raging on the Kansas plains would soon blow itself out. At first, it looked like he might have his wish. Not long after the Democratic party, meeting in Cincinnati, had nominated Buchanan as its presidential candidate for 1856, Franklin Pierce made one of the few worthy decisions of his presidential career: he sent John Geary out to Kansas to be its new governor.

Men did not trifle with John Geary. Standing six and a half feet tall and not yet forty, he expected to be obeyed and usually was. Arriving in Kansas on September 11, 1856, he dealt severely but impartially with all agitators whether free-soil or proslavery. Less than three months after Geary had come out to the territory, President Pierce could refer with some degree of truth to "the peaceful condition of things in Kansas,"[17] and Buchanan, at his inauguration, was able to say of the problems of slavery in the territories, "May we not, then, hope that the long agitation on this subject is approaching its end?"[18]

Buchanan wanted to forget about Kansas. The South did not, and the South was used to having its way in the Democratic party. For as long as most men could remember, the South had held a veto power over any Democratic presidential nomination. It was to the South that Buchanan owed not only his nomination but his election as well. In 1856 only four Northern states had voted for him.[19] The South was not long in attempting to collect the Buchanan debt.

To the South, Kansas had both symbolic and real importance. It was a symbol of the whole future course of slavery. If slavery

[17] Fourth Annual Message of President Pierce, December 2, 1856; ibid., pp. 405, 407.

[18] John Bassett Moore, ed., *The Works of James Buchanan*, X, 320.

[19] The four Northern states were Illinois, Indiana, New Jersey, and Pennsylvania. These, plus California, were the only free states Buchanan carried in 1856. *The Tribune Almanac and Political Register for 1862*, p. 64.

could prosper there, it would attest to the vigor of the institution. Slavery would be not only surviving, but actually expanding. An uneasy South would be reassured. Should slavery be kept out of Kansas, many Southerners would be confirmed in their fears that it was a dying institution.

There was a more immediate and pragmatic facet of the Kansas problem. Ever since California had joined the Union in 1850 as a free state, the national political balance had been tilted against the South: the score stood at sixteen free states to fifteen slave. Making Kansas a slave state would restore the sectional balance that the South was coming to equate with survival.

Buchanan's attitude toward the South was one of sympathy devoid of any real understanding. He seems genuinely to have felt that the South had in recent years been slighted in national politics and that it deserved a better deal,[20] but he shared with the majority of Northerners a profound ignorance of the forces behind Southern behavior. The President respected the talent of Southern politicians and relied heavily upon their counsel throughout most of his administration, but Buchanan and the South remained fundamentally strangers. Above all, Buchanan feared the South in general and secession in particular. While it is commendable that at an early date he recognized the very real dangers to the Union posed by Southern fire-eaters, to recognize a danger is one thing, to be thrown into a panic by it is quite another. Buchanan had not even taken the oath of office before he seemed obsessed by the belief that the South must be placated whatever the cost. Only days after his election he reinterpreted the Democratic platform of 1856 in such a way as to give the South a better chance to hold Kansas for slavery. What had appeared to be an endorsement of self-determination for the territories on questions of slavery now looked like a refusal to permit any unfriendly action toward the institution until time for statehood. There is evidence that early in 1857 he was quietly working to ensure that when the Dred Scott decision came it would be in a form pleasing to the South.[21] Whenever a sectional

[20] Richardson, ed., *Messages and Papers of Presidents*, V, 626–627.

[21] Nevins, *The Emergence of Lincoln*, I, 104ff.

difficulty had to be resolved during his administration, Buchanan automatically assumed that any concession would have to come from the North, and if it did not, he would in exasperation denounce his own section for being unduly rigid.[22] This kind of bias toward the South soon brought down upon Buchanan the suspicion of the North. Tolerated but never fully trusted by the South, Buchanan was now distrusted by the North as well. Suspected by both sections, admired by neither, he was in a poor position to settle the Kansas question in a way that would earn the approval of both North and South.

When the Kansas crisis began to reach a climax late in 1857, Stephen Douglas had at first appeared to be far better qualified than the President to deal with it. His flexible, practical approach to any problem had raised hopes that once again he would come forward with a compromise that would ease the tensions incident to westward expansion. His doctrine of popular sovereignty had promised to provide a framework for conducting any sectional dispute over slavery in the territories. Douglas' closest ties were to neither of the two older sections of the country where the most bitterness over Kansas was to be found. He was a Northwesterner, and the Northwest had the greatest interest of any part of America in the peace and prosperity of the trans-Mississippi West.

But as 1857 gave way to 1858, hopes of a quick and permanent answer to the Kansas question had begun to fade. Overheated tempers in the Capital had commenced to blow the controversy out of all proportion, and soon the whole matter had seemed beyond the help of well-intentioned men. By early 1858 Douglas' basic strategy had appeared to have changed from one of seeking an easy solution to one of postponement and delay. By May, the best he and the country could expect was an uneasy truce between pro- and antislavery forces. When Douglas left Washington the following month for Illinois, he must have known that if the Kan-

[22] Moore, ed., *Works of Buchanan*, X, 461–462.

sas crisis had eased somewhat in the past year, the Kansas question remained very much alive.

The little man was now coming back to his people without being able to show much in the way of positive success in Congress during the months just past. As he watched the Northwest slipping by outside the train window and reflected on the recent session, perhaps he began to realize for the first time the intricate nature of the problems posed by Kansas. Perhaps in the quiet hours of early morning there in the compartment, Douglas began to understand that the so-called Kansas crisis was in fact three different but simultaneous crises. The first concerned the violence that was tearing apart that unfortunate land. The second dealt with the admission of Kansas to statehood. The last involved the adoption of the Lecompton Constitution.

On the first point, Douglas had little quarrel with the President. Both men regretted that blood was being spilled in Kansas, and both sought an early end to agitation there. Nor does the list of shared viewpoints stop here. Although both thought of slaves primarily as property, they also privately found the institution of slavery repugnant.[23] Buchanan, like Douglas, felt that climate and economics, more than morality or legislative action, would determine the ultimate course of slavery. He declared in his Third Annual Message, "From natural causes the slavery question will in

[23] For Buchanan's views, see Klein, *President James Buchanan*, pp. 100, 147–150. Douglas' dislike of slavery is more difficult to establish because he was always careful neither to praise nor condemn the peculiar institution in his public pronouncements. But in less guarded moments of private conversation with his friends and family, his true feelings emerged: McConnel, *Transactions of the Illinois State Historical Society for 1900*, p. 49. Douglas declared to the author, "I am not proslavery. I think it a curse beyond computation to white and black." Also, see "Letter of a Native Southerner" in the *New York Tribune*, August 23, 26, and 27, 1859; important statements by James Lemen in Stevens, "Life of Douglas," pp. 655–656; Judge Robert A. Douglas, *Stephen A. Douglas' Attitude Toward Slavery* (n.p., n.d.), a reprint of a letter by Douglas' son, October 14, 1908, replying to an invitation to attend the semi-centennial celebration of the Lincoln-Douglas Debates; and Douglas' remarks in the Senate, April 20, 1848, *Cong. Globe*, 30th Cong., 1st sess., app., p. 507.

each case soon virtually settle itself."[24] Both men sought to rid the land of the pernicious slavery controversy once and for all, but in different ways. Buchanan tried to bury the question at the national level by admitting Kansas as a state; Douglas sought interment in the territories by way of his popular sovereignty formula. Both wanted to see Kansas, whether as a territory or a state, firmly in the Democratic column.

On the second point, the admission of Kansas to the Union, there was partial agreement. While Buchanan thought he saw in speedy admission an easy way out of a problem,[25] Douglas himself had no intrinsic objection to admission if Kansas could be brought into the Union in a fair manner.

It was on the question of the manner of admission that the two men disagreed violently. The focal point of their quarrel was the Lecompton Constitution.

In February, 1857, the proslavery Kansas Legislature had passed a bill calling for a convention to meet at Lecompton in September to draft a constitution preparatory to statehood. So blatantly did the voting requirements for convention delegates and the restrictions upon their work favor the proslavery forces that Governor Geary promptly vetoed the bill. The legislature quickly repassed it over his veto and Geary resigned in March. The crisis in Kansas had begun to heat up again.

On March 26, 1857, Buchanan sent the able Robert J. Walker of Mississippi out to Kansas as its new governor. It would have been difficult to imagine a less propitious time for undertaking what was at best a hazardous and unrewarding job. A rowdy and fraudulent election of convention delegates was held in June, and in the early fall the constitutional convention commenced its deliberations.

By any standards, the Lecompton Constitution, which was announced on November 7, was a farce. Its preamble both recognized the right of property in slaves and declared it inviolable. Free

[24] Moore, ed., *Works of Buchanan*, X, 342.

[25] Richardson, ed., *Messages and Papers of Presidents*, V, 478–480.

Negroes were barred from Kansas altogether. Furthermore, the constitution prohibited amendments for seven years.

When the news of the handiwork of the Lecompton convention began to spread beyond Kansas, there was an immediate uproar. Francis Lieber found the constitution a fraud unequaled in history and was reminded of Goethe's progress of shame in *Faust*.[26] The *New York Tribune* warned, "People of the United States! Unless your Representatives reject this Constitution, Kansas is forever enslaved."[27]

Douglas' reaction to the constitution was predictably hostile. He pronounced the Lecompton convention "irregular."[28] He held that by drawing up a constitution the convention had exceeded its authority merely to petition Congress for statehood,[29] and he lashed out against the built-in obstacles to amendment.[30]

Yet it was for those parts of the Lecompton Constitution governing a popular referendum on slavery that Douglas reserved his heaviest verbal artillery, and it was here that the Lecompton issue was joined with Buchanan in the clearest form.

The one thing the delegates to the constitutional convention at Lecompton feared was a genuine popular referendum on their handiwork. They had been chosen by a small minority of Kansans and had carried out their work under a shroud of secrecy. Only with the greatest reluctance did the convention consent even to a modified form of submission: not the whole constitution, but only those parts dealing with slavery would be submitted to a popular vote. Should the slavery clauses be rejected—an unlikely event in view of the proslavery oligarchy's control of the election machinery—existing slave ownership would remain unimpaired. Only

26 Comments written by Francis Lieber on the back of a printed copy of the *Senate Committee on Territories Minority Report on Kansas*, dated February 18, 1858; Lieber Collection (Henry E. Huntington Library), LI 381. Cited hereafter as Lieber Collection.

27 *New York Tribune*, November 19, 1857.

28 *Cong. Globe*, 35th Cong., 1st sess., p. 48.

29 Ibid., p. 16.

30 Ibid., p. 50.

the introduction of new slaves would be prohibited. Either way, slavery and slaveholders would win.[31]

Douglas' innate sense of fair play was outraged. He warned his Senate colleagues: "A constitution forced on a people against their will is not a republican constitution within the spirit of our institutions."[32] Douglas was always careful to stress that it was not the proslavery bias of Lecompton that upset him, but rather the lack of a genuine popular vote on the entire constitution. Such a contention contained the outward appearance of truth. After all, Douglas had announced his public stand against Lecompton two weeks before a referendum approved the proslavery clauses of the constitution.[33] It was clever political ground, too. It enabled Douglas to appear as the disinterested advocate of popular sovereignty, concerned only with learning and enforcing the public will. By avoiding any specific condemnation of the proslavery bias of the Lecompton instrument, he had some chance of retaining the confidence of the South as a moderate Northerner. By basing his whole case on popular sovereignty, he hoped to appear to both North and South as a man of principle.

But a thoroughly frightened James Buchanan had little use now for principle and moderation. The South was restless and there were murmurs of secession; it must be appeased. Kansas was erupting into violence again; it must be pacified. Casting about for a solution to both problems, he determined upon the speedy admission of Kansas under the Lecompton Constitution. As a sop to Northern sentiment, he would consent to a referendum on the slavery clauses

[31] Nevins, *The Emergence of Lincoln*, I, 235–239; Roy F. Nichols, *The Disruption of American Democracy*, pp. 132–133.

[32] *Cong. Globe*, 35th Cong., 1st sess., p. 50.

[33] Douglas made public his opposition to Lecompton in his Senate speech of December 9, 1857. *Cong. Globe*, 35th Cong., 1st sess., pp. 14–18. A plebiscite on the narrow question of whether the new constitution should prohibit the introduction of additional slaves into Kansas was held on December 21 and produced a proslavery majority. The results of this election were largely dismissed on grounds of fraud. Leverett W. Spring, *Kansas: The Prelude to the War for the Union*, pp. 229–230; William F. Zornow, *Kansas*, p. 78.

alone. Rising to new heights of sophistry, Buchanan explained that the phrase "domestic institutions," which under the Kansas-Nebraska Act were to be regulated by the people of the territory, meant "domestic" in the sense of familial and hence concerned only slavery.[34] In addition, Buchanan pointed out that the entire constitution could always be submitted to the people after Kansas had become a state.[35]

In fairness to Buchanan it must be said that there was something to his contention that since slavery alone was disturbing the country, only the slavery question deserved submission. His view drew support from the unlikely source of Abraham Lincoln.[36] Much of the difficulty had arisen from the fact that the American experience provided no ironclad rules for statemaking. Only in about one half of the territories prior to 1857 had the kind of submission now demanded by Douglas actually occurred, although a popular referendum had been held in almost every instance where there had been deep and fundamental cleavages in the body politic like those that now existed in Kansas. Finally, Buchanan's plan for partial submission was better than the opposition of some Southern Ultras to submission in any form.[37]

Although Lecompton provided the occasion for the formal break between Douglas and Buchanan, a conflict of personalities had been going on quietly between the two men years before the political clash erupted. They had almost nothing in common. There was Douglas, young, pushing, aggressive; Douglas, the extrovert; Douglas, to whom thought and action were synonymous; Douglas, whose boundless self-confidence and teeming imagination propelled him at times toward greatness and at times to the brink of folly. And there was Buchanan, who, as the cares of the presidency began to weigh heavily upon him, withdrew more and more into brooding

[34] Richardson, ed., *Messages and Papers of Presidents*, V, 452.

[35] Ibid., pp. 479, 499.

[36] Ibid., p. 452. John G. Nicolay and John Hay, eds., *Complete Works of Abraham Lincoln*, III, 161.

[37] *Charleston Mercury*, December 11, 1857.

suspicion and divided the world into those few who were for him and all the rest who were therefore against him.[38]

Buchanan had never wanted the Compromise of 1850 that Douglas had helped shape.[39] In 1852 Buchanan had privately worked against Douglas' try for the presidential nomination. He had given grudging formal support to Douglas' Kansas-Nebraska Act, but privately he despised it.[40] In the Cincinnati convention of 1856 Douglas, although incapable himself of coming away with the presidential nomination, could have blocked the nomination of any other Democrat. With that peculiar combination of political realism and magnanimity that marked so many of his public acts, Douglas at the crucial moment withdrew his name from the convention, which proceeded to nominate Buchanan.[41] Douglas did not stop here. He threw his considerable energies and a large part of his private fortune into Buchanan's campaign.[42]

Douglas expected Buchanan's gratitude. He received his disdain. Buchanan's first response was to pen a stiff note of thanks which has ever since delighted scholars with an eye for not wholly unintentional slips: it was addressed to "The Honorable Samuel A. Douglas"![43]

Buchanan had not even taken the oath of office before he yielded to Southern pressure and did a volte-face on the question of when a territory could bar slavery within its borders should it desire to do so. Douglas had maintained that the decision could come any time after the territory had been organized; Buchanan had apparently agreed, but later announced that formal prohibition of slav-

[38] E. Ramsay Richardson, *Little Aleck: A Life of Alexander H. Stephens*, p. 177.

[39] Klein, *President James Buchanan*, pp. 214–215; Robert W. Johannsen, ed., *The Letters of Stephen A. Douglas*, p. 193.

[40] Klein, *President James Buchanan*, pp. 263, 289–290.

[41] Johannsen, ed., *Letters of Douglas*, p. 361.

[42] Ibid., pp. 367–368. Estimates of Douglas' financial aid in the 1856 campaign run as high as $100,000.

[43] Nichols, *Disruption of American Democracy*, p. 59; Klein, *President James Buchanan*, p. 259; George Fort Milton, *The Eve of Conflict: Stephen A. Douglas and the Needless War*, p. 243. The original letter is in the Douglas Papers, University of Chicago.

ery could occur only at the time a territory achieved statehood. This was a direct slap at Douglas' cherished popular sovereignty.

Relations between the two men grew no better after Buchanan took office. Expecting the offer of a cabinet post, Douglas instead found himself excluded from even the Directory. Buchanan made it clear in the early days of his presidency that Douglas was to have little voice in the disposition of administration patronage. On important national appointments Buchanan merely ignored Douglas' advice. For lesser posts, particularly in Illinois, the President went out of his way to choose men unfriendly to Douglas, whose correspondence from the time Buchanan took office contains a surprising number of recommendations for government jobs that simply went unheeded.[44] In exasperation, Douglas wrote to Samuel Treat early in 1857: "At present, I am an outsider. My advice is not coveted nor will my wishes probably be regarded. I want only a fair share for my friends."[45] Buchanan's patronage war on Douglas took a novel twist with the President's attempt to name the Senator's father-in-law to a federal office. Douglas saw this as a cynical move by Buchanan to bring charges of nepotism down upon his head. When Douglas publicly expressed reservations about the appointment, the *New York Tribune* crowed, "He loved not Papa less, but the party more."[46]

For a man of his impetuous and combative temperament Douglas showed more restraint at this stage than at any other time in his career. When Buchanan in his Inaugural Address underwrote the Southern view on the timing of popular action on slavery in the territories, Douglas kept his peace.[47] When the Supreme Court three days later endorsed Buchanan's view in the Dred Scott decision, Douglas kept silent. When he did finally speak out against the decision at Springfield in June of 1857, he did so in such a mild fashion that the administration-controlled *Washington Union*

[44] Johannsen, ed., *Letters of Douglas*, pp. 376–379.

[45] Ibid., p. 372.

[46] New York *Tribune*, October 13, 1857; Johannsen, ed., *Letters of Douglas*, pp. 397–398, 401–402.

[47] Richardson, ed., *Messages and Papers of Presidents*, V, 431.

called his speech "One of the most powerful and convincing arguments ever made by the distinguished Senator of Illinois."[48]

Douglas could overlook petty slights and even the kind of abstract challenge to his views posed by the Dred Scott decision. He could not overlook Buchanan's determination to fasten the Lecompton Constitution upon the people of Kansas. Before Lecompton there was always the possibility of a reconciliation between the President and the Senator; after it there was none. Lecompton was an open and concrete challenge to Douglas' popular sovereignty. He could not ignore it. Neither could Buchanan. He had gotten his outsized ego involved with it.

Buchanan stressed the need for "localizing"[49] all distracting problems in Kansas and then went on to conclude that the best way to do so was for Congress to admit Kansas as quickly as possible with the Lecompton Constitution. This, in Buchanan's curious reasoning, would settle the Kansas question once and for all and provide the kind of final solution that he always sought.[50] Here indeed is the President at his most naive. Life offers very few final solutions, least of all in the field of politics. Buchanan never revealed how immediate admission would have cooled off the Kansas crisis, much less solved the infinitely more complex Kansas question. A bolder man looking for a final solution might have rejected Lecompton, admitted Kansas as a free state, dared the South to secede in 1857, and hoped for the best. But Buchanan was not a bold man.[51]

The President also had something besides the welfare of the country in mind when he urged a quick and easy solution to the

[48] *Washington Union*, June 20, 1857.

[49] Ibid., December 13, 1857; Richardson, ed., *Messages and Papers of Presidents*, V, 478–480.

[50] Moore, ed., *Works of Buchanan*, X, 83, 97.

[51] Three years after the Lecompton struggle, Douglas claimed that he had not feared Southern talk of secession in 1857 and hinted that perhaps he had even wanted to provoke the Ultras into a rash act which the heavily Unionist sentiment of the times would have quickly put down. Milton, *Eve of Conflict*, p. 281n.

Kansas troubles. Early in his term Buchanan had announced that he would not seek re-election, but there is evidence that whatever resolution he had upon this decision soon began to waver.[52] As early as September, 1857, the administration-controlled *Washington Union* dismissed the current wave of speculation over Buchanan's successor as an attempt "to distract, divide, and conquer the Democracy . . . upon a question to be decided three years hence."[53] By the end of the year the *New York Times* was saying: "The prominent leaders of the Democratic Party suspect the President of a desire for renomination."[54] Eighteen months later it could predict that Buchanan would seek the Charleston nomination in 1860.[55] Henry Wise, the governor of Virginia, wrote Fernando Wood in the July preceding the Charleston convention: "Indeed, there is no manner of doubt that the essay will be to nominate Mr. Buchanan again, and he is now moving unmistakably that way."[56] Alexander Stephens concurred.[57] The one great obstacle to Buchanan's re-election would be a continuation of the Kansas crisis. Even if Buchanan had not finally made up his mind in 1857 to run again, he quickly saw that his premature disavowal had weakened both the Democratic party and his control over it. Too many people were looking to Stephen Douglas as the next Democratic President. The aging Buchanan must have felt about the younger Douglas as Elizabeth did toward Mary Queen of Scots: "More people worship the rising than the setting sun." Buchanan resolved to remain in a position to dictate the 1860 nomination whether he himself sought it or not,[58] and he was determined to keep the am-

52 Moore, ed., *Works of Buchanan*, X, 105; Richard E. Stenberg, "An Unnoted Factor in the Buchanan-Douglas Feud," *Journal of The Illinois State Historical Society* 25 (January 1933): 273–274.

53 *Washington Union*, September 12, 1857.

54 *New York Times*, December 25, 1857.

55 Ibid., July 23, 1859.

56 Henry Wise to Fernando Wood, Richmond, Va., July 6, 1859; Brock Collection (Henry E. Huntington Library), Box 35. Cited hereafter as Brock Collection.

57 Phillips, ed., *Correspondence of Toombs*, p. 456.

58 Ibid., p. 450.

bitious Douglas from stealing the political spotlight in the Kansas controversy.

Stephen Douglas' attitude toward Kansas was much more complex. In his role as chairman of the Senate Committee on Territories he had presided over the birth of the Kansas Territory in 1854, and that deformed political stepchild haunted him for the rest of his life.

Douglas' motives in hastening the organization of Kansas and Nebraska are not always easy to fathom. His goal of a Pacific railroad[59] and his desire, with one eye on the presidency, to appease proslavery politicians like David Atchison tell only part of the story.[60] His deep and abiding belief in national expansion, probably the most consistent dynamic force in Douglas' long public life, helps to fill out the picture, but does not complete it.

Perhaps the ultimate force was basically an emotional one. If James Buchanan was usually moved out of his lethargy only by fear, Stephen Douglas seems to have been dominated by a love of action as an end in itself. He was a born doer and when his restless spirit was confronted with a problem his first response was most frequently to take some form of positive action. There were times when Douglas confused motion with action, and upon occasion he acted precipitately to the detriment of himself and his country.

This is exactly what happened in 1854. Douglas' action was a compound of haste and carelessness. Largely through his efforts Kansas and Nebraska were called into existence long before their white population was large enough to warrant a territorial government. By an ill-considered yielding to Southern pressure, he incorporated into his Kansas-Nebraska bill a repeal of the Missouri Compromise, which for more than a third of a century had governed the course of national expansion. While outwardly enshrining Douglas' beloved concept of popular sovereignty, the Kansas-Nebraska Act was essentially—perhaps purposely—ambiguous

[59] James C. Malin, *The Nebraska Question, 1852–1854*, pp. 443–448.

[60] P. Orman Ray, *The Repeal of the Missouri Compromise*, pp. 22–24, 201–219, 276–288.

with regard to the concrete application of that principle. In theory all decisions pertaining to slavery were left to the people of the territories, but when and how those decisions were to be made remained unanswered. Much of Douglas' political life after 1854 was to be spent alternately trying to define popular sovereignty and denying that any further definition was necessary.

The Kansas-Nebraska Act was a national tragedy. It destroyed the uneasy truce between sections that the Missouri Compromise had effected. It turned the tranquil land of Kansas into a bloody political cockpit. It also led to the formation of the Republican party, and six years later the election of the first Republican President would become the occasion for secession.

The legislation was a personal tragedy as well. It destroyed the aura of respectability Douglas had earned with his great work in the Compromise of 1850.[61] His maneuvering to repeal the Missouri Compromise brought him the suspicion of the North without the affection of the South. There was about Douglas' behavior over Kansas-Nebraska something not wholly honest, something close to political sleight-of-hand.[62] After 1854 most people did not quite trust Stephen Douglas. When he returned home to Illinois in the summer of 1854, angry mobs greeted him to protest his role in the repeal of the Missouri Compromise. Douglas remarked, "I could travel from Boston to Chicago by the light of my own effigy."[63] The November elections in Illinois witnessed a severe setback for the Democracy.[64] The Kansas-Nebraska Act had proved to be a political liability for the Little Giant.[65]

In the fall of 1857 Douglas knew that in just over a year he

[61] Holman Hamilton, *Prologue to Conflict*, p. 141.

[62] Nevins, *Ordeal of the Union*, II, 95.

[63] Milton, *Eve of Conflict*, p. 175. For Douglas' reaction to his hostile reception in Chicago upon his return from Washington after having passed the Kansas-Nebraska Act, see Johannsen, ed., *Letters of Douglas*, pp. 327–329.

[64] In the 1854 Illinois elections the Douglas Democrats lost control of the legislature and elected only four out of nine Congressmen. Arthur C. Cole, *The Era of the Civil War, 1848–1870*, pp. 133–134.

[65] H. S. Foote, *War of the Rebellion*, p. 183.

would face a campaign for re-election to the United States Senate. Always a political realist, he grasped the fact that his chances against the newly formed Republican party were not good. Almost in desperation he cast about for a way to remove the stain left by Kansas-Nebraska upon his career. The urgent need was to strengthen his free-soil credentials. His eye fell on the Lecompton Constitution, which was then being fashioned into its final grotesque shape out in Kansas. When Douglas visited the Illinois state fair in September of 1857 to take political soundings, his worst suspicions that he could not support Lecompton and be re-elected were confirmed.[66] By the end of October Douglas had probably decided that he would have to oppose admitting Kansas under Lecompton, but he still hoped Buchanan would not throw the immense power and prestige of the presidency behind the Southern slaveholders' position.

He was not optimistic. For Douglas, the anti-Lecompton stand was a carefully calculated political risk. He fully understood the consequences of challenging the President and the Democratic establishment. He also knew that if he did not, not only would he himself go down to defeat in 1858, but many of the Democratic voters in the North would bolt to the Republican standard.[67]

Douglas naturally rested his entire case against Lecompton on the principle of popular sovereignty.[68] Yet had his stand been wholly due to principle, he would probably have taken it earlier,

[66] Cole, *Era of the Civil War*, p. 176.

[67] *New York Tribune*, December 21, 1857; James Ford Rhodes, *History of the United States, 1850–1909*, II, 285; Nevins, *The Emergence of Lincoln*, I, 348; Nichols, *Disruption of American Democracy*, p. 135. For letters attesting the opposition of public opinion in the Northwest to Lecompton see: W. A. Cales to Douglas, Urbana, Ill., November 21, 1857; James W. Sheahan to Douglas, Chicago, Ill., December 4, 9, 1857; anonymous to Douglas, Boston, December 11, 1857; Edwin M. Stanton to Douglas, n.p., December 11, 1857; John W. Forney to Douglas, Philadelphia, Penn., December 13, 1857; B. M. Thompson to Douglas, Ann Arbor, Mich., December 15, 1857; James W. Sheahan to Douglas, Chicago, Ill., December 31, 1857; Will A. Hacker to Douglas, Jonesboro, Ill., February 26, 1858; James D. Eads to Douglas, Ft. Madison, Iowa, February 26, 1858; Stephen A. Douglas Papers, University of Chicago Library. Cited hereafter as Douglas MSS.

[68] *Cong. Globe*, 35th Cong., 1st sess., p. 1870.

perhaps in the early fall of 1857 when word of the emerging constitutional farce began to filter back from Kansas.[69] The *New York Tribune* came closest to truth when it referred to Douglas' policy as "enlightened expediency."[70] Douglas, in fact, in late 1857 was in what is for a politician the rare and happy situation where the expedient course of action is identical with the noble one.

It was perfectly natural for him to stress his idealistic motives and the sanctity of popular sovereignty, but in doing so he fell prey to the disease of the times: the tendency for public men first to become identified with some abstraction and then to be ensnared by it. States' rights, free soil, and abolitionism more and more dominated the actions of the politicians and limited their range of response to national problems. And now Douglas had elevated popular sovereignty from the status of a useful device to the level of a dubious ideal. Such was the price of refurbishing his political identity in the North.

By July of 1857 Buchanan had yielded to Southern pressure and withdrawn his support from Governor Walker, the one remaining hope for justice and fairness in Kansas. By October it was general knowledge that Walker was *persona non grata* at the White House. A month later the administration-controlled *Washington Union* had begun to hint broadly that Buchanan would support the recently finished Lecompton Constitution.[71]

Douglas' position was also hardening. Early in November the *Chicago Times*, a strongly pro-Douglas organ, announced: "When Kansas applies for admission, the only question will be—Is this Constitution the will of the people fairly expressed?"[72] On November 22 and 23 Douglas indicated in letters to friends his intention

[69] For Douglas' not wholly convincing explanation of his delay in opposing Lecompton, see his Senate speech of December 9, 1857; ibid., pp. 16–18.

[70] *New York Tribune*, May 11, 1858.

[71] *Washington Union*, November 18, 1857; Stenberg, "Buchanan-Douglas Feud," p. 279.

[72] *Chicago Times*, quoted in *New York Times*, November 12, 1857; also see *Chicago Times* editorial, November 18, 1857, quoted in *New York Tribune*, November 23, 1857.

to oppose Lecompton.[73] On December 2 Douglas returned to Washington. The *New York Times* commented: "He talks freely with reference to the Kansas question, sustaining Governor Walker boldly."[74] The next day Douglas called at the White House and took part in one of the great encounters of American history.

Douglas began the interview on a respectful note as befitted a visit to an older man in an august office. He had, he explained, come only to seek information. Did the President intend to endorse Lecompton? He did. Would the President consent to delay his endorsement for three weeks until after the results of the slavery referendum to be held in Kansas were known? He would not.

Now it was Douglas' turn to be angry. His reasonable attitude had been rebuffed. His voice louder now, he announced that when the question of Kansas was raised in Congress, he would oppose admission under the Lecompton scheme.

Buchanan, his face flushed with anger, half rose from his desk and with that peculiar arrogance weak men often show, reminded Douglas of the fate of Democrats like N. P. Tallmadge and William C. Rives, who had once run afoul of Andrew Jackson. This ludicrous analogy was too much for the Little Giant. He made for the door, but before leaving, turned and retorted, "Mr. President, I wish you to remember that General Jackson is dead."[75]

The gauntlet was down, the die was cast. There was no turning back now. In Douglas' own graphic phrase, "I have taken a through ticket and checked all my baggage."[76] On December 8 Buchanan, in his first Annual Message, seemed to support the handiwork of Lecompton and argued that a public referendum in Kansas on the entire Lecompton Constitution was not called for.[77]

The next day, before packed Senate galleries, Douglas delivered

[73] Johannsen, ed., *Letters of Douglas*, pp. 403–404.

[74] *New York Times*, December 3, 1857.

[75] The general outline of the White House showdown between Buchanan and Douglas soon became common knowledge, but Douglas' first public confirmation of the story occurred during an 1860 presidential campaign speech in Milwaukee. *Washington Daily National Intelligencer*, October 23, 1860.

[76] Horace Greeley, *Recollections of a Busy Life*, p. 356.

[77] Richardson, ed., *Messages and Papers of Presidents*, V, 449–454.

one of the great speeches of his career. He denounced both the Lecompton convention and the work it had done. The convention itself had exceeded its authority merely to petition Congress and had instead proceeded to draw up a constitution looking toward statehood. Douglas centered his comments on the constitution itself, particularly upon those clauses preventing the full submission of the whole constitution to a popular vote: "If the President be right in saying that, by the Nebraska bill, the slavery question must be submitted to the people, it follows inevitably that every other clause of the constitution must be submitted to the people."[78] Ringing the changes of reason, invective, and sarcasm, the Little Giant recalled Napoleon's address to his troops at the time of his election as First Consul: "Now, my soldiers, you are to go to the election and vote freely just as you please. If you vote for Napoleon, all is well; vote against him, and you are to be instantly shot."[79] A ripple of laughter swept the Senate.

As a way out of the Kansas impasse, Douglas recommended discarding both the Lecompton Constitution and the free-soil Topeka Constitution,[80] resurrecting an older Kansas Enabling Act (usually called the Toombs bill), and attaching to it a clause borrowed from the Minnesota Enabling Act requiring full submission, thus beginning the process of constitution-making in Kansas anew.[81]

Although the December 9 Senate speech climaxed the Buchanan-Douglas feud, Douglas, in spite of his earlier apparently implacable attitude, did not intend it as a declaration of war on the administration. The opening paragraphs of the speech betrayed a remarkably conciliatory attitude on the part of the Illinois Senator. Douglas expressed pleasure that a careful reading of the President's Annual Message revealed no specific endorsement of the Lecompton convention and no concrete recommendation that Congress admit

[78] *Cong. Globe*, 35th Cong., 1st sess., p. 15.

[79] Ibid., p. 17.

[80] The Topeka Constitution, drawn up in 1855, prohibited slavery in Kansas after July 4, 1857. William F. Zornow, *Kansas: A History of the Jayhawk State*, p. 71. In 1855 and again in 1857 this constitution was overwhelmingly accepted at popular referendums conducted by free-state forces; ibid., pp. 71, 77.

[81] *Cong. Globe*, 35th Cong., 1st sess., pp. 18, 24.

Kansas under the constitution that convention had produced. "I rejoice," Douglas continued, "on a careful perusal of the message, to find so much less to dissent from than I was under the impression there was, from the hasty reading and the imperfect hearing of the message in the first instance."[82] By appearing to denounce not Buchanan, but Lecompton, Douglas was extending a last olive branch to the President.

Buchanan did not take it. The fury of the long-gathering storm now broke upon Douglas. Buchanan set out neither to convert Douglas to his views nor merely to punish him for his political sins. He determined to put an end to his career as United States Senator. There would be no quarter from Buchanan. On December 23 the *Union* placed Douglas among the "agitators" whose object was to block a peaceful and final settlement of the Kansas question. Less than a month later the *Union* had grown bolder and asked that its readers bear in mind the fate of previous party rebels who "were driven into political exile and stripped of their power and influence."[83]

Buchanan's basic strategy in the long fight that followed was to make what was essentially a personal feud appear to be a question of party loyalty. He would first try to equate Douglas' dissent on the specific issue of Lecompton with a general bolt from the Democratic party by the Illinois Senator. Having isolated Douglas from the Democratic party, Buchanan hoped to be able to threaten him with defeat in his bid for re-election in November. By stressing the partisan nature of the quarrel, Buchanan could also avail himself of the most powerful weapon in the arsenal of a nineteenth-century President: federal patronage.

Early in 1858 the *Union* announced officially what had long been common knowledge: the admission of Kansas under Lecompton was now a party measure.[84] Though the announcement came as no surprise to Douglas, it left him uneasy.[85] While his active

[82] Ibid., p. 14.

[83] *Washington Union*, January 16, 1858.

[84] Ibid., February 18, 1858.

[85] For Douglas' reaction to the news that Lecompton had now become a test

imagination and restless spirit had usually placed him on the left wing of the Democratic party, he had always sought to avoid open rebellion. Douglas might want to reform the Democratic party and restore the sectional balance Buchanan's dalliance with the South had upset, but he did not wish to bolt.

He had always been a good party man.[86] As early as 1835 he had denounced Joseph Duncan, the Illinois Democratic governor, as a traitor for his opposition to President Jackson over the Bank.[87] Douglas owed a great debt to the Democracy. His meteoric rise through the political ranks paralleled the growth of formal party machinery in the Northwest. To the end of his life much of his political power and fame rested on a base of firm control of the Democratic organization in Illinois.

Yet something more than sentiment caused Douglas' reluctance to be cast in the role of party rebel. He was aware that only a small portion of the Democrats in Congress would actively support his Lecompton stand. In the Senate he could count on help from only three members of his party: David C. Broderick of California, George E. Pugh of Ohio, and Charles E. Stuart of Michigan. Broderick was, however, vulnerable to administration patronage pressure, and Pugh would eventually support the administration-sponsored English bill. In the House only about a fifth of the Democrats were certain to rally to the Douglas standard in the Lecompton fight. There were in both houses of Congress many members who were either apathetic or purposely noncommittal on the whole dispute.

Douglas knew that in the late 1850's the Democratic party establishment was a formidable enemy. Its long, if lethargic, domination of American politics had given it a firmly entrenched base of support. It controlled all three branches of the national government and a vast amount of patronage, and it was on the anvil of patronage that Buchanan hoped to break Stephen Douglas. The

---

of party loyalty, see his February 28, 1858, letter to Samuel Treat; in Johannsen, ed., *Letters of Douglas*, p. 418.

[86] Louis Howland, *Stephen A. Douglas*, p. 286.

[87] Johannsen, ed., *Letters of Douglas*, pp. 12–13.

New York Tribune commented that Buchanan "treasured his patronage as a miser does his gold."[88]

Although Buchanan had largely ignored Douglas' advice on new appointments since the beginning of his term, after the formal break over Lecompton in December the President began to wield the patronage axe in Illinois against incumbent Douglas sympathizers, many of whom had held their offices for years. Scores of United States marshals, customs officials, and postmasters were removed each week.[89] In February of 1858 Douglas wrote to his friend Samuel Treat: "It has become apparent that the Administration is more anxious for my destruction than they are for the harmony & unity of the Democratic Party. You have doubtless seen that they are removing all my friends from office & requiring pledges of hostility to me from all persons appointed to office."[90] The administration began a skillful, if somewhat diabolical, letter-writing campaign to key individuals on the Illinois political scene, promising the best offices to anyone who would desert Douglas. James Sheahan has written: "On successive days a letter like this would arrive from a member of the Cabinet, then from a Senator, until before the week was out four or five letters would have arrived."[91] There was evidence that postal officials were interfering with the delivery of Douglas' personal mail.[92] In March of 1858 the pro-Douglas postmaster at Chicago was summarily removed from office. In May, 1860, Douglas announced with some slight exaggeration to the Senate, "For three years no friend of mine has been permitted to hold a crossroads post office, or even to circulate the public documents under my frank, as a general thing, in my own State."[93]

After Douglas' Senate speech of December 9, 1857, events moved

[88] *New York Tribune*, December 2, 1857.

[89] Albert J. Beveridge, *Abraham Lincoln*, II, 551.

[90] Johannsen, ed., *Letters of Douglas*, p. 418.

[91] James W. Sheahan, *The Life of Stephen A. Douglas*, p. 387.

[92] O. Jennings Wise to Douglas, Richmond, Va., September 27, 1858; Douglas MSS.

[93] *Cong. Globe*, 36th Cong., 1st sess., p. 2156.

rapidly. On December 15 Governor Walker resigned. Six days later a referendum on the narrow issue of slavery under the Lecompton Constitution was held in Kansas. In an election largely boycotted by free-soilers and marked by open fraud, the slavery clauses carried by a vote of 6,143 to 569.[94] On January 4, 1858, in what was for Kansas an orderly referendum called by a special session of the newly elected territorial legislature, which now had a free-soil majority, the entire Lecompton Constitution was defeated by 10,226 votes to 161.[95] The North largely accepted this verdict as final. Buchanan did not. On February 2, 1858, he sent the Lecompton Constitution to Congress with a formal recommendation that Kansas be admitted under it.[96]

Douglas' strategy now begins to grow clear. First, he would avoid making the fight seem one between himself on the one hand and the Democratic party on the other. That would be playing Buchanan's game. Douglas would instead reserve his verbal artillery for Lecompton and Buchanan. On February 8, 1858, Douglas demanded in the Senate that the President transmit whatever information he might have regarding alleged frauds in the recent Kansas elections.[97] He was not successful;[98] he never expected to be, but this deft maneuver had put the spotlight squarely on Buchanan, tacitly associated him with the frauds perpetrated in Kansas, and placed him on the defensive.

Second, Douglas continued to appear to conduct his attack on Lecompton from the high ground of principle. In a Senate speech on February 4, he again stressed that the only real question at issue was whether or not Lecompton genuinely reflected the will of the people of Kansas.[99]

[94] *Tribune Almanac for 1859*, p. 33.

[95] Ibid., p. 34; Zornow, *Kansas*, p. 78; Spring, *Kansas*, pp. 228–229. The October, 1857, elections had given the free-state forces control of the territorial legislature, which was called into special session in December and immediately arranged for this referendum on the entire Lecompton constitution.

[96] Richardson, ed., *Messages and Papers of Presidents*, V, 471–481.

[97] *Cong. Globe*, 35th Cong., 1st sess., p. 607.

[98] Ibid., p. 1438.

[99] Ibid., p. 570.

Third, although the Senate was Douglas' great forum, he knew that administration control there was strong and that if Lecompton were to be defeated, it would have to be blocked in the House.[100]

Finally, although Douglas never actually admitted it, his words and actions from early 1858 onward suggested that his main goal was to delay the admission of Kansas for as long as possible. This is the best explanation of his insistence that the Senate turn its attentions in the early spring of 1858 to the admission of Minnesota as a state.[101] His immediate purpose here was probably twofold: first, to admit a free state to serve as a counterweight in the national sectional balance if a slave Kansas should come in under Lecompton in spite of his efforts; second, to distract congressional attention from the Lecompton debate and thereby delay admitting Kansas for as long as possible. Consummate politician that he was, Douglas had probably by early 1858 realized that whether Kansas was admitted as a free state or slave state, he would be the loser. If admitted as a slave state under Lecompton, it would be a personal satrapy of the administration forces that now sought to crush him. But even if Kansas entered the Union as a free state after a fair referendum on a new constitution, the long pent-up anger of the free-soil forces would probably push it into the Republican camp by 1860, and Douglas had had his eye on the 1860 election for a long time.

On March 22, 1858, Douglas left his sickbed to deliver his final Senate attack on Lecompton. The *New York Times* correspondent wrote: "The chamber was thronged as it is only on great occasions. Galleries, lobbies, floor, even the seats of members, were filled with spectators. A crowd of ladies had been for hours awaiting the time when the Illinois Senator should come. . . . Mr. Douglas' appear-

100 The Democratic majority in the Senate was much greater than in the House and, in addition, the South, which favored Lecompton, was proportionately stronger in the upper house. The 1st session of the 35th Congress found the Senate divided: 37 Democrats, 20 Republicans, and 5 Americans; in the House, 128 Democrats, 92 Republicans, and 14 Americans.

101 *Cong. Globe*, 35th Cong., 1st sess., p. 1446.

ance was greeted with demonstrations of applause, which testified how strongly the popular heart is moved by the spectacle of duty contending against wrong and defying power."[102]

The Little Giant, still pale from his recent illness[103] and concerned about Mrs. Douglas, who had almost died a few weeks before,[104] made his way slowly to the front of the Senate chamber. A stillness fell over the galleries.

Douglas lashed out against the authority of the Lecompton Convention to draft a constitution and questioned the legality of the elections that followed. He professed not to care about the proslavery bias of the Lecompton Constitution and reminded his audience again that his opposition to that constitution was made public before Kansas allegedly voted to accept that document with the slavery clauses attached. He based his opposition solely on the high ground of popular sovereignty, which, he said, in this instance meant that the people of Kansas be left "perfectly free to form and regulate their domestic institutions in their own way, subject only to the Constitution." Douglas remained unimpressed by administration arguments that Kansas could always amend its constitution after statehood. Summoning all that was left of his wasted strength, Douglas admonished the hushed chamber, "It is a mockery, nay, a crime, to attempt to enforce this constitution as an embodiment of the will of that people."[105]

With an eye toward the Southern Senators he warned that if the federal government could run roughshod over the will of the people of a territory, it could do the same thing to the people of a state. In a subtle fashion he reminded his fellow Democrats that they were not immune from sharing his fate of being ostracized from the party for daring to differ with the President: "Are you to read

[102] *New York Times*, March 24, 1858.

[103] Johannsen, ed., *Letters of Douglas*, p. 419.

[104] Mrs. Douglas had suffered a miscarriage in February; ibid., pp. 411–417; Milton, *Eve of Conflict*, p. 289.

[105] Douglas' Senate speech of March 22, 1858, is in *Cong. Globe*, 35th Cong., 1st sess., app., pp. 194ff.

out of the party every man who thinks it wrong to force a constitution on a people against their will?"[106]

That speech, Douglas reflected, had been one of his finest. It had contained just that right balance of cajolery and warning, of principle and realism, that was basic to his political character. But it had been to no avail. The next day the Senate had passed the Lecompton bill by a vote of 33 to 25.[107] The scene of battle had then moved to the House of Representatives.

The little man noticed that the cigar had gone out. Just as well. He rose, braced himself for a moment against the side of the swaying car, and called for the porter. It would soon be time for the first of several appearances he would make that day from the rear of the train when it stopped at the small towns along the line in Ohio and Indiana. And then would come the endless parade of visitors through the private car as more and more Douglas supporters climbed aboard the train to ride with the champion over the last few miles of the long journey that had begun in Washington.

To them Stephen Douglas, not James Buchanan, was the real head of the Democratic party. Throughout the long bitter feud with Buchanan, the Illinois Senator had never let the fight for his own political survival blind him to the larger interests of his party and his country. Although the Little Giant had neither asked for nor received any quarter, he had never closed his mind to some form of reconciliation in the interest of Democratic harmony. Beginning in early April, 1858, he had actually appeared to be taking the initiative in effecting a truce with Buchanan over Kansas.

Douglas regretted the quarrel between himself and Buchanan, and no doubt felt uncomfortable in his current role as the renegade of the Democratic party. Good party man that he was, Douglas would probably have described his attitude toward the administration as one of loyal opposition. There was another consideration at work by April of 1858: in a few weeks time Douglas would

[106] Ibid., p. 201.

[107] For the roll-call vote in the Senate, see the *Tribune Almanac for 1859*, p. 25.

begin his campaign for re-election. Given the choice, he would prefer to return to Illinois with the blessing of Buchanan or at least his indifference, rather than his outright hostility. From April, 1858, onward Douglas avoided direct attacks upon the President, and reserved his verbal barbs for the Directory.[108]

For a while a rapprochement seemed within reach. Perhaps Buchanan was beginning to sense that his merciless attack on Douglas had made the Little Giant something of a hero to the American public, with its characteristic sympathy for an underdog. Hoping to destroy Douglas, Buchanan may have seen that he had elevated him to the position of the most famous and popular Democrat in the land. By late March the *Washington Union* was denying that it had ever read Douglas out of the Democratic party.[109] By April attacks on Douglas in its columns had ceased altogether. Buchanan began looking about for a face-saving avenue of retreat. He eagerly seized the opportunity presented by the English bill; indeed, he may have written much of it.[110]

Although the Democrats enjoyed a nominal majority in the House of Representatives, party discipline was much weaker there than in the Senate. When the Senate passed the Lecompton measure and sent it to the House, a combination of Republicans and Douglas Democrats prepared to give it a rough reception. The lower house voted to add on to Lecompton the so-called Crittenden-Montgomery Amendment,[111] which would have admitted Kansas under

[108] In a Senate speech of April 2, Douglas seemed to be trying to narrow the gap between his policy on Kansas and that of the administration. He adopted one of Buchanan's favorite phrases and stressed the need to "localize" the Kansas controversy. *Cong. Globe*, 35th Cong., 1st sess., p. 1443. Also see Douglas' attack on the Danites in Illinois in which he studiously avoided blaming Buchanan, who was their sponsor; ibid., 35th Cong., special sess., pp. 3055–3058. Douglas' correspondence from April, 1858, suggested that his supporters felt that a rapprochement with Buchanan was in the air. James M. Davidson to Douglas, Chicago, Ill., April 27, 1858; Usher F. Linder to Douglas, Charleston, Ill., May 15, 1858; James W. Sheahan to Douglas, Chicago, Ill., May 30, 1858; Douglas MSS. Also see the *New York Journal of Commerce*, May 7, 1858.

[109] *Washington Union*, March 25, 1858.

[110] Klein, *President James Buchanan*, p. 311.

[111] The vote for amendment was 120 to 112. *Tribune Almanac for 1859*, p. 28.

Lecompton on the condition that the entire constitution first be submitted to the Kansas voters in a fair election. If Lecompton were subsequently rejected, a new constitution was to be drawn up looking toward prompt admission to statehood.[112] Because the administration obviously would not accept such an amendment, it amounted to a defeat of Lecompton in the House. It now fell to a conference committee to work out the differences between the two houses of Congress. The result was a bill named for William H. English, Democratic Representative from Indiana. The English measure provided for the admission of Kansas with a grant of almost four million acres of federal land plus 5 percent of the cash realized from the forthcoming sale of two million additional acres. Under the guise of holding a popular vote on the question of the land grant, the bill provided an indirect popular referendum on Lecompton. If Kansas voted to accept the grant, she would be admitted under Lecompton; if she rejected it, she would remain a territory until obtaining the requisite population for a congressional district. This would be about ninety thousand inhabitants, and Kansas was at least two years away from that figure.[113]

Buchanan represented the English bill as a final and magnanimous concession in the interest of party harmony to the recalcitrant Douglas faction. He wrote Jeremiah Black, the Attorney-General: "If the English Bill had been especially designed to afford . . . Douglas an honorable opportunity to escape from the dilemma in which he had placed himself, it could not have been more ingeniously contrived. It was the last plank held out to him and yet he refused to seize it."[114]

Magnanimity was not one of Buchanan's strong points. A better explanation of his support of the English bill would seem to be that if Kansas voted to accept the tempting land grant, Buchanan

112 The Crittenden-Montgomery Amendment also included a plan for rigorous supervision of the loose electoral machinery in Kansas. The complete text of the Crittenden-Montgomery Amendment is found ibid., pp. 25–27.

113 The text of the English bill is found ibid., pp. 29–30.

114 A memorandum from Buchanan to Black, undated, but written before September 18, 1859; Jeremiah S. Black Papers (Library of Congress), volume 26, items 53891–53898. Cited hereafter as Black Papers.

Representative William H. English of Indiana. His bill broke the congressional deadlock over Lecompton.

would have his victory over Lecompton. If, on the other hand, Kansas voted to reject the offer, as Buchanan probably expected it to, it would be left in the territorial condition for at least two more years. Thus the national dirt could be swept under the territorial carpet, and Buchanan could serve out the rest of his term in peace. Under the guise of generosity toward his opponents, Buchanan was in effect making a face-saving retreat.

Douglas' attitude toward the English bill was complex. Allen Johnson was no doubt correct when he wrote that Douglas' decision to oppose it was probably the most painful one he had ever taken.[115] He could not easily object to the *de facto* referendum on the constitution. Although the English arrangement was somewhat devious, it implemented the essence of his demand for popular submission. It was this demand that had led Douglas to support the Crittenden-Montgomery compromise plan. Nor did Douglas seem unduly upset by the large federal land grant the *New York Times* labeled as little more than a bribe.[116] Instead, he hammered away at the inequity of agreeing to admit Kansas with its present population of perhaps forty thousand if it accepted Lecompton, but forcing it to wait until it had ninety thousand inhabitants should it prefer to come into the Union under any other constitution. Douglas argued that should Kansas reject Lecompton, it must be allowed to draw up another constitution looking toward immediate admission. Alternately, Douglas would accept the ninety thousand population requirement if it were henceforth made a general rule for all territories awaiting statehood. But to make a special case of Kansas constituted unwarranted congressional intervention and made a travesty of his beloved popular sovereignty.[117] The English bill gave tacit approval to popular sovereignty as a principle, only to hamstring its workings in practice.

As with Buchanan, one has to look below the surface of professed reasons for a true explanation of Douglas' anti-English position.

[115] Allen Johnson, *Stephen A. Douglas: A Study in American Politics*, p. 345.
[116] *New York Times*, April 26, 1858.
[117] Douglas' speech opposing the English bill was made on April 29, 1858, and may be found in the *Cong. Globe*, 35th Cong., 1st sess., pp. 1868ff.

Douglas had little to gain from supporting the measure. His anti-Lecompton stand had earned the vocal support of Democrats in the East and the crucial Northwest and had brought Douglas closer to his goal of appearing to be a man of principle. To have modified his views at this juncture would have undone much that Douglas had recently accomplished in the North, but would not really have reconciled the South.

Douglas may have been a national political figure, but his first job was to win re-election in Illinois that fall. His mail left no doubt what the reaction of the Northwest to the passage of the English bill would be. Daniel O. Morton wrote from Cleveland, Ohio: "What we must fear now is a *compromise* at Washington. For Gods [*sic*] sake put your foot on every proposition looking that way."[118] From Chicago James M. Davidson admonished Douglas: "Yield not one inch. Consent to no compromise. Stand firm by the right and God and the country will stand by you."[119] George Buell of the *Cincinnati Enquirer* encouraged Douglas with these words: "I tell you I have not during the last three weeks met one man in this city of 225,000 people whose heart and soul indorse either the English or the Lecompton proposition."[120]

Douglas would lose by publicly supporting the English bill, yet privately he must have been quite pleased with it. He must have known that the election to be held under the English scheme would result in the defeat of Lecompton. Keeping Kansas in the territorial condition for a few more years would serve Douglas' presidential ambitions better than admitting a state that would vote with the administration in the Democratic convention in 1860 and probably with the Republicans in the election that followed.

In short, in his stand on the English bill, the crafty Illinois Senator had the best of both worlds: he received credit for opposing a measure that was unpopular in Illinois, and yet he was not unduly upset when the English bill passed the Senate on April 30 by a

[118] Daniel O. Morton to Douglas, Cleveland, Ohio, February 22, 1858, Douglas MSS.

[119] James M. Davidson to Douglas, Chicago, Ill., April 27, 1858; ibid.

[120] George P. Buell to Douglas, Cincinnati, Ohio, May 4, 1858; ibid.

vote of 31 to 22 and the House by 112 to 103.[121] Indeed, it may well have been that one reason Douglas voted against the English bill was to insure Southern support of it, for Douglas' acceptance of an administration measure would have been looked upon by the South with suspicion. When the people of Kansas in the election held pursuant to the English bill on August 2 voted down Lecompton 11,300 to 1,788,[122] Douglas' entire Kansas position received a belated vindication, and his political fortunes for 1860 began to look brighter.

With the passage of the English bill, the Kansas crisis was, for the time being, quiescent. Furthermore, the ostensible cause of the friction between Buchanan and Douglas had been removed, and many observers felt their long and costly feud would now end. The *New York Journal of Commerce* for May 7, 1858, commented: "The tone and bearing of Senator Douglas since the Kansas question was disposed of do not indicate a disposition to provoke a renewal of hostilities or to prolong unnecessarily the unpleasant controversy which has existed between the Administration and himself." Usher Linder felt constrained to warn Douglas: "You cannot return to the Administration without (excuse the word) political infamy. . . . Any reconciliation between you and the Administration party soils you, yes to be plain, degrades you and strikes you down from that high position where you have fearlessly and disinterestedly battled and which has endeared you to all disinterested and high-minded men."[123]

Linder need not have worried. After a brief respite, Buchanan

[121] *American Almanac for 1859* (Boston, 1859), XXX, 369.

[122] Ibid., for the vote on Lecompton under the English scheme. While the actual vote was on the question of whether or not to accept the federal land grant incorporated into the English Act, the referendum was in fact on the larger issue of accepting or rejecting Lecompton and was so regarded by the people of Kansas. English, in his legislation, had included safeguards against the kind of electoral frauds that had plagued Kansas for so long, and the August 2, 1858, vote was generally considered a fair one. For the most balanced discussion of the English bill and its effect on Lecompton see Frank H. Hodder, "Some Aspects of the English Bill for the Admission of Kansas," *Annual Report of the American Historical Association for 1906* 1: 201–210.

[123] Usher F. Linder to Douglas, Charleston, Ill., May 15, 1858; Douglas MSS.

began to swing his patronage axe once again, and the Little Giant resumed his defiant mood. That the feud between the two men did not end with the temporary resolution of the Kansas problem, but continued unabated for three more years, is perhaps the best proof that the differences between Buchanan and Douglas went much deeper than Lecompton.

For James Buchanan, the fight with Douglas was almost a total disaster. It exposed to public view the personal shortcomings his intimates had long suspected. The petty intrigue that Buchanan confused with statesmanship, the vicious patronage war on the Illinois Senator, the sight of the President of the United States stooping to such tactics as having the post office open Douglas' mail or having a brass band blare forth while Douglas was making a speech,[124] quite simply disgusted the country. Buchanan's stand alienated moderate opinion in the North, but it did little to satisfy the South. The primary beneficiaries of the feud were Buchanan's two worst enemies: Douglas and the Republican party. It is hard to disagree with the later verdict of the *New York Times* when it held that Buchanan's stand on Lecompton ultimately destroyed him.[125]

Perhaps the most harmful effect of all was of a more subtle nature. The Lecompton feud went on too long. For almost a year Buchanan and Kansas dominated the news coming out of Washington, and Buchanan's personality did not wear well under the hot light of publicity. He soon began to suffer from overexposure. If by the middle of 1858 America was tired of Kansas, it would also soon be tired of Buchanan. The *New York Times* commented in July of 1859: "The story of Buchanan's Presidency thus far is a chronicle of lost opportunities, of indecisive temporising at decisive moments, of timid inaction when courage and energy might have secured important benefits for the country."[126] Perhaps the most ironical outcome of all was that one of the last acts of the Buchanan

124 Nevins, *The Emergence of Lincoln*, I, 396.
125 *New York Times*, June 29, 1860.
126 Ibid., July 23, 1859.

administration would be to admit Kansas early in 1861 as a free state.

From Douglas' point of view, the feud had somewhat better results, at least in the short run. His audacity in successfully challenging the President of the United States and the Democratic establishment did serve to cast Douglas in the pleasant, if unusual, role of the underdog waging a battle of heroic proportions. It attracted a great deal of national attention. His stand on Lecompton rallied Illinois to his standard and made possible his re-election to the Senate. It partially removed the shadow of suspicion that had lingered for years over his role in repealing the Missouri Compromise. A typical reaction on this point was contained in a letter to Douglas comparing him to a sinner who had repented.[127]

So pleased with the new Douglas was Horace Greeley that in the early spring of 1858 he encouraged the Republicans in Illinois not to oppose the Little Giant's bid for re-election. Douglas was shrewd enough to realize that Greeley's primary aim was probably to deepen the split in the Democratic party to the benefit of Republicans nationally. He also knew that to accept Greeley's aid formally would be to incur the suspicion of his Democratic supporters in Illinois. If Douglas had been ready to take that kind of risk, he would probably have formed his own third party.[128] Nevertheless, the spectacle of some Eastern Republicans seeking to work for his re-election must have been privately very pleasing to the Little Giant.

James G. Blaine has written: "Until his break from the regular ranks in his opposition to the Lecompton Constitution, Douglas had enjoyed boundless popularity with his party in the South."[129] Did Douglas' anti-Lecompton stand therefore mark the sudden and

[127] Anonymous to Douglas, n.p., December, 1857 (filed between December 31, 1857 and January 1, 1858); Douglas MSS.

[128] Douglas apparently gave some thought early in 1858 to forming a Constitutional Union party based on the doctrine of popular sovereignty and composed of anti-Lecompton Democrats and Republicans. Milton, *Eve of Conflict*, p. 283.

[129] James G. Blaine, *Twenty Years of Congress*, I, 150.

complete alienation of the South from his cause? While it is true that Douglas' attitude toward Lecompton, much more than his later reply to Lincoln's Freeport Question in the joint debates, angered the South, its effect was less abrupt than is commonly assumed. In the last analysis, Douglas' Lecompton policy probably served merely to confirm the suspicions the South now tended to have toward any Yankee politician, especially one as unimpressed by its threats as Stephen Douglas. The effects of Douglas' stand were mitigated by a tendency of many Southerners, with their predisposition to see politics mainly in human terms, to look upon the feud with Buchanan largely as a personal quarrel. At most it was to them a dispute within the Democratic party and not a matter of vital national importance. Much southern anger with Douglas was short-lived. In September of 1858 a correspondent in Shreveport, Louisiana, would write to endorse Douglas' bid for re-election. The writer regretted Douglas' attitude on Kansas, but added, "I am disposed to forgive and forget the past and I think that is the feeling in the South."[130]

For Douglas himself, the stand on Lecompton symbolized the end of that part of his public career during which he sought largely to appease the South. In the next stage of his career he would adopt a public attitude of sectional neutrality, which did not always succeed in hiding his growing bias toward the North.

If his quarrel with Buchanan helped Douglas in many respects, it hurt him in others. At times he seemed to have won a Pyrrhic victory. He had less power in Congress now. William Seward had once labeled him a "legislative dictator, intolerant yet irresistible."[131] Now he spoke for a minority of the Democrats on Capitol Hill; in a few more months he would lose his coveted chairmanship of the Committee on Territories. Outside the halls of Congress, he was the member of a confused and divided party. It no longer

[130] Roland Jones to Douglas, Shreveport, La., September 20, 1858; Douglas MSS.

[131] Howland, *Stephen A. Douglas*, p. 286.

seemed quite so likely that Stephen Douglas would be the next Democratic candidate for the presidency.

Although Douglas won most of his encounters with Buchanan, each victory served to narrow his political base. While the anger with which the South had greeted Douglas' stand on Lecompton would abate, long-standing Southern suspicions of the Illinois Senator had been confirmed. If the Southern people did not regard Douglas as an outright enemy, it was nonetheless going to be much more difficult for him to appear as a friend. Nor was Douglas' setback in the South offset by comparable gains in the East. The enthusiasm of the New England and Middle Atlantic States for Douglas' opposition to Lecompton did not mean a long-range victory for his cause there. When the Lecompton clamor had faded away, somehow the East still did not seem to trust Douglas. Louis Howland has commented that this was too much to hope for since Douglas had long been associated with the proponents of slavery and was known first of all as a good party man.[132] Always striving to be a statesman of national proportions, Douglas found himself with only the Northwest as a sure source of political strength.

Finally, by conducting his fight on Kansas largely at the national level and by relying on Congress to shape the future of that territory, Douglas, although he had claimed to be defending popular sovereignty, had in fact acted in a manner contrary to one of its constituent principles: nonintervention by the federal government in the affairs of a territory.

From the larger point of view, the Buchanan-Douglas feud was both a cause and an effect of the pernicious disease that was infecting American politics with alarming rapidity as the 1850's drew to a close. The democratic process was dissolving into petty personal quarrels on the one hand, and unrealistic concern with abstractions on the other. There was less and less room for the down-to-earth bargaining and give-and-take that are at the heart of any successful political system. Kansas was intrinsically of only marginal impor-

[132] Ibid., pp. 296–297.

tance, but it had the misfortune to become a symbol of the whole future of slavery in America. In the name of free-soil or states' rights, of abolitionism or popular sovereignty, politicians, both North and South, were recklessly straining the few national ties that still bound their increasingly antagonistic sections to the Union.

But those were long-term considerations. On this pleasant July morning Stephen Douglas was thinking of such immediate problems as getting re-elected.

The establishment of an uneasy truce over Kansas had not altered Buchanan's aim to block Douglas' return to the Senate. While the *Union* piously professed a "serene indifference"[133] toward the outcome of the Illinois race, the Buchanan forces had deliberately set out to defeat Douglas' try for re-election. On June 9 the Buchanan faction of the Illinois Democracy had met in convention at Springfield to endorse an alternate slate of candidates. They called themselves National Democrats; Douglas contemptuously labeled them Danites.[134] They denied the validity of the regular Democratic convention, which two months earlier had met in the same city and supported Douglas. While avowedly seeking to elect Douglas' old enemy Sidney Breese to the Senate, the Danites knew he had no chance and covertly threw much of their support to the Republican candidate.

On June 16 the Illinois Republicans had also held a convention at Springfield and chosen their candidate for the United States Senate. That same evening he had warned them of a "house divided against itself." His name was Abraham Lincoln.

One of Douglas' aides entered his car to tell the Senator that the train was approaching Toledo. Douglas thanked him. He would have to get ready for his first speech of the day.

He turned his glance one last time to the broad blue expanse of

133 *Washington Union*, October 29, 1858.

134 *Cong. Globe*, 35th Cong., special sess., pp. 3056–3058.

Lake Erie, now shimmering under the bright July sun. With the Democratic establishment out for his defeat and the most able Republican in the Northwest in the field against him, Douglas knew that he would face in Illinois the greatest challenge of his long political career.

Stephen Douglas must have smiled to himself. He loved a fight, and that summer promised a good one.

3. Popular Sovereignty

Stephen Douglas rode into the Illinois lists as the champion of principle.[1] In an age when politicians felt constrained to identify their names with some doctrine, and more often than not became the prisoners of it, Douglas chose to wear the favor of that whimsical lady, Popular Sovereignty.

Most observers found her attractive, those who looked closer dubbed her superficial, and the most acute of all pronounced her ambivalent. Douglas himself appears to have discovered her charms rather belatedly. He then wooed her furiously, placed her on a pedestal, and proclaimed her to the world. He would one day largely cast her aside. His long relationship with her had about it the aura of romance, but cynics labeled it a liaison of convenience. Few doubted her utility before the tournament in Illinois that summer of 1858, few did so when it had ended. But after several sallies by the tall challenger from Springfield, many began to question the lady's virtue.

Popular sovereignty was at least four ideas under one name. No

[1] See Richard Allen Heckman, "The Lincoln-Douglas Debate, Freeport, Illinois, August 27, 1858," (M.A. thesis, Indiana University, 1956), pp. 50–51; Edwin Erle Sparks, ed., *The Lincoln-Douglas Debates of 1858*, p. 321.

small part of the confusion surrounding the term can be traced to a failure to define which aspect of the doctrine is under consideration. Popular sovereignty was a theory of government, a prescription for settling territorial questions, a framework in which to conduct national disputes over slavery, and a philosophical extension of the political personality of one man: Stephen A. Douglas.

As a theory of government, popular sovereignty simply meant that all political power resided ultimately with the people. The doctrine was synonymous with democracy and basic to the American political experience. Alexis de Tocqueville commented: "If there is a country in the world where the doctrine of the sovereignty of the people can be fairly appreciated, where it can be studied in its application to the affairs of society, and where its dangers and advantages may be judged, that country is assuredly America."[2]

In the American political experience the primary political devices for giving expression to the idea of the sovereignty of the people were universal suffrage and majority rule. Even so implacable a foe of Douglas and his doctrine as James Buchanan observed that popular sovereignty was, in effect, "a self-evident political maxim. It is nothing more than to say the majority shall rule."[3]

If popular sovereignty was a general theory of politics, it was also a specific prescription for curing the territorial ills of America in the 1850's. It proposed to solve the problems presented by widely differing territorial areas by granting them a high degree of autonomy from the government in Washington. "What is called Popular Sovereignty in the Territories," wrote one commentator, "is a phrase used to designate the right of the people of an organized Territory, under the Constitution and laws of the United States, to govern themselves in respect to their own internal polity and domestic affairs."[4] As a territorial policy, popular sovereignty was made up of two constituent principles, one positive, the other

[2] Alexis de Tocqueville, *Democracy in America*, ed. Phillips Bradley, I, 55.

[3] Memorandum of Buchanan to Jeremiah Black, undated, but before September 18, 1859. Black Papers, vol. 26, item 53892.

[4] J. Madison Cutts, *A Brief Treatise upon Constitutional and Party Questions and the History of Political Parties*, pp. 123–124.

negative: self-government by the people of the territories and non-intervention in territorial affairs by the federal government.

Popular sovereignty, as a territorial policy for America, was of dim origin and uncertain parentage. Its growth was gradual and largely paralleled the development of the American nation itself. The doctrine fit America well and the Western frontier best of all. Its essential ingredients—localism and majority rule—were basic to the whole political experience of the frontier, with its love of individualism, its suspicion of centralized political power, and its bias in favor of home rule. Frederick Jackson Turner called popular sovereignty in the territories "a natural outcome of the combined influences of Puritan political philosophy, in its Scotch-Irish form, the revolutionary spirit, and the forest freedom . . . the doctrine that the people in an unoccupied land have the right to determine their own political institutions."[5]

The great test for the doctrine of popular sovereignty in the territories involved the status of slavery along the frontier. Throughout early American history there was a strong predisposition to leave the fate of the institution of slavery in the hands of those most closely affected by it. Each state was to decide for itself whether it would be slave or free. In the territorial experience of the country there was a similar bias in favor of decentralized control. Although the Ordinance of 1787 found the national government seeking to bar slavery throughout the Northwest Territory, the ultimate effectiveness of the statutory provision was strongly influenced by the attitudes of the local settlers. In the Missouri Compromise of 1820, slavery was prohibited in all the territory acquired under the Louisiana Purchase north of the line 36° 30′, but the future of the institution below that line was left up to the local inhabitants. The Compromise of 1850 in effect recognized the right of the residents of the new Utah and New Mexico Territories to decide the future of slavery for themselves; the Kansas-Nebraska Act of 1854 purported to enshrine the principle of popular sovereignty in the territories.

[5] Frederick Jackson Turner, "Western State-Making in the Revolutionary Era," *American Historical Review* 1, no. 2 (January 1896): 266.

No one man fathered popular sovereignty as a means for deciding the status of slavery in the territories; many adopted it. A principle as intrinsic to the political spirit of a people as popular sovereignty was to Americans is rarely invented or even discovered by a single person. It almost seems to grow up *sui generis* and is from time to time clarified and expanded by the best political minds of the day.

Popular sovereignty had a long and distinguished list of contributors. Thomas Jefferson, Edward Livingston, Zachary Taylor, James L. Orr, and Daniel Dickinson all played a part in its development and clarification. Although John C. Calhoun detested the whole idea of popular sovereignty applied to the question of slavery in the territories, his notion of the concurrent majority closely resembled the positive side of the doctrine: self-determination. Popular sovereignty on the frontier was in many respects Calhoun's concurrent majority applied to territories as well as to states. His doctrine of nullification may be compared to the negative side of the idea of territorial popular sovereignty: nonintervention.[6]

Lewis Cass contributed more to the development of popular sovereignty as a territorial principle than any other American prior to 1850. It was Cass who, in his celebrated letter to A. O. P. Nicholson late in 1847,[7] molded the vague but familiar components of popular sovereignty into a concise formula for dealing with the immediate and specific problem of the status of slavery in the territories. Cass's biographer has written that he "took the wandering, tentative suggestions of statesmen and people, and combined them and arranged them in a clear and succinct statement of a great political principle."[8]

If Cass and others clarified popular sovereignty, Stephen Douglas popularized and mobilized it. He did not create the doctrine; he never claimed to. Douglas was not an original political theorist, although he had one of the most active imaginations in American

[6] An admirable discussion of Calhoun's views may be found in Charles M. Wiltse, *John C. Calhoun, Sectionalist, 1840–1850*, pp. 414–417.

[7] Andrew C. McLaughlin, *Lewis Cass*, pp. 235–239.

[8] Ibid., pp. 235–236.

politics.[9] The term popular sovereignty no doubt conjured up in Douglas' mind memories of the town meetings he had witnessed as a small boy back in Vermont. It must have also appealed to the Westerner's love of local self-government and his inveterate suspicion of too much centralized authority.

Douglas' long relationship with the fundamental tenets of popular sovereignty had its beginnings as early as 1845 when, as a member of the United States House of Representatives, he tried to write a primitive version of the doctrine into the joint resolution for the annexation of Texas.[10] Three years later, in a speech at New Orleans, Douglas endorsed the right of the citizens of a territory to control their own affairs.[11] Ever since the Wilmot Proviso, which sought to have Congress bar slavery from all land acquired as a result of the Mexican War, had been proposed in 1846, Douglas had denounced the measure as arbitrary interference with the right of the people of the territories to decide the question of slavery for themselves.[12]

The year 1850 marked the first time that Douglas attempted to incorporate the essence of popular sovereignty into a major piece of territorial legislation. Although Henry Clay continues to receive the major share of the credit for the Compromise of 1850, it was young Senator Stephen Douglas who guided it through the tortuous legislative channels and who left his mark on many of its measures.[13] The acts organizing the New Mexico and Utah Territories did not explicitly endorse the principle of territorial control over slavery, but Douglas, by refusing to include in his legislation a clear prohibition against any action on slavery by the territorial legislature, in effect left the way open for the people of the territory

[9] Frank E. Stevens, "Life of Stephen Arnold Douglas," *Journal of the Illinois State Historical Society* 16: 666.

[10] Albert J. Beveridge, *Abraham Lincoln*, II, 177 n. At this early stage of his relationship with popular sovereignty Douglas was concerned primarily with the control by states, rather than territories, over the institution of slavery within their boundaries.

[11] Ibid., pp. 176–177.

[12] Robert W. Johannsen, ed., *The Letters of Stephen A. Douglas*, pp. 241–242.

[13] Holman Hamilton, *Prologue to Conflict*, pp. 133–150.

to erect legal barriers to slavery on the one hand, or to give it legal protection on the other.[14]

Douglas' actions at this stage of his relationship with popular sovereignty did not, however, suggest the attitude of an idealist. His efforts in 1850 were largely governed by expediency, and the set of compromise measures themselves were arrived at in a rather *ad hoc* fashion. The preconditions for the successful application of the doctrine of popular sovereignty to the territories were present in the 1850 settlement, but nowhere in the territorial bills was there a positive statement of principle. It was only during the debates on the Kansas-Nebraska bill four years later that Douglas revealed that the earlier compromise had established a universal principle controlling all future territorial policy. In 1854 Douglas, perhaps feeling that only the cause of principle could make the repeal of the Missouri Compromise acceptable to the people of the free states, refined his 1850 position, wrapped his machinations in a cloak of idealism, and proclaimed to the world his Kansas-Nebraska Act as the embodiment of the universal principle of popular sovereignty for the territories.[15]

As the doctrine of popular sovereignty began to achieve a concrete identity in the public mind, as it began to mature and Douglas' name became more closely associated with it, a fundamental duality in the entire notion began to appear.

There was a hard side to popular sovereignty—the side of principle. That principle was best expressed in the Kansas-Nebraska Act: "it being the true intent and meaning of this Act not to legislate slavery into any territory or state, nor to exclude it therefrom; but to leave the people thereof perfectly free to form and regulate their domestic institutions in their own way, subject only to the Constitution of the United States."[16]

The hard side of popular sovereignty was narrow in its focus. It purported to be concerned only with slavery in the territories. It carried the unmistakable implication that, left to themselves, the

[14] Johannsen, ed., *Letters of Douglas*, p. 192.

[15] *Cong. Globe*, 33rd Cong., 1st sess., pp. 222, 240, 275–280.

[16] Ibid., p. 421.

people of the territories could settle the question of slavery quickly, easily, and permanently. Yet there was about the hard side of the doctrine much that was artificial, unrealistic, and basically two-dimensional. It sought to solve the territorial slavery problems in a political and moral vacuum.

The hard side oversimplified the process of arriving at a decision on slavery. It too easily assumed that all the people of a territory needed was to be left alone by the rest of the country. Basic to the hard side of popular sovereignty was the notion of absolute nonintervention by the federal government where the question of the status of slavery in a territory was concerned. The hard side went a step farther and seemed to imply that any territorial decision on slavery was to be reached through a process of simple majoritarianism, uncomplicated by any ethical or moral considerations.

The hard side of popular sovereignty became the object of fervent praise and bitter denunciation, but in the end it remained basically an abstraction, sterile and inoperative. A degree of nonintervention by the federal government, the negative side of the doctrine, was of course the corollary to the positive side, self-determination, which, through the emphasis it placed on the force of local habits and custom, found wide support among the best political thinkers. Had Douglas been somewhat better read, he could have summoned up a worthy ally on this point in Rousseau.[17] American experience with prohibition and civil rights legislation supports Douglas' contention that the fundamental area for determining the efficiency of a given law is usually a local one.

But the idea of absolute nonintervention by the federal government in the domestic affairs of a territory found little support in the constitutional theory of American government.[18] It found even less in practice.

When Stephen Douglas qualified the powers the citizens of a territory might exercise over slavery with the phrase "subject only to the Constitution of the United States,"[19] he left the door open

[17] Jean Jacques Rousseau, *The Social Contract*, ed. G. D. H. Cole, Chapter III.
[18] Allan Nevins, *Ordeal of the Union*, I, 32.
[19] *Cong. Globe*, 33rd Cong., 1st sess., p. 421.

for intervention in territorial affairs from a number of quarters, principally the Supreme Court, whose job it was to interpret the Constitution. In writing the Kansas-Nebraska bill, Douglas provided that the governor, appointed by the President, should have a veto over the acts of the territorial legislature. When Douglas expounded the virtues of nonintervention by the federal government in the affairs of a territory, he was in fact censuring intervention by only one branch—Congress—while giving his tacit approval to intervention by the President and the Supreme Court. In practice, Douglas would at times even approve a rather broad area of congressional intervention. The 1850 Compromise required congressional approval of all territorial legislation; the Kansas-Nebraska Act, while less stringent, left the door open to congressional revision of acts of the territorial legislature.[20] Douglas based his campaign against Lecompton in part on the need for Congress to pass an enabling act before Kansas could legitimately seek statehood.[21] In 1857 Douglas shocked a number of people by announcing that popular sovereignty was a gift from the federal government to the people of the territories and as such could be revoked by Congress at any time.[22] Douglas was among the first to urge Buchanan to send federal troops to Utah in response to rumors of a Mormon uprising in 1857. At one point he suggested that if less drastic measures failed, Congress should simply rescind the territorial status Utah had acquired as a result of the 1850 Compromise.[23] As civil war drew nearer, Douglas more and more tended to look to Congress for a solution of the problems posed by slavery in the territories.[24]

Although after his death Douglas would be eulogized as the

20 Hamilton, *Prologue to Conflict*, pp. 203–204; George Fort Milton, *The Eve of Conflict: Stephen A. Douglas and the Needless War*, p. 133.

21 *Cong. Globe*, 35th Cong., 1st sess., p. 15.

22 Beveridge, *Abraham Lincoln*, II, 501–502.

23 Harry V. Jaffa, *Crisis of the House Divided*, p. 358.

24 See, for example, Douglas' proposed compromise of December, 1860. *Cong. Globe*, 36th Cong., 2nd sess., app., p. 41. Also his plan to prohibit the territory of Colorado from barring slavery; ibid., p. 764.

champion of "absolute non-intervention by Congress,"[25] Henry Foote was probably closer to the truth when, in a perhaps not wholly unintentional slip of the tongue, he referred to Douglas as the "fearless champion of intervention and popular sovereignty."[26]

Yet such was the ritual of the hard side of popular sovereignty that Douglas could never openly admit that he sanctioned intervention by the federal government over matters that concerned the status of slavery in the territories. As late as 1860 Douglas proclaimed, "So long as Congress does not touch the question there will be peace, and whenever Congress does interfere there is strife."[27]

Far from nonintervention resulting in peace in the territories, the reverse would seem to be nearer the truth. It was the prospect that the federal government would continue to sit idly by that encouraged extremist elements in Kansas to turn to violence. Far from nonintervention furthering the cause of expression of popular opinion on slavery, it took very real intervention in the form of a strong governor and federal troops to safeguard the honest working of election machinery on the Kansas frontier. Federal intervention in the affairs of a territory reached its climax in the Douglas-sponsored move, undertaken in the name of popular sovereignty, to block the admission of Kansas under the Lecompton Constitution.

The hard side of popular sovereignty proposed to settle all territorial questions, including the difficult issue of slavery, through the simple expedient of putting into effect the wishes of the majority of voters in each territory. Here again, in its search for a quick and easy solution to problems of awesome difficulty, popular sovereignty began to lose contact with political reality.

While the notion of majority rule is a basic component of any democratic system, it is essentially a means that must ultimately be judged by its ends. Douglas, when expounding the hard side of

[25] Ibid., 37th Cong., 1st sess., p. 36.

[26] H. S. Foote, *War of the Rebellion*, p. 247.

[27] Stephen A. Douglas, "The Montgomery Address of Stephen A. Douglas," ed. David R. Barbee and Milledge L. Bonham, Jr., *Journal of Southern History* 5, no. 4 (November 1939): 550. See also *Cong. Globe*, 36th Cong., 2nd sess., pp. 643, 661.

the doctrine, as he did during the assault on Lecompton, professed to disregard ends—to "care not" whether slavery was approved or forbidden in a territory so long as a fair plebiscite was held on the question.[28] Douglas overlooked the ethical framework in which any political decision, minority or majority, must be evaluated. It was upon just this ethical, or as he called it, moral, omission from the doctrine of simple majoritarianism that Lincoln was to concentrate his attacks on Douglas during the 1858 senatorial campaign in Illinois.

The only acceptable defense for a nonethical approach to majority rule is the contention that the majority will always choose the just course. History, unfortunately, does not bear out this easy assumption. Nor does it bear out another implicit in the simple majoritarianism of the hard side: that a minority will always acquiesce in the decisions of a majority. In the decade prior to the Civil War the most vocal and implacable elements in American politics, both in the states and the territories, were minorities: Southern Ultras and Northern abolitionists.

If the hard side of popular sovereignty too readily accepted whatever a territorial majority wished as right, it also oversimplified the factors which conditioned the most important decision that majority would have to make. The Douglas doctrine maintained that popular opinion on slavery was largely determined by narrow economic self-interest, which in turn was held to be primarily a function of climate.[29] Such reasoning is valid up to a point. Economics obviously plays a role in determining political behavior. As for climate, Montesquieu and others have readily conceded its influence.[30] The error on the hard side of the doctrine of popular sovereignty was basically one of proportion. To say that economic factors and climate influence political behavior is one thing; to hold that they are its sole, or even primary, determinants is quite

[28] *Cong. Globe*, 35th Cong., 1st sess., pp. 14–18.

[29] Paul M. Angle, ed., *Created Equal? The Complete Lincoln-Douglas Debates of 1858*, p. 375.

[30] W. T. Jones, ed., *Machiavelli to Bentham*, vol. II of *Masters of Political Thought*, ed. Edward McChesney Sait, pp. 242–244.

another. The latter approach erects artificial and unrealistic barriers against the entry of ethical considerations into the political decision-making process. Just as Douglas' career was a compound of principle and expediency, of magnanimity and self-interest, so was the political behavior of individual Americans in the 1850's and so it is today. Montesquieu himself could never quite bring himself to approve of slavery even under the most propitious climatic conditions.[31] It was this artificial, incomplete, needlessly amoral aspect of popular sovereignty that prompted Carl Schurz to dismiss the whole notion as totally lacking in both logic and humanitarianism.[32]

Perhaps the basic shortcoming of the hard side was that it was too exclusively a political concept. It readily accorded the inhabitants of a territory the political right of self-determination, but its moral neutrality toward slavery was indicative of a serious disregard for the human or natural rights of mankind. The kind of community relevant to popular sovereignty in its usual form was primarily a political one. In order for people to exercise control over their domestic affairs, all the doctrine seemed to require was that they formally be granted the status of territory by Congress. It made no provision for the existence of the kind of underlying social community that is basic to the smooth functioning of any political system. Much of the trouble that beset Kansas can be traced to the fact that a political community was created before there was a sound underlying social community. A territory was called into being long before there was a large, permanent group of white settlers with a history of shared experiences and outlooks that might have enabled Kansas to withstand the strains the slavery controversy placed upon its political fabric.

There was another side to popular sovereignty. It had less of principle about it, more of policy. It was less an ideal than it was a device. It was more practical and flexible, somewhat subjective

31 Ibid., p. 244.

32 Heckman, "Lincoln-Douglas Debate, Freeport," p. 131.

and less doctrinaire. If the hard side was concerned primarily with the institution of slavery in the territories, the soft side was broader in its focus. It sought to resolve, or at least discipline, the larger question of the fate of slavery not just on the frontier, but throughout America. The soft side proposed a set of rules for determining the status of slavery in the American territories and hoped that both North and South would agree to abide by the outcome of any decision that might be taken under these rules. The soft side was essentially a way for those Americans who favored slavery and those who opposed it to agree to disagree over its fate in the newer parts of the country. It tried to turn many of the flaws of the hard side into positive virtues.

The soft side of popular sovereignty was also more closely attuned to the political needs of Stephen Douglas. If both North and South would agree to it as a means of settling the growing slavery dispute, his role as a national leader in an age beset with sectionalism would take on new life.

For a while the soft side of popular sovereignty seemed to be succeeding. The two compromises of 1850 and 1854 do seem to have calmed tempers on both sides of the Mason-Dixon Line temporarily. Although the Kansas-Nebraska Act, by repealing the Missouri Compromise at the insistence of the Southerners in Congress, angered many in the North as an attempt to appease the South without exacting any *quid pro quo*,[33] James G. Blaine probably assessed its short-run effect accurately when he wrote: "the North was consoled, it would not be unfair to say cajoled, with the doctrine of popular sovereignty as defined by Mr. Douglas."[34] The South temporarily accepted the popular sovereignty aspects of the Kansas-Nebraska Act as the price for obtaining the repeal of the Missouri Compromise. The South also no doubt saw that the doctrine, by agreeing to permit the spread of slavery, carried an implied concession to the Southern position that slavery had a right to expand.

[33] Five free-state legislatures passed resolutions condemning Kansas-Nebraska; only one, Illinois, approved.

[34] James G. Blaine, *Twenty Years of Congress*, I, 147.

Yet acceptance of the idea of popular sovereignty by both the North and the South was in the end highly tentative. The North might grant slavery the right to expand, but would not tolerate expansion as a reality. The South would not forever content itself with rights alone. The North would permanently embrace popular sovereignty only if it proved an effective barrier to the spread of slavery. The South for its part would tolerate the scheme only so long as it produced popular majorities that favored slavery. When local control over slavery seemed to be working against the expansion of the institution, the South would turn from the concept of nonintervention to the opposite one of intervention in the form of a congressional slave code for the territories.

In its role as a means to sectional adjustment over slavery, the soft side took the inherent vagueness that characterized the principle of popular sovereignty on its hard side and tried to turn it to positive advantage.

In spite of the fact that the doctrine of popular sovereignty was frequently proclaimed as a clear and succinct principle, upon closer examination it was ambiguous, perhaps ambivalent. The Kansas-Nebraska Act professed to leave the fate of slavery in a given territory up to the local inhabitants, but it never spelled out how any decision for or against slavery was to be reached: through the territorial legislature? through a constitutional convention? through a popular referendum? The long dispute over Lecompton largely concerned the question of what constituted a valid expression of the popular will on slavery.

A much more serious shortcoming was the failure of the hard side of popular sovereignty to specify the time at which people living in a frontier area could make a decision for or against slavery. There were three basic schools of thought on this point. The first held that action on slavery could be taken by the first few white American settlers who arrived on the frontier long before it had been granted territorial status by Congress. This was the so-called squatter sovereignty view, which never found many serious advocates in Washington. The issue was largely joined between those who held that the people of a territory could legally bar slavery only at the time they drafted a state constitution just prior to being admitted into the Union, and those who felt that the same people could arrive at a decision any time after having achieved territorial status.

The advocates of postponing any action on slavery maintained that the institution existed in the territories by virtue of the United States Constitution. It would be superfluous for a territorial legislature to sanction slavery, illegal to forbid it. Only when a territory was ready for statehood could it decide the matter of slavery for itself. This school of thought was composed largely of Southerners, together with an occasional Northerner like Benjamin Hallet of Massachusetts and, of course, James Buchanan. As the 1850's progressed, many Southerners would exchange this position for an even more extreme one, demanding not only that slavery be allowed in the territories, but also that the federal government be made responsible by statute for protecting it there.

Those who held that the citizens of a territory could decide for or against slavery at any time they chose were mainly Northern Democrats like Cass and Dickinson.[35] Both political theory and historical precedent tended to favor their side of the controversy. The Southern view presupposed too wide and unrealistic a gulf between the powers of a state and the powers of a territory. Furthermore, the people most directly affected by the question, the people of Kansas and other territories, overwhelmingly endorsed the Northern version.[36] Perhaps the strongest argument of all in favor of the Northern view was that the Kansas-Nebraska Act, which purported to enshrine the principle of popular sovereignty in the territories, replaced the Missouri Compromise, which had dealt with slavery not in states, but only in territories. At the bottom of the tangled constitutional argument over the exact timing of a decision on slavery in the territories lay the awareness of leaders both North and South that if slavery were kept out of an area during

[35] *Cong. Globe*, 35th Cong., 1st sess., p. 2205.

[36] Robert W. Johannsen, "Stephen A. Douglas, Popular Sovereignty, and the Territories," *The Historian* 22, no. 4 (August 1960): 395.

the territorial stage, it stood almost no chance of ever being allowed there after statehood.[37]

There could be little doubt which view of popular sovereignty Stephen Douglas favored. During the negotiations that went into forging the Compromise of 1850, he and Henry Clay had successfully foiled a Southern attempt to prohibit the territorial legislatures of Utah and New Mexico from taking any action on slavery.[38] Yet if the interests of principle required Douglas to clarify his views in the Kansas-Nebraska Act, his idea of political expediency required that he keep them somewhat ambiguous. If his plans for national expansion were to be fulfilled, if Kansas and Nebraska were to be organized in 1854, Douglas would need Southern help in Congress. It would be best not to antagonize that section through a premature and perhaps unnecessarily precise definition of the principle of popular sovereignty.

From a somewhat larger point of view, a certain amount of ambiguity in the concept of popular sovereignty would enhance Douglas' role as a national political figure—a man who could devise a scheme by which the North and South could agree to settle their differences over the course of slavery in the territories. When not pushed too far, when not defined too closely, popular sovereignty promised a remarkable solution to the conflict between states' rights and human rights—a conflict as old as the American political system itself. To the South, Douglas could proclaim popular sovereignty as an end in itself—an idea whose stress on the political autonomy of a frontier community drew its inspiration from the same wellsprings of political decentralization as the doctrine of states' rights. To the North, Douglas could present his program not only as one resting on the notion that ultimate sovereignty belonged to the individual citizen, but as one which, if fairly applied, could give expression to the growing sentiment on the Western frontier in favor of human rights in general and free-soil in particular.[39]

[37] Angle, ed., *Debates*, p 173; Wiltse, *Calhoun, Sectionalist*, p. 326.

[38] Hamilton, *Prologue to Conflict*, pp. 146–147.

[39] For an interesting attempt to show that popular sovereignty furthered both

But ambiguity, unaccompanied by any deeper agreement on the question of slavery in the territories, was an unstable basis for achieving sectional adjustment. Its continued existence presupposed either great restraint or great indifference on the part of the enemies and advocates of slavery alike. In the last analysis, North and South would both accept the ambivalent language of the Kansas-Nebraska Act only as long as they felt that events on the territorial periphery did not threaten their way of life. Kansas, which was the great proving ground for popular sovereignty, stirred relatively little excitement in the older sections of the country during the first two years of its territorial existence. Yet by 1856, when the fate of slavery in Kansas was felt to held the key not only to the political balance of power in Washington,[40] but to the whole future of slavery in America, both North and South took another look at the concept of popular sovereignty. Continued toleration of the idea would depend on its effects upon the existence of slavery. Douglas had offered each side in the sectional controversy a chance to perpetuate in the territories its own way of life. Now both demanded virtual certainty. The North attempted to interpret popular sovereignty in a manner that would further the cause of free-soil on the Western frontier. The South hoped to adjust the content of the scheme to suit the needs of slavery expansion. A program that served best as a kind of truce between the advocates and opponents of slavery, a device that was most useful as a kind of neutral recorder of the current state of public opinion on slavery in frontier areas, was seized upon by an anxious generation, snatched out of context, and used by each side of the sectional struggle as a makeweight in its favor. The benign ambiguity, the intentional equivocation, which Douglas, perhaps naively, depended upon to earn

---

the cause of states' rights and human rights, see Douglas' speech of July 9, 1858, at Chicago, Angle, ed., *Debates*, p. 19.

40 If Kansas were to enter the Union as a slave state, the sectional composition of the national government would be more evenly balanced: sixteen free states, sixteen slave. Should Kansas become a free state, the imbalance that had existed ever since 1850 when California entered the Union as a free state would be aggravated, and the South's position as the minority section confirmed.

the acceptance of his doctrine in all sections of the country, gave way to a growing demand for sharp definition.

Once more the crucial issue of the timing of a popular decision on slavery in the territories—the question Douglas had tried to repress on the one hand and answer with obfuscation on the other—began to rise to the surface of American politics. As late as 1856 the Democratic party, strained by growing animosity between its Northern and Southern wings, tried to paper over its profound internal disagreements on territorial policy by making explicit the ambiguity implicit in the heart of the Kansas-Nebraska Act. The Democratic national convention, meeting in Cincinnati in June, unanimously adopted a platform calling for "the uniform application of the Democratic principle to the organization of Territories and the admission of new states with or without domestic slavery as they may elect."[41] Southerners were for the time being mollified; so were Northerners. All thought that the party's 1856 platform embodied their particular interpretation of popular sovereignty. But neither side was any longer willing to delay clarification of the basic uncertainties in the creed of popular sovereignty. Northerners and Southerners both looked to the President-elect for confirmation of their views.

James Buchanan equivocated. In his letter accepting the Democratic presidential nomination he seemed to adopt the Northern, territorial sovereignty, point of view. Buchanan wrote that "the people of a territory, like those of a State, shall decide for themselves whether slavery shall or shall not exist within their limits."[42] As late as August, 1856, Buchanan appeared to hold to this view, but sometime between then and November 6 he did a complete political about-face and endorsed the Southern position.[43]

The reasons for Buchanan's sudden reversal only two days after his election have never become completely clear. Their deepest

[41] For the relevant passages of the 1856 Democratic platform see Horace Greeley and John F. Cleveland, *A Political Text-Book for 1860*, p. 25. Blaine (*Twenty Years of Congress*, I, 147) comments on their ambivalence.

[42] John B. Moore, ed., *The Works of James Buchanan*, X, 83.

[43] Ibid., pp. 87, 97.

roots probably were to be found in his weak personality. James G. Blaine felt that Buchanan had been planning such a move for months and was emboldened to act by his recent victory and by the fact that the Democrats would have a comfortable majority in all three branches of the government.[44]

A somewhat less harsh explanation might be that Buchanan had two primary tasks: to get elected and to appease a restive South. By appearing to adopt the territorial sovereignty view, he hoped to earn the support of the free states at the polls in November and achieve his first aim; by his subsequent *volte-face* he hoped to achieve the second.[45]

A historian kindly disposed toward Buchanan might conclude that the responsibilities of the office he was about to assume sobered the President-elect and inclined him to favor delaying a decision on slavery in Kansas until statehood, thereby easing the tension both in that unfortunate territory and in the nation as a whole. A more realistic observer might take note of a visit of Southern slaveholders to Wheatland shortly after the election. No record of that meeting has survived, but there is some indication that it must have been a stormy one and that the Southern visitors mingled expressions of dissatisfaction toward the territorial version of popular sovereignty with vague threats of secession. They may have even alluded to a plan to encourage members of the electoral college to vote against Buchanan should he not amend his position to please the South.[46] Whatever took place at Wheatland that day, it must have frightened Buchanan, for only fear could ever drive him out of his lethargy into the kind of action a reversal on popular sovereignty entailed.

Buchanan reiterated his new views on the timing of popular sovereignty in his Inaugural Address.[47] Two days later in the Dred

[44] Blaine, *Twenty Years of Congress*, I, 128–130.

[45] Buchanan's 1856 showing in the free states ultimately, however, proved disappointing. He carried only five: Indiana, Pennsylvania, New Jersey, Illinois, and California.

[46] David C. Mearns, ed., *The Lincoln Papers*, I, 283–284.

[47] James D. Richardson, ed., *A Compilation of the Messages and Papers of the Presidents, 1789–1902*, V, 431.

Scott decision the Southern-dominated Supreme Court wrote finis to the soft side of the concept of popular sovereignty. By strongly presuming that because Congress could not interfere with slavery in a territory, it could not authorize a territorial government to do so either,[48] the Court in effect made the Southern interpretation of popular sovereignty the law of the land. The rules of the popular sovereignty game that Douglas had proposed as a way to resolve differences between the sections over the future of slavery in the territories had now been sharply altered to favor the side of slavery. No reasonable proponent of free-soil in the North would commit the destiny of the Western frontier to a scheme that almost guaranteed the expansion and perpetuation of slavery.

Douglas himself, however, refused to acknowledge the demise of the soft side of his program. His long fight against Lecompton may be thought of as an attempt to show that if a fair referendum on the question of slavery took place, even a territory where slavery had existed and been sanctioned by territorial law might in the end still come into the Union as a free state. In his Freeport Doctrine, Douglas attempted to redress the legal imbalance the Dred Scott decision had produced in favor of slavery and argued that effective action against slavery could still be taken at the local level by the people of a territory long before statehood. This approach brought Douglas a measure of success in the Illinois campaign of 1858, but in its larger role as a national policy, a means by which the North and the South might readily agree to disagree over the future of slavery in the territories, the soft side of popular sovereignty from 1857 onward was largely a dead letter.

Judged by its effects upon both the nation and the career of Stephen Douglas, the doctrine of popular sovereignty was in the last analysis largely a failure on both its hard and soft sides.

The hard side of the concept—the rigid, impersonal, narrow, somewhat unrealistic side of the principle—was never actually given a fair trial. In the place of the nonintervention that was central

[48] For the relevant passages of the Dred Scott decision see 19 *Howard*, 451 (1857).

to it, there was in Kansas, the site of its first great test, intervention from the North, the South, and all three branches of the federal government. Nor was the fate of slavery in practice left up to the impersonal workings of climate and economics in a moral vacuum. Far from checking their moral baggage at the frontier, the immigrants who flooded into Kansas in the mid-1850's often seemed to be taking part in a moral crusade for or against the institution. Even Douglas at one point apparently modified the amoral tenets of the hard side of his doctrine. Speaking at Quincy during the 1858 campaign, he took cognizance of the role of moral and ethical considerations in any decision on slavery and asked only that each state and territory be allowed to choose its own peculiar moral code without any outside interference.[49]

Yet if the hard side of popular sovereignty never became a reality, it nonetheless had far-reaching repercussions in the America of the 1850's. Much that was central to the principle of popular sovereignty was unexceptionable. The influence of climate and economics on politics was self-evident. The notion of nonintervention and the concept of popular control of government through the rule of the majority were basic parts of the American political tradition. The doctrine's studied lack of clarity in its application to the territories also served to prevent a rigid and clear division of opinion over its essential worth. Yet not finding within the hard side of popular sovereignty the stuff from which real political issues are made, many politicians extracted false issues from it. They argued not over what the doctrine was, but over what it might do; not over a factual situation, but a legal tendency.[50]

In short, the doctrine of popular sovereignty on its hard side succumbed to the political disease of the times and, like positive protectionism, free-soil, and abolitionism, became an abstraction.

[49] Angle, ed., *Debates*, pp. 351–352.

[50] The best example of raising false issues from the doctrine of popular sovereignty is probably to be found in Lincoln's speeches during the 1858 campaign. He consistently equated the legal right of slavery to enter territories with its permanent establishment there. See especially the "House Divided" speech in ibid., pp. 1–12.

Most useful as a device, popular sovereignty became a symbol. Few judged it on its simple merits; most either loved or hated it. Emotion, not reason, determined its worth in the public eye. John Crittenden once tried to dismiss popular sovereignty as a "mere abstraction."[51] He was only half right. No abstraction in these overheated antebellum years could ever be termed mere. Too much concern for abstraction would one day tear a nation in two. In spite of the self-evident political maxims that lay at its heart and the vagueness that surrounded many of the finer points of the doctrine, the hard side of popular sovereignty in the end served to divide the American people more than it united them. During the 1858 campaign Lincoln's strategy called for portraying popular sovereignty as a device for furthering the aims of the Southern slaveholders. Yet in 1860 an observer at the Democratic convention in Charleston could write that many of the Southern delegates considered the doctrine of popular sovereignty "a great deal worse than the rankest sort of Abolitionism."[52]

The hard side of popular sovereignty was almost a complete failure when measured by the narrow standard of the personal political interests of Stephen Douglas. It at first promised to furnish him a rationalization in the North for his role in the repeal of the Missouri Compromise. It promised to give his career that veneer of principle which Americans in the 1850's were coming to demand of their public men. Popular sovereignty failed in the long run to achieve the first goal and did more harm than good to its arch exponent in attempting to reach the second.

Most Americans in the North remained unconvinced of the strength of the ties that bound this most practical and expedient of men to any principle. Douglas, who always seemed to have an opinion, was apparently trying to erect into a principle an attitude of "care not" where the future of slavery was concerned. The essential opaqueness of certain parts of the doctrine, particularly as it was embodied in the Kansas-Nebraska Act, struck some as simple

[51] Albert D. Kirwan, *John J. Crittenden*, p. 361.

[52] Murat Halstead, *Three against Lincoln: Murat Halstead Reports the Caucuses of 1860*, ed. William B. Hesseltine, p. 117.

opportunism—an idealistic cloak for disguising more of the political twistings and turnings that had marked so much of Douglas' career. Quite a few Northerners must have shared the view of Edward Everett[53] and Theodore Parker[54] that Douglas' principle was a mere personal and political expedient masquerading as a great national principle.

In the North the self-consciously amoral tenets of the hard side of Douglas' program were often simply dismissed as immoral.[55] Douglas' principle at times made him seem utterly unprincipled.

The South committed the opposite error. Instead of trying to cast doubt on Douglas' attachment to the principle, it preferred to tie Douglas' name to a misrepresented doctrine. *Douglasism* became a synonym for virtual abolitionism. It was symptomatic of just how far political thought had removed itself from reality that many Southern delegates to the Charleston convention regarded Douglas as more dangerous to the South than Seward.[56] Seeking to base his actions on principle, Douglas in the South had largely become the victim of his own abstraction.

Popular sovereignty on its hard side grew more unpopular with each passing year. Douglas seemed to sense this, but instead of disavowing his doctrine, he merely changed its name. A study of his speeches after 1858 reveals a tendency on his part to avoid referring to his program by its controversial title of popular sovereignty and to seek refuge instead in such euphemisms as Cincinnati platform and doctrine of nonintervention.[57]

Yet Douglas for too long identified himself with the hard side of popular sovereignty, by whatever name it was known. He continued to cling to an idea that was sterile and unrealistic in inspira-

53 Reinhard H. Luthin, "The Democratic Split During Buchanan's Administration," *Pennsylvania History* 11, no. 1 (January 1944): 15.

54 John Weiss, *Life and Correspondence of Theodore Parker*, II, 239.

55 *New York Tribune*, July 17, 1860.

56 Halstead, *Three against Lincoln*, p. 117.

57 See, for example, the speeches made by Douglas in Ohio in 1859, particularly the one delivered at Cincinnati. Harry V. Jaffa and Robert W. Johannsen, eds., *In the Name of the People: Speeches and Writings of Lincoln and Douglas in the Ohio Campaign of 1859*, pp. 151–172.

tion, inapplicable in practice, and damaging to his own political self-interest. Much has been made of the fact that in a noble, if somewhat frantic, attempt to arrive at a sectional compromise in those turbulent weeks of 1861 just prior to Fort Sumter, Douglas apparently finally surrendered much of his long-cherished principle. But what Douglas in fact did was merely to inter formally the hard side of his popular sovereignty—the side that never had much relevance or application to the territorial experience—in favor of a more realistic program. His compromise proposals embodied tighter congressional controls over any territorial decision on slavery and were more explicit as to the timing of any such decision. Absolute nonintervention and benign ambiguity had at last been discarded from the Douglas catechism.

Unlike its hard counterpart, the soft side of popular sovereignty in a sense achieved a limited degree of success for a brief period. With the passage of the Compromises of 1850 and 1854, Americans both North and South appeared to accept Douglas' program as a way to agree to disagree over the future of slavery not only in the territories, but throughout the entire country. But the apparent success of the doctrine in this capacity over the short run was deceptive. It was at heart less a shaper of consensus than a reflection of it. The soft side of popular sovereignty could only work as long as most Americans valued national unity more than victory in the territories for their particular views on slavery. This attitude in turn seemed to depend on the existence of a shared feeling that the prohibition or toleration of slavery in one territory was not a harbinger of the whole future of that institution in America.

Up to 1856 the soft side of popular sovereignty provided America with an excuse, if not a force, for national unity. Perhaps its most useful service to the nation was in allowing the people of the North and the South to continue to hope for victory in the territories for their way of life by peaceful means: by ballots rather than bullets. If the doctrine did not prevent sectional animosities and occasional clashes during the early 1850's, it probably helped to delay the Civil War until the North was clearly capable of winning it. Few Americans today would wish to reverse that verdict.

Yet if in the short run the soft side of popular sovereignty did contribute to the easing of sectional tensions over slavery, it may ultimately have made them much worse. When the brief honeymoon of obfuscation and tacit agreement was over, when the test case of slavery in Kansas arose and its outcome was felt to be indicative of the fate of slavery throughout America, both the North and the South ceased to regard popular sovereignty as an end in itself and instead judged it by its results. When the South, by virtue of its dominant position in both the Democratic party and the national government, attempted, through the Dred Scott decision and through proposals for a territorial slave code to alter the rules of popular sovereignty too sharply in favor of slavery, mutual sectional forbearance was replaced by mutual suspicion. The fate of slavery in the territories now seemed to depend upon which section controlled the presidency and the Supreme Court; the fulcrum of territorial policy on slavery now clearly rested in Washington. Northern aims could best be served by a party of clearly free-soil views gaining control of the national government.

The result was the election of a Republican President in 1860. Only after the Republicans had him elected did Northern free-soilers again seem receptive to the notion of popular sovereignty. When in 1861 the Republicans proposed to organize the new territories of Colorado, Dakota, and Nevada without any formal federal prohibition on slavery, Douglas represented their move as a belated vindication of his principle of popular sovereignty.[58] He implied that the Republicans had accepted the central tenet of the hard side of his doctrine: absolute nonintervention in territorial affairs.

They had in fact accepted only a specious form of the soft side of the idea. Republicans, like Southerners, valued popular sovereignty not as a national principle, as Douglas would have had it, but as a means to their sectional goals. With the climate of the new lands and the territorial officers the new Republican President would appoint hostile to slavery, the Republicans could afford to leave the future of slavery up to the will of the local inhabitants.

[58] *Cong. Globe*, 36th Cong., 2nd sess., p. 1391.

Yet the very fact that the Republicans preferred not to interfere with territorial control of slavery when interference would have been superfluous attested to the worth of Douglas' doctrine and the sympathetic chords it touched in the American political tradition.

From the standpoint of the career of Stephen Douglas, the soft side of popular sovereignty produced results that were at very best mixed. The ambivalent language of the 1854 legislation admittedly helped to permit the organization of Kansas and Nebraska. For a brief period Douglas' traditional goal of national expansion seemed to take on new life, even in an age of growing sectionalism. For a while North and South appeared to have agreed on a formula for handling territorial disputes. Douglas' role as a truly national political leader was temporarily enhanced.

Yet if North and South would apparently tolerate the Douglas doctrine before 1857, both would denounce it after that time for opposite reasons. The South charged popular sovereignty with the loss of Kansas to free-soil. Northerners, on the other hand, often blamed the concept for turning the entire West into the legalized prey of slavery.[59] Douglas' efforts in defense of his concept during the Lecompton struggle heightened Southern suspicions of the Illinois Senator without satisfying the whole of the North over the long term. Although the future of slavery in Kansas was at the bottom of the Lecompton controversy, the quarrel between the Northern and Southern wings of the Democratic party often took the form of a dispute over the exact meaning of popular sovereignty. By adding yet another issue to the sectional struggle, popular sovereignty in one sense hastened the demise of the Democratic party and with it Douglas' hope to unite the nation behind him.

In the campaign of 1860 Douglas' continued espousal of popular sovereignty as a way toward the resolution of sectional conflicts ultimately caused him to fall between two political stools. He failed to satisfy either those who regarded slavery as an evil and desired

59 Daniel J. Ryan, "Lincoln and Ohio," *Ohio Archaeological and Historical Quarterly* 32, no. 1 (January 1923): 24.

to curb it or those who considered it a worthy institution and wanted to see it not only survive but expand.

If the soft side of popular sovereignty largely failed Douglas in the long run at the national level, it did prove useful to him in Illinois in the 1858 campaign. In that essentially Western state the conflicts between pro- and antislavery opinion were much less bitter than in the nation as a whole. There was a large element of moderate opinion, which placed a high value on preserving the Union. There was a predisposition not to push definitions too far, and a great personal loyalty to Stephen Douglas. In this kind of political environment, popular sovereignty could help voters to see in Douglas what they wanted to see, to make him appear the candidate who was "the best means both to break down and to uphold the slave interest."[60]

If the Republicans were to win the 1858 Senate race in Illinois, they would have to refute both the hard side and the soft side of popular sovereignty. The second task was far more difficult than the first, but there was one man who thought he had found a way to do this. Abraham Lincoln would base his attack upon a denial that anyone could accept the soft side of popular sovereignty without accepting the hard; he would deny that anyone could embrace the practical virtues of popular sovereignty as a means to agree to disagree over slavery without being tainted by its essential immorality masquerading as amorality. He would deny that anyone had a right to do wrong.

[60] John G. Nicolay and John Hay, eds., *Complete Works of Abraham Lincoln*, V, 94.

4. The Lincoln-Douglas Debates

The Lincoln-Douglas Debates settled nothing and they settled everything with a terrible finality. Their focus was as narrow as the future of a dying institution in a single frontier territory that had already expressed itself unequivocally against slavery;[1] it was as broad as the American conscience itself. They contained much that was petty, irrelevant, and obfuscatory; they contained much that was of vital importance. They showed each man at his best; they showed each man at his worst. The debates were a prologue, yet they held within themselves the essence of the whole tragic story of slavery, secession, and civil war.

Abe Lincoln was no stranger to Stephen Douglas. They first met in 1834 when Douglas, only twenty-one years old, was running for state's attorney for the First Judicial Circuit of Illinois, and Lincoln, four years his senior, was a young member of the state House of Representatives from Sangamon County. Lincoln's first recorded

[1] The people of Kansas roundly defeated the Lecompton Constitution in an election held pursuant to the English Bill. This was on August 2, 1858. The first joint debate was not held until August 21.

comment on the diminutive Douglas was to pronounce him "the least man I ever saw."[2] From that time on their political paths were to cross many times. In 1839 they held a public dialogue over the choice of presidential electors,[3] and for the next twenty years the two men met in joint debate during every major political contest in Illinois.

By 1850 Douglas was the leading Democrat in the state, and the ambitious Lincoln, hoping to share in his fame, followed his trail relentlessly up and down Illinois. The year 1854 marked the first time the two men met to debate a vital and immediate issue of national importance: the repeal of the Missouri Compromise, which Douglas' Kansas-Nebraska Act had only recently accomplished. The debate opened at Springfield, and within a few days the two men rejoined the issue at Peoria.[4] During the next four years while Douglas was in Washington, Lincoln stumped the state of Illinois hammering away at the Senator's role in repealing the 1820 Compromise. Douglas had hung a political albatross around his own neck in the Kansas-Nebraska Act; Lincoln intended to keep it there.

It was a curious rivalry. It went deeper than politics, yet it never developed into a bitter personal feud. Lincoln and Douglas were bigger men than James Buchanan. They had once been attracted to the same woman, a pretty young girl named Mary Todd, who had moved to Illinois in 1839 from Kentucky.[5] Lincoln won that dubious prize. There were apparently no hard feelings. In 1847 Douglas signed Lincoln's note for $167[6] and years later wrote a letter of introduction to the president of Harvard College on behalf of Robert Todd Lincoln, then a young freshman.[7]

[2] Frank E. Stevens, "Life of Stephen Arnold Douglas," *Journal of the Illinois State Historical Society* 16: 290.

[3] Ibid., pp. 323–327.

[4] A good account of the 1854 contest may be found in Edwin E. Sparks, ed., *The Lincoln-Douglas Debates*, pp. 5–15; Lincoln's Peoria speech is in John G. Nicolay and John Hay, eds., *Complete Works of Abraham Lincoln*, II, 190–262.

[5] Stevens, "Life of Douglas," p. 323.

[6] Carl Sandburg, *Abraham Lincoln: The Prairie Years*, I, 356.

[7] Robert W. Johannsen, ed., *The Letters of Stephen A. Douglas*, p. 481.

Horace Greeley took the credit for suggesting the Lincoln-Douglas Debates of 1858;[8] so did Jesse Fell and the editors of the *Chicago Press and Tribune*.[9] It really does not matter very much who first proposed the contest, for if the suggestion had not come from these sources, Lincoln would no doubt have made it himself.

Abraham Lincoln had a rare gift for being able to put an opponent on the horns of a dilemma. Never was this talent shown to better advantage than on that day in July, 1858, when Lincoln wrote to ask Douglas, "Will it be agreeable to you to make an arrangement for you and myself to divide time and address the same audiences the present canvass?"[10] Lincoln had much to gain and almost nothing to lose from issuing such a challenge. He was very much the underdog of the campaign. His party had enjoyed considerable success in Illinois recently, but it was still new and unseasoned. Its organization was no match for the sophisticated and well-entrenched Douglas machine. Lincoln's political record prior to 1858 was at best undistinguished. He was still almost unknown outside of Illinois, and even within the confines of the state his fame was no match for that of the senior Senator. Lincoln did not expect to rival the Little Giant as a popular drawing card, but he thought he saw in the device of the joint debates a way to share his fame. He was right. It was Douglas most Illinoisans came to hear that summer of 1858; it was Lincoln they remembered.[11]

Douglas had very little to gain from accepting the challenge. He was at the peak of his fame, the best known politician in America, unbeaten on any major issue. He did not take kindly to the idea of letting Lincoln ride to political prominence on his coattails.

There was a deeper reason for Douglas' reluctance to accept Lincoln's challenge. Douglas' ultimate success in political joint debate had been limited. Although he usually won the argument, he some-

[8] *New York Tribune*, July 12, 1858.

[9] Richard A. Heckman, "The Lincoln-Douglas Debate, Freeport, Illinois, August 27, 1858," p. 41.

[10] Nicolay and Hay, eds., *Works of Lincoln*, III, 189.

[11] C. Gillisler to Douglas, Ottawa, Illinois, August 17, 1858; Douglas MSS.

times lost the campaign. In 1838 he had run for Congress from the Third District of Illinois against Major John T. Stuart. The candidates met in public debate and the Little Giant lost the election.[12] When he was challenged over the Kansas-Nebraska Act upon his return to Illinois in 1854, Douglas' forensic skill by itself proved unable to bring his followers victory at the polls. Anti-Nebraska men swept the state.[13] There is no reason to doubt Douglas' sincerity when, upon learning of Lincoln's nomination in June of 1858, he remarked to John W. Forney, "I shall have my hands full."[14]

The obvious thing for Douglas to do was to refuse Lincoln's challenge. But matters were not that simple. Ever since Douglas had returned to Illinois early in July, Lincoln had been following the Little Giant from town to town. When Douglas made a speech, Lincoln would make one in reply, sometimes the same day, sometimes the next. Thus Lincoln not only had the advantage of attracting to his audience a large part of the crowd that had gathered to hear Douglas; he also usually had the last word, or, to use the expression of the day, "concluded on" his opponent.[15]

The nature of the dilemma Lincoln's challenge posed to Douglas now becomes clearer. A refusal by the Little Giant would carry the appearance of running away from Lincoln and would in itself be no guarantee that Lincoln would stop pursuing Douglas on his campaign trail. If, on the other hand, Douglas accepted, he would make Lincoln the beneficiary of a substantial part of his great fame and prestige.

Douglas accepted. On the twenty-fourth of July he wrote Lincoln a long and rambling letter that betrayed the discomfort he was feeling from Lincoln's shrewd challenge. The Little Giant began by alluding to "difficulties in the way of such an arrangement." He then went on to chastise Lincoln for not having made his sug-

12 Stevens, "Life of Douglas," pp. 315–322. Douglas nonetheless waged an impressive campaign for a man only months past the age of twenty-five.

13 George F. Milton, *Eve of Conflict: Stephen A. Douglas and the Needless War*, p. 185.

14 Albert J. Beveridge, *Abraham Lincoln*, II, 572.

15 Stevens, "Life of Douglas," pp. 551–552.

gestion earlier and concluded by giving Lincoln's proposal his grudging consent "in order to accommodate you as far as it is in my power to do so."[16]

Six days later Douglas wrote to Lincoln setting out the terms of the contest. There were to be seven joint debates altogether. This would mean that, in view of the speeches both had already made at Springfield and Chicago, joint discussions would be held in all of Illinois' nine congressional districts. The places and dates named by Douglas were as follows:

Ottawa	August 21
Freeport	August 27
Jonesboro	September 15
Charleston	September 18
Galesburg	October 7
Quincy	October 13
Alton	October 15

Douglas went on to add: "We shall alternately open and close the discussion. I will speak at Ottawa one hour, you can reply occupying an hour and a half and I will then follow for half an hour. At Freeport you shall open the discussion. . . . We will alternate in like manner at each successive place."[17]

Historians often pause here to praise Douglas' shrewdness in turning the tables on Lincoln and gaining the crucial concluding speech in four out of the seven encounters, including the important first and final debates.[18] But look deeper. Of the sites named by Douglas, Ottawa and Freeport were in safe Republican territory, Alton and Jonesboro were firmly Democratic. Only in the remaining three towns was there much chance of the debates themselves turning the electoral tide in one direction or the other. Of these three, Galesburg was on balance moderately Republican, Quincy and Charleston moderately Democratic. Thus under Douglas' arrangement Lincoln stood a chance of bringing two unstable Democratic districts into the Republican camp while exposing to Democratic cap-

[16] Johannsen, ed., *Letters of Douglas*, pp. 423–424.

[17] Ibid., pp. 424–425.

[18] Allan Nevins, *The Emergence of Lincoln*, I, 374.

ture only one uncertain district of his own. Although in his letter accepting Douglas' terms Lincoln complained that "you take four openings and closes to my three,"[19] he must have been secretly pleased at the arrangement.

The Lincoln-Douglas Debates were rich in the kind of dramatic content that delighted contemporary journalists and continues to delight historians today. They pitted against one another the two leading men of the Democratic and Republican parties in Illinois and saw them locked in combat over crucial issues in a crucial state in a crucial time in the history of our country.

There was the tall challenger from Springfield standing six and a half feet tall. There was Douglas, the champion, who one spectator in Alton said had difficulty in being seen over the railing of the speakers platform. The railing was four feet high.[20]

There was the well-dressed Douglas turned out in what was in those days known as plantation style, complete with ruffled shirt, dark blue coat with shiny buttons, and a broad-brimmed felt hat. There was Lincoln with his old tall stovepipe hat and the coat with the sleeves that were too short and the ill-fitting pants that stopped long before they reached the tops of his outsized boots.[21] There was Douglas whose rapid, impassioned delivery seemed to make his words almost tumble over one another. There was the calmer, more deliberate, almost bashful Lincoln. His voice was, surprisingly, pitched higher than that of the diminutive Douglas; he talked more slowly but somehow seemed to say more. His words appeared to lack much in the way of making an immediate impression, but they stayed with people longer. They had less impact than Douglas' but more power.

It was a highly personal struggle in an age when United States Senators were still selected by state legislatures. Nowhere in Illinois

[19] Nicolay and Hay, eds., *Works of Lincoln*, III, 197.

[20] Edmund Beall, "Recollections of the Lincoln-Douglas Debate Held in Alton, Illinois, October 15, 1858," *Journal of the Illinois State Historical Society* 5, no. 4 (January 1913): 487.

[21] Milton, *Eve of Conflict*, p. 320; Sparks, *Lincoln-Douglas Debates*, p. 207.

in 1858 did the names of Lincoln and Douglas appear on a ballot, the contest being ostensibly for the election of state senators and representatives. Yet few students would wish to quarrel with Allan Nevins' verdict that in these debates we have one of the best examples in the history of our country of a dramatic and direct appeal to the will and judgment of the American people by the two contenders themselves.[22] The debates reminded a young spectator named Carl Schurz of one of those epics from an age long past which tells of two great armies pausing to watch the issue of battle being decided by two champions locked in single combat between the lines.[23]

Contemporary witnesses greeted the debates with more levity and good-natured common sense than have scores of posthumous commentators. There is a stubborn tendency to become overawed by the godlike figure of Lincoln and the seriousness of the issues he discussed. It is easy for the student to receive the impression that the debates were basically a rather ponderous affair.

They were nothing of the sort. Illinois was not many years removed from the frontier, and on the frontier politics was a prime source of amusement in the monotonous, isolated life of the settlers. Most people in the Illinois of 1858 were vaguely aware of the dangers that had begun to gather on the American political horizon, but the great majority of people did not journey many long miles over dusty roads to the debate sites primarily to be alarmed or impressed or made wise. They came to be entertained, and they were not disappointed.

What they saw was partly a debate, partly a canvass, partly a trial, and partly a spectacle. It was wholly American. It was a state fair, a school picnic, and the Fourth of July all rolled into one. To the accompaniment of booming brass bands, torchlight parades, and scores of pretty girls, the two contenders made their way up and down Illinois that hot summer of 1858. Douglas traveled in a style

[22] Allan Nevins and Willard L. King, "The Constitution and Declaration of Independence as Issues in the Lincoln-Douglas Debates," *Journal of the Illinois State Historical Society* 52, no. 1 (spring 1959): 12–13.

[23] Carl Schurz, *The Reminiscences of Carl Schurz*, II, 88.

one might call frontier-regal. He went from town to town in an elegant private train, often over the rails of the Illinois Central he had helped to build. The long line of coaches was broken by a single flatcar on which the irrepressible Little Giant had mounted a six-pounder to boom the announcement of his arrival when his train approached the outskirts of a populated area.[24] The man charged by the Illinois Central with the responsibility for the safe passage of Douglas' train over its right-of-way was a young vice-president not many years out of West Point. His name was George B. McClellan.

Although the issues involved went to the very foundations of American life, the conclusion is irresistible that for those fortunate enough to be there, the debates must have been a great deal of just plain fun. Something of the sheer wonder and delight the Lincoln-Douglas Debates brought into the simple and routine lives of those who heard them occasionally cuts through the mists of the years, as in this account by an eyewitness: "The then famous 'Little Giant' of the Senate was the first United States Senator I ever saw and of course I fell into line at his reception at the Brewster House and was presented."[25] This was written half a century after the last debate, but the impression made by Mr. Lincoln and Mr. Douglas was as vivid in the memory of the old man as it had been to the boy who had seen them early on that morning in 1858.

The peculiar geopolitical structure of Illinois largely determined the strategy of the two participants in the debates and went far toward deciding the results of the election.

Illinois in 1858 was a big state and growing bigger. Its population, already estimated at a million and a half, was each day increasing with the arrival of immigrants from both Europe and the older sections of America. It was physically big too, slicing more than four hundred miles through the heart of the North American continent from Wisconsin in the north to Kentucky in the south.

24 Sparks, *Lincoln-Douglas Debates*, p. 259; Milton, *Eve of Conflict*, p. 320.

25 J. W. Clinton, "Polo [Illinois] in War Time," *Journal of the Illinois State Historical Society* 4, no. 2 (July 1911): 202.

In order to cover such a large area, each candidate during the 1858 campaign traveled over five thousand miles and made scores of speeches. The joint debates themselves represented only a small portion of the whole contest.

Water played an important role in Illinois. Lake Michigan washed it on the northeast, the Wabash and the Ohio bounded it on the southeast, and the mighty Mississippi formed its entire western border: Douglas took careful note.

With its elongated north-south shape, Illinois in many respects represented in microcosm the sectional forces that were tearing at the political fabric of America itself. The first area of the state to have been settled was that lower third beginning where the Mississippi and Ohio meet at Cairo and running north to a line roughly even with St. Louis. It was called Egypt and was colonized largely by white farmers from below the Mason-Dixon Line, principally from the Border states. The Mississippi reinforced the commercial ties of lower Illinois with the South, and the area was Southern in origin, culture, and sympathies. Although the large majority of the Southerners who came to Egypt had belonged to the yeoman class of white farmers and had never themselves owned slaves, and although slavery had been technically illegal in Illinois since the time of the Northwest Ordinance, the institution persisted in one form or another until about 1850, either clandestinely or through the extralegal device of indentures.[26] Not having a direct financial stake in slavery, most people in southern Illinois sympathized with Southern slaveholders more on social than economic grounds. Like thoughtful persons throughout America they asked themselves what alternative there was to slavery as a means to race adjustment. Free Negroes presented a growing social problem in Illinois and were generally unwelcomed in all parts of the state, north as well as south. In 1853 the legislature at Springfield prohibited their entering Illinois altogether.[27]

[26] T. C. Pease, *The Story of Illinois*, pp. 147–148.

[27] Don E. Fehrenbacher, *Prelude to Greatness*, p. 31; Eugene H. Berwanger, *The Frontier against Slavery*, pp. 45–48. Chaplain W. Morrison, *Democratic Politics and Sectionalism: The Wilmot Proviso Controversy*, and V. Jacque Voegeli, *Free but Not Equal: The Midwest and the Negro during the Civil War*,

The northern portion of Illinois had gotten off to a slower start, but had recently been making great strides. Highlighted by the vibrant, robust boomtown of Chicago that Douglas had helped to found, nourished by wave after wave of newcomers from New England, Ireland, and Germany, and providing a healthy economic climate for new and thriving industries like iron and steel, it was now the most rapidly growing part of the state. Southern Illinoisans, like citizens of the slave states, saw the sectional balance slowly tilting against them throughout the 1850's.

If Illinois possessed an identifiable north and south, it also had a very real central section bounded roughly by the towns of Ottawa, Paris, Belleville, and Oquawka.[28] If the northern part of the state was Republican and the southern part Democratic, the center was less certain in its political allegiances.[29] In the old days it had been primarily Whig and American. With the virtual disappearance of these parties by 1858, its residents were casting about for a new political home. Their votes could go in either direction. If the geographical extremes of the state were also its political extremes, if the north was tolerant of abolitionists and the south of proslavery men, the center was distinguished by its moderation. Its political disposition leaned slightly in the direction of free-soil, but its actions were determined largely by a deep-seated suspicion of radicalism of any description.[30]

It was here in the center section of Illinois, no part of which was more than eighty miles from Springfield, that the election of 1858 would be decided, and it was the inveterate moderation of this area that largely determined the campaign strategy of the two contenders.

---

provide convincing evidence of the anti-Negro bias in the Midwest prior to the Civil War.

28 Allen Johnson, *Stephen A. Douglas: A Study in American Politics*, p. 363.

29 Paul M. Angle, ed., *Created Equal: The Complete Lincoln-Douglas Debates of 1858*, p. xxiv; Arthur C. Cole, *The Era of the Civil War, 1848–1870*, pp. 175–178.

30 Cole, *Era of the Civil War*, pp. 175–176.

Historians have tended to concentrate too much on what was said in the debates and too little upon how it was said. They have often become preoccupied with an unrealistically long list of issues, while neglecting the important subtleties of rhetoric, tactics, and timing. The two candidates professed to see the differences between themselves as broad, irreconcilable, and crucial for the future of America. Although such an approach had obvious value for enhancing the dramatic content of the campaign, there is little reason to doubt the sincerity of the contestants in stressing the extent of their differences.[31]

Yet a closer look reveals that a number of potential issues were never even brought up, others were mentioned only to betray a wide area of agreement between the two men, and still others were raised but never really joined. In those rare instances where there was a genuine clash over an issue, it usually occurred along a very narrow front.

To audiences still shaken from the financial panic of the year before. neither Lincoln nor Douglas had anything to say about money, banking, or securities reform. In a world only recently made smaller by the laying of the Atlantic cable, no mention was made of trade, tariff, foreign policy, or immigration. In a state not many years removed from the frontier, nothing was said about homestead lands or the Pacific railroad.

As long as the campaigners could confine their discussion to vague, general principles, there was a chance that they might convince their audiences of the very real differences between them. But as soon as the abrasion of debate began to force a clarification and definition of those principles, and as the focus of the contest later turned from the niceties of principles *per se* to a study of their application, the chasm separating Lincoln and Douglas began to close. It became apparent that neither really wanted absolute equality in all areas of American life for the Negro, that both agreed to support the Fugitive Slave Law, and that neither man

[31] Angle, ed., *Debates*, p. 23.

really wanted to admit any more slave states into the Union. Both regarded the Dred Scott decision as an obstacle to their peculiar solution to the problem of slavery in the territories.

Spectators who came looking for a resounding clash of ideas were usually disappointed. The two forensic knights would come charging through the Illinois lists, verbal lances poised for impact, the audience holding its breath in anticipation. More often than not they rode quite past one another without ever striking a blow. Lincoln would say that slavery showed a legal tendency to expand; Douglas would imply that it showed a pragmatic tendency to remain stationary. Douglas defended one interpretation of the Dred Scott decision; Lincoln accused him of trying to nullify another. Douglas would maintain that the founding fathers created a Union half-slave, half-free; Lincoln would reply that they had placed slavery in the course of ultimate extinction. Douglas exclaimed that ours was a white man's government; Lincoln would answer that he did not want a Negro for his wife.

When the broad regions of tacit agreement on the one hand and false and irrelevant issues on the other are swept away, the area of true and meaningful discussion between the two men proves to have been small and basically abstract. Lincoln and Douglas did not divide over the existence of slavery in the United States, but only over the future of that institution along the frontier. The concrete territorial case of Kansas provided no real issue. Both condemned Lecompton and argued only over who should get the credit for defeating it: Douglas or the Republican party. Lincoln and Douglas were much closer to one another on Lecompton than Douglas was to his own party. When the issue of slavery was joined at all, it was on essentially hypothetical ground.

Unlike the differences of the two candidates over issues, the contrasts between their debating styles were obvious, vivid, and possibly more meaningful for the final outcome of the election.

The Lincoln-Douglas contest observed few of the niceties of the debate form. It was closer to a series of joint stump speeches, and

Douglas was a born stump speaker. For Douglas, speech was merely an extension of action, and the debating platform, a genteel substitute for the prize fight ring. In debate he was quick, tough, spontaneous, and occasionally vulgar. Isaac Arnold commented that "his style was bold, vigorous, and aggressive, and at times defiant. He was ready, fertile in resources . . . terrible in denunciation, and handled with skill all the weapons of debate."[32] He must have spoken faster than Lincoln, for although each man was allotted the same amount of time in every debate, the written versions of Douglas' speeches are consistently longer than those of his opponent.

Although more forceful than eloquent, most of Douglas' speeches are marked by an admirable clarity. In an age when overblown oratory on the classical model was the rule, Douglas' relentless logic and concise, thrusting argument came as a refreshing change of pace. Douglas knew how to laugh, but humor was not really his stock in trade. He preferred the quicker and more biting effects of wit. The homely parables that brought a broad, slow smile to the face of the listener he would leave to Abe Lincoln. Douglas' delivery was more heated, more emotional, but its fundamental appeal was to the minds of those who heard him; Lincoln was calmer, more deliberate, almost detached, but his words spoke to the heart, and the response they evoked was basically a sentimental one.

Lincoln and Douglas planned their strategy and tactics with all the care a field general would lavish upon a major campaign. Indeed, the debates in more than one respect resembled a military clash, complete with feints, flanking movements, and an occasional frontal assault. If the engagement never produced a rout for either party, it did witness a few hasty retreats from advance positions. The two political warriors conducted themselves for the most part with honor and valor. Their performance sometimes showed flashes of brilliance, and only rarely was it worthy of censure.

Each man sought to take the offensive while keeping his oppo-

[32] Isaac N. Arnold, *Reminiscences of the Illinois Bar Forty Years Ago*, p. 150.

nent on the defensive.[33] Each man tried to occupy and hold the high ground of principle while forcing his adversary to conduct his attack from less noble terrain. Yet, of the two, Douglas found it more difficult to mount a strong offensive. In his role as incumbent, his actions restricted by the responsibilities of his high office, Douglas knew that his campaign would be essentially a holding action. Douglas' arguments were marked by an occasional brilliant sally in the direction of the enemy camp, but for the most part he was content to remain within his own lines.

It was a wise choice. In the Lincoln-Douglas Debates the contestants usually found it easier to hold and defend old positions than they did to occupy new political ground. Whenever either candidate mounted an attack, it usually proved short-lived and ineffective. More often than not it ended in a somewhat ragged retreat. Douglas might call Lincoln an abolitionist, Lincoln might charge Douglas with being the tool of Southern slaveholders, but their audience for the most part was not greatly moved. What appeared at first glance as a genuine offensive move on the part of one of the candidates, more often was in fact something akin to guerrilla warfare. Both men were better at laying traps for their opponent than at destroying him outright. If the audience had come expecting a frontal assault by the challenger, they usually had to be satisfied with a verbal state of siege. Lincoln told a man who came to visit him while he was resting in his hotel room at Quincy, "You can't overturn a pyramid, but you can undermine it; that's what I've been trying to do."[34]

Since Douglas' basic strategy from the outset of the campaign was primarily defensive, he understandably sought to narrow the front he had to defend by limiting the scope of the issues under discussion. Douglas would have been content to confine the argument to the present. He prided himself on being a practical man and professed disdain for hypothetical questions.[35] Douglas partic-

[33] Beveridge, *Abraham Lincoln*, II, 641–642.

[34] Sandburg, *Lincoln: Prairie Years*, II, 161.

[35] Adlai E. Stevenson, "Stephen A. Douglas," *Transactions of the Illinois State Historical Society for 1908*, p. 62; Angle, ed., *Debates*, p. 152.

ularly despised legalisms, which he equated with abstractions and dismissed as worthless.[36] He praised the Constitution and the positive law that emanated from it, but he had a deep-seated suspicion of anything resembling natural law. For Douglas, the best laws were those that reflected the economic self-interest and public opinion of those whom they sought to discipline. No mere entry on the statute books could take the place of climate and economics as a determinant of human behavior.[37] Whenever Lincoln in the course of the debates would point to the Northwest Ordinance as the ultimate cause of Illinois being free-soil, Douglas would give the credit to the influence of climate and soil working through his beloved popular sovereignty.[38]

If Douglas concentrated on the present, Lincoln talked more of the future. If Douglas sought to solve practical problems, Lincoln dealt more with abstract questions. If Douglas praised positive law, Lincoln inclined to talk of natural rights, which he loosely equated with morality.

It was Lincoln who held that Jefferson's greatest contribution to the Declaration of Independence was to introduce an abstract truth into what had been only a revolutionary document.[39] He attacked the Dred Scott decision not only as wrong in itself, but also because it foreshadowed a future and much more serious kind of decision that would impinge on the right of the free states to forbid slavery within their borders.[40]

While Douglas stressed the sanctity of the Constitution, Lincoln concentrated his attentions on the preamble of the Declaration of Independence. Lincoln always invoked the entire document as an ideal, but when he came to cite specific references, it became apparent that one small phrase in the preamble overshadowed all others

[36] See Douglas' Senate speech of May 15 and 16, 1860, in *Cong. Globe*, 36th Cong., 1st sess., app., p. 301.

[37] Angle, ed., *Debates*, pp. 364 and 375.

[38] Ibid., pp. 58–60. Harry V. Jaffa and Robert W. Johannsen, eds., *In the Name of the People: Speeches and Writings of Lincoln and Douglas in the Ohio Campaign of 1859*, pp. 225–226.

[39] Merrill D. Peterson, *The Jefferson Image in the American Mind*, p. 162.

[40] Angle, ed., *Debates*, pp. 144, 329.

in importance: "that all men are created equal, that they are endowed by their Creator with certain unalienable Rights, that among these are Life, Liberty and the pursuit of Happiness."[41] Here indeed was a worthy vehicle for the propagation of Lincoln's cause. It permitted him to appear conservative by identifying with the sentiments of the founding fathers, while the appeal of the phrase itself was essentially radical. Lincoln was not naive enough to believe that all men in America were in fact given an equal chance at birth. He saw in the preamble of the Declaration a worthy ideal to strive for, a program for future action, and a fitting reply to a Douglas preoccupied only with the present. It enabled him to throw down before those defenders of the sanctity of the Constitution, with all its cynical compromises and emphasis on positive law, the challenge of natural law and human rights.

The election of 1858 was a struggle over political middle ground. Lincoln and Douglas, like the majority of people of Illinois, were basically conservative in their political orientation. The decisive electoral battleground lay in the center of the state, which had for so long been a Whig stronghold. Each man attempted to portray himself as a moderate while labeling his adversary as a dangerous radical. Douglas' major goal throughout the campaign was to convince his listeners that popular sovereignty was a program in the best American tradition for furthering the cause of free-soil in the territories—a cause toward which the majority of Illinoisans were sympathetic. Popular sovereignty was therefore represented by Douglas as a conservative means to a conservative end.

It followed that Lincoln's foremost task in the campaign was to invalidate Douglas' credentials as an effective, though not admitted, free-soil champion. Lincoln seemed to spend most of his time attacking the Douglas of 1854—the Douglas who was openly sympathetic toward slaveholders and slavery—without acknowledging that during the last four years the Little Giant had made a series of impressive strides in the direction of free-soil.[42]

41 Ibid., p. 101.

42 Douglas' fight against Lecompton was, of course, the great turning point in this direction.

Each man adopted a conservative pose on the major issues of the campaign. In central Illinois, both sought to identify their careers with the old Whigs in general and with Henry Clay in particular. On the crucial slavery question, the differences were not those between extremists. Douglas would tolerate slavery but not a slave code; Lincoln's dislike of slavery stopped far short of abolitionism.

Each man sought to stand on strong national ground while placing his opponent in the light of a narrow sectionalist who would recklessly destroy the Union. Douglas attempted to cast discredit on Lincoln's patriotism during the Mexican War,[43] while Lincoln argued that the Douglas position on slavery was contrary to the intentions of the founding fathers, who placed that institution "in the course of ultimate extinction."[44] In fact, both men were deeply loyal to their country, and the differences between them were much narrower than they cared to admit. The only major point of disagreement was over the subtleties of the definition of the word *nation.* For Douglas, the nation was primarily a political entity held together by ties of positive law and patriotic emotion. It was no accident that his great hero was Andrew Jackson. To Douglas' way of thinking, the nation equaled the sum of its sectional parts.

Lincoln, on the other hand, looked upon the Union as mystical more than political. In Alexander Stephens' perceptive phrase, "With Lincoln the Union rose to the sublimity of religious mysticism."[45] For him, the basic bonds of the Union were moral rather than political or emotional. The nation was greater than the mere sum of sectional political interests; somehow it possessed a unique and noble spirit. Lincoln seems to have been feeling his way toward a concept of nationhood strikingly similar to Rousseau's General Will.[46] While Douglas' loyalty was to the nation *qua* nation, Lincoln's allegiance was more specific. He would identify with only a particular kind of nation, and his judgment upon its worth was

[43] Angle, ed., *Debates*, p. 108.

[44] Ibid., p. 353.

[45] Edmund Wilson, "Abraham Lincoln: The Union as Religious Mysticism," in *Eight Essays*, p. 197.

[46] Jean Jacques Rousseau, *The Social Contract*, ed. G. D. H. Cole, Chapter III.

ultimately a moral one. In Douglas' hierarchy of values, the nation—its health, preservation, and expansion—stood at the very top. Lincoln was less absolute in his loyalties. He declared in a speech in New York early in 1861: "There is nothing that could ever bring me to consent—willingly to consent—to the destruction of this Union . . . unless it would be that thing for which the Union itself was made."[47] Lincoln had expressed similar sentiments seven years before at Peoria.[48]

For Douglas, maintaining a moderate pose was easier than it was for Lincoln, but potentially less productive. Because he was a practical man, the incumbent, and the leader of the moderate wing of a reactionary party, Douglas' conservatism was deep-seated, sincere, and convincing. Yet the device he had seized upon to give voice both to his own conservatism and to that of his fellow Americans was basically fragile and unstable. Popular sovereignty served best as a bridge between moderate schools of thought, but public opinion in America had by 1858 begun to polarize around extreme positions. Furthermore, the Dred Scott decision had exposed the very real flaws embedded in the legal foundations of popular sovereignty, and Lincoln with his logical and relentless mining and sapping tactics promised to expose them still more.

Lincoln too was at heart a conservative; indeed many of his friends complained that he was too conservative.[49] But his strategy in the 1858 campaign called for doing far more than simply issuing an appeal to conservative sentiments. In the first place, Lincoln was the candidate of a new and progressive party. He was also closely identified with the northern part of the state, where liberal ideologies received their most favorable reception. In the second place, if the campaign were to resolve itself into a straight contest for the conservative vote, Douglas would be an easy winner. Lincoln's fundamental task was to appeal to the radical free-soil and abolitionist sentiment in Illinois without sacrificing his hold on

[47] Nicolay and Hay, eds., *Works of Lincoln*, VI, 149–150.
[48] Ibid., II, 248.
[49] Cole, *Era of the Civil War*, p. 155.

more conservative points of view. He had to stand on moderate ground while swinging out to gather in more extreme positions. He could not openly identify himself with radicals and abolitionists, but he could not afford to alienate them either. Like Douglas, Lincoln knew that majority opinion in Illinois was essentially moderate, but unlike his opponent, Lincoln seems to have grasped just how potentially immoderate it really was. What Lincoln did in the 1858 campaign was to put into words the gnawing moral anxiety moderate elements in America were coming to feel toward the institution of slavery. He expressed and focused the latent discontent of thoughtful, reasonable men, without ever explicitly prescribing a radical cure for the ills of conscience.

All the many strategic threads of Lincoln's campaign were brilliantly prefigured in the speech he delivered before the Republican convention that had just nominated him as its candidate at Springfield on June 16.

Lincoln spoke briefly, yet he touched on a wide variety of subjects. One passage, however, stood out above all others:

> A house divided against itself cannot stand. I believe this government cannot endure permanently half slave and half free. I do not expect the Union to be dissolved—I do not expect the house to fall—but I do expect it will cease to be divided. It will become all one thing, or all the other. Either the opponents of slavery will arrest the further spread of it, and place it where the public mind shall rest in the belief that it is in the course of ultimate extinction or its advocates will push it forward, till it shall become alike lawful in all the states, old as well as new—North as well as South. Have we no tendency to the latter condition?[50]

Here is the Lincolnian concern for the future. Here is Lincoln in the role of prophet, a role he was to assume often in the debates, a role many historians—with their predisposition to see him in retrospect as a kind of Messiah—readily accord him: "It will become all one thing, or all the other." Here is Lincoln growing

[50] Angle, ed., *Debates*, p. 2.

alarmed over a legal "tendency." Here is Lincoln giving us a hint of the kind of absolute moral alternatives he would pose in the campaign that was to follow.

Here also is Lincoln, the shrewd politician who knew that as the less-famous contender he would have to strive hard to steal the political spotlight from the senior Senator from Illinois. The House Divided speech promised to produce just the kind of shock his campaign needed to attract public attention. It would give Lincoln a unique and indelible political identity in the eyes of both his own fellow Republicans and the uncommitted voter.

The House Divided speech was sensational in its impact but basically ambivalent in its content. This is the way Lincoln wanted it. The subjective impression it made was radical, but its objective form was moderate. It carried with it a flavor of crusading zeal and intolerance for the status quo, yet Lincoln did not advocate any definite changes. He did not "expect" the Union to be dissolved, he only "believed" the government could not endure "permanently" in the state it was in. He predicted change but shied away from being the one to effect it. Avoiding a more specific prediction, he declared only, "It will become all one thing, or all the other."

As a political gambit, the speech passed every test with flying colors. It called Lincoln to the public's attention, it enabled him to seem both liberal and conservative. It answered the main requirement of a good political slogan: it could mean many things to many people holding a wide variety of opinions. It could comfort moderate free-soilers without alienating radicals and abolitionists. Standing objectively in the center, Lincoln had begun his subjective swing to the left.

If the House Divided speech proved a political asset for Lincoln in many respects, it also brought its share of liabilities that Douglas was quick to exploit. If each man sought to appear a moderate, the other side of the strategic coin found each trying to brand his opponent as a dangerous radical. Lincoln would portray Douglas as sympathetic to slavery and accuse him of conspiring with Southern slaveholders to extend it not only into the territories, but into the free states as well. Douglas, in turn, sought to label Lincoln as an abolitionist in free-soil disguise.

Lincoln's House Divided speech provided Douglas with an excellent weapon for this purpose. If the most consistent theme of Lincoln's speeches during the debates was an attack on popular sovereignty, each of Douglas' seven speeches hammered away at the implicit radicalism of the notion of the house divided. He charged Lincoln with wantonly destroying the status quo on slavery erected by the founding fathers; he interpreted the speech as calling for a uniformity of institutions in a country whose strength lay in its diversity. In a brilliant tactical appeal to proponents of natural and positive law alike, Douglas warned that the program set forth by Lincoln "would be destructive of state rights, of state sovereignty, of personal liberty and personal freedom."[51] Douglas next went beyond the familiar confines of politics and admonished his listeners that "uniformity is the parent of despotism the world over, not only in politics but in religion."[52] Stretching the credulity of those who had come to hear him, Douglas went one step farther and announced that "Mr. Lincoln advocates boldly and clearly a war of sections, a war of the North against the South, of the free states against the slave states—a war of extermination—to be continued relentlessly until the one or the other shall be subdued and all the states shall either become free or become slave."[53] Douglas here was probably closer to the truth than either he or Lincoln imagined in the still-tranquil atmosphere of 1858.

Lincoln in turn charged Douglas with participating in a national conspiracy to make slavery legal throughout America. He saw the Kansas-Nebraska Act and the Dred Scott decision as laying the groundwork for a future Supreme Court ruling prohibiting the citizens of a free state from forbidding the entrance of slavery. He argued that it was not he but Douglas who was disturbing the status quo created by the founding fathers. Lincoln, oriented to-

[51] Ibid., p. 19.
[52] Ibid.
[53] Ibid., p. 18.

ward the future and delighting in the role of prophet, was particularly adept at parading a rather unlikely series of horrors. He argued that Douglas' view of slaves as property destroyed any logical and legal opposition to the revival of the African slave trade and that the attempt to find a means of coexistence between the Dred Scott decision and popular sovereignty in fact made Douglas as much a nullifier of federal law as the most radical Northern abolitionists.

Douglas retaliated by claiming that Lincoln's goal of containing slavery would mean virtual starvation for a rapidly multiplying Negro population confined within a fixed area. Always anxious to paint Lincoln as a dangerous extremist, Douglas, in his opening speech of the debates, was intent upon tying his opponent to a radical antislavery platform allegedly adopted by a Republican state convention at Springfield in 1854.

Both candidates found difficulty in making these charges of radicalism stick, and they retreated from advanced offensive positions as the debates wore on. Lincoln qualified his conspiracy charge by confessing that he was talking more about a tendency than a reality. Douglas found himself in an uneasy position when Lincoln successfully refuted the charge that he had supported the radical 1854 platform. A highly agitated Stephen Douglas, who was beginning to suspect that he had based his charges upon false evidence, fired off a telegram to his old friend Usher F. Linder: "The hell-hounds are on my track. For God's sake, Linder, come and help me fight them."[54] The telegram fell into Republican hands and was immediately published. Douglas' embarrassment was compounded, and Linder, for his part, had the dubious distinction of living out the rest of his life known as "For-God's-Sake-Linder."

If these extremist charges were of little use in scoring debating points, they had a certain value for somewhat less noble ends. Each candidate's speaking time was rigidly limited under the terms of the debate—indeed, a timekeeper was always present on the platform. By making a charge against his opponent, no matter how ridiculous

[54] Johannsen, ed., *Letters of Douglas*, p. 427.

and unrealistic it might have been, each man hoped to force his adversary to waste much valuable time in removing the smear he had applied. Lincoln found himself explaining at great length that he really was patriotic during the Mexican War and that he did not actually want a Negro for his wife.[55] Douglas, for his part, expended much time and effort denying that he had conspired in the unlikely company of James Buchanan and Roger Taney to make slavery legal throughout the Union.

This was not the only example of the use of tactics that, if not unethical, were at least something less than honorable. Although both men posed as consistent advocates of principle, they were not above slanting a speech to suit a given audience. At Charleston, in the southern half of Illinois, Lincoln began his speech by reassuring the crowd: "I am not, nor ever have been in favor of bringing about in any way the social and political equality of the white and black races."[56] In Egypt, where his views were not well received, Lincoln concentrated more on personalities than issues.

Douglas was sometimes guilty of similar tactics, although in Alton, far down in southern Illinois, he lashed out against Lecompton and the English bill in strong and unequivocal language. His sin was more one of evasion and obfuscation. Although he loved a good fight and was usually the first to pick up any challenge that was flung down before him, Douglas was not above resorting to red herrings or turning to ridicule when Lincoln had driven him into an uncomfortable position and a direct answer might have been harmful. When Lincoln asked Douglas at Freeport if he would support a Supreme Court decision abrogating the right of states to exclude slavery, the Little Giant was content to reply that he was "amazed that Lincoln should ask such a question" and chided his opponent for trying to cast an imputation upon the Supreme Court.[57] Lincoln never really got an answer to his question.

All of the many issues discussed during the debates—popular

[55] Angle, ed., *Debates*, pp. 118, 358.
[56] Ibid., p. 235.
[57] Ibid., p. 154.

sovereignty, the repeal of the Missouri Compromise, Kansas, the Fugitive Slave Law, the role of the Northwest Ordinance, the Dred Scott decision, states' rights, and the Declaration of Independence —were concerned with the place of the Negro in America in general and with slavery in particular.

Neither candidate had a very high opinion of the Negro. Douglas saw him as a member of an inferior race; Lincoln concurred.[58] Both men realized that if majority sentiment in Illinois was opposed to slavery, it was not pro-Negro. Quite the opposite. Northwesterners in the 1850's, unlike some of their Eastern brothers, professed little love for the Negro. They did not even like him. His political and social behavior was governed by Black Codes fully as notorious as any adopted by the South during Reconstruction.[59] If the Negro wished to live in Illinois, he would have to do so on the white man's terms.

From the very outset, the indifference of public opinion in Illinois toward the plight of the black race, coupled with the basic moderation of both candidates, guaranteed there would be no sharp issue drawn along radical-conservative lines where the Negro was concerned. The differences that did appear between Lincoln and Douglas were very narrow in their scope and more relative than absolute.

The candidates showed almost complete agreement in their opposition to any form of social equality for the Negro. Lincoln in practice stopped far short of the logical implications of the abstract position he had adopted in the House Divided speech. He was much more complacent toward the inferior status of the Negro in society than he ever was toward slavery. Far from advocating social equality between the races, Lincoln recognized that "there is a physical difference between the white and black races which will ever forbid the two races living together on terms of social and political equali-

[58] Ibid., pp. 22–23, 235.

[59] Henry C. Hubbart, *The Older Middle West*, pp. 44–51. The existence of widespread anti-Negro feeling in the Northwest is discussed at length in Berwanger, *Frontier against Slavery*; Morrison, *Democratic Politics and Sectionalism*; and Voegeli, *Free but Not Equal.*

ty."[60] He went a step farther and maintained that, since "there must be the position of superior and inferior, I am as much as any other man in favor of having the superior position assigned to the white race."[61]

Douglas attempted to drive Lincoln off this moderate middle ground: "I have not the slightest idea but that he conscientiously believes that a negro ought to enjoy and exercise all the rights and privileges given to white men."[62] Douglas played on the fear that has always been at the bottom of the resistance on the part of the white race in America to granting social equality to the Negro: that the ultimate outcome of any concession would be racial amalgamation. Lincoln recognized the seriousness of the specter Douglas had raised and chose to blunt its force by exaggerating it to the point of the ludicrous: "Judge Douglas will have it that I want a negro wife. He can never be brought to understand that there is any middle ground on this subject."[63]

If in the social sphere there were few real differences between Lincoln and Douglas on the position of the Negro, the political sphere disclosed few more. Lincoln and Douglas went on record as being opposed to according the Negro all the rights of citizenship, yet neither was unalterably opposed to expanding the meager political privileges already enjoyed by the free blacks. Douglas argued that "this government was made by our fathers on the white basis. It was made by white men for the benefit of white men and their posterity forever, and was intended to be administered by white men in all time to come," but went on to add that the Negro nonetheless "ought to possess every right, every privilege, every immunity which he can safely exercise consistent with the safety of the society in which he lives."[64] Lincoln in turn accepted that part of the racial status quo that placed the Negro in an inferior political position, but unlike Douglas he refused to recognize any given

60 Angle, ed., *Debates*, p. 326.

61 Ibid.

62 Nicolay and Hay, eds., *Works of Lincoln*, III, 91.

63 Angle, ed., *Debates*, p. 358.

64 Ibid., pp. 294–295.

status quo as permanent. By basing much of his case for the Negro on the preamble of the Declaration of Independence, Lincoln was holding forth the ideal of equality at some distant future time, while accepting the inferior status of the Negro for the present. It was an approach wholly typical of Lincoln, who often in the course of the debates showed himself to be both the conservative and the radical.

The significant differences between the two men on the political position of the Negro were subtle and relative. For Douglas, the Negro was not quite a full-fledged human being.[65] In August of 1858 Douglas, in an apparent deviation from his erstwhile faith in the effectiveness of climate as a determinant of human behavior, told a delegation of Germans in Chicago that "the experience of the world in all ages proves that the negro is incapable of self-government in all climes."[66]

Douglas refused to recognize the concept of natural rights where the Negro was concerned. He would accord him political rights under positive law, but these would have to be granted by the dominant white group at the state level and were always subject to the qualification "consistent with the safety of society."[67] Lincoln, with his moral awareness and frequent references to the Declaration of Independence, looked more to human rights under natural law. For Lincoln, unlike Douglas, the Negro was first of all a human being, albeit an inferior one.

Only in the economic sphere did Lincoln and Douglas show clear differences over the role of the Negro in America. Speaking at Quincy, Lincoln said of the Negro, "I agree with Judge Douglas that he is not my equal in many respects, certainly not in color—perhaps not in intellectual and moral endowments; but in the right to eat the bread without leave of anybody else which his own hand

[65] *New York Tribune*, December 6, 1858.

[66] Printed copy of a speech by Douglas to a delegation of Germans in Chicago, August, 1858 (exact date not given, but probably August 28); catalogued under "Stephen A. Douglas" in the Huntington Library; not in a named collection.

[67] Angle, ed., *Debates*, p. 22.

earns, he is my equal and the equal of Judge Douglas, and the equal of every other man."[68]

Lincoln attacked slavery along a broad front and issued a sweeping moral indictment of the whole institution, but when he moved from general criticisms to specific ones, the only concrete aspect of slavery he censured was the economic exploitation of the Negro. But slavery was much more than an economic system; it was a method of political and social adjustment between the races. Lincoln neither condemned the kind of racial adjustment proffered by slavery nor suggested a clear alternative system of his own.

What is usually referred to as the slavery issue in the Lincoln-Douglas Debates was in fact two separate issues: Is slavery wrong? If so, where and how should it be checked? On the first point there was no clear division between the candidates. Lincoln said slavery was wrong, but Douglas never really said that he thought it was right. On the second question the area of division was narrow—so narrow that at times the campaigners seemed to be arguing entirely over hypothetical situations. Neither man wanted to disturb the existing status of slavery in any state. Neither would oppose unequivocally the admission of any more slave states. Neither wanted to reopen the African slave trade. Both agreed to enforce the Fugitive Slave Law. The conflict in the debates was not between Ultra and abolitionist points of view, but between two shadings of essentially moderate Northern opinion on slavery. The main point at issue was the status of slavery in the territories in general and the role of the federal government in determining the status in particular. Yet here again the issue was elusive. The only immediate territorial slavery dispute had been settled in August of 1858 when the voters of Kansas had roundly defeated admission under Lecompton.

Lincoln was actually arguing that at some undisclosed future date in some territory yet unborn Congress should have the power to prohibit slavery. Douglas naturally held that the question should

[68] Ibid., p. 327.

be left to the decision of the citizens of the territory through the workings of popular sovereignty. Yet even here the issue has about it a hollow ring, since in the autumn of 1858, with the Democratic party firmly entrenched in all three branches of the government, neither Lincoln nor Douglas could have seriously thought that Congress would make a move to interdict the spread of slavery in the foreseeable future. When all the eloquent posturing is swept aside, both candidates were tilting at windmills: Lincoln attacked not a reality but a legal tendency of slavery to expand into some hypothetical future territory; Douglas defended his popular sovereignty against an onslaught from a free-soil Congress which was nowhere to be found. Their argument becomes at once even more pointless and unfortunate when one bears in mind that both men wanted to see an end to slavery expansion, although Douglas, because of his national political ambitions, kept his wishes on the point to himself.[69] Furthermore, the popular sovereignty of Douglas would probably in the end have been as potent a tool for containing slavery as Lincoln's congressional prohibition.[70]

If the issue between Lincoln and Douglas was often specious, a fundamental ambivalence contained in both men's views on slavery was partly to blame. The Little Giant detested slavery in private and sought to ignore it in public. Slavery was alien to Stephen Douglas with his Vermont background, his instinctive sense of justice, and his ties to industry more than agriculture. To his close friends and family he confided his abhorrence of the institution. Following a trip through the South he remarked in private that he had seen "three hundred of those recently imported miserable beings in a slave-pen at Vicksburg, Mississippi, and also large numbers at Memphis, Tennessee."[71] For obvious political reasons Doug-

[69] *Washington Union*, October 29, 1858; Sandburg, *Lincoln: Prairie Years*, II, 152.

[70] J. G. Randall, *Lincoln the President: Springfield to Gettysburg*, I, 124; Charles W. Ramsdell, "The Natural Limits of Slavery Expansion," *Mississippi Valley Historical Review* 16, no. 2 (September 1929): 162.

[71] See the correspondence of a "Native Southerner" in the *New York Tribune*, August 23, 26, 27, 1859; McConnel, *Transactions of the Illinois State Historical Society for 1900*, p. 49; letter of James Lemen in Stevens, "Life of Douglas,"

las had refused the gift of a large plantation stocked with 150 slaves in Lawrence County, Mississippi, offered him by his first father-in-law, Colonel Robert Martin. After the Colonel's death Douglas did, however, become the executor of his estate and administered the Martin holdings for the benefit of his wife and children until the time of his own death. The concern Douglas felt for the field hands is readily seen in the care his overseers took to reassure him of their welfare.[72] In the campaign of 1858 Douglas successfully refuted every charge by Republicans and Buchananites that the family's slaves were being mistreated.

Yet the smooth workings of popular sovereignty and his own career as a national political figure dictated that Douglas suppress in public the revulsion he felt toward slavery in private. Douglas would neither praise nor condemn slavery openly. He sought to ignore it. Douglas did not seek the slavery issue: it was forced upon him. Although in the debates he would tacitly accept Lincoln's contention that slavery was the major cause of unrest in America, Douglas always seems to have considered the problem essentially a nuisance that was interfering with the much more important work of peaceful national expansion. Given the choice, Douglas would have preferred to turn his back on the slavery question altogether. As late as 1859 he would announce to the Senate: "I regret these frequent discussions upon the question. This subject would never have been introduced into the Senate this year, if it had been left to me."[73] Even when Douglas appeared to face the slavery question squarely, his favorite prescription of popular sovereignty was in some respects a formal device for allowing both himself and the federal government to avoid responsibility for the problem and hand it back to the people of the territories.

---

pp. 655–656; remarks by Douglas, *Cong. Globe*, 30th Cong., 1st sess., app., p. 507; reprint of Judge Robert A. Douglas' letter of October 14, 1908.

[72] R. I. Ward to Douglas, New Orleans, Louisiana, November 30, 1857; Douglas MSS. See also Robert W. Johannsen, "Stephen A. Douglas and the South," *Journal of Southern History* 33, no. 1 (February 1967): 30–31. In 1857 the Lawrence County plantation was sold and Douglas moved the Martin family's slaves onto a new plantation in Washington County, Mississippi.

[73] *Cong. Globe*, 35th Cong., 2nd sess., p. 1256.

Douglas' attitude was conditioned by many forces. There was the obvious personal factor that continued discussion of slavery went contrary to his basically conservative nature and made his posture as a national political leader awkward to maintain. There were more enlightened reasons as well. Douglas felt that, while economic and climatic forces were working for the eventual disappearance of slavery, any attempt to abolish it in the short run would result in an unhealthy mixture of morals and politics, quite probably culminating in civil war.[74]

It was Lincoln's refusal to ignore the moral implications of slavery that created the impassable ideological gulf between the two candidates. We have seen them to have been in substantial agreement on the range of objective controls the American people could legally put upon slavery. At a more subtle level, both seem to have felt that in the long run slavery was doomed. Douglas saw economic forces working against it. Lincoln, by arguing for the containment of slavery as the first step toward its ultimate extinction, adumbrated the Ramsdell view that slavery in the late 1850's was a dying institution that could survive only as long as it found an abundance of rich new land to cultivate.[75]

It was the introduction of the moral issue that prevented any compromise over the rather narrow differences the two contenders had over the workings of slavery. Douglas' popular sovereignty implied the kind of tacit acceptance of slavery Lincoln's advanced moral position could not admit. Furthermore, the idea that slavery was a local political problem was basic to the whole notion of popular sovereignty, but Lincoln's moral approach made even the most isolated instance of slavery a national question. To Lincoln, slavery was the kind of moral disease that leaped across mere political boundaries to infect the whole way of life of a nation tolerating it in any part of its domain. Permit slavery in one territory and you sap the moral strength of an entire nation and prepare public opinion for tolerating it everywhere.[76] It was this subtle moral aggres-

[74] Angle, ed., *Debates*, pp. 59, 352, 402.
[75] Ramsdell, "Natural Limits of Slavery Expansion," p. 171.
[76] Angle, ed., *Debates*, p. 128.

sion of slavery that Lincoln primarily had in mind when he opened the 1858 senatorial campaign with a warning that the proponents of slavery "will push it forward, till it shall become alike lawful in all the states, old as well as new—North as well as South."[77]

Slavery for Lincoln was a national ill demanding a national remedy. For Douglas it was a local abscess to be ignored as long as possible, until it either disappeared through the workings of nature or was quietly excised by those most immediately affected.

In the struggle for the respectable middle ground of political moderation, Lincoln's major objective was to cast doubt on Douglas' credentials as a conservative champion of free-soil. The main point of his attack was popular sovereignty. When Douglas had concluded the opening speech of his campaign from the balcony of the Tremont House in Chicago, his admirers set off a large fireworks display that lit up the night sky and spelled out POPULAR SOVEREIGNTY.[78] Thus was proclaimed the keynote of Douglas' campaign. He was to spend the next four months defending his favorite doctrine with varying degrees of success against the repeated sallies of the challenger from Springfield.

In planning his strategy against popular sovereignty, Lincoln grasped the fundamental duality of the idea better than Douglas himself. His attack on the hard side of the notion was twofold. First, he questioned whether popular sovereignty was in fact made of the stuff of genuine principle and hinted broadly that it was much closer to a mere makeshift expedient.[79] Second, he condemned its professed amorality on the stern moral ground that it gave men the right to do wrong. Lincoln refused to grant Douglas' proposition that popular sovereignty was an enlightened way to preserve the valuable parts of a status quo while opening the door to reasonable change. Far from viewing popular sovereignty as progressive, he saw in the Kansas-Nebraska Act a step backward, since that piece of legislation had repealed the Missouri Compromise with its legal restraints on slavery and its implied moral censure of the entire

[77] Ibid., p. 2.

[78] Beveridge, *Abraham Lincoln*, II, 598.

[79] Angle, ed., *Debates*, p. 302.

institution. Yet nowhere did Lincoln take exception to what was perhaps the central and most sound aspect of popular sovereignty: that local habits and customs in all countries, especially America, do go far toward determining the effectiveness of a given law. Shrewd strategist that he was, Lincoln merely ignored the most challenging parts of popular sovereignty, bypassing them in favor of more vulnerable aspects.

Moving his attack to the soft side of popular sovereignty, Lincoln returned a double indictment of the Douglas doctrine. First, he argued that the Dred Scott decision had knocked out whatever legal underpinnings territorial control over slavery might once have had. Second, turning his attention to the results produced by popular sovereignty, Lincoln held that it led to the hegemony of slaveholders in a given territory. A territory remained free not because of the forces of climate working through popular sovereignty but because of a rigid prohibition against slavery at positive law. If Illinois was free-soil, it was because of the Northwest Ordinance. Lincoln was in fact saying that wherever popular sovereignty was tried, the result was slavery; where freedom obtained, it was because the scheme had been superseded by positive law. Lincoln therefore dismissed popular sovereignty as wrong at both natural and positive law, and productive of only bad results on those occasions when it worked at all.

He explicitly ignored the value of popular sovereignty as an agreement to disagree and maintained that any attempt to approach slavery from the standpoint of moral detachment was in fact immoral. Lincoln was really saying that one could not take advantage of whatever benefits popular sovereignty offered on its soft side without at the same time embracing the immoral tenets of the hard side. His advanced moral position prohibited Lincoln from granting his adversary any tenable middle ground. It was a shrewd approach, but one which played reckless with his country's future.

The Dred Scott decision is usually portrayed by historians as an unmitigated political disaster for Stephen Douglas. Responsible scholars like Jaffa stress that Taney and his court with one stroke destroyed the shaky legal foundations of popular sovereignty and exposed the logical flaws that were never really very far below the bland surface of Douglas' doctrine. It is true that, given the choice, Douglas would have preferred that the Court had never ruled on Dred Scott's case. When the decision was announced in March of 1857, Douglas and his followers maintained a public silence, but privately expressed their displeasure in unequivocal language.[80]

Douglas could hardly have been pleased with the implicit threat the decision posed to the powers a territorial legislature might exercise over slavery. Again, the decision itself, coming as it did from the highest court in the federal judiciary, represented the kind of national interference in territorial affairs that was an anathema to popular sovereignty with its strong localistic bias.

At the same time, if the Dred Scott decision caused Douglas discomfort in some respects, it must have reassured him in others. The declaration that no Negro could be a citizen of the United States was to Douglas unexceptionable, although he would have preferred to leave the question of citizenship to the individual states.[81] That part of the decision pronouncing the Missouri Compromise unconstitutional must have comforted Douglas, who for the last four years had been burdened with the charge that he had been responsible for its repeal in the Kansas-Nebraska Act. Furthermore, it had always been central to the Douglas version of popular sovereignty that neither Congress nor any other branch of the federal government should intervene in a territory either to prohibit or to perpetuate the institution of slavery. The Court agreed.

Only the passage that seemed to curb the powers of a territory itself to exclude slavery within its confines posed a real threat to the doctrine of popular sovereignty. Yet Douglas found consolation in the fact that the Court did not explicitly forbid exclusion by a territory, but only "presumed" that if Congress did not have the powers to keep slavery out of a territory "it could not authorize a territorial government to exercise them."[82]

[80] Harry V. Jaffa, *Crisis of the House Divided*, p. 110; Nevins, *The Emergence of Lincoln*, I, 141–143.

[81] Angle, ed., *Debates*, pp. 60–61.

[82] The Dred Scott Decision may be found in 19 *Howard*, 393 (1857).

The best judgment upon the Dred Scott decision would seem to be that, although it thwarted Douglas at some points, it still left him room for maneuver. If there was one man in America who could make the most of such an opportunity, it was the wily and imaginative Stephen Douglas. He was quick to see that the Supreme Court had not really spelled out just what a territory could or could not do to encourage or discourage slavery. Douglas, like the Southern slaveholders, joined the Court in recognizing that slaves were property and as such entitled to protection under the Fifth Amendment.[83] At the same time, uncertainty over the peculiar nature of slave property and over just how far government at the territorial and local level could go toward discouraging a particular kind of property opened up a wide range of possibilities for the Little Giant. Far from causing Douglas to surrender his belief in popular sovereignty, the Dred Scott decision made him cling to his pet doctrine all the harder and started him on the tortuous course of trying to adapt it to the changed legal climate.

Douglas succeeded magnificently. The Dred Scott case had presented Lincoln with a rare opportunity, but he never seemed able to bring the full force of his forensic charges to bear against either the decision or Douglas' position on it. Lincoln's handling of the Dred Scott issue was the least satisfactory part of his 1858 campaign. He paraded the ludicrous notion of Douglas' somehow being in collusion with James Buchanan on the decision. He raised the specter of a future decision that would bar the prohibition of slavery by states. It was a shallow move that pulled the Dred Scott case entirely out of context and overlooked the obvious fact that there was no such case currently pending anywhere in the federal judicial system. Furthermore, such a decision might have caused some Southern advocates of states' rights as much discomfort as it would have Northern abolitionists. He described Taney's decision as "political,"[84] as if all other Supreme Court judgments had been formed in a political vacuum.

Since Lincoln erroneously assumed that the Dred Scott case had

[83] Angle, ed., *Debates*, pp. 216–217.

[84] Ibid., p. 36.

unequivocally prohibited territorial legislatures from barring slavery, he was in fact attacking one kind of decision while Douglas was defending another. At bottom, the simple truth was that neither man liked the Dred Scott decision. Lincoln denounced it outright, and Douglas sought to modify it to suit his needs. In the end, Lincoln found himself in the awkward position of castigating both the decision and Douglas' attempts to change it.

Lincoln had one last arrow in his verbal quiver, and he let fly with it at Freeport one August afternoon. True to its aim, it hit the soft side of popular sovereignty.

Lincoln posed four questions to Douglas that day at Freeport, but it is the second history remembers best. Anxious to seize the initiative in his first chance at an opening speech in the debates, Lincoln demanded to know: "Can the people of a United States Territory, in any lawful way, against the wish of any citizen of the United States, exclude slavery from its limits prior to the formation of a state constitution?"[85]

In asking a series of formal questions, Lincoln was adopting a tactic Douglas had introduced earlier at Ottawa. But at the same time it was a typically Lincolnian move in its attempt to put an opponent on the defensive and place him in a position where any move he might make would mean the loss of votes.

Historians nonetheless often exaggerate the shrewdness and foresight of Lincoln in asking what has come to be known as the Freeport Question.[86] Perhaps the favorite explanation is that Lincoln realized at the very outset that Douglas would take an affirmative position. By doing so, he would keep the free-soil vote in Illinois and probably win the senatorial election, but would at the same time alienate the Southern vote and doom his chances to be elected President in 1860. Lincoln, according to legend, is supposed to have confided to his closest friends that he was searching for bigger game than the Senate seat and that the presidential battle of 1860 was a hundred times more valuable than the 1858 contest.[87]

[85] Ibid., pp. 143–144.
[86] Cole, *Era of the Civil War*, pp. 170–171.
[87] Schurz, *Reminiscences*, II, 98.

Such an explanation is a bit too neat and logical to be very convincing. It assumes a degree of foresight and long-range planning that simply does not fit the fluid, rough-and-tumble political setting of 1858. It has about it the specious ring of hindsight and of commentators projecting their own logical and analytical discoveries onto the motives of their subject, and the wisdom born from years of study long after an event onto the frenetic, *ad hoc* atmosphere of a political campaign.

There is actually very little reason to believe that Lincoln in 1858 was primarily concerned with winning the presidency two years later. He had more ambition than his modest demeanor conveyed, and most certainly he dreamed great dreams at times, but in 1858 Lincoln was almost unknown outside of Illinois. William Seward was generally acknowledged to be the most likely Republican presidential nominee for 1860. Henry Villard, who knew Lincoln well, has written: "I had it from Lincoln's own lips that the United States Senatorship was the greatest political height he at the time expected to climb."[88] Lincoln's famous letter to Henry Asbury suggests strongly that Lincoln felt Douglas had already lost whatever following he had once had in the slave states and that the next object was to destroy whatever sympathy remained in the southern part of Illinois. Lincoln declared confidently that Douglas "only leans Southward more to keep the Buchanan party from growing in Illinois."[89] Lincoln focused his Freeport Question on Illinois, not on the country as a whole.

If a candidate in the campaign had genuinely national ambitions and could realistically look beyond 1858 to 1860 with some hope, it was Stephen Douglas and not Abraham Lincoln. Finally, the usual contention that Lincoln in asking the Freeport Question deliberately sacrificed victory in 1858 for a larger victory in 1860 reduces itself to the absurd proposition that defeat is the precondition of success. If Lincoln had been elected United States Senator in 1858, he would have been in a much stronger national position for a bid at the Republican nomination in 1860.

[88] Henry Villard, *Memoirs*, I, 96.

[89] Nicolay and Hay, eds., *Works of Lincoln*, III, 198.

A more realistic analysis of the Freeport Question would show that it was less logical in its content, less far-reaching in its results, and that Lincoln was less certain of its precise purpose and value at the time he posed it. Lincoln's primary aim in asking the Freeport Question was to expose the logical contradictions, always implicit in the doctrine of popular sovereignty, as well as the legal contradictions that had recently begun to appear. In the Freeport Question Lincoln asked if the people of a territory could exclude slavery in any "lawful" way. Lincoln was questioning legal rights more than practical power. Douglas had been in an uncomfortable legal position ever since the Supreme Court had ruled on Dred Scott. In one of the many parades that accompanied the debates, a Republican delegation carried a banner showing Douglas as a circus rider attempting simultaneously to ride two horses labeled "Dred Scott" and "Popular Sovereignty."[90]

To accomplish his purpose Lincoln seized upon the favorite weapon in his logical arsenal: the dilemma. It was in fact a double dilemma: once the Freeport Question had been asked, Douglas would either answer it or ignore it. If he ignored it, he would appear to be dodging a fight—something Douglas had never done. If, on the other hand, he answered in the negative, Douglas would be acknowledging the demise of his cherished popular sovereignty and would alienate a large portion of the crucial moderate free-soil vote in central Illinois. If he answered in the affirmative, he would further alienate an already suspicious South and those voters in Illinois who sympathized with it.

The true focus of Lincoln's probe was much narrower than is usually assumed. He sought to make Douglas choose, not between abolitionists and fire-eaters—those extremes had long ago been irretrievably lost to the Little Giant—but between Northern moderates and Southern moderates. Lincoln sought to cut away the middle ground from under Douglas and to deny him the reputation of a moderate that he had labored to build up since 1854.

Did Lincoln expect Douglas in his answer to embrace the North-

90 Sparks, ed., *Lincoln-Douglas Debates*, p. 374.

ern or the Southern position? A political realist like Lincoln probably knew what answer Douglas would give at the time he posed his famous question and was not displeased with the reply he received. His defense of the right of the people of a territory to forbid slavery prior to statehood indirectly attested the worth of Lincoln's contention that territories should be free-soil. At the same time, it widened the split in the Democratic party, for the Buchanan-Douglas feud had erupted on this very point. Thus the question whether Lincoln at Freeport had his eye on 1858 or 1860 becomes irrelevant. The most realistic result to have been expected from that question was the deepening of the Democratic split. As such, the question served the Republicans equally well for 1858 and 1860.

The Freeport Question could hardly have taken Douglas by surprise. His correspondence contains evidence that his supporters expected a move of this sort by Lincoln.[91] His speech at Bloomington some six weeks before had contained the essence of his reply at Freeport.[92] His answer was quick, unequivocal, and calm: "I answer emphatically, as Mr. Lincoln has heard me answer a hundred times from every stump in Illinois, that in my opinion the people of a territory can, by lawful means, exclude slavery from their limits prior to the formation of a state constitution."[93]

Douglas maintained that he had held such a position for ten years.[94] His answer was consistent with his earlier views and readily predictable from them. It was, in fact, the natural result of the whole course of his career since 1850.

If Lincoln in his more hopeful moments expected to discomfit Douglas or perhaps even to force him to repudiate popular sovereignty, he was doomed to disappointment. What Douglas did was first to depreciate the significance of Lincoln's query: it was too abstract; and besides, he had answered it "a hundred times from

[91] S. W. Randall to Douglas, Joliet, Illinois, August 28, 1858; Douglas MSS. The letter seems to have been composed without its writer's knowing that a question similar to the one he predicted had been asked the day before at Freeport.

[92] Milton, *Eve of Conflict*, pp. 321–322.

[93] Angle, ed., *Debates*, p. 152.

[94] Johannsen, ed., *Letters of Douglas*, p. 455.

every stump in Illinois."[95] He then faced squarely the dilemma posed by Lincoln, and in answering he seized the blunter horn at the risk of alienating some proslavery sympathizers. Far from destroying popular sovereignty, Lincoln's Freeport Question gave Douglas a golden opportunity to expound the free-soil virtues of his pet doctrine at the northernmost site of the debates before twenty thousand listeners who had little use for slavery.[96]

Yet if Douglas' answer to the Freeport Question caused him little trouble in the short run, the long-term results were less satisfactory. Douglas was soon forced to modify the position he had taken in the debates. In the overheated atmosphere of Freeport he had flatly maintained that the people of a territory could exclude slavery and effectually prevent the introduction of it into their midst.[97] But after the debates had ended, Douglas began to have second thoughts. He told an audience in New Orleans in December of 1858, "We hold that slaves are property, and that the owner of a slave has the same right to move into a territory and carry his slave property with him, as the owner of any other property has to go there and carry his property."[98] Once there, however, the newly arrived slave property would of course be subject to local laws.

Douglas modified his views in another subtle but significant way. In the joint debates he had indicated that it would be the territorial legislature that would decide whether or not slavery got a favorable legal reception in a given territory.[99] Yet perhaps the strong presumption the Dred Scott opinion contained against the legality of any unfriendly action toward slavery by a territorial legislature, plus widespread fear of a future decision removing any lingering doubt on this point, caused Douglas to change his approach without ever really announcing that he had in fact done so.

Douglas began to talk less about laws passed in a territory at the legislature level and more about local laws. There is a strong indi-

95 Angle, ed., *Debates*, p. 152.

96 *Chicago Journal*, August 28, 1858, in Sparks, ed., *Lincoln-Douglas Debates*, p. 198.

97 Angle, ed., *Debates*, p. 152.

98 Stevens, "Life of Douglas," p. 596.

99 Angle, ed., *Debates*, p. 152.

cation that what Douglas now had in mind were municipal ordinances. In the 1860 campaign he compared the regulation of slavery to the control of alcoholic beverages, which in America has traditionally been carried out at the county level. Douglas was also coming to rely more on the taxing power to drive slavery from a given area and on judgments handed down by local juries.[100] Both operated primarily on the county or municipal level.

This approach to decentralized control of slavery was perfectly in keeping with that valid premise of popular sovereignty holding that local habits and customs go far toward determining the effectiveness of a given law. At the same time, Douglas' new tack was at odds with the changing national legal climate, especially after the Dred Scott decision.

The Little Giant considered his scheme for local control of slavery moderate and well suited for reassuring the South. His approach granted the Southerners the right to take their slaves into any territory they might desire. He joined the Supreme Court and the South in recognizing that slaves were first of all property. But the South was no longer satisfied with being granted a right. It wanted a reality. In the course of a New England tour in 1858, Jefferson Davis seemed to endorse Douglas' views when he declared that unless a territory passed laws protecting slave property "it would be rendered more or less valueless, in proportion to the difficulty of holding it without such protection . . . the insecurity would be so great that the owner could not ordinarily retain it. Therefore, though the right would remain, the remedy being withheld, it would follow that the owner would be practically debarred by the circumstances of the case from taking slave property into a territory where the sense of the inhabitants was opposed to its introduction."[101]

Yet although Davis and other Southerners shared Douglas' opinions, they drew quite opposite conclusions and began to talk of a federal slave code to remedy the practical disadvantages slavery

[100] Emerson D. Fite, *The Presidential Campaign of 1860*, p. 283. *Cong. Globe*, 35th Cong., 2nd sess., p. 1258.

[101] Dunbar Rowland, ed., *Jefferson Davis, Constitutionalist*, III, 299.

might face in a territory where public sentiment was hostile to it. Perhaps embarrassed over the possible implications of what he had said in New England, Jefferson Davis hastened to reassure his constituents. In a speech before the Mississippi Legislature in November, 1858, he admitted, "It is true . . . all property requires protection from the society in the midst of which it is held," but concluded that "this necessity does not confer a right to destroy, but rather creates an obligation to protect."[102] Unless Douglas would agree to safeguard slave property once it got to a territory, his granting it a right of entry was a meaningless gesture, since no sane slaveholder would take his valuable property where it would not be protected.

Douglas made one more concession to the South in the months after the debates. He would not only recognize slaves as property, but would also accord them the same protection in the territories as any other property.[103]

The South was unimpressed. It maintained, with much cogency, that slaves were a very special form of property demanding a very special form of protection, presumably a federal slave code. The *Richmond Enquirer* for October 19, 1858, complained, "In Virginia, the man who steals a slave is punished more than a man who steals ten times his value. . . . How is slavery to exist in a Territory which punishes the stealing of a negro as simple grand larceny?" Douglas knew the answer, but kept silent.

In appraising the results of the Freeport Question, historians have tended to fall into an error more common to journalists: making what is essentially a dramatic incident into a major turning point in the American past. What happened at Freeport made news but not history. One commentator in an excess of enthusiasm has ranked Freeport, Illinois, beside Plymouth Rock, Independence Hall, and Valley Forge in the annals of our country. Invoking the now familiar image of Lincoln-the-prophet, he professed to see in

102 Ibid., p. 345.

103 Stevens, "Life of Douglas," pp. 596–597; *Chicago Times*, November 11, 1858.

the Freeport Question the progenitor of secession, a bloody civil war, the Emancipation Proclamation, Lee's surrender at Appomattox, and the rebirth of a new and united nation.[104] But a closer and more reasoned analysis of the Freeport Question suggests that its effects were on the whole mild and short-lived. Far from causing a revolution in public opinion, it served merely to reinforce existing points of view.

In the North, Douglas' reply to the Freeport Question produced positive but not sweeping benefits. It gave new life to the tottering idea of popular sovereignty and reinforced Douglas' moderate credentials as an effective, if not admitted, champion of free-soil. In so doing, it strengthened his hand in the crucial central section of Illinois. In a year when Democratic candidates sympathetic to the administration's views on slavery in the territories were going down to defeat throughout the North, Douglas' answer helped carry him to victory. If the reply did not by itself account for his success against Lincoln, it is safe to assume that had Douglas answered in any radically different way he quite probably would have lost what was a very close election anyway.

If Douglas' answer produced immediate benefits in the North, it had positive long-range effects as well. Two years later Douglas entered the Charleston convention with the strong support of the Northwest and much of the East. As late as 1859 Lincoln was genuinely fearful that the Republican party might support Douglas for the presidency.[105] In the election of 1860 Douglas received an impressive popular vote throughout the North. Perhaps the most important effect that Douglas' reply at Freeport had upon the North was to make people there believe that he had adopted a position more anti-Southern than either the Little Giant or many citizens of the South in fact believed he had taken. Northerners in 1858, like generations of historians after them, demonstrated a tendency to overestimate the role played by the Freeport Question in the alienation of the South from the Douglas cause.[106] A fairer

[104] W. T. Rawleigh, ed., *Freeport's Lincoln*, p. 74.

[105] William Baringer, *Lincoln's Rise to Power*, p. 74.

[106] Nevins, *The Emergence of Lincoln*, I, 392; James F. Rhodes, *History of*

conclusion would seem to be that, if the reply at Freeport did not help Douglas in the South, neither did his answer by itself seriously impair any important segment of his support below the Mason-Dixon Line.

The moderates from whom Douglas had always drawn his greatest strength in the South remained steadfast in their loyalty to the Little Giant. After all, the position he adopted at Freeport had found support earlier among an impressive list of Southerners, including Cobb, Breckinridge, Stephens, Benjamin, Butler, and Toombs.[107] Douglas' correspondence contains many letters from the South warmly endorsing his stand.[108] The moderate Southern press was not unduly upset,[109] realizing that Douglas' position was far more reasonable than the kind of federal prohibition on slavery many Northerners were beginning to demand.

As for the Southern Ultras, what Douglas said at Freeport did not alienate them; they were irreconcilable long before the campaign ever got under way. Furthermore, Douglas' subsequent declaration at Jonesboro against any federal slave code for the territories was much stronger medicine than anything he had come out with at Freeport.[110]

Yancey and company were probably secretly quite pleased by Douglas' Freeport answer. What they feared most was the possibility of a moderate Northern Democrat getting the nomination at Charleston in 1860. Douglas' great victory in 1858 made him a very real threat to the fire-eaters, who eagerly seized upon his Freeport speech to brand him as a dangerous radical not far removed from the abolitionists. The Freeport reply gave the Ultras a convenient weapon with which to harry Douglas and a handy excuse for demanding at Charleston the one plank in the platform they knew Douglas would not accept: a federal slave code for the territories.

---

the United States from the Compromise of 1850, II, 328; Henry P. Willis, *Stephen A. Douglas*, pp. 292–294.

107 Sheahan, *Stephen A. Douglas*, p. 429.

108 See for example A. Rust to Douglas, Arkansas, September 25, 1858, and W. J. Pegram to Douglas, New Orleans, La., September 29, 1858; Douglas MSS.

109 *Richmond South*, October 30, 1858.

110 Angle, ed., *Debates*, p. 229.

Thus, far from upsetting the Southern radicals, Douglas had played into their hands. Lincoln, hoping at Freeport to draw a sharp differentiation between Douglas and himself, had in fact succeeded in having Douglas denounced in the South not because he was different from Lincoln, but because he was too much like him!

The Freeport answer then effected no revolutionary changes in Douglas' position in the South. Those Southerners who were loyal to him before the reply were loyal to him afterwards. Those who disliked him before were simply confirmed in their animosity. The query had almost no immediate effects; its real impact was a delayed one: it gave the fire-eaters an excuse to destroy Douglas two years later at Charleston.

One might therefore conclude that the Freeport debate brought as many assets as it did liabilities into the Douglas camp. Far from being caught by surprise, Douglas seemed almost to welcome Lincoln's query as an attempt to clarify an awkward and misunderstood position. He avoided having to repudiate his favorite scheme of popular sovereignty. He strengthened his hand throughout the North while at the same time retaining the allegiance both of Egypt and those people in the slave states who had traditionally supported him.

On the other hand, if Douglas' answer helped to confirm his position as the leading member of the Democratic party, it perpetuated the split that plagued that party. It was to be used by the administration and its sympathizers as an excuse to remove Douglas from the chairmanship of the Senate Committee on Territories. Although Douglas' handling of the dilemma Lincoln had posed was a remarkable piece of political agility, it nonetheless saw him forced off the high ground of principle onto less noble pragmatic terrain. The kind of reasoning Douglas might have called imaginative impressed others as sophistry and confirmed the widespread impression of a man who was slightly devious and not altogether to be trusted.[111] At Freeport Douglas showed himself to be a master politician, but his credentials as a statesman were open to question.

111 *New York Tribune*, November 5, 1858; *Washington Union*, September 10, 1858.

If Lincoln attacked the soft side of popular sovereignty with his Freeport Question, he challenged the hard side with morality. In the first debate at Ottawa, Lincoln unleashed his moral assault and said of Douglas, "When he invites any people willing to have slavery, to establish it, he is blowing out the moral lights around us. When he says he 'cares not whether slavery is voted down or voted up,'—that it is a sacred right of self-government—he is in my judgment penetrating the human soul and eradicating the light of reason and the love of liberty in this American people."[112]

With one stroke Lincoln had raised the level of the whole contest. He had done more than that: he had aroused the conscience of a nation and asked questions that America is still trying to answer today.

Lincoln used the term *morals* as a synonym for human rights. The choice of words was a good one for the kind of impression he was trying to make. Lincoln did not set out to teach or convert his listeners. He sought only to appeal to that latent sense of decency and right which he felt was basic to the American national character. Lincoln was more than moral: he was a moralist, but he had the gift of never appearing unduly pious.

There is no reason to doubt the sincerity of Lincoln's moral concern over slavery, but one should not be blind to the real and immediate political benefits such a posture brought to the man and his party. It attracted widespread attention and helped to awaken America from its normal state of political apathy. It enabled Lincoln to conduct his campaign on higher and simpler ground and to avoid being entangled in legalisms. It gave new life to the Republican party, which had been searching for a useful issue ever since Lecompton. It created a new and positive identity for a party that, since its inception as an anti–Kansas-Nebraska force, had been distinguished primarily by its negativism. The moral issue gave Lincoln a chance to threaten with a single thrust, at the one point where it was truly vulnerable, the whole position on slavery that Douglas had so laboriously built up. There was an intimation of

[112] Angle, ed., *Debates*, p. 130.

Lincoln's strategy in a speech he made at Edwardsville early in the campaign: "All, or nearly all, of Judge Douglas's arguments are logical, if you admit that slavery is as good and as right as freedom, and not one of them is worth a rush if you deny it."[113]

Yet Lincoln never put into practice all of the logical implications of his advanced moral position. When it came up against hard realities, Lincoln's morality demonstrated a peculiarly political dimension. He denounced slavery unequivocally, but was content to confine it to its existing area. His concession that each state might determine the status of slavery within its boundaries was a political solution to what Lincoln claimed was a moral problem. He refused to pass moral censure upon the South for holding slaves and seemed almost to adopt an attitude of dialectical materialism toward morality when he said of the Southern people: "They are just what we would be in their situation."[114] At one point he announced that "public opinion is founded, to a great extent, on a property basis."[115] In later years, with all the power of the presidency at his command, Lincoln showed a persistent tendency to compromise with slavery. In 1862 he wrote Horace Greeley: "If I could save the Union without freeing any slave, I would do it; and if I could save it by freeing all the slaves, I would do it."[116]

This tendency to compromise with reality in no way detracted from the impact of Lincoln's moral attack on slavery and its defenders. Quite the opposite. His flexible and moderate approach probably reassured his listeners and showed him to be an idealist without illusions. What Lincoln did was to channel and give expression to the growing current of moral unrest over slavery that was abroad in the land without getting too far ahead of public opinion. Lincoln not only entered a plea for morality, he made his kind of morality palatable to a large number of Americans.

Douglas could not follow Lincoln onto this high moral ground.

[113] Nicolay and Hay, eds., *Works of Lincoln*, XI, 109.

[114] Ibid., II, 205.

[115] Ibid., V, 330.

[116] Abraham Lincoln to Horace Greeley, Washington, August 22, 1862, in Henry S. Commager, ed., *Documents of American History*, pp. 417–418.

It was not that he was immoral or even amoral. Douglas knew from long years in public life that no politician who flouted the moral sense of the community could long survive.[117] At the same time, he had a deep-seated suspicion of mixing morals and politics. The result, he felt, was quite likely to be specious at best and dangerous at worst.[118] The moral neutrality with which Douglas approached politics not only fitted his philosophical predisposition, it had produced impressive concrete results. It lent his behavior the kind of flexibility and detachment needed to effect the compromises of 1850 and 1854. Douglas' popular sovereignty was in a sense his professed attitude of indifference and moral neutrality toward the institution of slavery transformed into a principle and a device.

There were, at the same time, instances in Douglas' career when, far from ignoring morality or denying its relevance to politics, he appeared to summon it to his aid. He denounced the Lecompton Constitution as immoral in 1857, and three years later, with civil war imminent, he reminded a Senate colleague from Virginia that he was "under the highest moral obligation to revise his own work, and give us a good law, and not break up the Government because he framed a bad law, and refuses to correct the error."[119] Yet the kind of morality Douglas occasionally invoked was somehow different from Lincoln's. It was less abstract, less absolute. The moral choice between good and evil alternatives was ultimately a human one.[120] Most of Douglas' references to morality have a distinctly political orientation. He spoke often of "moral treason."[121] In 1860 he stressed the need for a large popular vote in his race for the presidency because it could mean the "moral power to sustain me in the performance of my duties."[122]

Douglas' approach to morality must therefore ultimately be

[117] Johannsen, ed., *Letters of Douglas*, p. 237.

[118] Angle, ed., *Debates*, pp. 351, 352.

[119] *Cong. Globe*, 36th Cong., 2nd sess., p. 57.

[120] Angle, ed., *Debates*, p. 351.

[121] Ibid., p. 154.

[122] Ollinger Crenshaw, *The Slave States in the Presidential Election of 1860*, The Johns Hopkins University Studies in Historical and Political Science, series 63, no. 3 (1945): 86.

judged in relation to his scale of political values. He felt that there were greater wrongs than slavery, foremost among them the dissolution of the Union. He did not so much deny the existence of natural rights as he thought it the better part of political wisdom not to insist fully on each and every one of them in practice. In a speech startlingly reminiscent of the words of Edmund Burke, Douglas warned the Senate, "It is one thing to have the right, it is another thing to exercise it . . . we have the right to do a great many foolish things, a great many silly things."[123] Douglas did not deplore morality so much as mixing morality with politics in an unstable and explosive atmosphere.

There was much about Douglas' political neutrality toward slavery that was sound. If he denounced those abolitionists who castigated slavery as contrary to natural right, he dealt just as severely with those Southern politicians who went beyond their traditional reliance upon the Constitution and attempted to justify slavery at higher law.[124] While many of his colleagues on both sides of the Senate aisle wrapped their real interests in a specious cloak of morality, Douglas did the reverse and masked an inner moral concern with the objective appearance of indifference. An accurate assessment of him might be that he was moral but not a moralist.

Douglas' basic error with regard to the moral issue of slavery was less one of judgment than of timing. Douglas' approach not only fitted in with the American pragmatic political tradition in general but with the outlook of the age he knew best. Douglas had grown to political maturity and greatness at a time in our history when most Americans cared little about the moral implications of slavery and were in a hurry to get on with the larger task of nation-building.

But in retrospect it is clear that by 1858 the dominant American outlook had changed radically although almost imperceptibly, and Douglas had not kept up with the times. While he was content to dismiss the moral concern over slavery as just another bothersome abstraction that was interfering with the more important work of

[123] *Cong. Globe*, 36th Cong., 1st sess., p. 2155.

[124] Ibid., 35th Cong., 1st sess., app., p. 199.

the political process, other Americans in the North had begun to sense that the peculiar institution was casting a long shadow over the whole quality of national life. From the perspective of a hundred years, Douglas seems to have been blind to the growing, if still latent, sense of moral outrage around him. Perhaps his fundamental error lay not so much in appearing indifferent toward the future course of slavery, but in failing to realize how his country would react once its conscience was aroused.

The last joint debate was held at Alton on October 15, less than three weeks before the election for the state legislature. The results of the election itself were outwardly simple. On a cold, wet November 2 the people of Illinois made their way over muddy roads to the polling places in the firehouse or country school or crossroads store and returned Stephen Douglas to the United States Senate.

Yet the story was really much more complex. The Douglas Democrats did not get a majority of the popular vote cast; they did not even get a plurality. The final count showed 125,430 votes for the Republicans, 121,609 for the Democratic followers of Douglas, and 5,071 for the Buchananite slate. But in 1858 the popular vote did not determine a senatorial election. United States senators were still elected by the state legislature, where Democrats outnumbered Republicans 54 to 46. The real contest was decided January 6, 1859, at the capitol in Springfield, where the assembled senators and representatives in a straight party vote sent Douglas back to Washington.[125]

Looking at their party's victory in the popular vote and its defeat in the Senate race, some Republicans were quick to allege gerrymandering. They maintained that if the legislative districts had been fairly drawn Lincoln's preponderance in the popular vote

[125] The popular vote figures are for the race for state treasurer, a statewide election and the best indicator of relative party strength in Illinois in the 1858 campaign. *Tribune Almanac for 1859*, pp. 60–61. The Republican strength in the total popular vote in all legislative races may have been proportionately even greater. Milton, *Eve of Conflict*, p. 351; Willis, *Stephen A. Douglas*, p. 288. The figures on the partisan composition of the legislature are found in the *Tribune Almanac for 1859*, p. 61.

would have been accurately reflected in the composition of the new legislature. Aside from overlooking the obvious difficulty that no reapportionment scheme could have changed the fact that in 1858 only part of the membership of the predominantly Democratic state senate was up for re-election, the charge upon close analysis is not very convincing.

It is of course true that apportionment in Illinois was based on the census of 1850 and therefore failed to give the rapidly growing northern part of the state, which was the great stronghold of Republicanism, the proportional voice it deserved. At the same time, the apportionment scheme obtaining in 1858 was the same one under which the Republicans had defeated the Douglas Democrat, James Shields, in the Senate race of 1854. Furthermore, as recently as the last session of the Illinois legislature, Governor William Bissell, a Republican, had vetoed a new apportionment bill. Most Republican candidates throughout the Northwest faced similar handicaps in 1858, yet the majority of them, unlike Lincoln, went on to victory. Lincoln himself seems to have been less exercised by the apportionment situation than the commentators who came after him. He accepted the system as a hard fact of political life and, long before the election, actually predicted he would win the popular vote but lose the indirect election in the legislature.[126]

Douglas carried Egypt by a heavy majority and drew impressive strength in central Illinois from old Whig and American elements.[127] This combination of areas of support potentially hostile to one another attested to the effectiveness of Douglas' shrewd reply to the Freeport Question and confirmed Lincoln's conclusion that Douglas had obtained his victory by portraying himself as "the best means to break down and to uphold the slave interest."[128]

Douglas' marriage to a Catholic, his own Scotch-Irish background, his innate conservatism, and his defense of Chief Justice Taney no doubt made a profound appeal to the growing Irish vote.

126 Sandburg, *Lincoln: Prairie Years*, II, 161.

127 See the excellent election map of Illinois in 1858, Cole, *Era of the Civil War*, p. 178.

128 Nicolay and Hay, eds., *Works of Lincoln*, V, 94.

So did his exuberant, irrepressible, somewhat intemperate nature. Lincoln in turn probably won the German vote. Douglas generally made a favorable showing among the propertied groups in urban areas, but his strength in the city of Chicago, which he helped to found and called home, was disappointing. Douglas not only failed to carry Chicago, but actually ran behind his ticket there. The strong influence of administration patronage might possibly hold the explanation.[129]

Students of the 1858 campaign usually conclude that Douglas' great strength was in the southern part of the state and Lincoln's in the north.[130] This statement is of course true as far as it goes, but a close analysis of the election results suggests strongly that the true basis of Douglas' political strength in Illinois may have been basically riparian more than southern. Douglas may have run well in Egypt less because it was in the extreme south of the state and more because it was at the juncture of the two most important river systems in the Northwest. Wherever the Mississippi or the Ohio or the Wabash ran, Douglas ran well. His southern strength extended farthest north precisely along the water's edge. The only exceptions to the rule were those Illinois counties directly opposite St. Louis, which was a hotbed of free-soil activity, and little Edwards County, which for as long as most people could remember had been an outpost of Whiggery and free-soilism down in the depths of darkest Egypt.[131]

Douglas' strength along the rivers has several explanations. Partly it reflected his record of favoring public works projects, especially flood control and improvement of navigation. It also in part expressed the sympathy of the people of the river towns, which had a large stake in trade with the South, toward Douglas' faith in the traditional ties of the Northwest to the Southwest and toward the kind of economic nationalism he was now offering as an antidote to the growing political threat of sectionalism. Again, in the course

129 Cole, *Era of the Civil War*, p. 177.

130 Nevins, *The Emergence of Lincoln*, I, 366, 398; Angle, ed., *Debates*, p. xxiv; Cole, *Era of the Civil War*, p. 179.

131 See election map in Cole, *Era of the Civil War*, p. 178.

of westward migration in America it had always been the propertyless—the dispossessed, the drifters—who settled along the river bank. This group gave its overwhelming political allegiance to the Democratic party.

Yet this was not the whole story. Douglas consistently ran ahead of his party in those counties which bordered on the major north-south waterways. Perhaps the river dwellers saw in the Little Giant something of themselves. He too had come West without any money, and he too was most at home dealing with practical problems like trade and levees and harbors. Like the great river and those who dwelled beside it, he was always anxious to be moving on. Perhaps it was no mere accident that one admirer welcomed Douglas to his town with the greeting "Abolitionism might as well talk of caging the mighty Mississippi in a pint bottle . . . as to talk of the demolition of the lion of the matchless talents . . . which you possess."[132] Under the hyperbole basic to the political oratory of the frontier was a metaphor that tells us a great deal about why some people felt toward Stephen Douglas as they did.

The long-standing feud with Buchanan in the end produced only a negligible effect on the Douglas cause. The administration backed its own slate of legislative candidates and carried on the patronage war unabated throughout the campaign. Buchanan was predictably hostile to the whole idea of holding the joint debates in the first place. At one point he announced that he would view the outcome of the campaign as a referendum upon his administration.[133] A few days later he attempted to correct this political blunder by professing indifference to the outcome of the Illinois election.[134] Buchanan in fact worked hard for Douglas' defeat. Taking his cue from the White House, Lincoln disdained the help of the administration publicly while gladly availing himself of its fruits.

If the stunning defeats suffered by the Democratic regulars in

[132] "Address of Welcome to Stephen A. Douglas Upon the Occasion of his Visit to Vermilion County," September 21, 1858; Lamon Collection (Henry E. Huntington Library), LN2312.

[133] *Washington Union*, August 28, 1858.

[134] Ibid., September 3, 1858.

the October election in Pennsylvania or Vice-President Breckinridge's belated decision to campaign actively for Douglas in Illinois made Buchanan have second thoughts about the wisdom of the reckless course he had embarked upon, they caused no outward change in his anti-Douglas onslaught.

There is no reason to feel that Douglas was displeased. By casting him in the role of underdog the administration had unwittingly helped the Little Giant overcome the handicap of the vulnerable position in which national fame and success had placed him vis-à-vis the challenger. It is quite plausible, as the *Union* charged, that Douglas was ready to make up with Buchanan until his return to Chicago in July convinced him of the very real benefits of the administration's continued hostility toward him.[135]

In the end, the Buchananites made a pitiable showing in Illinois, polling only 5,071 votes, or less than 2 percent of the total. On the other hand, had all these votes gone to Douglas Democrats, they would have won the statewide popular vote by a slight majority. Perhaps these few thousand votes do not quite tell the whole story of Buchanan's impact upon the 1858 election. It would be safe to assume that his assault upon Douglas served mainly to confuse Democratic voters and may have had its most telling effect in simply keeping many of them at home on election day.

If the Illinois election of 1858 had a true loser, it was James Buchanan. In a final desperate maneuver, the administration's henchmen in Illinois tried to influence the legislature to disregard its popular instructions and vote against Douglas when it met to ratify the results of the election the following January.[136] Far from succeeding, this kind of move merely confirmed the public in its tendency to view James Buchanan as a petty political intriguer who would stop at nothing.

The results of the debates themselves are much more difficult to estimate than the outcome of the election. Their clearest effect was to stimulate public interest and get out a popular vote in Illinois far

135 Ibid., August 11, 1858.

136 Cole, *Era of the Civil War*, p. 179.

larger than the one in the presidential election year of 1856. Whether the debates really changed many of the votes they helped to bring out is less certain. Shrewd observers of the campaign, like Carl Schurz, felt that traditional party loyalties, more than anything that was said in the debates, determined most voters' behavior on election day.[137] On the other hand, it is of more than passing significance that Lincoln's party carried four of the seven counties that played host to the joint debates. Here the contest might be expected to have had its most immediate impact upon the voters.

No one really won the debates. There was no formal account kept of the points scored, and the highly partisan nature of the press that reported them made it an unreliable judge of their outcome. Nor was the content of the debates the kind of material from which a neat tally can be adduced. Many issues were not joined at all, many charges were simply left unproved. The debates served more to dramatize issues than to clarify, much less to resolve.

The real impact of the debates was at once more subtle and less immediate than is usually assumed. Although the campaign was only statewide, the issues and the participants involved raised it to national importance. It was the most widely reported political contest in America up to that time. Reporters using the recently invented streamlined form of shorthand accompanied the contenders wherever they went and telegraphed verbatim reports of the debates to every corner of the Union. The Atlantic cable had only recently parted, and the sudden lack of foreign news left editors with plenty of space on the front page for Mr. Lincoln and Mr. Douglas out in Illinois.

The major result of the debates was essentially a delayed one. The immediate reaction was usually to underestimate their importance. The *American Almanac* failed to include them among the two hundred most important events for 1858. Yet with time the debates grew in stature, and understandably so, for when read as a whole their impact is much greater than the sum of the rather mediocre constituent speeches themselves. They came to be valued

[137] Schurz, *Reminiscences*, II, 100.

largely as a dress rehearsal for the greater drama of the election of 1860, with the same leading characters, the same script, and the same sectional backdrop.

The passage of time seemed to strengthen Lincoln's claims to victory in the debates. It was Lincoln who in 1860 took the initiative to have them published in book form, and it is his name that always comes first in their title.

In contrast to their positive value to the careers of Lincoln and Douglas and their undeniable function as a source of popular entertainment, the debates left less beneficial results in their wake. Although matters of great national importance had been discussed, the debates actually covered very little new ground. They contributed almost nothing to finding a practical solution to the slavery problem. They did not even provide much in the way of a clear-cut referendum on popular sovereignty.

They did little and yet they did much. The kind of relentless moral onslaught Lincoln launched upon the status quo in his House Divided speech may, from the perspective of a hundred years later, have been historically necessary to awaken the American conscience and prepare the people for the end of a doomed institution. Yet from a more immediate point of view, it fueled the flames of intolerance and preoccupation with abstractions. It cut away at the pitiful amount of political and ideological middle ground that was left in America. It drove compromise farther way and brought civil war nearer.

Perhaps if there was a tragic element in the Lincoln-Douglas Debates, it is to be found in the fact that the alternative solutions to the slavery question offered by each man were not really antithetical at all. They were basically complementary. If the moral fervor unleashed by Lincoln could have been allowed to work through the moderating device of Douglas' popular sovereignty, and if Douglas could have given up the unrealistic demand that immigrating Yankees check their moral baggage at the territorial border, slavery might well have been first contained and then eradicated without a nation having to pay the terrible price of civil war.

But in November of 1858 most Americans, including Lincoln and Douglas themselves, were not taken up with considerations of the broad sweep of history. Their concern was more immediate.

Lincoln took his defeat hard and seems to have lapsed briefly into one of his moods of deep melancholia and introspection. Those who knew him well claimed that on that election night in Springfield, when the returns from all over Illinois were beginning to confirm the Douglas victory Lincoln had privately predicted, he said simply, "It hurts too much to laugh and I am too big to cry."[138]

Yet when the first shock of defeat had passed, Lincoln came to a more realistic verdict on the outcome of the campaign: "It's a slip and not a fall."[139] If the election had not brought him victory, it had brought him something even more valuable—the kind of national fame that he could never have achieved by the persistent political plodding that had heretofore marked his public career. Lincoln got the best of both worlds. He suddenly had the national political stature that made him a force to be reckoned with in the 1860 Republican National Convention. Yet his fame was not so great that it placed him in the vulnerable position of an acknowledged favorite like Seward. In short, after 1858 Lincoln was admirably suited for the role of dark horse of the Republican party.

The debates not only brought Lincoln fame, they also brought him the right kind of fame. They not only enhanced his reputation, they started him on the road to greatness. It was not so much what he had said but how he had said it. The words of the fiery Douglas might have made more of an immediate impact, but Lincoln's in the end had more power. His logic had been sharp and relentless, but it was not his logic the people of Illinois and the world longest remembered. It was more the man's candor and magnanimity and sincerity—that subtle subjective appeal which made its way into the hearts of his listeners through the gauze of mere words. It was the humility of the tall, sad man who somehow made his listeners partners with him in the slow, painful, uncertain search for a solu-

138 Charles S. Zane, "Lincoln as I Knew Him," *Journal of the Illinois State Historical Society* 14, no. 1 (April 1921): 76.

139 Baringer, *Lincoln's Rise to Power*, p. 43.

tion to the curse of slavery. He had not come to preach, but he ended up by converting.

Lincoln in 1858 had shown himself to be not only a good politician, but a good man. He had found himself in that unusual and happy position where the course of self-interest is also the course of justice. The verdict of Isaac Arnold, who knew both men well and attended the debates, has remained unchallenged for more than a century: "Lincoln had two advantages over Douglas: he had the best side of the question and the best temper."[140]

Lincoln had shown himself to be an idealist without ever ceasing to be a realist. The House Divided speech had staked out new moral ground, but it also formed the high-water mark of his moral attack upon slavery. Lincoln had defined and focused the growing uneasiness that the majority of Americans throughout the North were beginning to feel toward slavery. He had succeeded in arousing the conscience of a nation. He refused to try to alarm it.

This Lincoln, now steadily more moderate and responsible, this Lincoln, whose oratory would improve each day from the halting effort at Ottawa until it crested at Gettysburg, had suddenly become the foremost obstacle between Stephen Douglas and the presidency of the United States.

The 1858 election was a great personal and political triumph for the Little Giant. It marked the apogee of a long and distinguished public life. Against enormous odds Douglas had beaten his two most powerful political enemies: the Republican party and James Buchanan. In a year when Democrats were going down to defeat everywhere throughout the North, not only did Douglas win his election, but his party also received a larger popular vote in Illinois than it had in the presidential election of 1856.[141] His victory confirmed his title of leading Democrat and made him very much the man to beat in 1860.

Success has a way of breeding success, and even some Southerners were sufficiently struck by the scale of Douglas' victory to

140 Arnold, *Reminiscences*, p. 151.

141 In 1856 Buchanan polled 105,348 votes in Illinois. Douglas Democrats in 1858 received a total of 121,609 votes. *Tribune Almanac for 1859*, pp. 60, 64.

forget, at least temporarily, their animosity toward him. A man from Warren County, Virginia, wrote a few weeks after the election to say, "Last winter it was considered almost abolitionism here in Virginia to speak a word in your behalf. . . . But many that were forward in condemning you last winter are now strongly in your favor. It is not your principles or arguments so much that has made them so, but it is your *success*."[142]

But if 1858 was the high point of Douglas' political fame and power, it also marked the beginning of his decline. If he was the leading member of his party, that party was now irreparably broken. An angry and stunned administration would soon remove him from the chairmanship of his beloved Senate Committee on Territories. He had paid the price of political isolation for his victory. He emerged from the campaign unacceptable to much of the South, much of the Democratic party, and all of the Republican party, which had once thought of adopting him as its own. The man who always aspired to be a truly national political figure found himself thrown back upon a rather narrow political base. He was stronger than ever in his own Northwest, but much of the South now looked upon him with hostility, and the East regarded him with suspicion.

He suffered in ways other than political. The high cost of the campaign, probably close to $50,000,[143] had placed a severe strain on his personal finances, which were at best always in something of a state of crisis. His Washington bankers sent word that he was $220.72 overdrawn.[144] The real estate firm of McCarty and Brown in Austin, Texas, wrote to make a pointed reference to the desperate condition of Douglas' finances and asked if he would therefore be interested in selling the land he owned in Texas in "Peter's Colony —lying in the vicinity of Fort Belknap, and on the Brazos River and its tributaries." They suggested a price of $1.50 to $3.50 an acre and offered their services.[145]

[142] Reuben Finnell to Douglas, Warren County, Virginia, December 1, 1858; Douglas MSS.

[143] Sparks, ed., *Lincoln-Douglas Debates*, p. 589.

[144] Bank of the Metropolis to Douglas, Washington, D.C., August 5, 1858; Douglas MSS.

[145] The firm of McCarty and Brown to Douglas, Austin, Texas, September

The campaign had cost Douglas something more valuable than money. The almost constant travel, the long days on the platform in the open air, the short, fitful hours of sleep caught in some strange hotel room or sitting up in his private train had severely taxed a constitution that at best was never particularly robust. The physical decline that ended in his early death less than three years later probably began in that strenuous autumn of 1858.[146]

Nor was Douglas' trouble just physical. He was drinking more than usual now, and his behavior was increasingly disorganized. He was growing careless of his once immaculate personal appearance. Even the lovely and patient Adele Douglas, who accompanied him everywhere on the campaign trail, complained of his tendency to lose things.[147]

The battle had left Douglas permanently scarred in other ways, too. His shrewd handling of Lincoln's logical and moral thrusts had confirmed his long-standing credentials as a politician, but the country now needed a statesman. The kind of maneuvering and sophistry Douglas had to resort to in the debates was not fundamentally dishonest or devious or deceptive, but neither was it the stuff from which greatness is made.

Douglas had not changed; the times had. To the problems of the day he offered the same hardheaded, down-to-earth approach that had stood him and his country in such good stead for so long. But the American people wanted something more now. One shrewd contemporary observer put it this way: "They were looking for a god, but they found a man."[148]

When the legislature had met and confirmed his election, and his old friend Charles Lanphier had sent him the good news over the telegraph, Douglas wired back, "Let the voice of the people rule."[149]

13, 1858; ibid. The lands described were in what is today Young County, Texas. A search of Young County records failed, however, to produce any evidence of land held in the name of Stephen A. Douglas.

[146] Stevens, "Life of Douglas," p. 589.

[147] Nevins, *The Emergence of Lincoln*, I, 385.

[148] The *Vermilion County* (Illinois) *Press*, September 29, 1868.

[149] Johannsen, ed., *Letters of Douglas*, p. 433.

What he said was wholly typical of the brash self-confidence of the Little Giant, but what he did betrayed a certain uneasiness. He had won his election in the North, but if he had not permanently alienated his supporters in the South, he had made them suspicious. The situation below the Mason-Dixon Line in late 1858 was probably not beyond repair, but there was very definitely some political fence-mending to be done.

Whenever Douglas faced a serious problem, he moved. Less than two weeks after his November victory he headed south.

5. 1859: The House Dividing

Stephen Douglas would not have looked good on a veranda. He probably would not have been comfortable there either. He was no stranger to the South. He had visited it often, studied it carefully, and courted it assiduously. Yet Douglas and the South were never completely at ease in one another's company.

Douglas was neither hostile to the South nor ignorant of its manifold peculiarities. He never made the mistake of ignoring it. He had many friends there and a profound respect for the statesmen it had produced.[1] Both of his wives had been Southern girls. The first, Martha Martin Douglas[2] of North Carolina, bore him two sons and a daughter[3] before her death in 1853. In 1856, Douglas married Adele Cutts of Washington.[4] During the 1850's he came south often

1 Frank E. Stevens, "Life of Stephen Arnold Douglas," *Journal of the Illinois State Historical Society* 16: 379.

2 Douglas married Martha Martin in 1847. Her family came from the Dan River Country in Rockingham County, North Carolina, just below the Virginia line.

3 Robert Martin Douglas was born January, 1849. Stephen Arnold Douglas, Jr., was born November, 1850. A daughter was born in January, 1853, but lived only briefly.

4 Miss Cutt's family was mostly from Maryland and Virginia. She was a grandniece of Dolly Madison.

on business or pleasure, and his family continued to draw much of its income from the rich Mississippi soil of the Martin family plantation.[5]

Stephen Douglas may have had strong ties to the South, but he never fully succeeded in understanding it. The South did not even try to understand the Little Giant. It would use him when it could and at best ignore him when it could not. Its leaders would one day turn on him and seek his defeat in the presidential campaign of 1860. The South repaid Douglas' long years of concession and conciliation first with distrust and then with hostility.

Slavery was the great barrier between them, but slavery does not tell the whole story. The South was more complex than that; so was Stephen Douglas. The South and Douglas were never really strangers, but they remained fundamentally alien to one another throughout most of the 1850's. The mere fact of the Little Giant's Vermont background was enough to discredit him in the eyes of a people who were each day growing more isolated and suspicious of the rest of America. The South was agrarian, while Douglas stood for the advancing forces of industrialization symbolized by the thriving boomtown of Chicago and the Illinois Central whose rails he had helped push down to where the South began. Perhaps most important of all, the South was sectional in its approach to politics, while Douglas was, first of all, national.

Douglas, who seemed to worship action almost as an end in itself, stood in sharp contrast to that leisurely, almost lethargic section so firmly wed to the status quo. He was not quite genteel, this man Douglas. His family background was unimpressive and his manners left much to be desired. In debate he was quick and thrusting, upon occasion rude and vulgar. He was swift to anger, but his anger

[5] Robert Martin, the father of Douglas' first wife, Martha Martin Douglas, acquired a sizable plantation in Lawrence County, Mississippi, in the early 1840's. Following Martin's death in 1848, Douglas, as executor, managed the plantation for the benefit of Martha and their two sons. In 1857 the Lawrence County holdings were sold and its approximately 150 slaves were moved onto a new plantation—a joint venture between Douglas and James McHatton—located in Washington County, Mississippi. Robert W. Johannsen, "Stephen A. Douglas and the South," *Journal of Southern History* 33, no. 1: 29–30.

never caused him to bear a grudge or resort to violence. The South's emotional pendulum swung much farther in both directions and oscillated between an exaggerated politeness on the one hand and the code duello on the other. He was militant but not militaristic. He was a gutfighter wholly at odds with the Southern ideal of chivalry.[6] In all the literature on Stephen Douglas there is no evidence that he ever rode a horse, much less a white charger.

Douglas' relationship to the South passed through four distinct phases. The first was marked by a spirit of appeasement and conciliation wrapped in the guise of compromise. It lasted through 1856 and was climaxed by the Kansas-Nebraska Act. The second period began in 1857 with Douglas' firm stand against Lecompton. During this period the Little Giant publicly extolled popular sovereignty and sought to portray himself as neutral on the pressing sectional questions of the day while steadily working to postpone any showdown between North and South. The South, however, was unconvinced of Douglas' avowed neutrality and, after Lecompton, tended to regard him with increased suspicion and hostility. The third stage began in 1859 and lasted until midway in the presidential campaign of 1860. Douglas now freely acknowledged his sectional bias in favor of the North, but still sought to placate the South through reassurance, compromise, and even an occasional concession. The beginning of the last period can be placed somewhere in the summer of 1860, when Douglas seemed to realize that Lincoln would be elected President and that secession was now a serious threat. He still refused to close his eyes to any possibility of compromise, but for the first time he supported those Northern men who would approve the use of force against a seceding state.[7]

Douglas spent much of his early political life in an ill-considered attempt to woo the South. He worked hard for the annexation of Texas; he was one of the most vocal Northern supporters of the

[6] The *Richmond Enquirer*, for September 4, 1860, contained some disdainful remarks on Douglas' lack of chivalry.

[7] See Douglas' 1860 campaign speech at Raleigh, North Carolina, in Emerson D. Fite, *The Presidential Campaign of 1860*, pp. 276–300, especially p. 282.

Mexican War and the great territorial annexations that followed it. He hammered out the Compromises of 1850 and 1854, which contained significant concessions to the South. He realized better and earlier than most Northerners that slavery was principally an institution of race adjustment and that there was no easy substitute for it.[8] Yet the South remained unimpressed by the Little Giant. To its way of thinking, Douglas was first of all a Yankee, and in the 1850's the South might tolerate a Yankee as a political servant, but would never consent to be led by one.

In 1852 Douglas, then only thirty-nine years old, came very close to walking off with the Democratic presidential nomination. Had he been successful he would quite probably have become the youngest President in our history. In the end, it was the South that thwarted Douglas' bid by exercising the *de facto* veto that it had enjoyed over every Democratic nomination since most people could remember.[9] Far from growing angry or revengeful toward the South, Douglas, who could take comfort from the fact that he was still very young for a politician of national stature and would have many more chances to be President, redoubled his efforts to strengthen his position below the Mason-Dixon Line.

James Ford Rhodes felt that it was a desire to stand well with the South that prompted Douglas' leading role in the Kansas-Nebraska Act.[10] Although this may be an extreme conclusion, there is little doubt that it was Senator Archibald Dixon of Kentucky who took the lead in encouraging Douglas to incorporate a specific repeal of the Missouri Compromise into that act,[11] and that Douglas saw repeal as the price that had to be paid if the South were to accept the popular sovereignty aspects of the legislation.

If Douglas hoped to curry favor in the South through Kansas-Nebraska, he was soon disappointed. If the South was pleased with the repeal of the Missouri Compromise, it was suspicious of popular

[8] Allen Johnson, *Stephen A. Douglas: A Study in American Politics*, p. 91.

[9] Ulrich B. Phillips, ed., *Correspondence of Toombs*, p. 298.

[10] James F. Rhodes, *History of the United States from the Compromise of 1850*, I, 429–430.

[11] Allan Nevins, *Ordeal of the Union*, II, 95–96.

sovereignty. The net result of Douglas' efforts seems to have been apathy more than enthusiasm.[12] The South's leaders might put up with Douglas' territorial programs for a while longer, not because they now thought of him as pro-Southern, but because they felt he might be easy to control after all.[13] Douglas' gesture to the South therefore came to be regarded as a sign of weakness by the slavocracy.

Seeking conciliation, Douglas had instead sown the seeds of disillusion. The South looked upon the Kansas-Nebraska Act as carrying an implied promise on the part of Douglas and other Northern Democrats not only to permit the expansion of slavery, but to work covertly to facilitate its spread. It was a curiously naive assumption. No Northern politician could realistically make, much less keep, such a promise in the face of the rapidly growing antagonism above the Mason-Dixon Line to the spread of slavery.

The meager amount of goodwill that Douglas' solicitous attitude toward the South had fostered in the first half of his national political career reached its peak in 1854 and decreased steadily thereafter.

While the South for a few more years after 1854 accepted Douglas' domination of the narrow field of territorial affairs, far from showing any gratitude toward him for past services, it seems to have set out deliberately to hamstring Douglas' pet projects in other areas of national life. It was Southern opposition in Congress that year after year caused Douglas' grandiose scheme of a Pacific railroad to be tabled. It was the South that consistently blocked the kind of homestead legislation Douglas advocated. Southern obstructionism reached the height of its pettiness in repeated attempts to stall Douglas' projects for federal improvement of the port of Chicago in the annual Rivers and Harbors legislation.[14]

While the South was on balance more helpful than the North toward Douglas' bid for the Democratic nomination at Cincinnati in 1856, the slave states would support Douglas only as long as the

[12] Ibid., pp. 145, 157–158.

[13] John B. Moore, ed., *The Works of James Buchanan*, IX, 486 n.

[14] *Cong. Globe*, 35th Cong., 2nd sess., pp. 1619–1620.

ambiguity inherent in his cherished popular sovereignty permitted them to make of that doctrine whatever suited their peculiar needs. When the Buchanan-Douglas feud forced the Little Giant to clarify his popular sovereignty in a manner unacceptable to the South, a major segment of its leaders then placed him squarely in the enemy camp.

While Lecompton alone did not cause the rupture between Douglas and the South, it was nonetheless a major turning point in their long and uneasy relationship. It climaxed the years of suspicion and mistrust. It gave those Southerners who had always disliked Douglas an excuse to make a formal break with him; it focused and gave expression to the latent hostility a much larger group of Southerners was coming to feel toward all Yankees. It severely tried those in the South who were determined to persevere in their loyalty to the Little Giant. The *Mobile Daily Register*, perhaps a little too eagerly, regretted Douglas' anti-Lecompton stand "as it will at once sever the ties which have hitherto bound this able statesman and the people of the South together in such a cordial alliance," and concluded flatly, "there must henceforth exist an impassable gulf between the Southern people and the Illinois Senator."[15] The *Union*, usually too prejudiced against Douglas to be very reliable, accurately assessed immediate reaction to the break with the administration over Lecompton: "There is no quarter in the South in which he can hope to be regarded in any other character than as a disorganizer and an apostate."[16]

Lecompton symbolized the end of any chance of a close political alliance between Douglas and the South, but it did not mark the end of any further relationship between them. Douglas was now thrown back more upon his sectional base in the North, but he did not for this reason cease to court the South. In 1858 he led the attack in the Senate against Buchanan's alleged subservience to the British in suppressing the African slave trade.[17] To the end of his

[15] *Mobile Daily Register*, December 13, 1857.

[16] *Washington Union*, August 14, 1858.

[17] *Cong. Globe*, 35th Cong., 1st sess., pp. 2348, 2496–2497. Douglas here was probably motivated largely by a desire to embarrass Buchanan rather than to

life he strove to effect a workable compromise with the South, but with this difference: he would no longer sacrifice Northern interests to do so.

The South for its part after 1857 distrusted Douglas more than ever, but was not quite ready to discard him. It was impressed by his great victory in 1858.[18] The South could never again really accept Douglas, but it might continue to try to use him.

Stephen Douglas lived out the last years of his life in the most sectional age in American history, and in any sectional choice he was first a Northwesterner and second a Northerner. After all, it was Vermont that had borne him and Illinois that had sent him on to national political fame. It was the Northwest that had given him an unshakeable base of support within the Democratic party. But Douglas avoided making a choice between sections for as long as possible. In many ways he was the least sectionally oriented of any of the political figures of his day. His first loyalties were to the nation and the Democratic party. Throughout the decade before the Civil War, Douglas tried repeatedly to sublimate sectional allegiances into a larger and more noble identification with the nation, its welfare and expansion.

There was in Douglas' public utterances throughout the last few years of his life an almost total absence of the kind of sectional demagoguery that often passed for statesmanship during this unfortunate period in our history. Although acquiring an anti-Southern reputation would have been a great help to Douglas' political career in the North from 1857 onward, he stubbornly refused to stoop to this kind of maneuver. Conversely, while Douglas recognized the force of Southern sectionalism, he never became its tool. On those occasions during the first half of his career in Washington when he seemed to identify with the narrow interests of the South, his actions were in fact the by-product of his role as a na-

---

reopen the African slave trade, to which Douglas was steadfastly opposed. See Robert W. Johannsen, ed., *The Letters of Stephen A. Douglas*, pp. 446–447, 452.

18 Reuben Finnell to Douglas, Warren County, Virginia, December 1, 1858; Douglas MSS.

tionalist, not a sectionalist. Although the Compromises of 1850 and 1854 involved very real concessions to the South, Douglas' primary motive in helping to pass them was national rather than sectional. In both 1850 and 1854 he was seeking an acceptable national territorial policy that would enhance the opportunities for the kind of peaceful expansion of the national domain that was always foremost in Douglas' scale of political values.[19]

In the Kansas-Nebraska Act, the Little Giant was willing to pay the price demanded by Dixon and other Southerners in order to achieve the larger national goal of development of the West in general and the building of the Pacific railroad in particular. Thoughtful Southerners must have realized that their section was not the direct beneficiary of Douglas' policies, but the residual legatee of his role as nationalist. Pierre Soulé wrote in 1858 to urge Douglas to visit New Orleans and described the citizens of that city as "being desirous of testifying to you their approbation of your truly national position in your late contest in Illinois in defense of the principles of States Rights."[20]

Douglas often seemed to recognize the power of Southern sectionalism only to try to direct it into more national channels. This is the true explanation of the occasional eruptions of jingoistic fervor on the part of the Little Giant: his open endorsement of the acquisition of Cuba and the indirect references he made from time to time about seizing more territory from Mexico.[21] When Douglas could no longer hope to sublimate Southern interests into some larger national scheme, he sought to appeal to the South's memories of a common national past. He told an 1859 audience at Wooster, Ohio, "There was no sectional strife in Revolutionary days. There were no sectional jealousies in Washington's camp. On every battlefield North and South—at Camden, Yorktown, Saratoga, and Trenton—Northern and Southern blood flowed in common streams in a common cause. . . . On every battlefield Southern chivalry has been

[19] James C. Malin, *The Nebraska Question, 1852–1854*, pp. 443–448.

[20] Pierre Soulé et al. to Douglas, New Orleans, La., December 2, 1858; Douglas MSS.

[21] *Cong. Globe*, 36th Cong., 1st sess., app., p. 314.

conspicuous by the side of Northern chivalry."[22] He used almost identical language in a similar appeal to patriotism on the 1860 presidential campaign trail.[23]

Only in the closing weeks of his life, with secession and civil war now upon the country, did Douglas publicly acknowledge the existence of sectionalism and its terrible power. Yet even here, Douglas recognized sectionalism only to deny that he had ever been a sectionalist. He told an audience at Springfield two weeks after Fort Sumter, "I have never pandered to the prejudice or passion of my section against the minority section of this Union." Far from having been a narrow Northern sectionalist, Douglas confessed that if he had ever deviated from his strong national position, it was to commit the opposite sin of being too much concerned with the welfare of the South.[24]

Stephen Douglas began the year 1859 by trying to woo the South in his role as an unbiased national figure; he ended it by losing the South altogether.

Douglas had won a great victory in Illinois, but if his views on popular sovereignty and slavery in the territories had reassured moderate opinion in his own state, they had confirmed the old suspicions of Douglas in the South and created some new ones. Douglas' remarkable electoral triumph had strengthened more than ever his ambitions to be elected President in 1860. Yet he knew that before that victory could be his, he must have at least the acquiescence of the South, if not its wholehearted acceptance. Three weeks after the election, Senator and Mrs. Douglas boarded the *City of Memphis* at Alton. Their destination was New Orleans.

He came south partly in triumph and partly as a supplicant and above all he came to explain. Yet he came more out of strength than weakness. The first letter Douglas received from the South

[22] Harry V. Jaffa and Robert W. Johannsen, *In the Name of the People: Speeches and Writings of Lincoln and Douglas in the Ohio Campaign of 1859*, p. 228.

[23] Fite, *Campaign of 1860*, p. 299.

[24] *Speech of Senator Douglas, Before the Legislature of Illinois, Springfield, April 25, 1861*, n.p., n.d.

inviting him to come stressed that the Little Giant's popularity there was strong and growing stronger every day.[25] The South was not ready to give up its lingering mistrust of Douglas altogether, but it was undeniably impressed by the scale of his victory in what was otherwise a disastrous year for the Democratic party.[26]

But if Douglas came to receive the plaudits of his Southern admirers, he came with misgivings as well. He knew that his forthright stand on Lecompton the year before had damaged his political future in the South,[27] and he must have realized that his recent answer at Freeport had served only to reinforce existing Southern suspicions of popular sovereignty. While Douglas would never have endorsed Lincoln's observation to Asbury in July of 1858 that "he cares nothing for the South; he knows he is already dead there,"[28] he nonetheless sensed that at best he could hope to turn Southern hostility toward him into toleration, but not affection.

There was just possibly another reason behind Douglas' decision to embark on his southern tour. Throughout his long public career, he demonstrated a consistent tendency to stay out of Washington when it might have been awkward for him to be there. He had won a victory at the polls in November, but the Illinois Legislature would not meet to ratify his re-election as Senator until the first week of the new year. The Buchanan forces were working night and day now to block Douglas at the legislative level. It was a desperate move and ultimately an utter failure, but it did serve temporarily to cast a shadow over Douglas' credentials. An extended trip south and a leisurely ocean voyage from New Orleans to New York would serve well as a means to avoid embarrassment in Washington. Furthermore, if Douglas could turn his visit into a

25 George W. Lamar to Douglas, Augusta, Georgia, October 23, 1858; Douglas MSS.

26 Reuben Finnell to Douglas, Warren County, Virginia, December 1, 1858; Douglas MSS. Austin L. Venable, "The Conflict Between the Douglas and Yancey Forces in the Charleston Convention," *Journal of Southern History* 8, no. 2 (May 1942): 229.

27 Allan Nevins, *The Emergence of Lincoln*, I, 263.

28 John G. Nicolay and John Hay, eds., *Complete Works of Abraham Lincoln*, III, 198.

triumphal tour through the very heartland of administration political power, he might dissuade the Buchananites in Illinois from pursuing the reckless course they had now embarked upon. At very least he would give a few wavering legislators second thoughts about yielding to administration pressure.

The theme of Douglas' speeches in the South during the 1858 trip may be described as nationalistic with pro-Southern overtones. He did not suddenly and cynically alter his principles to suit a new environment. He did not retract anything he had said during the debates with Lincoln, but through subtleties of emphasis and phrasing he was clearly trying to make what he had to say more palatable to the South. In St. Louis he stressed the sanctity of the Union and the importance of national expansion, but he did not forget to praise the notion of states' rights.[29] At New Orleans on December 6 he called for the annexation of Cuba and made a point of receiving in public a delegation of surviving veterans of the War of 1812.[30] It was that war which best symbolized the national period in which Douglas felt most at home. It also called up memories of his great hero, Andrew Jackson, the Southerner who was first of all a nationalist.

Douglas did not disown popular sovereignty when he crossed the Mason-Dixon Line, but just as in the North he had attempted to place it in a favorable light before moderate free-soil opinion, so in the South he stressed those shadings that would convince moderate proslavery opinion that his doctrine offered the best means to protect and perhaps even to expand the institution of slavery. Douglas in no way ignored or misrepresented the answer he had given Mr. Lincoln at Freeport, although the trip confirmed his fears that his reply had done more than anything else recently to stimulate ill-feeling toward him in the South.[31] As his tour drew to a close, Douglas did, however, offer a significant clarification of the so-called Freeport Doctrine. He told his audience at New Orleans that he had not intended to imply that a territory could legally

[29] *Memphis Daily Appeal*, November 30, 1858.

[30] *New Orleans Daily Picayune*, December 7, 1858.

[31] Johnson, *Stephen A. Douglas*, p. 394.

forbid the entry of slaves, or that it could refuse to grant them the protection accorded any other form of property. Douglas would only draw the line at requiring a territorial government to afford slave property any *special* form of protection.[32] Since no prudent slaveholder would take his valuable property where it could not be adequately protected, Douglas' modification represented a concession to the South more in form than fact, but a concession nonetheless.

A few days earlier at Memphis Douglas had returned to the theme of the racial inferiority of the Negro. What he said in Tennessee was in fact not very different from what he had maintained a few weeks before up and down Illinois, but in saying it Douglas dropped the polite talk about racial inferiority, which was more acceptable to Northern ears, and announced to the Southerners who had come to hear him that "between the negro and the crocodile, he took the side of the negro. But between the negro and the white man, he would go for the white man."[33]

This was the same Douglas who had recently won in Illinois, but he was now somehow different. In essence his platform was identical with the moderate one that had brought him victory in the North, but, through changes in language and timing, the Little Giant was trying desperately to make it acceptable to Southern ears. He still stood objectively on the moderate middle ground of neutrality toward slavery, but subjectively he was reaching out toward the South. If he would not grant all that the South demanded, he could at least identify himself with its problems and convey a feeling of sympathy based on understanding. The hard side of Douglas' doctrine remained unchanged in Southern latitudes. He never dropped his pose of professed amorality to tell the South that he thought slavery was right, but he went far toward implying that in his view it was not wrong.[34] Yet it was the soft, subjective side of his views that he sought to turn toward his Southern audiences.

[32] *New Orleans Daily Picayune*, December 7, 1858. The *Chicago Times* had hinted at such a change on November 11, 1858.

[33] *New York Tribune*, December 6, 1858.

[34] Ibid.

Where the application of his ideas could be reasonably modified to please the South, he would do so. But Douglas knew that too much alteration would arouse suspicion in the North. For the most part, he sought merely to calm and reassure Southerners, to reconcile them to his creed without materially changing it. He would stress the soft side of his beliefs and give the people in the South who were favorably disposed toward him an opportunity to see in Stephen Douglas what they wanted to see.

Douglas' 1858 trip was by almost any standard a great success. Everywhere he had gone he had been greeted warmly. He had not scheduled a speech at Memphis, but when its leading citizens learned he was coming down the Mississippi, they chartered a steamboat and went upriver to meet the Little Giant and urge him to visit them.[35] In New Orleans he was greeted by a brass band and a military escort, and spoke to a capacity crowd at the Odd Fellows Hall.[36]

He had crossed the Mason-Dixon Line under a cloud of suspicion. The South had followed the debates carefully and had come to suspect more than ever the man's platform and his motives. During his two-week visit Douglas made much of the South tolerate his ideas if not love them. He allayed their suspicions that he was on just another campaign trip. After all, had he not recently announced that the South was entitled to the next President of the United States?[37] Not all the South was now sure it was really necessary for it to produce the next President. A man who had heard Douglas speak in Memphis wrote him: "If you will administer the Government consonant with the views and principles therein expressed, I shall not object to you as our next President."[38]

The trip ended far better than it had begun. When the time had come to leave New Orleans and the South, Senator and Mrs. Douglas were escorted from the St. Charles Hotel through cheering mobs

[35] *Memphis Daily Appeal*, November 30, 1858.

[36] *New Orleans Daily Picayune*, December 7, 1858.

[37] Nevins, *The Emergence of Lincoln*, I, 420.

[38] W. C. Phillips to Douglas, Tennessee, December, 1858; Douglas MSS. (City and exact date not given on letter, filed in Douglas MSS between December 28 and December 31, 1858).

to the wharf where the *Black Warrior* was waiting to take them to New York. Farther upriver a hundred guns along the levee boomed their own farewell.[39] Douglas had come to the South an alien, he left once more a friend, if not an ally.

When Douglas sailed from New Orleans on December 12, 1858, he could hardly have been displeased to learn that the *Black Warrior* would call at Havana prior to making for New York. Indeed he may have planned things that way. It would have been the kind of shrewd political move typical of the Little Giant and wholly in keeping with his unique peripatetic political style.

Most of Douglas' biographers[40] either ignore his Cuban visit altogether or dispose of it in a single sentence, yet it is an incident rich in significance and dramatic content. The visit would give concrete expression to his recent pronouncement in New Orleans that it was America's destiny to have Cuba. Douglas' new expansionist fervor was no mere impulsive outburst of jingoism, but a calculated move that promised large political returns on a number of fronts. His correspondence shows that friends in the South had been urging just such a move to strengthen his credentials in the slave states.[41] If Douglas was too much of a realist to expect that a gesture of this sort would by itself reconcile the South to his cause, he probably felt that it at least would curb Southern hostility to the homestead legislation he would be introducing when Congress reassembled. Again, the demand for the annexation of Cuba fitted in nicely with Douglas' long record of fostering national expansion and with his obvious desire to sublimate the pernicious forces of sectionalism into some more worthy national purpose. To enrich the drama of his visit, Douglas would be arriving in Havana Harbor on board the same *Black Warrior* which in 1853 had touched

[39] *New York Tribune*, December 13, 1858.

[40] George F. Milton, *The Eve of Conflict: Stephen A. Douglas and the Needless War*, p. 362; Stevens, "Life of Douglas," p. 598.

[41] Edward Deloney to Douglas, Clinton, La., November 8, 1858; John T. Reid to Douglas, New Orleans, La., November 13, 1858; Douglas MSS.

off the famous incident with Spain that still rankled in the hearts of patriotic Americans everywhere.

Douglas may have had one other motive in mind. Buchanan had been pressing for the acquisition of Cuba for some time now.[42] Douglas no doubt hoped for a reconciliation with the administration following his great victory in Illinois. The Democratic convention of 1860 was only sixteen months off and Douglas would need the acquiescence, if not the active support, of the Buchanan faction in any bid he might make for the presidential nomination. Although Douglas probably knew that there was little chance of getting both Spain and the free states to consent to any annexation of Cuba by America in the near future,[43] he saw a chance to make a gesture of friendship toward the President and the Directory.

In the end, no one took Douglas' Cuban visit very seriously. He was received warmly in Havana, where he was regarded as the great rival of Buchanan, toward whom the Cuban press was at that moment especially vituperative because of the President's demand for annexation in his recent Annual Message.[44] Douglas, for his part, had the good sense to keep silent in Havana about his own plans for Cuba. That city's leading newspaper disposed of the whole visit in one sentence: "The distinguished American Senator, Mr. Stephen A. Douglas, arrived at this city on board the 'Black Warrior,' accompanied by his family and intends to spend several days among us."[45]

[42] Philip S. Klein, *President James Buchanan*, p. 324. Years before, in 1854, Buchanan, while minister to England, had been one of the authors of the Ostend Manifesto looking toward American annexation of Cuba.

[43] Douglas' interest in Cuba stopped far short of seizing that island by conquest, and his public pronouncements on the subject were highly qualified and circumspect, betraying a certain lack of enthusiasm. In 1859 he advocated the acquisition of Cuba "whenever the Island can be fairly obtained consistent with the laws of nations and the Honor of the country." "Autobiographical Notes" in Johannsen, ed., *Letters of Douglas*, p. 473.

[44] Second Annual Message of James Buchanan, December 6, 1858. James D. Richardson, ed., *A Compilation of the Messages and Papers of the Presidents*, V, 510–511.

[45] *Habana Crónica de la Marina*, December 17, 1858.

The North was predictably hostile to any scheme for the expansion of slavery, and the *New York Times* dismissed Douglas' call for the annexation of Cuba as an "excessive and not very creditable subservience to the Executive."[46] The South remained unimpressed. Douglas' gesture on Cuba was essentially a national move with pro-Southern side effects, and in the late 1850's the South thought and acted first as a section and only reluctantly as part of America.

More seriously, Douglas' power to effect policy had been suddenly and sharply curtailed by events in Washington.

On December 9 the Senate Democrats had met in caucus and removed Stephen Douglas from the chairmanship of the Committee on Territories. If the Little Giant had suspected that such a move was afoot and hoped to forestall it by staying away from Washington, he had overestimated the sense of honor of his political enemies. Succumbing to administration pressure, his Senate colleagues had decided to strip Douglas of the chairmanship while he was still a thousand miles away from Capitol Hill.[47] They offered the lame excuse that Douglas was absent and that there was pressing business for his committee to attend to. The *Washington States* retorted that if this was true, why not remove Douglas from membership on the committee altogether?[48] Months later the administration would reluctantly admit what Douglas had claimed all along: that it was his reply at Freeport that caused his discharge from the chairmanship.[49] From the larger point of view, the Freeport reply was probably more an excuse than a cause. It provided the angry and frustrated Buchanan with an opportunity to administer a schoolmasterish rap across the knuckles of an especially recalcitrant pupil. As a final insult, the chairmanship was given to

[46] *New York Times*, February 21, 1859.

[47] Douglas' deposition was made public December 13, 1858. *Cong. Globe*, 35th Cong., 2nd sess., p. 45. Thus, since he left New Orleans on the 12th, he probably did not learn of his removal until arriving in New York on December 30, 1858.

[48] *Mobile Daily Register*, December 17, 1858.

[49] James W. Sheahan, *The Life of Stephen A. Douglas*, p. 500.

James S. Green of Missouri, an outspoken advocate of slavery and a political opponent of Stephen Douglas.

It was the most drastic blow the administration could have dealt the Little Giant. It was also the most cruel. Douglas had served as the committee's chairman in the Senate for eleven years. During his brief stay in the House of Representatives from 1845 to 1847 he had also headed the House Committee on Territories. From these posts he had been the moving force behind the organization of the territories of Oregon, Minnesota, Washington, Utah, New Mexico, Kansas, and Nebraska. He had supervised the admission of Texas, Iowa, Wisconsin, California, Minnesota, and Oregon into the Union as states. Largely through his efforts, the national domain had more than doubled.

The fact that Douglas may have been expecting a move of this sort from the administration—indeed he had once before come close to losing his chairmanship in 1854 in the uproar that followed Kansas-Nebraska—in no way diminished the force of the blow. When he was deeply moved, as he had been after the Dred Scott decision and as he was now, the usually bumptious and loquacious Stephen Douglas lapsed into periods of prolonged silence. He made no public comment upon his removal for six weeks. When he finally did speak out, it was to portray himself as suffering the fate of a martyr who had stuck by his principles.[50] The *New York Journal of Commerce* tended to agree, observing that Buchanan's actions might once again serve to cast Douglas in the role of underdog that he had exploited so well the year before.[51]

While Buchanan no doubt saw his purge as a way to strengthen his ties with the South, many Southerners felt Douglas' punishment had been too severe. An indignant correspondent from Georgia saw the jealous hand of Howell Cobb behind the move.[52] A man in Florida compared Douglas to Martin Van Buren when Calhoun

[50] *Cong. Globe*, 36th Cong., 1st sess., p. 421.

[51] *New York Journal of Commerce* quoted in *Richmond Enquirer*, December 17, 1858.

[52] Dr. Henry Green to Douglas, Macon, Ga., December 10, 1858; Douglas MSS.

blocked his nomination in the Senate as minister to the Court of St. James.[53] The fact that Van Buren later became President would not have been lost on Douglas. A "Committee of Printers" in Galveston, Texas, wrote to express their support and indignation, although they were "employed by an anti-Douglas office."[54]

The removal from the chairmanship of the Senate Committee on Territories may have stunned Douglas, but it did not cripple him. By 1859 most of the great work of territorial expansion and organization was over. He remained on the Senate Foreign Relations Committee and, at least for the time being, on the Committee on Public Buildings. As consolation he was offered the chairmanship of the Senate Commerce Committee, which he declined. Although no longer its head, Douglas stayed on the Committee on Territories, and his great prestige and unrivaled knowledge of territorial matters still gave him a large voice in its affairs. Taking away his official rostrum on territorial matters did not silence the irrepressible Senator from Illinois; it merely forced him to seek other outlets for his views, such as newspapers, national magazines, and, of course, the stump.

Most important of all, Douglas' deposition made him mad. He had a score to settle now with Buchanan and the radical Southerners whose favor Douglas' ouster was intended to cultivate. There would be no more polite talk about it being a Southerner's turn to be President. If in fact Buchanan was thinking about running again, Douglas would not step graciously aside as he had done at Cincinnati in 1856. Early in 1859 Douglas definitely resolved to seek the Charleston nomination.[55]

53 "A Slaveholder" to Douglas, Florida, December 28, 1858; Douglas MSS (no city given).

54 "A Committee of Printers" to Douglas, Galveston, Texas, December, 1858; Douglas MSS (exact date not given, but filed between December 28 and December 31, 1858).

55 Johannsen, ed., *Letters of Douglas*, p. 439. Douglas on March 31, 1859, wrote to James Singleton, regarding the Charleston convention, "I do not intend to make peace with my enemies. . . . The time has arrived when our friends should prepare for organized action." Also see Milton, *Eve of Conflict*, pp. 365–366, 378–379.

The latent good will toward Douglas that the Southern tour of 1858 made manifest and the sympathy and support to which his removal from the chairmanship gave rise in the South formed an impressive tribute to the man, but good will and sympathy are not the same as political strength. Douglas' following in the South was impressive for a Northerner, yet upon close analysis, his political base there was dangerously narrow. It was limited to the areas along the major river systems of the South—primarily the Mississippi—to the Border states, to certain ethnic groups in the few large urban areas, and to those politically moderate commercial classes from which the old Whig party had once drawn its strength.

Douglas in 1858 actually visited the one area of the South where his popularity had always been greatest. He spoke at only a handful of towns along the Mississippi: St. Louis, Memphis, Vicksburg, and New Orleans. As in Illinois, Douglas always ran well along the river. In the election of 1860 Douglas made a far stronger showing in the western part of Tennessee, which was washed by the Mississippi, than he did in the central and eastern sections of the state.[56] An anonymous correspondent in Nashville had written Douglas at the height of the Lecompton controversy: "I fear you put little faith in Southern support after the shameful way in which they treated you in Cincinnati, but remember, Tennessee is also a western state, one of the Mississippi Valley states, and in that great valley, the heart and strength of the nation, lies your strength."[57]

Douglas' riparian strength in the South was partly due to the same factors that caused the Little Giant to run well in Egypt: his long record of favoring public improvement of rivers and harbors, his ties to the commercial classes who depended so heavily on the waterways for their economic welfare, and the sympathy the restless ever-moving Douglas evoked on the part of the uprooted folk who had come to settle along the rivers.

[56] Ollinger Crenshaw, *The Slave States in the Presidential Election of 1860*, p. 185 n.

[57] Anonymous to Douglas, Nashville, Tenn., December 28, 1857; Douglas MSS.

Perhaps most of all, Douglas and the Mississippi symbolized those bonds between the Southwest and the Northwest that had for so long been a part of the American scene and that were now being strained by the newer forces of sectionalism. Shortly before coming south in 1858 Douglas wrote of his vision of the time when "the Mississippi valley shall have doubled and trebled its population, and become the heart of the Republic, more extensive, powerful and glorious than any empire that the world ever beheld."[58] As late as 1860 Douglas would be preaching to the South the identity of its interests with those of the Northwest and the irreparable harm secession would do to commerce along the Mississippi.[59] The South, at least in part, shared Douglas' faith. In December of 1860, with civil war only a few months away, a Mississippi man wrote to Senator Douglas, "We cannot live at peace with New England. But the great Northwest is by nature our ally."[60]

Douglas and his Southern allies were on sound national ground. But it was the misfortune of Douglas and of the times in which he lived that many Americans, North as well as South, were no longer motivated by national considerations. Sectionalism was the order of the day, and the most vocal elements in the South would continue to honor the traditional ties with the Northwest only if that section would do its bidding on the overriding question of slavery.[61]

If the river areas of the South were bound to Douglas by ties of economics and tradition, the Border states' consistent loyalty to the Little Giant had essentially political roots. After all, Douglas' own state of Illinois had been settled largely by immigrants from along the Southern border, and in the late 1850's the dominant attitude of Illinoisans toward slavery and the Negro was not markedly different from that of the small white farmers who made up the bulk of the Border state population. Like their counterparts over in

[58] Johannsen, ed., *Letters of Douglas*, p. 430.

[59] Crenshaw, *Slave States*, p. 80.

[60] Quoted in Percy Lee Rainwater, *Mississippi: Storm Center of Secession: 1856–1861*, p. 170 n.

[61] W. E. Dodd, "The Fight For the Northwest, 1860," *American Historical Review* 16, no. 4 (July 1911): 778.

Egypt they did not themselves own slaves, but were tolerant of slavery and sympathetic toward the plight of the slaveholder in a rapidly changing world. Historians often overlook the fact that there were Border states in the North as well as in the South and that Illinois, with its long common boundary with Missouri and Kentucky, was, at least down in Egypt, very much a Border area. As the Civil War drew nearer and the supply of tenable political middle ground grew steadily smaller, Douglas, anxious to avoid an overt identification with any of the sectional extremes that were tearing the nation apart, tended to stress his role as a citizen of a Border state.[62]

Throughout the decade of the 1850's it was the Border states that provided Douglas with an impressive base of support below the Mason-Dixon Line. In the Cincinnati convention of 1856 it had been the delegations from Kentucky, Tennessee, and Missouri that had joined with the Northwest to spearhead Douglas' bid for the presidential nomination. A year later when Douglas took his highly controversial stand against Lecompton, the few letters he received from outside the North endorsing his position came from Kentucky, Maryland, Missouri, and Virginia.[63] In the campaign of 1858 Crittenden and Breckinridge of Kentucky added their immense prestige to Douglas' cause, and it was in the Border states that Douglas' reply to Lincoln at Freeport received its most favorable reception outside Illinois. Douglas came to the Border states twice during his campaign for the presidency in 1860, and the Border returned his interest with what was for a Yankee a very large popular vote.

The case of Virginia is especially interesting. In spite of its deep bonds of culture and sympathy with the lower South, it always gave Stephen Douglas a warm welcome and considerable political support. Two of its governors, Henry Wise and John Letcher, were at one time leading members of the Douglas camp. Virginia's at-

[62] *Cong. Globe*, 36th Cong., 1st sess., p. 558.

[63] See Thomas G. Addison to Douglas, Louisville, Ky., and James Harlan, Jr., to Douglas, Harrodsburg, Ky., both dated December 24, 1857; also Charles D. Drake to Douglas, St. Louis, Mo., December 26, 1857; and A. G. Southall to Douglas, Williamsburg, Va., December 21, 1857; Douglas MSS.

tachment to the Little Giant might in part be explained by its location along the Border and its nearness to Washington, which was for so long Douglas' great forum. Its innate conservatism, its long historical ties to the Union, and the fact that Douglas' bailiwick, the Northwest, had once belonged to Virginia, deepened its understanding and affection toward the man.

Douglas' political power in the South was characterized primarily by its lack of organization. The Little Giant never had the kind of machine below the Mason-Dixon Line that he could rely upon throughout the entire Northwest and much of the East. In the South he had to count for support on a few leading politicians, a smattering of newspapers, a somewhat larger circle of friends, and the ephemeral and steadily diminishing moderate vote.

Few people in the South in the years just prior to the Civil War were neutral or uncommitted, fewer still where a controversial, outspoken figure like Stephen Douglas was concerned. Political opinion in the South toward Douglas showed a tendency to crystallize into three identifiable and consistent attitudes. There were the irreconcilables led by Rhett and Yancey, who would not accept the Illinois Senator under any circumstances on any platform. Their inveterate hostility toward the Little Giant increased throughout the 1850's until it passed into an almost pathological hatred greater than they had for any other Yankee, including Lincoln and Sumner. They had decided to ruin Douglas, even if it meant the demise of the Democratic party and the destruction of the Union.

The second group consisted of those Southern leaders who would, at least temporarily, tolerate Douglas if not embrace him permanently and wholeheartedly. Alexander Stephens and Pierre Soulé were the most consistent and vocal among their ranks, which also included at one time or another Robert Toombs, James H. Hammond, John A. Quitman, William Walker, David Atchison, and Thomas Clingman, as well as Governors Wise and Letcher of Virginia and Governor John Winston of Alabama. The strong Whig antecedents of several of this group are unmistakable. Below the leading politicians stood those Southern newspaper editors whose allegiance to Douglas was important, but at best conditional and often short-lived. Douglas had no counterpart in the South to the *Chicago Times*, which served as his unofficial mouthpiece in Illinois. Although J. D. B. De Bow, editor of the influential review which bore his name, expressed strong disapproval of Douglas' reply at Freeport, he nonetheless supported Douglas throughout most of 1859 "In common with most of the States' Rights men of the South . . . whatever differences of opinion may exist between us on minor points."[64] De Bow's support was, however, to prove brief. Southern papers that at one time endorsed the Little Giant included both the *Richmond Enquirer* and *Examiner*. In 1859 Douglas made surprising strides in Florida, and one editor from there was able to write him: "Six months ago the *Florida Republican* was the only paper in the state which had the boldness to defend you. Now there are seven more defending your cause. A great reaction has taken place."[65]

The third group of Douglas' adherents in the South was less influential but more consistent in its allegiance. Its members remained loyal to the Little Giant and his cause right up to the election of Abraham Lincoln in 1860. Editors such as John Forsyth of the *Mobile Register* and J. S. Seibels of the *Montgomery Confederation*, together with the owners of the *New Orleans True Delta*, the *Augusta Constitutionalist*, and the *Memphis Appeal*, were the most prominent members of this group. Their support was steadfast and vital to the Douglas cause, but it is not clear whether the editors were motivated more by affection for the Little Giant and what he stood for, or by more personal motives. John Forsyth, probably the most influential of them all, had a grudge against the President dating from the time he had resigned as Buchanan's minister to Mexico in a pique over the rejection of his scheme to acquire more territory south of the border.[66] Douglas' following in the South was at times impressive, but it was at best highly individual-

[64] J. D. B. De Bow to Douglas, New Orleans, La., October 28, 1858; Douglas MSS.

[65] Thomas Floyd to Douglas, Jacksonville, Fla., July 16, 1859; Douglas MSS.

[66] Klein, *President James Buchanan*, p. 322.

istic, geographically narrow, and not particularly reliable. It was not the kind of political base from which a presidential victory might easily be fashioned.

Deprived of any thoroughgoing organized support in the South, Douglas came more and more to rely on the amorphous, inarticulate but hopefully vast area of moderate opinion in the slave states. He hoped to appeal over the heads of their implacable leaders to the latent good sense and conservatism of the people of the South.[67]

He partially succeeded. Those Southerners who remained loyal to Douglas were characterized by strong common sense and a practical approach to politics in an age that was becoming more and more unrealistic. Like Alexander Stephens they were disturbed by a growing preoccupation with symbols on the part of political leaders North as well as South.[68] In 1859 the *Mobile Register* warned the South not to destroy itself over a "barren abstraction" like a congressional slave code.[69] These Southern moderates realized the value of the benign ambiguity contained in popular sovereignty and the dangers inherent in pressing too hard for a definition in unstable times. If they could not like the Douglas doctrine, they would at least consent to ignore it. They were first of all Southerners, but unlike some of their more volatile neighbors, they refused to believe that Douglas represented any real threat to their vital interests. Had he not told people all across Illinois in the summer of 1858 that he would protect slavery in the states where it existed, and did not popular sovereignty represent a tacit approval of its expansion? Thoughtful Southerners were beginning to feel that slavery had just about reached the natural limits of its expansion anyway, and they saw in the proponents of a territorial slave code the same brand of irrationality that prompted radicals in the North to demand federal prohibition of slavery in the territories.[70] They may not have loved Douglas, but as Southerners they realized they needed him. The *New York Times* remarked, "As nothing would

[67] *Cong. Globe*, 36th Cong., 1st sess., p. 2152.

[68] Henry Cleveland, *Alexander H. Stephens*, p. 687.

[69] *Mobile Register*, July 7, 1859.

[70] Crenshaw, *Slave States*, p. 57.

be more hopeless than the condition of the South without Northern support, Southern Senators will wait awhile before closing the door of reconciliation forever with Mr. Douglas."[71] Douglas' stand on Lecompton did not please them, and his answers at Freeport did nothing to improve his image in their eyes, but the Southern moderates would still tolerate the Little Giant as a useful ally in an imperfect world.

If the moderate Southerners were loyal to their section, they were also devoted to the Democratic party and the Union. They refused to join the Ultras in pulling the Democratic house down around themselves in order to destroy an imagined enemy. They hesitated to accept the Buchanan view that by breaking with the administration Douglas had also broken with the Democratic party. They would not tolerate the mad cant of the fire-eaters that it would be better to elect a Black Republican President than the Little Giant. As Southerners they still cherished the hope that their section would produce the next President, but as political realists they had come to feel by 1859 that only Douglas could lead a united Democratic party to victory over the Republicans the following year. A correspondent from Macon, Georgia, conveyed that quality of enlightened political realism that was the trademark of Southern moderates when he wrote Douglas, "I am for you for President because you are right and nobody else can beat the Black Republican candidate."[72]

Those moderates in the South who rallied around the Douglas banner were also motivated by a strong desire to see the Union preserved. With the Irish and German elements of the South who, especially in New Orleans, provided Douglas with important political support,[73] it was a matter of recent immigrants with no traditional sectional roots pledging their loyalties to the nation that had given them a new home. But one did not have to be an immigrant to support the Little Giant. Among Douglas' adherents were men whose families had lived in the South sometimes for generations.

[71] *New York Times*, December 14, 1857.

[72] James A. Nisbet to Douglas, Macon, Ga., June 24, 1859; Douglas MSS.

[73] *Charleston Mercury*, November 6, 1860.

Their first loyalties were to the South, but they would not accept the Ultra view that you could not be a good Unionist and a good Southerner at the same time. They refused to love the Union less because they loved the South more.

With his strong unionism, his innate conservatism, and his ties to commerce, Stephen Douglas was particularly popular with the old Whigs in the South. His persistent stand in favor of a revenue tariff was sufficiently ambiguous not to alarm them, his record in support of public works pleased them, and his long service on behalf of the West, national expansion, and sectional compromise in the great tradition of Henry Clay delighted them.

Douglas was quick to grasp the importance in the South of the old Whig vote and directed his appeals toward it as he had done in Illinois in 1858. The hostile *New York Tribune* scorned such an approach, coming as it did from one who was "once the leader, not to say the idol, of the Democratic Party, and especially the ultra-Southern wing."[74] But Douglas' courtship of the Southern Whigs was reaping impressive political rewards. John Forsyth, editor of the *Mobile Register*, wrote, "I have drawn to me many of the most reputable and conservative of the old Whigs."[75] Douglas' correspondence is full of letters from other Southern supporters describing themselves as "old Clay Whigs."[76] One writer, in an excess of enthusiasm, compared Douglas' strong national position to that of Henry Clay when he declared that he would rather be right than President.[77] In 1859 Douglas still had hopes that he might be both.

Douglas stood well with the Southern moderates, whether of Whig or Democratic background, but by the end of 1858 they were a rapidly diminishing group. Some of its leading members, like Governor Henry Wise of Virginia, finally yielded to pressure for a congressional slave code and defected from the Douglas camp alto-

[74] *New York Tribune*, August 31, 1860.

[75] John Forsyth to Douglas, Mobile, Ala., July 30, 1859; Douglas MSS.

[76] L. C. Leland to Douglas, Panola, Miss., November 6, 1858, and John Wills to Douglas, Baltimore, Md., June 14, 1859; Douglas MSS.

[77] D. P. Henderson to Douglas, Louisville, Ky., December, 1857; Douglas MSS (exact date not given, but filed with letters of December 19–20, 1857).

gether during 1859.[78] Others, like John Forsyth, remained nominally loyal to Douglas, but interpreted his doctrines to suit their own ends. The *Mobile Register* announced in September, 1859, that the Douglas version of popular sovereignty could be stretched to permit the reopening of the African slave trade, since regulation of that trade was properly a matter for the individual states.[79] The few remaining genuine pro-Douglas moderates in the South felt more and more constrained to warn Douglas to make no compromise with extreme political elements of whatever complexion.[80] The sad thing was that compromise and benign ambiguity were Douglas' great political stock in trade. They were at the heart of the concept of popular sovereignty, and it was through them that Douglas had always sought to woo those same moderates who now warned against a flexible approach.

The *Black Warrior* landed at New York on December 30, 1858, and Douglas was immediately the object of spontaneous outbursts of public enthusiasm and affection that rivaled those he had recently enjoyed in the South. Manhattan gave him a reception at City Hall, and thousands of New Yorkers waited outside in a cold, driving rain to cheer the Little Giant.[81] He continued on his triumphal way to Philadelphia and then Baltimore where, on January 6, 1859, his joy at the warmth of his reception was climaxed by the news that the Illinois Legislature had just formally re-elected him to another term in the United States Senate.[82]. When his train arrived at Washington, thousands of admirers were waiting at the station to escort him to the Douglas home on Minnesota Row.[83]

78 Henry Wise to Fernando Wood, Richmond, Va., July 6, 1859; Brock Collection, Box 35.

79 See editorial of *Mobile Register* quoted in *New York Times*, September 26, 1859.

80 Crenshaw, *Slave States*, p. 75.

81 *National Intelligencer*, January 3, 1859; *New York Times*, January 1, 1859. On December 31, 1858, Douglas appeared at City Hall at 1 p.m. and that evening addressed a large crowd outside his New York hotel, the Everett House.

82 See Douglas' telegram to Charles Lanphier, Baltimore, January 6, 1859. Johannsen, ed., *Letters of Douglas*, p. 433.

83 Douglas arrived in Washington on January 6, 1859. For an account of his

The Little Giant no doubt saw in the warm welcome accorded him in the East, coming as it did on the heels of his triumphal tour of the South, a much needed fillip to his ambitions as a truly national political leader. But beneath the bland surface of nationwide enthusiasm for the Douglas cause, the rumblings of sectionalism were growing steadily louder and more ominous. Washington was full of rumors of an Ultra plot to assassinate Douglas, and for the first time in his life the Little Giant thought it wise to retain the services of a professional bodyguard.[84]

By the start of 1859, Douglas himself, like most of his colleagues in an unfortunate age, was basically a sectional political figure. The Southern tour of 1858 had evidenced much warmth and friendship, but if it was political power Douglas was after, he would have to look for it in the North.

In his quest for national unity, Douglas now shifted his tactics from an appeal to patriotism in all parts of the land to a shrewd but unstable balancing of sectional interests. More than ever, Douglas' nationalism came merely to equal the sum of its sectionalist parts, and his conservatism to resemble a loose and highly *ad hoc* adjustment of extreme points of view.

The year 1859 began on a deceptive note of calm and optimism. The financial panic that had struck in 1857 had now run its course and prosperity was beginning to return to the land. The elections were over for two more years. There were no pressing territorial questions to disturb the country. America in 1859 would have done well to have rested and to have sought to bind up its sectional wounds. Stephen Douglas would have too.

But Douglas was uncomfortable in a world where public opinion was polarizing around sectional and political extremes. He had grown up in a national and conservative age and the new order was

---

warm reception there and of the previous day in Baltimore, see the *National Intelligencer*, January 7, 1859. For his visit to Philadelphia, see ibid., January 5, 1859.

[84] Douglas' bodyguard was Major Tom Hawkins, one of the best shots of his day. Milton, *Eve of Conflict*, p. 364; Stevens, "Life of Douglas," pp. 658–659.

strange and awkward to him. Whenever Douglas was ill at ease, his first response was to do something. In 1859 he did too much. Deprived of the concrete problems that had challenged him in his role as chairman of the Committee on Territories and now lacking the kind of public rostrum with which the chairmanship had provided him, Douglas turned to less pragmatic pursuits and to other ways of making his views known to the American people. In so doing, he fell prey to the disease of the times: an exaggerated concern for abstractions and a reckless urge to define much that served best when left ambiguous. He announced prematurely in an open letter[85] the terms upon which he would accept the presidential nomination the following year, and then largely retracted much that he had said in the months that followed. He wrote a very bad article for a national magazine[86] and went out to Ohio in an unsuccessful attempt to help Democratic candidates in the state elections of 1859. He sought to mollify the South by pressing for legislation to prevent a recurrence of raids like the one John Brown staged at Harpers Ferry in October, and succeeded only in drawing down upon his head Southern scorn and suspicion.[87] By the time the year was out, Douglas was standing on far less secure political ground than he had been when it began.

If there was much that was new about the Douglas of 1859, there was much that was familiar as well. The long-standing feud with Buchanan lingered on, but public opinion was now more than ever on the side of the Little Giant. The President continued to wield the patronage ax against Douglas and introduced several new features into the struggle that seemed almost to have become by now a permanent part of the American political scene. Buchanan encouraged administration Democrats to launch a pamphlet war against the Little Giant.[88] In April he forced the Illinois Demo-

[85] The Dorr Letter.

[86] The *Harper's* article.

[87] *Cong. Globe*, 36th Cong., 1st sess., p. 553.

[88] The most famous pamphlet was written by Jeremiah Black, the Attorney-General. It was first published anonymously in the *Washington Constitution*, September 10, 1859, although its authorship did not long remain a secret. For its text see Jaffa and Johannsen, eds., *Name of People*, pp. 173–199.

cratic Committee formally to expel Douglas from the ranks of the party in that state. Whereas in years past Buchanan had sought mainly to alienate Douglas from any substantial support in the South, he now sensed the fundamentally sectional nature of Douglas' political strength and concentrated more in destroying the Little Giant in the North.

Douglas responded in kind. He was less polite now and frequently attacked Buchanan by name on the floor of the Senate. He used his post on the Foreign Relations Committee as a platform from which to criticize administration handling of American relations abroad.[89] He hammered away at the need to cut down on the amount of discretion left to the executive branch in carrying out public policy in a variety of areas.[90]

1859 was a disastrous year for James Buchanan. He had long since exhausted whatever supply of good will he might once have had among the American people, and they were now willing ing to believe the worst about the President. In March the press began to carry the first hints of the scandals of waste and corruption that were to leave an indelible black mark upon the history of the Buchanan administration.[91] The *Washington Union* would no longer be around to paper over any shortcomings in the official household. It ceased publication in the spring of 1859.[92] In April Governor Wise of Virginia announced his formal estrangement from the Buchanan camp.[93] In October the Eastern papers carried the news that Senator Broderick of California, one of the few Democrats in the Senate who had stood by Douglas throughout the whole Lecompton crisis, had been killed by an enraged Southern partisan.[94] The usually circumspect *New York Times* attributed

89 *Cong. Globe*, 35th Cong., 2nd sess., p. 1123.

90 Ibid., p. 1316.

91 *New York Times*, March 1, 1859.

92 *Washington Union*, April 9, 1859. The *Washington Constitution* now came to be considered the official spokesman of the Buchanan administration.

93 *New York Times*, April 27, 1859.

94 Broderick was killed in California by Judge David Terry on September 16, 1859. Roy F. Nichols (*Disruption of American Democracy*, pp. 263–264) has a good account of the background of the murder.

the murder to Broderick's differences with the administration and added, "We are equally convinced that Mr. Douglas has encountered personal as well as political perils from the course which he saw fit to take."[95]

Douglas returned often in 1859 to the familiar theme of popular sovereignty. He clung to it as the one hope for preserving the unity of the Democratic party and with it, "the peace and harmony of the Union."[96] He felt constrained to try to explain away the many shortcomings and contradictions which Lincoln had uncovered in the debates of the year before and which continued to bother the Little Giant. But Douglas' explanations seemed somehow less consistent now and less productive of any important results.

In a sectional period, popular sovereignty could only maintain its pretenses to nationalism by growing more ambivalent, displaying one face to the North and another to the South. For the benefit of the Northerners, Douglas softened the blatant amorality of his doctrine and modified his professed attitude of "care not" where slavery was concerned so that he might appear less callous.[97] He grew more realistic and finally admitted that the kind of sovereignty he was willing to accord a territory, far from being absolute, was limited, conferred from without, and thus by implication not sovereignty in its pristine form at all.[98] In his desire to convince the North of the virtues of his scheme, Douglas moved in 1859 from his sound traditional view that popular sovereignty was an implied right under the American system of government to the much less convincing position taken in his *Harper's* article[99] that it was positively and explicitly endorsed by the Constitution.

For the benefit of the South, Douglas again stressed the nonintervention aspects of popular sovereignty and played up its close ties with the doctrine of states' rights.[100] He showed a willingness to let the ambiguities inherent in his platform be settled by the Supreme

95 *New York Times*, October 13, 1859.

96 Johannsen, ed., *Letters of Douglas*, p. 440.

97 *Cong. Globe*, 36th Cong., 1st sess., p. 559.

98 Ibid., 35th Cong., 2nd sess., p. 1256.

99 Jaffa and Johannsen, eds., *Name of People*, pp. 63–67.

100 Ibid., pp. 106–109, 127, 213.

Court. This approach was not only a useful way to buy time and delay a conflict; it was also designed to soothe the Southerners, who would probably continue to dominate the Court for a long time to come.[101]

Douglas was wasting his time. Many of his moderate supporters in the South, for whom popular sovereignty had the greatest potential appeal, chose simply to ignore what they considered to be an unpopular doctrine and a great handicap to Douglas' cause below the Mason-Dixon Line. Others joined the Ultras in their demand for a congressional slave code for the territories. It was an old political ally of Stephen Douglas, Senator Albert G. Brown of Mississippi, who rose in the Senate on February 23, 1859, to give the rest of the nation formal notice that the South would now settle for nothing less than positive protection of slavery in the territories by federal law.[102]

There was a third group in the South who would endorse Douglas' popular sovereignty as a handy device to effect the ends of the slavocracy. Alexander Stephens in his "Letter to the Gentlemen of Macon" reassured Southerners that as far as popular sovereignty was concerned, "no serious practical danger to us could result from it. Even according to that doctrine we have the unrestricted right of expansion to the extent of population. It is admitted that slavery can, and will go, under its operation wherever the people want it."[103] Others pointed out that popular sovereignty and the reopening of the African slave trade were not incompatible. Lincoln had reached the same conclusion during the 1858 campaign.[104] Statements like these did little to help Douglas in the South, while doing much to blacken the image of popular sovereignty in Northern eyes.[105]

[101] *Cong. Globe*, 35th Cong., 2nd sess., pp. 1245–1246.

[102] Ibid., pp. 1241–1244.

[103] Alexander H. Stephens, *A Constitutional View of the Late War Between the States*, II, 683–684.

[104] *Mobile Register*, editorial quoted in the *New York Times*, September 26, 1859; Angle, ed., *Debates*, p. 8.

[105] *New York Tribune*, September 10, 1859; *New York Times*, September 26, 1859.

The South had little use for either the hard or the soft side of the Douglas doctrine. It was no longer impressed by moral neutrality toward slavery; it now wanted something more. In Lincoln's words, Southerners were now demanding that the rest of the country "cease to call slavery wrong, and join them in calling it right."[106] A section whose leaders would do much to bring about civil war through a reckless and neurotic preoccupation with abstractions had the audacity to criticize popular sovereignty for being abstract. The *Union*, always anxious to incur the favor of the South, remarked of Douglas, "He would tempt slavery into the Territories by a barren concession of the abstract right to carry them there."[107] More and more the South would use *Douglasism* as an expression of its disdain for popular sovereignty.[108]

If the Southerners condemned popular sovereignty on its hard side, it was because they judged it on its soft side. If they appeared to become exercised over the remote implications of that doctrine, it was because some of their very immediate interests were affected by it. Southerners had shown a persistent tendency in the past to judge popular sovereignty by its effects upon slavery and to tolerate it only as long as it did not seriously threaten that institution. By 1859 it was more than ever the future of slavery and not the idea of popular sovereignty *per se* that concerned the South. The *Richmond Enquirer* confessed that its differences with popular sovereignty were "not upon principle but on expediency."[109] Modern scholars[110] have tended to treat the South's apparent concern with states' rights, to which Douglas hoped to appeal with his popular sovereignty, as merely an ideological cloak for fostering the perpetuation and expansion of slavery. At the beginning of 1859, Stephen Douglas had almost arrived at the same conclusion.[111]

Douglas' approach to the South appears to have grown increas-

106 Nicolay and Hay, eds., *Works of Lincoln*, V, 325.

107 *Washington Union*, September 10, 1858.

108 *Vicksburg Weekly Sun*, June 24, 1859.

109 *Richmond Enquirer*, December 15, 1857.

110 Arthur M. Schlesinger, Sr., *New Viewpoints in American History*, pp. 220–244.

111 *Cong. Globe*, 35th Cong., 1st sess., app., p. 197.

ingly anachronistic. Popular sovereignty suited the South of an earlier era—the South that was still content to rely on the doctrine of local self-government and states' rights to protect its way of life. By the late 1850's the South was concerned not so much with nonintervention as with demands which a large portion of the North found intolerable.[112] Douglas was right in his repeated protests beginning in 1859 that not he, but the South, had changed.[113] But being right did not alter his position of growing isolation from the South. The doctrine with national pretensions that had been designed by a Northerner to placate the South was now denounced by the Southerners because they thought Northerners too fond of it.[114] As a final bit of irony, Douglas in mid-1859 witnessed the popular sovereignty, upon which he had hoped for so long to unite the Democracy, being put forward as a possible platform for Black Republicans throughout the Northwest![115]

On June 13, 1859, an old and loyal political ally of Stephen Douglas in the Northwest wrote the Little Giant a letter. He was J. B. Dorr, owner of the *Dubuque* (Iowa) *Herald and Express*, and he was brief and to the point: "Permit me to say that your friends in this state of whom there are large numbers feel somewhat embarrassed by the want of definite knowledge of your position in relation to the Charleston Convention of 1860."[116] Dorr went on to add that Douglas' reluctance to disclose the kind of platform he would agree to run on was causing confusion among Democrats and working against Douglas' chances to be President. The Iowa Democratic State Convention was to assemble within a week, and Dorr urged Douglas to make some kind of public statement of principles to clear the air.

Dorr's was only the most recent of a growing number of letters

112 See Jesse T. Carpenter, *The South as a Conscious Minority*, for a brilliant study of the changing approach of the South to the defense of its interests.

113 *Cong. Globe*, 36th Cong., 1st sess., app., p. 311.

114 Henry Wise to Fernando Wood, Richmond, Va., July 6, 1859; Brock Collection, Box 35.

115 *New York Times*, May 7, 1859.

116 J. B. Dorr to Douglas, Dubuque, Iowa, June 13, 1859; Douglas MSS.

John Forney, owner of the *Philadelphia Press* and a leading Douglas supporter in the North.

urging that Douglas clarify his position. As early as December, 1858, John Forney had written, "You are understood as occupying a position of entire submission to Charleston. This will never do."[117] H. B. Payne of Ohio and Jonathan T. Reid of New Orleans offered much the same advice.[118]

On June 22, 1859, Douglas issued his famous reply in what has come to be known as the Dorr Letter. He would, he said, be willing

[117] John W. Forney to Douglas, Philadelphia, December, 1858; Douglas MSS; exact date not given but filed between December 28, 1858 and December 31, 1858. This letter was marked "answered," but no known reply by Douglas has been found.

[118] Jonathan T. Reid to Douglas, New Orleans, La., June 14 and 20, 1859; H. B. Payne to Douglas, Cleveland, Ohio, April 12, 1859; Douglas MSS.

to accept the Democratic nomination on a platform incorporating the principles of the Compromises of 1850 and 1854, together with the Cincinnati platform of 1856 "as expounded by Mr. Buchanan in his letter accepting the nomination."[119] Buchanan's letter had led people to believe that a decision on slavery could be taken long before a territory was ready for statehood.[120] Douglas went on to say that he would, however, have to refuse a nomination entailing a commitment to any program that either called for the reopening of the African slave trade, a congressional slave code, or "the doctrine that the Constitution of the United States either establishes or prohibits slavery in the Territories beyond the power of the people legally to control it as other property."[121] This last stipulation, a reiteration of the Freeport Doctrine, was no doubt aimed at the proponents of slavery who felt in 1859 that a congressional slave code might not be necessary as long as the courts would protect slavery in the territories at common law and strike down any local legislation hostile to it.

Douglas had several motives in making this kind of statement at this particular point in his career. It is of more than passing significance that he wrote to Dorr just after he had returned from one of his trips to Mississippi, ostensibly to inspect the Martin family holdings.[122] His letter contained bitter medicine for the South. Had he been emboldened to write it because he had discovered a surprising store of good will toward himself in the South that might serve to cushion the effects of his stand? Or had he, on the other hand, found such hostility among Southerners that he despaired of ever appeasing them and determined once and for all to cast his lot with the North? The best explanation would seem to be

119 Douglas' reply to Dorr is in Johannsen, ed., *Letters of Douglas*, pp. 446–447.

120 Buchanan's letter of acceptance is found in Moore, ed., *Works of Buchanan*, X, 83.

121 Johannsen, ed., *Letters of Douglas*, p. 447.

122 Certainly a most curious business trip. Douglas was gone from mid-May to mid-June and spent considerable time visiting with political cronies in Georgia and Tennessee, which would send key delegations to the Charleston convention. *Memphis Daily Appeal*, June 3, 4, 1859.

that Douglas was anxious to reassure the North, which had always been suspicious of his dalliance with the South, that he had made no deals or concessions on his recent visit below the Mason-Dixon Line. Douglas had not despaired altogether of his political chances in the South, but was merely trying to warn its leaders and to cut down at an early stage any move to write a slave-code plank into the Charleston platform. One of his most trusted lieutenants in the slave states had only recently written the Little Giant: "Would it not be well for you to make some move to stir up the thoughts of the South to the dangers it is running under the advisement of its would-be leaders?"[123] Douglas no doubt saw in his reply to Dorr another opportunity to clear up the confusion over the exact meaning of popular sovereignty that had resulted from Lincoln's persistent probing during the Illinois campaign of the year before. By setting out the conditions on which he would accept the Democratic presidential nomination in 1860, Douglas was also trying to make himself seem less available and to avoid the perils that always go with being too early the clear party favorite. Finally, an open letter like the one he wrote to Dorr would serve to define and strengthen his political identity and to comfort those of his followers who were beginning to fear a rapprochement with Buchanan.[124]

Taking a larger view of the Dorr Letter, it would seem that Douglas had now firmly decided that his political future must rest first of all on an unshakable base of Northern support. To stand with the South on slavery would ruin him in the North without in any way guaranteeing ultimate success in the slave states. The letter was intended to appeal to the North and largely reflected the stiffening of Northern opinion on slavery. The *New York Times* remarked that "there is not a single free state in the Union which will vote for Congressional intervention in favor of slavery in the Territories, or for the abrogation of the Federal laws against the African slave trade. Any politician with his eyes half open can see

[123] Jonathan Reid to Douglas, New Orleans, La., June 14, 1859; Douglas MSS.

[124] Anonymous to Douglas, New York City, July 14, 1859; Douglas MSS. Nichols, p. 262.

that the Democrats of the North have yielded all the ground on this subject which they intend to yield."[125] Douglas had apparently decided to take the Charleston nomination out of Northern strength and not through following the unsuccessful course of appeasing the South. He knew that the Dorr Letter would be poorly received in the South, and he expected some Southern leaders to use it as an excuse to block his bid for the presidency.[126] But Douglas felt that a combination of Northern support and acquiescence by Southern moderates would gain him the nomination over the opposition of Southern Ultras. Once the nomination was his, he expected even the more extreme Southerners to unite behind him as the Democratic standard-bearer. Douglas' strategy was to prove unduly optimistic in the end.

The Dorr Letter actually contained little that was new. In the Jonesboro debate of 1858 and on the Senate floor in February of 1859, Douglas had stated his unalterable opposition to anything resembling a federal slave code.[127] Yet in the overheated sectional atmosphere of the summer of 1859 the letter produced results out of all proportion to its intrinsic value. The *New York Times* praised it as "clear and consistent" and saw it as a welcome relief from the traditional vagueness of Douglas' public pronouncements.[128] A correspondent in Indianapolis said that the letter had confounded Douglas' enemies who "have waited for you to show signs of a craven spirit."[129] Democrats in Ohio now thought Douglas sufficiently sound to extend him an invitation to speak there on behalf of their party's candidates in the upcoming state elections. That Douglas seemed to repudiate much of the Dorr Letter at Pittsburgh in September by agreeing to "submit to the organization of the party in all things"[130] does not seem to have upset anyone in the North, with the possible exception of John Forney.

125 *New York Times*, September 12, 1859.

126 Johannsen, ed., *Letters of Douglas*, p. 469.

127 *Cong. Globe*, 35th Cong., 2nd sess., p. 1246; Angle, ed., *Debates*, p. 229.

128 *New York Times*, June 24, 1859.

129 W. W. Wick to Douglas, Indianapolis, Ind., July 7, 1859; Douglas MSS.

130 John W. Forney to Douglas, Philadelphia, September 26, 1859; Douglas MSS.

In the South the Dorr Letter did not alienate Douglas' moderate supporters so much as it confused them. A man in Virginia wrote to inquire innocently if he was to take it to mean that "you had declined the Charleston nomination in favor of Governor Wise."[131] The *Richmond Enquirer*, which had been friendly toward Douglas, first reprinted the letter without comment and only after more than two weeks reflection decided that it must oppose Douglas' bid for the nomination.[132] The Southern fire-eaters professed dismay. Rhett's *Charleston Mercury* pronounced the Dorr missive "impertinent."[133] Privately, they were pleased. They now knew that all that had to be done to thwart Douglas was to enter an irrevocable demand on the part of the lower South for a slave-code plank in the Democratic platform of 1860. But other Southerners like Henry Wise of Virginia were deeply concerned. Wise wrote to Fernando Wood that the platform set forth by Douglas in his reply to Dorr "will assuredly break up the convention."[134]

Douglas stayed in Washington throughout most of the summer of 1859. He labored long hours over the article he was writing for *Harper's Magazine*, but he must have felt uncomfortable in the capital. He missed the old days when he could hold forth in the Senate from the Olympian heights of his committee chairmanship. The kind of political stalemate that had settled over the legislative process in 1859 was alien to one who thrived on work that produced tangible and immediate results and who saw in concrete accomplishment the true end of all government.[135] He found the Washington atmosphere stifling and yearned to be out on the political hustings once more. When the invitation came from the Ohio Democrats to help in a close off-year contest for the governorship

[131] J. F. Simmons to Douglas, White Sulphur Springs, Va., July 1859; Douglas MSS (exact date not given, but filed between July 7 and July 11, 1859).

[132] *Richmond Enquirer*, June 24 and July 8, 1859.

[133] *Charleston Mercury*, June 27, 1859.

[134] Henry Wise to Fernando Wood, Richmond, Va., July 6, 1859; Brock Collection, Box 35.

[135] Nichols, *Disruption of American Democracy*, pp. 226–245; Nevins, *The Emergence of Lincoln*, I, 427–459.

and the control of the state legislature, Douglas accepted. There were other motives besides party loyalty at work. Douglas knew that the political complexion of the new legislature would determine the fate of his old ally of Lecompton days, Senator Pugh, who would soon be facing re-election against an upstart named Salmon P. Chase. Perhaps more to the point, the Ohio Democrats would be meeting in district conventions in early December to begin the selection of delegates to Charleston, and Douglas was anxious to strengthen his credentials in this key state of the Northwest.

The Little Giant made three major speeches in Ohio that September, addressing large crowds at Columbus, Cincinnati, and Wooster.[136] When Lincoln learned of Douglas' intervention in the Ohio campaign, he immediately decided to come over from Illinois to enter the fray on behalf of the Republican ticket. Although the two men did not meet in formal joint debate, Lincoln also spoke at Columbus and Cincinnati, conducting a running dialogue with Douglas reminiscent of the Illinois campaign the year before. Perhaps sensing that in the Dorr Letter he had spoken largely as a sectionalist, Douglas in Ohio tried hard to adopt a highly national posture. He appealed to memories of Revolutionary times, declaring, "There were no sectional jealousies in Washington's camp."[137] He invoked recollections of Clay and Webster and of the high national period they represented.[138]

In the Ohio speeches Douglas once more presented popular sovereignty as the only practical middle ground between the demands of extremists North and South for federal intervention for or against slavery in the territories. Only this time, knowing that in Ohio he was on even more strongly free-soil political terrain than he had been in Illinois the year before, Douglas hesitated to mention slavery by name and instead spoke of "local and domestic concerns."[139] The phrase *popular sovereignty* had itself come under

[136] Douglas also spoke en route at Pittsburgh on September 6, 1859, and was warmly received. *New York Times*, September 7, 1859; *New York Tribune*, September 6, 1859.

[137] Jaffa and Johannsen, eds., *Name of People*, p. 228.

[138] Ibid., pp. 153, 159–161.

[139] Ibid., p. 210.

such suspicion in the North that Douglas relied more and more on the term *self-government.*[140]

Yet the Douglas of 1859 seemed to lack the incisiveness and the vigor of the Douglas who had defeated Lincoln the year before. He had never fully recovered from the strain of the long Illinois campaign. At Cincinnati his voice became so hoarse he could talk only with difficulty.[141] Then too, he had other things on his mind besides politics in the late summer of 1859. Mrs. Douglas was expecting a child in a few weeks and his mind probably went back to that day six years before when his first wife, Martha, had died in childbirth.[142]

Douglas' defense of popular sovereignty, always at best a bit awkward, now became strained and, upon occasion, ludicrous. He was more emphatic now, but less convincing. His continued insistence that all the troubles associated with slavery could be solved by banishing the question once and for all from the halls of Congress seemed out of date and much too simple for the seriousness of the times and the lateness of the hour.[143] His analogy between the relationship of a territory to Washington and an American colony to Great Britain in 1776 was specious at best.[144] A schoolboy could have refuted his argument that America rebelled against the mother country solely in defense of popular sovereignty. His statement at Columbus to the effect that in parts of the Constitution the word *territory* is used interchangeably with *state*[145] would have astounded the founding fathers. At Wooster Douglas declared that

140 Ibid., pp. 131, 135, 146, 166, 211. When Douglas did use the term *popular sovereignty*, he consistently coupled it with *nonintervention*; ibid., pp. 167, 169.

141 Ibid., p. 151.

142 Douglas' fears would have been well founded. On September 30, 1859, Adele Douglas gave birth to a daughter, Ellen, who lived only a few weeks. Mrs. Douglas herself fell seriously ill and hovered near death for six weeks. Johannsen, ed., *Letters of Douglas*, pp. 473–479, 482–483. Douglas was forced by his wife's illness to cancel another speaking tour of Ohio before the elections in October. See his letter of October 1, 1859, to George W. Manypenny; ibid., p. 476.

143 Jaffa and Johannsen, eds., *Name of People*, pp. 135, 155–161, 165, 223–224.

144 Ibid., p. 133.

145 Ibid., p. 142.

"so far as the slavery question is involved in the contest, it is simply a proposition of whether slavery is a federal or a local question."[146] The tendency to use *federal* as a synonym for *national* —and hence the opposite of *local*—was at best an example of purposeful deception, and at worst a shocking admission of ignorance of the nature of the American political system in which Douglas had operated with such success for so long. At Cincinnati the Little Giant accused the Republicans of wanting Congress to exercise sovereign power over the territories in all matters,[147] when only the question of slavery really interested them.

Douglas' Ohio speeches grew steadily more ragged and his defense of popular sovereignty more reckless in proportion to his frustration. He was tired now, probably sick,[148] and his heart was not in the contest. This is the only reasonable explanation for his statement at Wooster during his final appearance of the campaign that "if New Mexico wants slavery she has a right to it."[149] The Northern audience must have been amazed by the implication that desire makes right.

Douglas would have done well never to have gone out to Ohio that September of 1859. In the end he helped neither himself nor his party. He undid much of the favorable impression the Dorr Letter had created throughout the North, without in any way reconciling the South to his cause. In the elections that followed, the Ohio Republicans swept the governorship and both houses of the legislature.[150] It was a rehearsal for 1860.

Still, the trip reaped some rewards. In its December district con-

[146] Ibid., p. 201.

[147] Ibid., p. 154.

[148] Douglas' speaking engagement at Cincinnati was postponed until September 9 because of illness. *New York Times* for September 9, 1859. Douglas remained unwell throughout the fall and in November grew desperately ill. Johannsen, ed., *Letters of Douglas*, pp. 480–481; *National Intelligencer* for November 16, 1859.

[149] Jaffa and Johannsen, eds., *Name of People*, p. 224.

[150] Ohio Republicans won the governorship by 17,000 votes. The new State Senate found 25 Republicans facing 10 Democrats. The House was divided 64 to 40 in favor of the Republicans. *New York Times* for October 14, 1859.

ventions, the Ohio Democracy instructed its delegates to Charleston overwhelmingly in favor of the Little Giant.[151]

In the early spring of 1859 the editors of *Harper's* had consented to Douglas' request to publish an article he would write setting forth his views on popular sovereignty in the territories. The inconsistencies that Lincoln had exposed in the Douglas doctrine during the 1858 debates had continued to worry the Little Giant. Douglas himself was not really satisfied with the connotations of what he had said at Freeport. Deprived of his voice as committee chairman, Douglas no doubt saw in the *Harper's* article an opportunity to present his views to a large and influential national audience and to answer the recent wave of attacks upon popular sovereignty.

It was nonetheless highly unusual in mid-nineteenth-century America for a politician to use a sophisticated monthly journal as a vehicle for expounding and popularizing his ideas. What Douglas did was as novel as a presidential aspirant of today going on nationwide television one hour a week for a month to appeal to Americans a full year before the next election. But Stephen Douglas was never one to stick to the mere niceties of custom.

He threw himself into preparing the article with all the vigor and enthusiasm he brought to any task. He read widely in history and political science for the first time in his life.[152] Whole cartloads of books were sent over to his office from the Library of Congress. He asked scholars like George Bancroft long and detailed questions about American government and history.[153] There were rumors that the Little Giant was about to make a major and perhaps startling statement of policy, but the details of the project remained a well-kept secret.[154]

[151] Milton, *Eve of Conflict*, p. 406.

[152] For Douglas' usual aversion to extensive reading see Representative Cox's eulogy in *Cong. Globe*, 37th Cong., 1st sess., p. 36.

[153] Milton, *Eve of Conflict*, p. 386; Johannsen, ed., *Letters of Douglas*, pp. 442–443.

[154] Ibid., p. 449. Douglas in this July 17, 1859, letter to William A. Seaver

The article was published in the September number of *Harper's* under the title "The Dividing Line between Federal and Local Authority: Popular Sovereignty in the Territories." It was a literary disaster. When Douglas stood up to speak, he enthralled his audience; when he sat down to write, he bored them. The restless, energetic Little Giant found himself constricted by the limitations of the written word and the stuffy *Harper's* format. He was more at home with the spontaneity of speech, the give-and-take of debate, and the stimulation that comes from rapport with flesh-and-blood spectators. He had not spent his public life in the study of books but of men and concrete problems like public works and the national domain. He was not at ease with the close analysis of history and positively uncomfortable in the heady world of political theory. The smooth flow of words Douglas always enjoyed on the speakers platform left him as soon as he picked up his pen. His style became turgid and ponderous, his distinctions pedantic, his logic forced and strained. His tortuous arguments carried the flavor less of reason than of sophistry. Douglas was as emphatic as ever, but an annoying habit of resorting to bold and unsubstantiated assertions at awkward moments suggested that he was not quite convinced himself of the value of what he was saying. His admirers pronounced the piece unanswerable, a favorite adjective of the day, but unreadable would have been a fairer verdict.

Douglas' major goal in writing the *Harper's* article was to persuade his countrymen that popular sovereignty was still a valid solution to the problem of slavery, in spite of the doubts raised by Abraham Lincoln on the one hand and the Supreme Court on the other. 1859 was not far along when Douglas began to sense just how rapidly events were changing as the country moved inexorably toward civil war. He was anxious lest in the rapidly shifting political climate of America popular sovereignty be dismissed as just another *ad hoc*, temporary expedient for handling the crises that now seemed to break one upon the other. He sought to dig-

---

appeared anxious to keep the details of his work on the *Harper's* article a secret even from close friends.

nify the ancestry of his doctrine by showing that it had roots going back to the American Revolution and beyond, and that it was the kind of long-standing principle that could not be destroyed by something so immediate and transitory as the Dred Scott decision or a little violence in Kansas or a few awkward questions posed by a prairie lawyer.

Douglas began by taking his reader on a long and not always coherent journey through American history back to colonial times. In his pitch for popular sovereignty he drew an analogy between the relationship of the territories to the national government and that of the American colonies to Great Britain.[155] He professed to see in the colonists' struggle against Westminster the same kind of drive toward local self-government that now prompted the citizens of a territory to demand the right to control the institution of slavery within their frontiers, "the right of every distinct political community—dependent Colonies, Territories, and Provinces, as well as sovereign States—to make their own local laws, form their own domestic institutions, and manage their own internal affairs in their own way."[156] It was not the first time that Douglas had cited such a parallel. In his speech before the Senate the previous February—the same speech in which he had reiterated his opposition to a congressional slave code—Douglas had flatly announced that "the doctrine that Congress is to regulate the rights of person and property, and the domestic concerns of a Territory, is the doctrine of the Tories of the Revolution. It is the doctrine of George III and Lord North, his minister."[157] Douglas returned to the same theme during the Ohio speeches of September, 1859.

The colonial analogy, like so much else that Douglas said, was attractive and plausible on the surface, but specious and unconvincing when examined in depth. The alleged similarity between Washington in 1859 and London in 1776 simply would not stand the test of close analysis. The American national government was only one part of a larger federal system characterized by decentralization

155 Jaffa and Johannsen, eds., *Name of People*, pp. 65–73.
156 Ibid., pp. 67–68.
157 *Cong. Globe*, 35th Cong., 2nd sess., p. 1246.

and the interworking of the various layers of local, state, and national authority. England, on the other hand, enjoyed one of the most highly centralized systems of government in the western world. Again, the American colonies had been founded largely as business ventures, and the English mercantilists of the late eighteenth century still continued to regard them mainly as objects of economic exploitation. The federal government, on the other hand, looked upon the idea of a territory primarily as a useful political device to bridge the somewhat awkward gap between the time of settlement and statehood.

In the case of the territories, only the fact of dependence and subservience to a central government created any similarity to the American colonies prior to the Revolution. The territorial stage of the state-making process was for the most part relatively brief. Ten or twenty years was the average length of time between organization and statehood, although some territories had to wait much longer. The territorial period was considered temporary and without much intrinsic value. In the British Empire of the eighteenth century, however, colonies were looked upon as permanent political forms. There was none of the saccharine talk of preparation for independence that characterized the remnants of that same empire almost two centuries later. Some of the American colonies had been in the same essential political condition for a century and a half before the Revolution, and by 1776 they possessed a certain degree of maturity—that underlying sense of community which John Locke felt to be a prerequisite for the survival of any system of government.[158] The territorial phase, on the other hand, following as it usually did by only a few years the settlement of a given region, was likely to be marked by political immaturity on the part of its people and their institutions.[159] Their dependence on the parent government was more the product of need than coercion. It was this unformed political condition that Republicans like William

[158] John Locke, "Second Treatise on Civil Government," in *John Locke on Politics and Education*, ed. Howard R. Penniman, Chapter XIX.

[159] Kansas, of course, being the outstanding example.

Seward had in mind when they called for a "higher law"[160] to govern the American territories and to keep them unsullied by slavery while they were still in their pristine state of political innocence. Lincoln wrote in the fall of 1858, "In our new free territories, a state of nature does exist. In them Congress lays the foundations of society."[161]

If Douglas was stretching the credulity of his readers with the colonial analogy, he insulted their intelligence when he took the next step and suggested that the whole American Revolution had been fought in defense of popular sovereignty in general and the right of each colony to control slavery in its own way in particular.[162] Douglas was writing history backward now and projecting his views formed in the overheated atmosphere of the late 1850's back upon the sharply different political climate of 1776. By holding that the American Revolution was fought mainly over the issue of popular sovereignty, he had not only fallen into the error of *pars pro toto*, but had overlooked the fact that if the colonists had really been concerned only with obtaining the same kind of limited self-government he was offering the territories, they would have accepted the British Peace Plan of 1778 with alacrity. Not content to stop here, Douglas went on to argue that the Articles of Confederation, by creating a loose, decentralized system of government for the states as well as for the territories, had embodied the spirit of popular sovereignty.[163] He failed to mention that the Articles had proved a dismal failure.

In the *Harper's* article Douglas was still trying to reconcile popular sovereignty with Taney's words in the Dred Scott decision, which declared that since Congress could not legislate on slavery in a territory, "if it is beyond the powers conferred on the Federal Government—it will be admitted, we presume, that it could not authorize a territorial government to exercise them. It could con-

160 Seward had expounded his "higher law" doctrine during a Senate speech against passage of the 1850 Compromise. *Cong. Globe*, 31st Cong., 1st sess., app., p. 265.

161 Nicolay and Hay, eds., *Works of Lincoln*, V, 88–89.

162 Jaffa and Johannsen, eds., *Name of People*, pp. 67–78.

163 Ibid., pp. 78–87.

fer no power on any local government, established by its authority, to violate the provisions of the Constitution."[164]

Douglas readily accepted Taney's contention that Congress could exercise no power over slavery in the territories.[165] He devoted much space to supporting the rather doubtful argument that the Constitution, in permitting Congress to "make all needful rules and regulations respecting the territory or other property belonging to the United States,"[166] used the word *territory* only in the sense of land and not in reference to an identifiable political community.[167] Therefore Douglas concluded that the kind of power granted Congress over a territory did not extend to interfering with "the domestic institutions and internal polity of the people."[168] Douglas had apparently disregarded Chief Justice Marshall's opinion of fifty years before that the power to acquire territory carries with it the power to govern.[169]

Yet Douglas was not many pages along in his *Harper's* article when he parted company with the Taney Court and its Southern adherents who presumed that if Congress could not exercise any powers touching slavery in the territories, it could not authorize a territorial government to exercise them either.[170] Rising to new heights of sophistry, the Little Giant drew an extremely pedantic distinction between the powers Congress could exercise but not confer, and those it could confer but not exercise.[171] In the first category were the classic powers of levying taxes, establishing a postal system, declaring war, and maintaining an army and a navy. In the second group were such tasks as setting up a system of courts, and, according to Douglas, conferring upon the individual territories the powers of self-government over slavery.

Douglas' choice of words was as bad as his distinction between

[164] 19 *Howard*, 451 (1857).

[165] Jaffa and Johannsen, eds., *Name of People*, p. 98.

[166] U.S. Constitution, Article IV, Section 3.

[167] Jaffa and Johannsen, eds., *Name of People*, pp. 89–92.

[168] Ibid., p. 91.

[169] *American Insurance Company* v. *Canter*, 1 *Peters*, 511 (1828).

[170] 19 *Howard*, 451 (1857).

[171] Jaffa and Johannsen, eds., *Name of People*, pp. 63ff.

the various kinds of powers was strained. *Confer* carried with it the flavor of a relationship between a superior and an inferior. It also strongly implied the notion of the partibility of sovereignty, which most political philosophers have rejected. The Little Giant would have done more to convey the idea of the federal government dealing with the territories as a *primus inter pares* had he used a word like *recognize*, in the sense that one nation recognizes the sovereignty of another nation without really giving up anything of its own to do so.

Douglas went even farther and, in an attempt to justify a larger amount of autonomy for the territories, suggested throughout the *Harper's* article that for practical purposes territories were virtually the same as states and should be accorded much the same control over local matters like the regulation of slavery. Here he committed an error opposite from that of the states' rights followers of Calhoun, who tended to endow the idea of a state with some almost mystical and wholly unwarranted degree of sovereignty. Abe Lincoln saw the flaw in Douglas' easy assumption and innocently asked in his speech at Columbus in September, "If there is no difference between them, why not make the Territories States at once?"[172] Lincoln in fact directed most of his 1859 Ohio campaign speeches at the *Harper's* article and with a few carefully chosen phrases toppled the unsteady platform that Douglas had labored to construct out of sophistries and half-truths. At Columbus he reduced Douglas' whole argument in defense of popular sovereignty in the face of the Dred Scott decision to the absurd proposition that "a thing may be lawfully driven from where it has a lawful right to be."[173] In the same speech Lincoln maintained that Douglas' professed moral neutrality and attitude of "care not" toward slavery implied that slavery was "one of those little unimportant, trivial matters which are of just about as much consequence as the question would be to me, whether my neighbor should raise horned cattle or plant tobacco."[174] Lincoln also argued that by leaving the

[172] Ibid., p. 246.
[173] Ibid., p. 258.
[174] Ibid., p. 244.

manifold ambiguities inherent in popular sovereignty to be defined by Congress, Douglas was implicitly sanctioning the kind of federal intervention in territorial affairs that his doctrine ostensibly was designed to prevent.

Yet a close study of Lincoln's Ohio speeches shows that his radicalism had crested during the Illinois campaign of the year before and that he was more moderate and circumspect in his later speeches. In Ohio he no longer issued a sweeping indictment against the entire Douglas doctrine. He was now willing to grant the validity of a "genuine"[175] popular sovereignty, and portrayed Douglas' version as a corrupt form, which reduced itself to the notion that "if one man chooses to make a slave of another man, neither that other man nor anybody else has a right to object."[176] Here we have a hint of the coming endorsement of a modified version of popular sovereignty by Republican candidates in the Northwest during the election of 1860 and their tacit acceptance of the doctrine in their territorial policy after coming to power in 1861. Lincoln, like Douglas, was suffering from the effects of some of his more reckless statements during the Illinois campaign and was anxious to re-establish his credentials as a responsible moderate. At Cincinnati he began by trying to correct the popular impression that his "House Divided" speech had carried any connotation of a declaration of war between sections. The use of any language implying such an idea, he said, was purely accidental: "I had no purpose of entering into the slave States to disturb the institution of slavery."[177] Thus, paradoxically, mid-1859 found the leading representatives of two parties that were ideologically farther apart than ever fighting over the rapidly diminishing supply of moderate political ground.

The impact of the *Harper's* article is easily exaggerated. *Harper's*, appealing primarily to the small educated elite in America, was very far from being a mass circulation magazine. Although Douglas sought to reach a national audience through its pages, the maga-

175 Ibid., p. 238.
176 Ibid.
177 Ibid., p. 274.

zine's readership was primarily Eastern. It had a small but influential following in the Northwest, but in the South its circulation was largely limited to a few cosmopolitan centers like New Orleans and Charleston. It is doubtful that many subscribers waded through the whole incredibly dull and ponderous twenty pages of fine print, and quite unlikely that many of those who did actually changed their political views as a result.

Perhaps the most immediate and visible effect of Douglas' *Harper's* piece was to set off a lively pamphlet war. Jeremiah Black, the Attorney-General and administration spokesman, later confessed to having written an anonymous rebuttal in the *Washington Constitution* for September 10, 1859. Reverdy Johnson[178] in turn wrote a pamphlet in support of Douglas' position, while George Ticknor Curtis responded for the Republicans with a reply entitled *The Just Supremacy of Congress Over the Territories.*[179] For the most part, the deluge of pamphlets produced no appreciable results. The literary offspring were fully as unreadable as their progenitor.

Northern reaction to the *Harper's* article was on balance mildly favorable. The *New York Times*' immediate response was to praise the article as "straightforward" and "masculine."[180] By the following June that newspaper had decided, upon reflection, that writing it had probably been a mistake. Douglas would have done better to stand still. The *Times* however recognized that "with him, to stand still, to rely upon what he has already done, is neither easy nor safe."[181]

The *New York Herald* was more perceptive and saw in the *Harper's* article the confirmation of Douglas' decision to base his politi-

[178] Douglas wrote Johnson on October 21, 1859, "I am extremely gratified that you are replying to Black," and indicated that he himself was also working on a reply. His serious illness in November put an end to this project. Also see Douglas to Johnson, November 4, 1859; Reverdy Johnson Papers (Library of Congress).

[179] George Ticknor Curtis, *The Just Supremacy of Congress Over the Territories.*

[180] *New York Times*, September 6, 1859.

[181] Ibid., June 25, 1860.

cal strength in 1860 firmly in the North. His view of Dred Scott would be bitter medicine to the South, and the *Herald* concluded that "if the Little Giant of the West is to ride his hobby in 1860, he must ride it exclusively on the north side of the Mason-Dixon line."[182] Out in Kansas, where people knew best how popular sovereignty worked in practice, public opinion remained dubious toward Douglas' exposition. The *Lawrence Republican* dismissed the whole article as an "electioneering ruse" and reminded its readers how locally elected probate courts in Kansas had been consistently overruled by the federal judiciary.[183]

In the South the *Harper's* article was received with much more hostility than the Freeport reply had been, in spite of Douglas' efforts to mollify that section by incorporating in his essay the Taney view of territories and the contention that slaves were first of all property.[184] Perhaps the best explanation was that *Harper's* dealt with abstractions and legalisms, Freeport with practical considerations, and in the 1850's it was preoccupation with abstractions that drove the South on its headlong plunge into self-destruction.

Douglas' essay went far toward alienating the support he had enjoyed among the moderate newspapers in the South. The once loyal *Richmond Enquirer* pronounced it "an incendiary document."[185] Even the faithful John Forsyth could make only an equivocal endorsement.[186] The editor of the *Dallas Herald* wrote to say that the reaction in Texas had been largely apathetic.[187]

Douglas' friends in the South were at best noncommittal. Senator Brown of Mississippi told Douglas in a brief note, "I think you have made the best of a bad cause."[188] Augustus Wright of

[182] *New York Herald*, September 9, 1859.

[183] *Lawrence Republican*, September 8, 1859.

[184] Jaffa and Johannsen, eds., *Name of People*, pp. 104–105.

[185] *Richmond Enquirer* quoted in *New York Herald*, September 9, 1859.

[186] John Forsyth to Douglas, New York City, September 1, 1859; Douglas MSS.

[187] Charles R. Pryor to Douglas, Dallas, Texas, September 21, 1859; ibid.

[188] Senator Albert G. Brown to Douglas, Hinds County, Miss., September 10, 1859; ibid.

Georgia provided scant comfort: "Whether correct or not, the argument is certainly a weighty and powerful one."[189]

Looked at from the perspective of more than a hundred years, the *Harper's* article contained little that was new and was largely a heavy restatement of Douglas' traditional moderate views. As such, it served to drive him farther from those Northern Radicals and Southern Ultras who had little use for any tenable middle ground. Yet it was Douglas' great misfortune that the manner in which he presented his platform served also to alienate moderate opinion, both North and South. Douglas in the pages of *Harper's* had unwittingly succumbed to the malady that was besetting most of the politicians of his day. He was making the practical, flexible device of popular sovereignty into a rigid and formal abstraction. He was turning a policy into a creed. He was becoming mired in legalisms. Douglas was, in short, becoming the victim of Douglasism. From the unlikely quarter of the South came the comment "Abstractions are not always sovereign over practical emergencies, and the statesman who, to inaugurate a favorable theory, is willing to annihilate rights and solid interests, is a political Jesuit, who, lost in the contemplation of his ends, is blind to the enormity of his means. It is to be seriously feared that this sort of Jesuitism is threatening to engulf Mr. Douglas' statesmanship."[190]

By September 22, Douglas was back in Washington.[191] Eight days later Mrs. Douglas gave birth to a daughter and came close to death in so doing. Her doctors gave her up for lost, and for six weeks her life hung in the balance. She eventually recovered, but the child, whom they named Ellen, was dead before the coming of winter.[192]

189 Augustus R. Wright to Douglas, Rome, Georgia, September 29, 1859; ibid.

190 Percy Roberts, "Popular Sovereignty," *De Bow's Review* 27, no. 6 (December 1859): 632.

191 Douglas' last speech in Ohio had been given at Wooster on September 16. By September 22, his correspondence shows, he was in Washington once more. Johannsen, ed., *Letters of Douglas*, pp. 467–468.

192 Ibid., pp. 473–479, 482–483.

Douglas himself had never fully recovered from the arduous campaign in Ohio. He returned to Washington noticeably unwell and in November fell desperately ill. He too now hovered near death and rumors of his passing flew through the capital.[193] It was long after Christmas before he could once more venture forth on his political sallies from the tall red-brick house on Minnesota Row.[194]

His body weakened by illness, his spirit despondent over the loss of his infant daughter and the failure of all his efforts throughout the long summer to produce any meaningful results,[195] the resourceful and resilient Douglas must have found himself desperately wishing for the first time in his life that events could somehow stand still until he could regain the strength to deal with them and get his bearings in a rapidly changing world that seemed intent on tearing itself apart.

But events would not stand still for Stephen Douglas or anyone else in 1859. In a pleasant little mountain town in northern Virginia, up where the Potomac joins the Shenandoah and the Baltimore and Ohio starts its long climb through the Blue Ridge, a madman was about to strike the first sparks that would light the flames of civil war. The town was Harpers Ferry and the man was John Brown. On the evening of October 16 the fanatical Brown and his small band of marauders moved on Harpers Ferry in what they hoped would be the start of a general slave uprising throughout the South.

It was really not much of a raid. Brown and his ragtag band

193 Ibid., pp. 480–481; *National Intelligencer*, November 16, 1859.

194 Johannsen, ed., *Letters of Douglas*, pp. 480–481. Douglas wrote George N. Sanders on December 15, 1859, "I hope to resume my seat in the Senate in the course of two or three weeks." In the same letter Douglas referred to a suggestion by his doctor that he go south to recover his health, but added that he had "given up the idea." A trip at that time to the South would have been politically unwise, since throughout 1859 Douglas was first of all interested in establishing his identity as a loyal and sound Northerner.

195 The *Harper's* article and the Ohio speeches of Douglas' in many ways had offset the favorable impression the Dorr Letter had made in the North. The Democratic defeat in Ohio marked the end of an unsuccessful summer for the Little Giant.

seized the strategic railroad bridge across the Potomac, followed by the important federal armory and arsenal that were the town's major industry. Then Brown's hastily drawn plans began to disintegrate. After the initial success that had come with surprise, no one had any clear idea what to do next. The much-vaunted Negro uprising remained only a dream in the mind of the man from Kansas. He could not go forward to other objectives, and he did not have enough men to hold those he had won. The local militia soon recaptured the railroad bridge leading to Washington, and thirty-six hours after it had been seized by Brown, the armory was retaken by a detachment of Marines that had been rushed to the scene by a frightened administration. They were led by Colonel Robert E. Lee of the U. S. Second Cavalry. His right-hand man that day was a young lieutenant named J. E. B. Stuart. Ten of the raiders were killed in the fighting; others managed to escape into the rugged countryside. John Brown himself was taken prisoner, tried and convicted on three counts of conspiring to insurrection, murder, and treason. On the morning of December 2, 1859, he was hanged by the state of Virginia.

Douglas' first public response was to denounce the Brown raid as a "monstrous and wicked outrage"[196] and to blame the whole thing on Republicans with their reckless talk of irrepressible conflicts.[197]

Southern reaction went deeper. The incident that Douglas was trying to make into a useful political weapon in the struggle between Republicans and Democrats, the South blew up out of all proportion and considered a threat to its very existence. The John Brown raid had in one dramatic incident focused the two great anxieties that were never far below the surface of the Southern mind and that were largely responsible for its sectional neurosis: fear of interference with its way of life by the North and fear of a slave uprising. In the overheated, unstable political atmosphere of 1859 a relatively small incident like the Brown plot was all that was needed to drive the South farther along its irrational course

[196] *Cong. Globe*, 36th Cong., 1st sess., p. 423.
[197] Ibid., p. 554.

marked by a preposterous demand for a slave code, secession, and civil war.[198]

The Little Giant also introduced in the Senate a resolution calling for a law that would make a federal crime of any conspiracy or combination in a state or territory to invade another state "with intent to steal or run away property of any kind, whether it be negroes or horses, or property of any description."[199]

If Douglas was trying to curry favor with the South or drive a wedge between it and Buchanan, who was predictably hostile to any plan that might increase the responsibilities of the presidency, he was wasting his time. Douglas' preoccupation with preventing one state from invading another seems irrelevant when considered a century later. That was not what John Brown's raid was all about, that was not what the South really feared, and that was not what ultimately brought on the Civil War. What is more, under Article I, section VIII, and Article IV, section IV, of the Constitution, as well as by virtue of the federal statutes of February 28, 1795, and March 3, 1807, the national government had ample powers to suppress an insurrection like Brown's. Even a timid President like Buchanan had not hesitated to use them.[200]

Douglas probably had another motive in proposing his legislation early in 1860. He was first of all a political realist, and he had no doubt come to feel that beneath all the apparent concern for states' rights voiced by the South lay the deeper determination of Southern leaders to resort to secession to protect Southern rights outside the Union rather than within it. Douglas in his resolution of January 23 intended to expose the Ultras' aim. Abe Lincoln

[198] An excellent account of the impact of the Brown raid on the South and upon Douglas' chances there for 1860 may be found in Nevins, *The Emergence of Lincoln*, II, 102–112. Also see the *National Intelligencer*, November 12 and 25, 1859, and Jefferson Davis' Senate speech of May 7, 1860; *Cong. Globe*, 36th Cong., 1st sess., pp. 1941–1942.

[199] *Cong. Globe*, 36th Cong., 1st sess., p. 553.

[200] Buchanan acted under these statutes in sending federal troops to Harpers Ferry in 1859, but refused to do so in December, 1860, at the start of the secession crisis. Richardson, ed., *Messages and Papers of the President*, V, 634.

was not the only politician who could pose a dilemma to his adversaries. Douglas would offer the South a measure for protecting the interests and security of the individual states at the price of increased vigilance and perhaps even intervention by the federal government. Strange language indeed coming from the onetime exponent of nonintervention!

The South played along with the game. If Douglas wanted to present his measure as a defense of states' rights, then it would reply in the same language. Jefferson Davis warned the Senate of the dangers of "investing the Executive with a discretion which would crush all the power of the States, and reduce the sovereignty of the States to merely a nominal thing.[201] The *Richmond Enquirer* responded by placing Douglas in the same company as John Brown and others who "undertake to coerce . . . the sovereign states of the South."[202] But the Southern leaders were primarily motivated by a desire to avoid giving the federal government any more authority or power to stop a state from seceding. Stephen Douglas knew their game, and during the campaign of 1860 he told an audience in Memphis that his John Brown legislation had been aimed primarily at forestalling the secessionist plans of the fire-eaters.[203]

For the Little Giant the year had finished far worse than it had begun. The warmth of the reception he had received at its start in both the North and the South had failed in the end to translate itself into a force sufficient to place Douglas once again in the position of an authentic national leader. 1859 was not many weeks old before the long night of sectionalism had begun to settle inexorably over the land.

Douglas' reaction was to move quietly and almost imperceptibly toward a more Northern sectional base, but he never ceased to try

[201] Dunbar Rowland, *Jefferson Davis, Constitutionalist*, IV, 146.
[202] *Richmond Enquirer*, August 31, 1860.
[203] *Memphis Daily Appeal*, October 25, 1860.

to pacify the South and perhaps even entice it into his political camp. In the end he failed. If the South's attitude toward Douglas was basically one of suspicion and mistrust at the beginning of the year, it was more akin to hostility at its close.

Douglas' failure in the South was ultimately one of timing and communication. Douglas preached nonintervention by Congress to the South at a time when the South had gone beyond faith in nonintervention to a demand for positive protection. He talked of states' rights at a time when Southern leaders were already thinking about secession. He offered the South compromise when it wanted capitulation and looked upon any concession on its part as tantamount to surrender. He offered it friendship when it demanded subservience. He sought its support for his bid for the presidency, yet the only presidential candidates the South had voted for in recent years had been either Doughfaces or military nonentities. Stephen Douglas was neither. He tried to remind the South of his long years of loyal service to its cause, yet it prejudged him along a narrow front and could remember only the apostasy of Lecompton and Freeport. Perhaps John Bell had been right after all when he told Douglas, "Those damned Southern Fools don't understand you. I do."[204]

In the end, Douglas' long courtship of the South proved a failure. In one of the last major public addresses of his life he acknowledged his mistake in "leaning too far to the Southern section of the Union."[205] Yet it is to Douglas' lasting credit that he never ceased to try to understand the South and, if possible, to pacify it and allay its dark suspicions. That was far more than most Northern politicians ever attempted.

In the North as well, Douglas during 1859 had shown himself to be somewhat out of joint with his times. His speeches were characteristically emphatic, but all his talk about national unity

[204] *Mobile Daily Register*, October 6, 1858.

[205] Douglas' speech of April 25, 1861, before the Illinois State Legislature at Springfield.

sounded strangely remote to a country marked by sectionalism,[206] and his professed moral neutrality seemed at odds with the growing tendency of pro- and antislavery forces alike to turn opinions into morals. By the end of 1859 the resourceful and adaptable Little Giant stood for the first time in danger of becoming a political anachronism.

Something else besides America had changed in 1859. On the surface Douglas was as ebullient and cocksure as ever, but perhaps down deep he was no longer quite so confident of his ability to meet any obstacle and to emerge victorious, either by surmounting it or going around it. His traditional response to any challenge had always been to launch himself into a frenzy of activity and arrive at a solution, often by hit-or-miss. Yet the kind of response he made in the Dorr Letter, in *Harper's*, and on the platform in Ohio, as well as the cure he proposed for future John Brown raids, succeeded only in sinking him deeper into the political mire of abstractionism and premature and exaggerated definitions of his policies. By 1860 people were beginning to find Douglas tiresome and repetitious, his programs irrelevant.[207] To a country in desperate need of action, Douglas seemed to offer only motion.

It was a sober Stephen Douglas, not yet fully recovered from his long illness,[208] who saw the old year out in Washington. His ambition was as strong as ever. He still wanted very much to be the next President. Yet now for the first time he must have begun to doubt his ability to seize the great prize toward which, in retrospect, his whole public career had been directed. Nor could Douglas comfort himself, as he had done in 1852 and 1856, with the knowledge that he was still young and would have many more

[206] See, for example, Douglas' speech in New York, December 31, 1858; *New York Times*, January 1, 1859.

[207] *New York Times*, June 25, August 10, September 29, 1860.

[208] Johannsen, ed., *Letters of Douglas*, pp. 480–481. Congress had convened on December 5, 1859, but it was not until January 12, 1860, that Douglas was well enough to participate in its deliberations. *Cong. Globe*, 36th Cong., 1st sess., p. 414.

chances to be President. Weakened by illness, dismayed at the sectionalism rampant in the land, Douglas at the end of 1859 probably felt for the first time in his life that time was running out for both himself and his country.

Douglas regarded the political wreckage that littered the course run that year by a nation driven on by the forces of sectional and idealistic folly, and he shook his head. He looked around him and saw a hostile President, a divided party, and a dividing nation.

And Charleston was less than four months away.

6. 1860: Victory, Defeat, Greatness

Charleston, South Carolina, was the most gracious city in America—when it wanted to be. With its narrow cobbled streets, its long and gently curving waterfront, and its stately townhouses, it shared with only a handful of other towns like Boston or Santa Fe or New Orleans a genuine old-world charm. It had for a century delighted a long series of captious European visitors and stuffy New Englanders like Henry Adams,[1] and it continues today to delight the scholar who comes to it in search of the Confederacy. The gates of its lovely homes swung open easily, and the warmth with which Charleston could greet a stranger was unique even in a part of America noted for its hospitality.

But the charm and graciousness of Charleston were deceptive. In the years just prior to the Civil War the warmth of its greeting was likely to prove ephemeral and its gaiety forced and superficial. Beneath the mask of confidence and ease lay the deeper and more powerful forces of concern and apprehension over a way of life that seemed out of step with the rest of the country. Like their homes, which were built to the curb and faced inward in the European

[1] Henry Adams, *The United States in 1800*, pp. 107ff.

fashion, the people of Charleston were withdrawing from the mainstream of American life. Their politics and culture took on the appearance of an almost frantic rearguard action by an aristocracy in a democratic age, a slavocracy in an age of freedom. And at the bottom lay fear and the guilt that bred it. Over half of the population of this city of 40,000 people was black, and Denmark Vesey and Nat Turner had not been entirely forgotten. John Brown had merely confirmed the long-standing suspicion that people in the North were actively working to foment a slave uprising.[2]

By 1850 this gracious and cosmopolitan city received all outsiders with suspicion and Yankees with distrust. When Charleston sensed a threat, real or implied, to its way of life, the warmth of its greeting could change in an instant to an icy stare and its famed hospitality to ill-disguised hostility. Those same gates that had once swung open so readily to admit a stranger were mounted in high stone walls and could slam shut with alarming suddenness.

In the early spring of 1860, Charleston closed its homes and its mind to the cause of Stephen Douglas.[3]

Charleston was a bad choice for a convention site. It was too small. It was too far away from the population centers of the East and the Northwest. It was too closely identified with the most implacable part of the most implacable section of the country at a time when America stood in urgent need of a workable compromise and a new infusion of the spirit of political moderation. It was also too hot. By late April the heavy coastal heat had already settled over Charleston and served only to aggravate tempers that were already too short.[4]

[2] Frederick L. Olmsted, *The Cotton Kingdom*, ed. Arthur M. Schlesinger, pp. 573–574; James F. Rhodes, *History of the United States from the Compromise of 1850*, II, 440.

[3] George F. Milton, *The Eve of Conflict: Stephen A. Douglas and the Needless War*, p. 426; Avery Craven, *The Growth of Southern Nationalism, 1848–1861*, p. 425; Allan Nevins, *The Emergence of Lincoln*, II, 203; Roy F. Nichols, *The Disruption of American Democracy*, p. 291; Rhodes, *History of the United States*, II, 440–441.

[4] Craven, *Southern Nationalism*, p. 324; Nichols, *Disruption of American Democracy*, pp. 291–292.

It had been chosen by a Democratic party anxious to appease the South and to give concrete expression to the notion, which had become popular in both the North and the South after the close of the Cincinnati convention, that the next Democratic President ought to come from below the Mason-Dixon Line. Some Democrats had seen in the selection of Charleston a means to proclaim to the world that their strained and uneasy party could maintain its unity on the extreme soil of South Carolina.[5] Others, particularly those close to the administration, had been attracted to Charleston because it promised to be the least favorable of all possible locations to the presidential aspirations of Stephen Douglas.[6] New York, Chicago, Baltimore, St. Louis, or even New Orleans would have been much better from the Douglas point of view.

The convention site was not the only cause for concern to thoughtful Democrats that spring. By 1860 the traditional give-and-take of American politics had almost totally surrendered to an inflexible insistence on rights, and concern for practical solutions to problems had been replaced by obsession with abstractions. The old national loyalties had given way to narrower and more emotional ties to one's section, the American gift for compromise to intransigence. Positions had begun to harden rapidly in the months before Charleston. In the closing weeks of 1859 the South put the rest of the Democratic party on formal notice that it would insist on a slave-code plank at Charleston.[7] Even the resilient and usually astute Douglas severely circumscribed his field of maneuver, announcing, "I do not intend to make peace with my enemies, nor to make a concession of one iota of principle, believing that I am right in the position I have taken, and that neither can the Union be preserved or [*sic*] the Democratic party maintained upon any other basis."[8]

[5] James G. Blaine, *Twenty Years of Congress*, II, 157.

[6] Reinhard H. Luthin, "The Democratic Split during Buchanan's Administration," *Pennsylvania History* 11 (January 1944): 30–31.

[7] Percy Lee Rainwater, *Mississippi: Storm Center of Secession, 1856–1861*, p. 109.

[8] Robert W. Johannsen, ed., *The Letters of Stephen A. Douglas*, p. 439; *Cong. Globe*, 36th Cong., 1st sess., p. 424.

The long overstrained democratic process was beginning to break down. Congress in early 1860 demonstrated neither the ability nor the inclination to deal effectively with the host of grave problems confronting the nation. Partisan and sectional considerations now dominated any discussion of public policy. Douglas complained to the Senate that every matter under discussion first became involved with the question of slavery and then turned into a hopeless stalemate.[9] It was February before the House could agree upon a Speaker, and the *New York Times* remarked sadly, "For the first time perhaps since the foundation of our Government our own future looks less clear and promising than that of old Europe."[10] In less than a year some of the members of this Thirty-sixth Congress would walk out of the Capitol not to return until a bloody civil war and the agonies of the Reconstruction that followed it had run their course. Even now, early in 1860, a few were planning to walk out of the Charleston convention.

An aura of impending tragedy hung over Charleston from the very beginning. More than a few delegates arrived actually wanting a rupture; most expected one. The *Charleston Mercury* greeted them with a front page editorial praising John C. Calhoun and quoting an 1849 speech in which he had admonished the South "to hold no political connection with any party at the North which is not prepared to enforce the guaranties of the Constitution in our favor and respect our rights."[11] Murat Halstead, who covered the convention for the *Cincinnati Commercial*, had confidently predicted a break before the proceedings were two days old.[12] The *New York Times* had been predicting one for a year.[13] Abraham Lincoln had foreseen a bolt as early as 1858, but he felt that in the end it would be the followers of Douglas and not the South that would walk out of the convention hall.[14]

Although never one to let the mere niceties of custom stand in

[9] *Cong. Globe*, 36th Cong., 1st sess., p. 1660.
[10] *New York Times*, January 2, 1860.
[11] *Charleston Mercury*, April 24, 1860.
[12] Murat Halstead, *Three against Lincoln*, p. 32.
[13] *New York Times*, April 5, 1859.
[14] Roy P. Basler, ed., *The Collected Works of Abraham Lincoln*, III, 345.

his way, Douglas did not dare to break the time-honored tradition that no major contender for a nomination ever went in person to his party's national convention. Perhaps it was not just good manners that kept the Little Giant away from Charleston that April. The effects of his long illness of the year before had not wholly passed. He came to the Senate less frequently now and usually spoke only briefly.[15] When he wrote to his friends, which was not often now, they must have been dismayed at how weak and scratchy the once firm and vigorous handwriting had become.[16] Although Douglas followed the convention closely from Washington, the tough, on-the-spot work of threats and cajolery, of bargaining and coercion, which is the essence of any close convention, was left to lieutenants like John Logan and John McClernand of Illinois, Senator George Pugh of Ohio, and George Sanders of New York, under the direction of the capable and loyal William A. Richardson of Illinois.

Theirs was not an easy task. There was a better-than-average chance that the Little Giant could be nominated, but that the Democratic party would unite behind him was doubtful and that he could in the end be elected President even more so. Still, there was some reason for optimism. Douglas went into the convention as the strongest single candidate and the only Democrat with truly national pretensions. He alone could hope to carry the Northwest and the East, together with the Border and a significant part of the South. Douglas was, in short, the only Democrat in 1860 who could unite his party and lead it to victory over the Republicans. The Douglas men could also take comfort from the fact that Sheahan's well-written campaign biography was just off the presses and selling briskly in all parts of the country.[17] Furthermore, the last two Democratic Presidents had come from the North, and the nomination had shown a tendency to move westward each time, from

[15] Douglas' only major speech in the first four months of 1860 was that of January 23 in favor of legislation to prevent future raids like that of John Brown. *Cong. Globe*, 36th Cong., 1st sess., pp. 552–559.

[16] See Douglas to Charles James Faulkner, Washington, March 24, 1860; Huntington Library, HM 23331.

[17] James W. Sheahan, *The Life of Stephen A. Douglas.*

Pierce of New Hampshire to Buchanan of Pennsylvania, and now, perhaps, to Douglas of Illinois.

Douglas' strategy at Charleston had been implicit in his cause ever since he had penned the Dorr Letter the year before. He would come to Charleston with a solid base of support from the entire Northwest and a majority of the Eastern states. He would seek to impress the South not by his talents as a compromiser or an appeaser, but with his power. He would take the nomination by force and on his terms.[18] He was not blind to the possibility of a bolt by disgruntled Southerners,[19] but he felt that it would be at the very worst of small proportions and quite probably short-lived.

Douglas did not expect the enthusiastic support of the South, but he did need at least the acceptance of a part of it. With 202 of 303 votes necessary for a nomination,[20] the slave states with 120 votes had a veto over any candidate. Even in the unlikely event that Douglas could carry the delegates from all other states, he would still require nineteen votes from the South to be nominated.

On the surface, Douglas' position in the South did not look bad. At the time the delegates began to gather in Charleston, only Alabama had formally resolved to leave the convention should the Douglas camp succeed in forcing the adoption of a popular sovereignty platform.[21] Mississippi would probably follow Alabama's lead,[22] but the course of the other Southern states was still unsettled at the time the convention began.

Douglas' attitude toward the South on the eve of the Charleston convention was a curious compound of realism and naiveté. He

18 See Douglas' letter to Peter Cagger of Albany, New York, February 19, 1860. Johannsen, ed., *Letters of Douglas*, p. 485.

19 Douglas had publicly recognized the possibility of a Southern bolt at Charleston in January, 1860. *Cong. Globe*, 36th Cong., 1st sess., p. 424.

20 There were 606 voting delegates to Charleston; each had half a vote.

21 On January 14, 1850, the Alabama State Democratic convention, meeting in Montgomery, had instructed its delegation to Charleston to seek a slave-code plank in the party platform and to bolt the convention if it did not get one; *Charleston Daily Courier*, January 16, 1860.

22 While Mississippi had not formally bound its delegates to any specific course, she was generally expected to follow suit. Rainwater, *Mississippi*, pp. 114–122.

knew that by the start of 1860 most Democratic state conventions in the South had passed resolutions opposing popular sovereignty and the Cincinnati platform. He realized that very few pro-Douglas Southerners would come to Charleston. Yet Douglas based his hopes on a belief that the majority of the people in the South still favored the maintenance of the Union. If they did not love the Illinois Senator, they might still disregard the rantings of the fire-eaters and vote for him as the one man above all others who could hold party and country together.

Douglas seriously overestimated the amount of pro-Union sentiment that still existed in the South in 1860, and as the convention drew near he appeared to be seized by a curious and quite unjustified optimism regarding his popularity below the Mason-Dixon Line. In February, 1860, he confided to Peter Cagger of New York, "There will be no serious difficulty in the South. The last few weeks has [*sic*] worked a perfect revolution in that section."[23]

Those moderate Southerners anxious to maintain the Union and to find at Charleston some practical compromise through which to preserve Democratic harmony were a rapidly diminishing group in an age when public opinion was moving swiftly and inexorably toward extreme positions. Even the reasonable Henry Wise had written to Fernando Wood, "We can't consent to leave a doubt about protection—to have a 'forked tongue' platform again," and predicted a breakup of the convention.[24] Those Southern moderates who did have a voice at Charleston generally failed to take Douglas' candidacy seriously and, like Andrew Johnson, felt that in the end he would either consent to run on almost any platform or throw his support to a Southerner in the interests of party unity.[25]

While Douglas represented his popular sovereignty platform as the one true means toward the preservation of party and national unity,[26] the majority of moderate men from the South at Charles-

[23] Johannsen, ed., *Letters of Douglas*, p. 485.

[24] Henry Wise to Fernando Wood, Richmond, Va., July 6, 1859; Brock Collection, Box 35.

[25] *Vicksburg Weekly Sun*, April 30, 1860.

[26] Johannsen, ed., *Letters of Douglas*, p. 440.

ton somehow hoped to achieve the same goals without having to nominate and support the Little Giant. Most came to the convention in a mildly anti-Douglas frame of mind and hoped in some vague way to thwart Douglas without having to break up the Democratic party to do it. In the end their nonchalance played into the hands of those Ultras who all along had been anticipating a rupture and actively working to bring it about.

It was the tragedy of the Charleston convention that the most vocal and best organized delegates were just those who had the least interest in its success. The Southern Ultras came to Charleston resolved to rule or ruin. They talked of Southern rights and defended slavery with the same moral fervor that the abolitionists used in condemning it.[27] In an age when slavery was a dying institution, they demanded a congressional slave code and perhaps even the reopening of the African slave trade.[28] If the rest of America would not meet their demands, they would leave the Democratic party and eventually the Union and ruin Stephen Douglas en route.

The Ultras at Charleston fell into two rather clearly defined groups. Some, like Jefferson Davis, came to the convention with the limited aim of seeing their views incorporated into the Democratic platform. They came with the intention of clearing up once and for all the ambiguities that had for so long been a part of official Democratic pronouncements on slavery. If they did not get their way on the platform, they were prepared to take more drastic steps. A second group, led by Yancey, probably intended to bolt the convention long before the temporary chairman first called for order in the stuffy and overcrowded atmosphere of the South Carolina Institute Hall. Unlike their somewhat more restrained fellow travelers, the future of slavery and the exact language of the new platform was of only secondary interest to Yancey and company. What really concerned them was which section should control the

[27] Halstead, *Three against Lincoln*, pp. 52–54; *Charleston Mercury*, April 24, 1860.

[28] The Majority (Ultra) Platform Report at Charleston contained a clause calling for the protection of slave property on the "high seas." Halstead, *Three against Lincoln*, p. 45. This was interpreted by some to mean the reopening of the African slave trade. For Benjamin Butler's comments see ibid., p. 50.

Douglas, 1857. He wore the beard for only a brief time.

James Buchanan, from an 1856 painting by William McMasters. *(Courtesy the James Buchanan Foundation for the Preservation of Wheatland. Lancaster, Pennsylvania)*

The Buchanan Cabinet. *Clockwise from top*: Howell Cobb, Treasury; Joseph Holt, Postmaster General; Isaac Toucey, Navy; Jeremiah Black, Attorney General; Jacob Thompson, Interior; John Floyd, War; Lewis Cass, State. The picture is undated, but it was obviously made after March 1859, when Holt replaced A. V. Brown as Postmaster General, and before the sweeping cabinet reorganization of December 1860.

(U.S. Signal Corps photo, Brady Collection, National Archives)

Constitution Hall, Lecompton, Kansas. Site of the Lecompton Constitutional Convention, fall 1857. (*Courtesy Kansas State Historical Society, Topeka*)

U.S. Senate Chamber as it looked during Douglas' last years. (*Library of Congress*)

Douglas' children: Robert Martin Douglas, *left*, and Stephen Douglas, Jr., about 1861.
(*Courtesy Illinois State Historical Library*)

Adele Cutts Douglas, the Senator's second wife, whom he married in 1856.
(*Brady-Handy Collection, Library of Congress*)

Douglas and Lincoln about the time of the 1858 joint debates.
(*Courtesy Chicago Historical Society*)

Kansas Territorial Governors: John W. Geary, *left*, and Robert J. Walker. *(Courtesy Kansas State Historical Society, Topeka)*

Chicago, 1858. Douglas began his campaign for re-election to the Senate in the rapidly growing city he called home. View of Randolph Street from the new dome of the Cook County Court House.
(Courtesy Chicago Historical Society)

Composite photograph of the Charleston Debate, September 18, 1858. (*Courtesy Illinois State Historical Library*)

Artist's impression of the Galesburg Debate, October 7, 1858. (*Courtesy Illinois State Historical Library*)

The White House about 1861. It proved to be an elusive goal for Douglas.
(Brady-Handy Collection, Library of Congress)

U.S. Capitol, looking west, about 1858.
(Brady-Handy Collection, Library of Congress)

Douglas supporters, North and South: *upper left*, August Belmont of New York, from a portrait by Eastman Johnson (*Courtesy Museum of the City of New York*); *upper right*, Fernando Wood of New York (*Courtesy Museum of the City of New York*); *lower left*, Horace Greeley of New York (*Brady-Handy Collection, Library of Congress*); *lower right*, John Forsyth of Alabama. (*Brady-Handy Collection, Library of Congress*)

upper left, Pierre Soulé of Louisiana; *upper right*, Henry Wise of Virginia (*U.S. Signal Corps photo, Brady Collection, National Archives*); *lower left*, Robert Toombs of Georgia; *lower right*, Alexander Stephens of Georgia (*Brady-Handy Collection, Library of Congress*)

South Carolina Institute Hall, Charleston. Site of the 1860 Democratic National Convention. *(Courtesy Carolina Art Association)*

The Charleston Hotel, where many of the convention delegates stayed. *(Courtesy Carolina Art Association)*

Hibernian Hall, *left*, headquarters of the Douglas men at Charleston, and the Mills House, a leading Charleston hotel used by convention delegates. *(Courtesy Carolina Art Association)*

Caleb Cushing of Massachusetts, Douglas' adversary at Charleston and permanent chairman of the 1860 Democratic National Convention. (*Brady-Handy Collection, Library of Congress*)

Robert Barnwell Rhett, Jr., editor of th *Charleston Mercury*. (*Courtesy University of South Carolina*

John Slidell of Louisiana, leader of the anti-Douglas administration forces at the convention. (*Brady-Handy Collection, Library of Congress*)

William Richardson of Illinois, Doug chief lieutenant at Charleston. (*Courtesy Illinois St Historical Libra*

Presidential contenders, 1860: Abraham Lincoln (*Courtesy Illinois State Historical Library*); Stephen Douglas (*U.S. Signal Corps photo, Brady Collection, National Archives*); *lower left*, John Bell (*Brady Collection, Library of Congress*); *lower right*, John Breckinridge. (*Brady-Handy Collection, Library of Congress*)

Front Street Theatre, Baltimore, where Douglas finally received the presidential nomination in June 1860.
(From collections of the Maryland Historical Society)

The St. Charles Hotel, New Orleans. Douglas' favorite stopping place on trips south.
(Courtesy Tulane University Library)

Lincoln's Inauguration, March 4, 1861. Douglas is supposed to have held Lincoln's hat. *(Courtesy Chicago Historical Society)*

Stephen Douglas in 1860.
(*Courtesy Illinois State Historical Library*)

Herschel V. Johnson of Georgia, vice-presidential candidate on the Douglas ticket, 1860.
(*Courtesy Chicago Historical Society*)

The Tremont House, Chicago, where Douglas died June 3, 1861.
(Courtesy Chicago Historical Society)

Douglas' tomb and monument, south side of Chicago.
(Courtesy Chicago Historical Society)

William Lowndes Yancey of Alabama, architect of the strategy of disruption at the 1860 Democratic Convention.

government of the United States. 1860 was the year for a new national census, and by early April there was speculation that the slave states would lose at least seven members in the House.[29] Southern leaders saw the balance of sectional power shifting inexorably against them. Unless the rest of America would acquiesce in the continued dominance of what by 1860 was clearly a minority section, they were prepared to leave the Democratic party and the Union. They had nothing positive to offer at Charleston. They were united in their determination to block Douglas, but had no alterna-

[29] *New York Times*, April 5, 1860.

tive candidate of their own, unless it was Lincoln or Seward, whose election would provide them with a convenient excuse for secession. Their convention tactics were wholly negative: when things were not going well for them, the Ultras were ready with a filibuster and when that failed, they were prepared to bolt.[30]

Stephen Douglas probably understood the Ultras better than any other Northern Democrat. He never deceived himself about their goals or the reckless tactics they would use to reach them. As early as 1857 he believed that at least a few among them were motivated primarily by a desire to dissolve the Union.[31] Unlike Lincoln and most other Northern politicians, Douglas never dismissed the threats and belligerence of Yancey and company as bluff. His error lay rather in consistently underestimating the number of Southerners who eventually would consent to join them on their reckless course, and in his naive exaggeration of the countervailing force of moderate Southern opinion. Douglas persisted in trying to isolate the fire-eaters from what he felt was the much larger mass of reasonable and prudent men in the South. Not until secession was an accomplished fact did the Little Giant ever condemn the South by name, preferring to aim his verbal barbs only at Yancey and his lieutenants.[32] Douglas seemed almost to want to push his Southern antagonists into some reckless and ill-conceived act so that their folly would stand exposed before the wiser and more cautious men who, he thought, were still in the majority in the South.[33] This is the only possible explanation for the apparent nonchalance with which the Douglas men accepted the possibility of a bolt at Charleston by discontented Southerners and for their consistent tendency to underestimate both its size and its permanence.

Douglas was partially correct in his appraisal of the potential strength of the Southern radicals at Charleston. Although they were perhaps the best organized and most determined faction at the con-

[30] Halstead, *Three against Lincoln*, p. 62.

[31] George Fort Milton, "Douglas' Place in American History," *Journal of the Illinois State Historical Society* 26, no. 4 (January 1934): 342.

[32] *Cong. Globe*, 36th Cong., 1st sess., app., pp. 313–314.

[33] Ibid., 35th Cong., 2nd sess., p. 1255.

vention, they could not alone have thwarted the Little Giant and broken the Democratic party beyond repair. The Ultras needed outside help to effect their reckless scheme. James Buchanan gave it gladly.

Buchanan probably wished in his heart to seek a second term,[34] but he must have recognized that his chances for renomination were slim and those for re-election practically nonexistent. In March of 1860 a new wave of scandals involving the executive branch shook the Capital.[35] It was now general knowledge throughout the country that the effective power of the presidency had long since passed by default into the hands of the Directory. Only three days before the start of the Charleston convention, the press published a letter from Buchanan to Governor Robert Walker, written in July, 1857, in which the President had endorsed the Douglas version of popular sovereignty for Kansas. This document gave the lie to later claims that White House policy on Lecompton was merely the logical sequel to the true Cincinnati platform.[36]

But if James Buchanan in 1860 could not himself gain a second term, he could at least prevent Stephen Douglas from getting the Democratic nomination. He sent his political henchmen south in hordes for the one purpose of cutting down the Little Giant. John Slidell was the chief administration spokesman at Charleston, but he had plenty of help from such inveterate Douglas-haters as Jesse Bright of Indiana and William Bigler of Pennsylvania. The editor of the *Cleveland Plain Dealer*, who covered the convention, counted over five hundred Buchananites who had come to Charleston either as delegates or lobbyists with the overriding aim to wreck Stephen Douglas.[37]

Like the Ultras, the Buchananites played an essentially negative role in the 1860 Democratic convention. They had no candidate of their own, although the President probably continued to the very

34 Richard Stenberg, "An Unnoted Factor in the Buchanan-Douglas Feud," *Journal of the Illinois State Historical Society* 25 (January 1933): 273–274.

35 *New York Times*, March 27, 1860.

36 Ibid., April 19, 1860.

37 George Fort Milton, "Stephen A. Douglas' Efforts for Peace," *Journal of Southern History* 1, no. 3 (August 1935): 270.

end to hope that an unbreakable deadlock might just result in his being renominated as the only way out of the impasse. Buchanan had urged the selection of Charleston as the convention site largely because it would be hostile ground for the Douglas cause.[38] His lieutenants, liberally provided with the political currency of patronage, roamed the lobbies of Institute Hall and the delegates' suites at the Planters Hotel seeking to detach some of the Douglas men from several key delegations.[39]

In the end the administration forces achieved a measure of success in their cabal against Douglas. James Buchanan may have been repudiated by much of America and ridiculed by the rest, but he was still the President of the United States and the nominal head of his party. He controlled the extensive patronage of the executive branch, and his views were not to be taken lightly. His efforts succeeded in damaging the Douglas cause beyond repair in Oregon and California, and cut into his power in a number of other states, including New Jersey, Pennsylvania, New York, Massachusetts, and Delaware. Administration influence showed surprising strength in the Border states, and the Buchananites even managed to sway a few members of the Douglas camp from the Northwest. In the end it was the administration that made possible the cynical and dangerous design of the Southern Ultras at Charleston.[40] Alexander Stephens, writing ten years later, concluded that it was Buchanan who broke the Democratic party at Charleston and did more than anyone else to cause the election of Lincoln.[41]

To win at Charleston Douglas would need almost the solid backing of the free states, but it was in just those states that Buchanan

38 Philip G. Auchampaugh, "The Buchanan-Douglas Feud," *Journal of the Illinois State Historical Society* 25, nos. 1–2 (April–July 1932): 33.

39 Halstead, *Three against Lincoln*, p. 79.

40 Perhaps the Buchananite intrigues got out of hand. Slidell and his cohorts came to Charleston with the primary aim of stopping Douglas. Too late they realized they had been playing into the hands of those Ultras who wanted to break up the convention. The administration men made an unsuccessful last-minute attempt to forestall the Southern bolt. Richard Taylor, *Destruction and Reconstruction*, p. 12; Halstead, *Three against Lincoln*, p. 57.

41 Alexander H. Stephens, *A Constitutional View of the Late War between the States*, II, 259.

ultimately did him the most harm. The Northwest predictably provided Douglas with his great base of support at Charleston, as it had done throughout his long political career. Led by William Richardson of Illinois and Henry Payne of Ohio, the seven states of the Great Lakes area formed an almost solid phalanx behind the Little Giant. By the end of February, state conventions in Illinois, Iowa, Wisconsin, Ohio, and Indiana had met and instructed their delegates in favor of Stephen Douglas. Michigan was considered safe, and the new state of Minnesota was anxious to express its gratitude for the efforts the Illinois Senator had put forth on behalf of its admission to statehood in his former role as chairman of the Senate Committee on Territories.[42] An administration attempt at Charleston to seat a rival Danite delegation from Illinois would prove abortive.[43] While the Northwest entered the convention supporting the Little Giant, its allegiance was conditional: any attempt by Douglas to appease the South by compromising the principles set forth in the Dorr Letter could well produce a major defection on the part of the Northwesterners.[44]

The New England and Middle Atlantic States were somewhat less certain. Most of New England appeared safe, although part of the Massachusetts delegation would probably take its cue from Caleb Cushing and adopt an anti-Douglas position from the outset of the convention. There was also some uncertainty in Maine. Only a month before the convention began, J. G. Dickerson of Belfast had written Jefferson Davis that Douglas' strength there was greatly exaggerated.[45] The large Pennsylvania delegation had yielded to administration pressure, and its loyalties were divided among a

[42] *Cong. Globe*, 35th Cong., 1st sess., pp. 1265, 1300, 1446. Minnesota joined the Union May 11, 1858.

[43] Halstead, *Three against Lincoln*, pp. 20–22, 36–37.

[44] H. B. Payne to Douglas, Cleveland, Ohio, March 17, 1860; Douglas MSS.

[45] Dunbar Rowland, ed., *Jefferson Davis, Constitutionalist*, IV, 210. In the vote on the crucial platform question, only in the Massachusetts delegation did any New Englander oppose the Douglas position. In the balloting for nominees, however, Maine's 8 votes were divided 5 for Douglas, 3 for James Guthrie; Connecticut's 6 votes went 3½ for Douglas, 2½ for Isaac Toucey; Massachusetts divided its 13 votes 5½ for Douglas, 6 for R. M. T. Hunter, and 1½ for

Pro-Douglas members of the key New York delegation: Peter Cagger, Dean Richmond, and George Sanders.

number of candidates. New Jersey entered the convention backing James Guthrie. New York held the key to Douglas' chances in the North, but it was far from being firmly in his column. One delegation, led by Dean Richmond, including August Belmont and Peter Cagger, was squarely behind the Little Giant, but the once loyal Fernando Wood was now heading a rival delegation that sought admission as the legitimate voice for the Empire State.[46]

California and Oregon voted consistently at Charleston with the slave states on procedural matters and in the balloting for candidates threw their support to Dickinson and Lane.[47] One explanation might be that the Far West had not forgotten that in 1858 Douglas had been lukewarm to the admission of Oregon as a state and preferred instead to devote his efforts to bringing another northwestern state, Minnesota, into the Union.[48] Perhaps equally important, isolated as it was from the other states by a thousand miles of thinly settled lands still in the territorial phase of political development, the Pacific Coast was not really an extension of the typical American frontier and shared few of the traditional values and interests that had always attracted the West to the cause of Stephen Douglas. Furthermore, the Far West, with its large military establishment and its high proportion of civil servants to a rather small white population was, perhaps more than any other part of the country, peculiarly responsive to administration pressure.

If Douglas hoped to do well among the Border states, he was doomed to disappointment. Although he had always been popular along the Mason-Dixon Line and would draw a large popular vote there in the election of 1860, the Border state delegates did as much as anyone to destroy Stephen Douglas at Charleston. It was partly a matter of several states clinging stubbornly to the cause of favor-

---

Jefferson Davis. The other 3 New England States—New Hampshire, Vermont, and Rhode Island—cast their total of 14 votes solidly for Douglas. Halstead, *Three against Lincoln*, pp. 70 and 99.

46 Douglas to Fernando Wood, February 16, 1860 (n.p., but almost certainly Washington, D.C.); Brock Collection, Box 280.

47 Halstead, *Three against Lincoln*, p. 99.

48 *Cong. Globe*, 35th Cong., 1st sess., p. 1324.

ite sons: Kentucky to James Guthrie, Tennessee to Andrew Johnson, and Virginia to R. M. T. Hunter. In all the Border states, Douglas could count on only six or seven votes. Missouri might in the end split its allegiance between Douglas and Guthrie, and the strenuous efforts of the loyal Reverdy Johnson in Maryland might detach one or two delegates from Hunter, but beyond that there was nothing. While the lower South was laying plans to bolt over the platform, more than a few of the Border delegates were preparing to leave the convention should it become apparent that Douglas would be nominated.[49] It was the Border states who in the closing hours of the convention joined forces with the New York delegation to require that any candidate must receive two thirds of all 303 votes in the convention to be nominated, and thereby in one stroke prevented the nomination of Stephen Douglas at Charleston.[50]

The best explanation of Border state hostility toward Douglas would seem to be that he had traditionally drawn most of his support in that area from the old Whig elements who were either not represented at all at Charleston or stood very low in party circles. The party machinery in the Border states remained very much in the hands of administration men or slavery sympathizers.

Douglas won more than his share of political battles down in the Palmetto State that steamy April of 1860, but in the end he lost the war. Whenever an issue reached the convention floor, the Douglas managers could, barring an occasional blunder, count on carrying a majority of the delegates—all that was needed for most of the business of the convention. In committee, the story was different. There, membership was on the basis of one man per state, and Douglas could never rely on more than sixteen of the thirty-three delegations represented.[51]

[49] Halstead, *Three against Lincoln*, p. 39.

[50] Ibid., pp. 95–98.

[51] Blaine, *Twenty Years of Congress*, I, 160; Nichols, *Disruption of American Democracy*, pp. 294–295.

Douglas benefited greatly from the position of his old friend and fellow Vermonter, David Smalley, as chairman of the Democratic Executive Committee.[52] His bid for the nomination got off to a good start on the opening day of the convention when Thompson B. Flournoy of Arkansas, one of the few Southerners sympathetic to Douglas, was chosen temporary chairman. But the initial optimism of Douglas' followers soon turned to apprehension when Caleb Cushing of Massachusetts, generally acknowledged to be pro-Southern in his political loyalties and openly hostile to popular sovereignty, was made permanent chairman. It was the first major setback of the convention, but it probably upset the Little Giant less than it did his supporters in Institute Hall. When the news reached Douglas' Washington home, his mind no doubt went back to that day more than ten years before when Cushing had written as a friend to ask Douglas to recommend someone "perfectly trustworthy to be employed as land agent and attorney" to supervise some of the Bay State politician's extensive holdings in Rock Island County, Illinois.[53]

Richardson and company won a major victory when the convention adopted a version of the unit rule peculiarly well suited to the ambitions of the Little Giant. Instructed delegations were to vote on the convention floor as a unit, but individual members of uninstructed delegations were left free to vote as they pleased.[54] Since most of the instructed delegations were pledged to Douglas, the new rule was a major victory for the Little Giant and left between thirty and forty Douglas men in uninstructed delegations free to support their candidate.[55] The South was angry and professed to see

[52] It was Smalley who took the initial steps in barring from the convention the anti-Douglas delegations from Illinois and New York. Halstead, *Three against Lincoln*, pp. 11, 31.

[53] Caleb Cushing to Douglas, December 10, 1849; Caleb Cushing Papers (Library of Congress), Box 337.

[54] Halstead, *Three against Lincoln*, pp. 25–31.

[55] The unit rule effectively silenced anti-Douglas minority factions in the important New York and Indiana delegations while freeing pro-Douglas support in Pennsylvania and several Southern states, including Alabama and North Carolina.

in the unprecedented ruling confirmation of Douglas' reputation as a practitioner of political sleight of hand. What really upset it was the realization that the Illinois men and their followers could now block any effort to foist a slave-code plank upon the convention.

On April 25 the convention, now in its third day, decided in favor of the Douglas camp on two important contested delegations. The Danites from Illinois and the Fernando Wood group from New York were turned away in favor of delegations headed by William Richardson and Dean Richmond.[56] The outcome of the Illinois contest had never been in doubt, but Wood had represented a very real threat in what was perhaps the key state in the convention. Illinois and New York together accounted for a block of forty-six votes, or almost one sixth of the total at Charleston. It was a great victory for the Little Giant and a major setback for James Buchanan.

It was the platform that held the center ring in the political circus that was the Charleston convention. Major segments of the Democratic party came to Charleston in an uncompromising frame of mind. Douglas had announced almost a year before in the Dorr Letter the kind of platform he would consent to run on. Alabama, on the other hand, was pledged in advance to leave the convention should efforts to procure a slave-code plank fail. Not long after the convention had begun, Mississippi, Louisiana, Arkansas, Texas, Florida, and South Carolina determined in a midnight conference to adopt a similar strategy. The seven slave states went a step farther and decided that the usual order of procedure must be reversed and demanded that the convention write a platform before choosing a candidate.[57] Some of the Southerners were no doubt motivated by a sincere desire to have their views on slavery in the territories become part of the official Democratic creed, but the more cynical of the slave-state delegates joined the Buchananites in seeing the plat-

[56] Halstead, *Three against Lincoln*, pp. 38–39.

[57] The final decision by the South to insist on writing a slave-code platform before choosing a candidate was apparently reached at a conference on the evening of April 23. *New Orleans Picayune*, April 28, 1860. The following day, April 24, the convention agreed to the Southern demand by an overwhelming vote. Halstead, *Three against Lincoln*, p. 36.

form as a convenient means to break Stephen Douglas. Their aim was obvious: force through a platform on which the Little Giant could not stand, and then nominate in his place a candidate more amenable to the South.

It is more difficult to determine why the Douglas forces assented readily, almost eagerly, to the demand to write the platform first. Perhaps the decision was only the logical outcome of the determination their leader had expressed in the Dorr Letter not to be a candidate except on the right platform. Perhaps victory in the crucial New York delegation fight had prompted the Northwesterners to feel they could dictate the terms of the platform once it left committee and reached the floor. Perhaps they faced with equanimity, even anticipation, the prospect of a subsequent bolt by a few discontented Southerners. That would, after all, leave fewer anti-Douglas men in Institute Hall to oppose the Little Giant when the actual balloting for a candidate got under way. In the last analysis, Richardson and his team reasoned that even if the candidate were chosen before the platform and Douglas emerged victorious, he could still not consent to run on just any collection of planks. Should the coalition between the Ultras and the administration force through its version of the platform, Douglas would either have to withdraw or appear weak and irresolute in the eyes of the vital Northern voters. If he withdrew, the onus for wrecking the convention would then rest squarely upon the Little Giant. The Southern insistence upon writing the platform early in the convention seems in retrospect to have been curiously myopic and to have played into the hands of the man it was meant to thwart.

The central task of reasonable men at Charleston was to come forward with a platform that would reconcile the demands of the popular sovereignty school on the one hand and the congressional slave-code advocates on the other. There was no shortage of suggestions. William Bigler of Pennsylvania and John Cochrane of New York proposed that the Cincinnati platform be adopted along with what amounted to an endorsement of the Southern interpretation of the Dred Scott decision plus a vague commitment to consider a congressional slave code if it proved necessary to safeguard slavery in the territories.[58] Another proposal called for giving slave property all "legal" protection in the territories, leaving the problem of further definition to the courts.[59] Perhaps the most promising way out of the impasse was the so-called Tennessee Compromise, proposed by the Border states, but never formally voted on in the convention. It remained silent on the subject of a congressional slave code, but explicitly denied the right of intervention by Congress or the territorial legislatures to impair slavery in the territories.[60] The Tennessee proposal amounted to offering the South a favorable interpretation of Dred Scott and a denial of the Freeport Doctrine, if in turn it would drop its demand for a slave code.

In the end none of these possible compromises got very far. They all smacked too much of the kind of ambiguity and reliance upon the Supreme Court that had for so long held the Democratic party together and that too many delegates came to Charleston determined to do away with once and for all.

The platform committee labored for four days and in the end reported two distinct sets of resolutions. Because the slave states and their sympathizers dominated this committee, as they did all others, the Majority Report predictably denied the power of either Congress or the territorial legislatures to abolish slavery or prohibit the introduction of slaves or in any way impair the right of property in slaves. It further stated that it was the duty of the federal government "to protect, when necessary, the rights of persons and property on the high seas, in the Territories, or wherever else its constitutional authority extended,"[61] and thus opened the door to a congressional slave code and perhaps even the revival of the African slave trade. Other articles called for the construction of a Pacific railroad, the acquisition of Cuba, and an end to legislation by some states designed to frustrate the enforcement of the Fugitive Slave Law.[62]

58 Halstead, *Three against Lincoln*, pp. 48, 57. W. W. Avery of North Carolina made a similar proposal; ibid., pp. 59–60.

59 *New York Times*, April 27, 1860.

60 Halstead, *Three against Lincoln*, p. 93.

61 Ibid., p. 45.

62 Ibid., pp. 45–46.

The Minority Report, offered by the Douglas men and their supporters, concurred with the majority on the last three points.[63] But it was silent on the African slave trade, and on the crucial question of slavery in the territories it simply reaffirmed the Cincinnati platform and added that "inasmuch as differences of opinion exist in the Democratic party as to the nature and extent of the powers of a Territorial Legislature, and as to the powers and duties of Congress, under the Constitution of the United States, over the institution of slavery within the Territories . . . the Democratic party will abide by the decisions of the Supreme Court of the United States on the questions of Constitutional law."[64]

These two clauses represented the most significant and least understood change in the whole strategy of the Douglas men at Charleston. It was not, as some observers concluded, merely an unexceptionable and meaningless pledge to abide by the law and hence, in the *New York Times* phrase, a plank that "therefore amounts to just nothing at all."[65] Nor was it, as some otherwise astute scholars have argued, merely a case of the Cincinnati platform plus Dred Scott.[66] Finally, it did not, as is often maintained, represent a major retreat by Douglas from the cherished doctrine of popular sovereignty.[67]

The Douglas men at Charleston appear in fact to have been trying to present one political face to the South and another to the North in a desperate attempt to hold the party together and strengthen their candidate's claim to being a truly national figure.

[63] The Minority (Douglas) Platform was slightly less strident than the Majority Report on its Cuba Plank. It called for the acquisition of Cuba "on such terms as shall be honorable to ourselves and just to Spain." The Majority position merely recommended acquisition "at the earliest practicable period." The Minority position was in keeping with Douglas' lukewarm attitude toward annexation of Cuba.

[64] Halstead, *Three against Lincoln*, pp. 60–61. This is the language of the amended Minority Report as presented to the convention April 28.

[65] *New York Times*, May 1, 1860.

[66] Robert W. Johannsen, "Stephen A. Douglas and the South," *Journal of Southern History* 33, no. 1 (February 1967): 39.

[67] Blaine, *Twenty Years of Congress*, I, 160–161; Nichols, *Disruption of American Democracy*, p. 302.

They could not offer the South a slave code such as the Majority Report demanded or even a favorable interpretation of the Dred Scott decision as envisioned by the Tennessee Compromise. But in the Minority Report Douglas seemed to be telling the South that if in the future the Supreme Court ruled in its favor and explicitly denied the right of territorial legislatures to curb the institution of slavery, he would support such a decision. Douglas' focus was on some future decision, the Ultras' on a favorable interpretation of a past decision.[68] To the North, on the other hand, Douglas seemed to be saying that the Freeport Doctrine was still intact since the Court had not specifically ruled against the power of the territorial legislatures over slavery. Even if the Court did one day so rule, it would not necessarily mean the end of popular sovereignty. For some time now Douglas had been less concerned with the role of the territorial legislature in effecting local control over slavery. He talked more of municipal police and court action. An unfriendly decision on the powers of the territorial legislature alone might not wholly collapse his doctrinal house of cards.[69]

The Douglas forces at Charleston had offered not so much a compromise as a truce. By appearing to draw closer to the administration interpretation of Dred Scott, Douglas hoped to detach those Democrats who were sympathetic to slavery, but who held that there was no need for a slave code, from those Southern Ultras who now demanded one. Furthermore, although Douglas could not agree at present with the views of most Southerners at Charleston, he could do the next best thing and agree to agree with them under some set of future circumstances.

The Minority Report inclined on balance to the South. If it did not meet all Southern demands, it was nevertheless more favorable to the South than any platform ever adopted by the Democratic party. But the Southerners remained unenthusiastic. They were tired of the kind of ambiguity and delay that had held the Union together for a decade. They wanted clarification and definition, followed by victory for their peculiar views. Some Southerners like

[68] *Cong. Globe*, 36th Cong., 1st sess., p. 421 and app., p. 311.

[69] George Murray McConnel, *Presidential Campaigns*, p. 130.

Jefferson Davis argued that there was at that moment in the federal judiciary no case pending which might decide the fate of Douglas' Freeport Doctrine and that it might be years before the Supreme Court could hand down any such ruling, if indeed it ever did so at all.[70] Privately, Southerners must have had deep reservations about committing the fate of their section to the hands of a Court whose membership in future years might well prove hostile. Yancey and his followers, on their part, were wary of any proposal that might carry with it the promise of a reasonable reconciliation between the sections and forestall their plans for secession.[71]

The voting on the various platform proposals began on the morning of April 30. The first motion came from Benjamin Butler of Massachusetts, later of silver spoons fame, who proposed the re-adoption of the 1856 platform unchanged. No one was particularly surprised when the administration men joined with much of the lower South and the Northwest to reject the Butler proposal 198 to 105.[72]

Now came the moment everyone had been waiting for. Chairman Cushing rose from his seat and called for a vote on the Minority Report. The Douglas forces' hopes began to rise as the roll call of states progressed from Alabama to Maryland and finally Wisconsin. They had, of course, been confident of their superb organization and carefully laid plans, but even the most optimistic among them was not prepared for the triumph that came with such suddenness. Within moments after the last delegation had cast its vote, the clerk rose to announce that the Minority Report had carried by 165 to 138.[73]

[70] Rowland, *Jefferson Davis*, IV, 291.

[71] *Richmond Enquirer*, September 4, 1860; *Memphis Daily Appeal*, July 19, 1860; Halstead, *Three against Lincoln*, pp. 8, 53, 80, 86; Nevins, *The Emergence of Lincoln*, II, 205, 221, 224, 227; Milton, *Eve of Conflict*, pp. 371, 441, 478–479; Nichols, *Disruption of American Democracy*, pp. 359, 368.

[72] Halstead, *Three against Lincoln*, pp. 60–61, 68–69. The South voted against the Butler proposal because it carried no provision for a slave code. The Northwesterners opposed it because it did not contain the Supreme Court plank that they erroneously felt would appease the South.

[73] Ibid., p. 70.

It was the highwater mark of Douglas' effort at Charleston. For a moment it appeared that he could in good conscience now go on to seek the Democratic nomination on a platform which did not conflict with the conditions set forth in the Dorr Letter, yet which, through the addition of the Supreme Court clause, strengthened his credentials as a reasonable man.

But the euphoria that seized the Douglas headquarters over at Hibernian Hall on Broad Street proved short-lived. The Buchananites were not going to let Douglas off with so quick and easy a victory. Butler again rose and this time proposed that a separate vote be taken on each of the two territorial planks contained in the Minority Report. His fellow Bay Stater, Cushing, readily agreed.[74] So did the Douglas men. Perhaps in the wake of the confidence and joy generated by their recent victory they felt they could win any vote handily and were anxious for a show of strength. Perhaps they still wanted to push the Southerners into a bolt. Most likely, they simply could not think of a reasonable excuse for rejecting Butler's proposal and failed to grasp the sinister nature of the trap that was being set for them. Douglas' enemies were trying to isolate the Supreme Court plank, which Southerners, upon reflection, were coming to regard with growing suspicion. If it were to be rejected by the convention, it would constitute a humiliating defeat for Douglas and would cast serious doubts on his claims to be a friend of the South and the only Democrat who could reconcile opposing sections and produce some semblance of harmony. His pretensions to being the candidate of national unity would receive a serious setback.

Once more the clerk called the roll. The first plank, which essentially reaffirmed the Cincinnati platform, carried resoundingly 237½ to 65,[75] albeit to the accompaniment of loud protests and threats by the South. Now Andrew Ewing of Tennessee called for a vote on the second plank, which would leave the job of clarifying the powers of Congress and the territorial legislatures over slavery to the Supreme Court. The Northerners at first voted for the propo-

[74] Ibid., pp. 70–71.
[75] Ibid., p. 71.

Interior of Douglas headquarters at Charleston.

Delegates to Charleston.

sition, but when they saw that the South was opposing what they had looked upon as a concession to it, they grew affronted and joined with the slave states to reject the controversial plank 238 to 21.[76] The Charleston platform, as finally adopted, consisted of the Minority Report minus the controversial and ambivalent Supreme Court proviso.

But the South was not ready to rest on its laurels after the stunning, if somewhat negative, victory on the platform. It was now time for the political wrecking firm of Yancey and company to ring up the curtain on the tragic drama of disruption and disunion whose script had been written many months before. L. P. Walker of Alabama rose to announce that his delegation had been instructed at the state convention to withdraw if no slave-code plank were adopted at Charleston. He then led his followers out of Institute Hall to the accompaniment of cheers and hoots. Mississippi followed suit immediately, as did Florida, Texas, and most of Louisiana, South Carolina, and Arkansas.[77] Two thirds of the Georgia delegation joined the bolters on the following day.[78] By noon of May 1, a total of forty-nine Southern votes had gone out of the Charleston convention for good.[79]

The Southern bolters professed to be fleeing a platform, but their protests and explanations have about them a hollow ring when read a hundred years later. The Minority Report, while not calling for a slave code or the reopening of the African slave trade, was the most pro-Southern platform in the long history of the Democracy. Even Jefferson Davis later admitted lamely that it did not really deny any Southern rights, it just did not sustain them vigorously enough.[80] Had a safe man been nominated on the same platform,

[76] Ibid., pp. 72–73.

[77] Ibid., p. 74.

[78] Ibid., p. 88.

[79] On May 1, Chairman Cushing made another one of his many anti-Douglas rulings and declared that the few Georgia delegates who had not bolted could not vote in the convention; ibid., p. 94. From the eight bolting Southern states, which together controlled 51 votes, only 2 votes—one each from Arkansas and South Carolina—were represented when the balloting for a candidate began.

[80] Rowland, *Jefferson Davis*, IV, 299.

the South would have found little difficulty in supporting him. Again, a close study of the convention records reveals that the Southern bolt came *after* the delegates had voted *down* the Supreme Court plank the South professed to detest and not when the really much more odious plank reaffirming the Cincinnati platform passed earlier.

The conclusion is inescapable that on April 30 many of the Ultras realized somewhat belatedly that the convention was going to produce a platform on which the hated Little Giant could stand. They talked of a platform, but in the end they ran from a man. They went into the convention demanding the very kind of platform Douglas long before had said he would not run on. D. C. Glenn, the leader of the Mississippi delegation, later confessed he came to Charleston determined above all else to stop Douglas.[81] There is some evidence that the Texas delegation had secretly determined to bolt if Douglas seemed about to be nominated.[82] Jefferson Davis later made the astonishing admission to the Senate that he "would sooner have an honest man on any sort of rickety platform you could construct, than to have a man I did not trust on the best platform which could be made."[83] Douglas shot back, "If the platform is not a matter of much consequence, why press that question to the disruption of the party?"[84] Alexander Stephens likewise felt that Douglas, and not the platform, was the real reason behind the Southern bolt.[85] Perhaps the most conclusive evidence is to be found in the fact that all the bolting states at Charleston, with the exception of Florida and South Carolina, agreed to send delegates to the Baltimore convention two months later, although it was commonly accepted long in advance that the Charleston platform would be readopted there substantially unchanged.

While it is easy to fathom the reasons for the Southern bolt, the equanimity with which some of the Douglas men anticipated a

81 Rainwater, *Mississippi*, pp. 121–122.

82 Nevins, *The Emergence of Lincoln*, II, 207 n.

83 Rowland, *Jefferson Davis*, IV, 335.

84 Ibid., p. 339.

85 Ulrich B. Phillips, ed., *The Correspondence of Robert Toombs*, p. 495.

walkout is much more difficult to explain. As early as February, 1859, Douglas had been hinting at the possibility of an Ultra bolt at Charleston.[86] By the beginning of the following year he was openly predicting one.[87] A bolt could help Douglas in more than one way. A walkout by some of the dissident Southerners would not only enhance Douglas' chances, under customary convention procedure, for gaining the nomination at Charleston, but, from a longer range standpoint, it might also strengthen his position against a Republican opponent by improving his image in the eyes of Northern free-soilers.[88] In the end, the Northwesterners probably felt any bolt would be short-lived. They no doubt expected the Southerners to reconsider and come back to the convention after tempers had cooled. At very least, they counted upon the South supporting Douglas in the November election. Although the Douglas partisans were the most responsible element in Charleston, they were not immune to the faults of their times. They underestimated the lengths to which the South was prepared to go and too readily accepted the breakup of one of the last surviving national institutions and the one great remaining hope for effecting some measure of sectional adjustment.

If the size of the Southern bolt surprised the Douglas faction, the next decision taken by the convention left them stunned and confused. John R. Howard of Tennessee offered a resolution demanding that any candidate must receive two thirds of *all* the votes originally represented at the convention in order to be nominated.[89] The Douglas men had based their whole strategy upon the assumption that only two thirds of the votes *remaining* in the convention after the bolt would be necessary. When the resolution passed 141 to 112, even the most optimistic among them began to lose hope.[90] With 202 of only 254 remaining votes needed to nominate, Douglas would now have to carry every free state delegation plus 19 votes

[86] *Cong. Globe*, 35th Cong., 2nd sess., p. 1246.
[87] Ibid., 36th Cong., 1st sess., p. 424.
[88] Halstead, *Three against Lincoln*, pp. 11, 13, 42.
[89] Ibid., pp. 93–98.
[90] Ibid., pp. 97–98.

from among the seven full slave-state delegations remaining in the convention.[91] That was impossible.

Historians have generally failed to note that the kind of two-thirds proposal that wrecked Douglas at Charleston came not from the Deep South but rather from Tennessee, and that it passed largely through the efforts of the Border states and the huge New York delegation.[92] One explanation might be that the Borderers, with their ties to both North and South, and the influential delegates from New York City, with its heavy participation in Southern commerce, realized better than anyone else at Charleston the need to preserve the Democratic party and, with it, the Union. They now sought to deadlock the convention until tempers could cool and the bolters were coaxed back into the party fold. The more cynical among them no doubt hoped that a stalemate would in the end result in the nomination passing to one of the favorite sons from the Border or perhaps to Horatio Seymour of New York.[93]

The balloting for the Democratic nominee for President of the United States commenced late on the afternoon of May 1. It lasted for two days. The delegates, now exhausted and irritable from the heat and frustration of Charleston, labored through fifty-seven ballots. The Little Giant led every one of them, but his strength crested at 152½ votes.[94] It was a majority of the total convention but 50 votes away from the needed two thirds. Douglas could at best muster only 9½ votes from the slave states.[95] Although he predictably ran strong in the North, only 45½ Douglas votes above the Mason-

[91] Missouri, Kentucky, Tennessee, North Carolina, Virginia, Delaware, and Maryland together represented 69 votes.

[92] Halstead, *Three against Lincoln*, pp. 97–98.

[93] A move was later made by the New York delegation at Baltimore to nominate Seymour.

[94] Douglas' peak strength of 152½ votes was reached on the twenty-third, thirty-second, and thirty-third ballots.

[95] Douglas' greatest strength in the slave states came on the twenty-third ballot when he received one vote each from Virginia and Tennessee in addition to the 4½ from Missouri, the 2 from Maryland, and the 1 from North Carolina that had remained loyal to him throughout the convention.

Dixon Line came from states that might go Democratic in November. Only about one third of the Little Giant's impressive convention strength would have cash value on election day.[96]

The proceedings were now deadlocked. Only a major compromise could save the Charleston convention in its closing hours. But with the platform already written, any compromise would have to be over the candidate, and that meant the withdrawal of Douglas' name from consideration by the convention. Thus paradoxically did the man whose great stock in trade had always been compromise discover that the only compromise he could now effect required his political self-denial.

Douglas would not withdraw. He had shown more flexibility than any other contender at Charleston. He had consented to modify his platform in spite of his rigid position in the Dorr Letter. He had gone a step farther and extended another olive branch to the South by offering the vice-presidency to Andrew Johnson of Tennessee, and Johnson had refused.[97] But he would not take the next step and pull his name out of the convention altogether. Douglas and his followers had put too much time and money into his bid for the nomination to quit now. They had forced through the kind of platform the Little Giant could accept, and their man had led the Democratic field on every one of the fifty-seven ballots that had been taken. Then too, Douglas had not forgotten the pain caused by being removed from the chairmanship of the Committee on Territories. [98] His followers came south with a score to settle with Buchanan, and they were not ready to counsel the kind of withdrawal that would perpetuate the President's control of the Democracy. But perhaps the most important factor in Douglas' refusal to withdraw was his feeling that time was running out for him, his party, and his country. He had come close to death the previous autumn and

[96] *Nashville Union and American*, May 15, 1860, in Dwight L. Dumond, ed., *Southern Editorials on Secession*, p. 96.

[97] Ollinger Crenshaw, *The Slave States in the Presidential Election of 1860*, pp. 178–179.

[98] *Cong. Globe*, 36th Cong., 1st sess., pp. 424–425, 2151–2152; Nevins, *Emergence of Lincoln*, II, 224 n.

months later was not fully recovered. For the first time, the Little Giant probably faced squarely the fact that he would not live forever. The future of the Union looked equally dubious. By April, Douglas must have come to believe that 1860 might be his last chance to win the presidency of an America that was still one nation.

The Charleston convention could only agree to try again. Shortly after 11 o'clock on the morning of May 3, the Democrats voted to adjourn to Baltimore in June, and Caleb Cushing rapped his gavel for the last time in Charleston.

Douglas had run a good race at Charleston and been very close to the nomination—closer than any of his lieutenants would have dared to predict at the start of the convention. But in the end he had failed to come away with the big prize. In spite of all of his rigid pronouncements to the contrary, he had entered the convention as the candidate of moderation and compromise and benign ambiguity, but too many people at Charleston had grown impatient with these old political virtues and preferred to embark on a course of reckless disregard for the future of their party and their country. In a move wholly in keeping with the suicidal predisposition of the times, many of the delegates had turned their backs on the one man who might have led them to victory in November. The old Democracy died at Charleston and the bolt that killed it was, in retrospect, the first overt act of secession by the South from the rest of America. Its mortal remains were unceremoniously shipped north to the cooler climes of Baltimore to avoid an unseemly decomposition.

By late afternoon on May 3, the South Carolina Institute was almost deserted. Only a handful of Negro porters remained to clean up the debris left in the wake of the convention: the posters and handbills and programs and the paper fans that the delegates had used in a futile attempt to fend off the heavy early spring heat of Charleston. The old hall would not witness such a spectacle again until much later in the year, when delegates from all over South Carolina assembled within its walls on December 20 to sign the first Ordinance of Secession of any Southern state. A year later, it would burn to the ground in the great Charleston fire of December, 1861.[99] The rest of the South was not far behind.

Instead of using the time between Charleston and Baltimore to bind up the wounds their party had suffered at its national convention, the Democrats seemed intent on making them worse. On Capitol Hill, Congress ceased altogether to be a forum for meaningful debate and productive discussion, and became instead a sounding board for the petty, internecine quibbles of the Democratic party. Insults and invective filled the Senate Chamber, where Douglasites, Southerners, and administration men kept up the verbal war that had broken out at Charleston. On May 8, in reply to some remark made by Jefferson Davis the day before, the Little Giant responded with that belligerent arrogance he could always summon when it suited his needs: "In regard to the Senator's declaration that he will grant no quarter to squatter sovereignty, I can only say to him that it will remain to the victor to grant quarter, or to grant mercy. I ask none."[100] On May 17 Douglas held the Senate floor for most of the day. While his tone was more restrained than that of Jefferson Davis, who frequently interrupted him, Douglas made it clear that he would tolerate no significant changes in the platform at Baltimore.[101] One Southern paper called the speech a "declaration of war against the South."[102] Hopes for a way out of the sectional impasse began to fade.

A spirit of futility marked the Baltimore gathering from its start. By June 18, when the convention was called to order by Caleb Cushing, the deadening heat of Charleston had moved north. Tempers were once again short, and the delegates hardly in the mood for effecting the kind of reasonable compromise that might hold their shattered party together for a few more months. Local resi-

99 The South Carolina Institute Hall stood on a site now occupied by a three-story building at 134 Meeting Street. A plaque on the exterior wall of the present structure commemorates the old hall and gives its history.

100 *Cong. Globe*, 36th Cong., 1st sess., p. 1970.

101 Ibid., p. 2153.

102 Dumond, *Southern Editorials on Secession*, p. 110.

dents grew angry at the rowdy behavior of some of the delegates, and the *Baltimore Patriot* complained of excessive drunkenness: "The hotels are crowded and doing a good business. The drinking shops are more crowded and doing a better business."[103] The *Charleston Mercury* gleefully predicted another rupture almost daily.[104]

Over in the mansion of Reverdy Johnson, where the Douglas men, once more led by Richardson, had set up their headquarters, the Little Giant's team had decided to adopt much the same strategy they had used at Charleston. They would go into the convention with a firm base of Northern strength and take the nomination by force. Yet they would do nothing to antagonize the South unnecessarily. Douglas had aimed most of his recent Senate speeches at isolating Yancey and his followers from the rest of the South and had not tried to make a frontal assault on the entire section.[105] But if the Douglas forces did not want another bolt, they were more prepared for a large one than they had been at Charleston and were in much tighter control of the convention machinery. The refusal of South Carolina and Florida to send delegations to Baltimore had altered the composition of all committees to sixteen members for Douglas, fifteen against him, even if all the remaining Southern delegations should prove hostile. Furthermore, the Committee on Credentials held the key to the Baltimore convention. While Douglas was no doubt pleased that of the eight states which had bolted at Charleston, only two refused to come to Baltimore, the returning seceders could still do more harm than good. Douglas' strategy called for trying to seat new delegations from the six discontented Southern states, rather than simply readmitting those delegates who had walked out in April. His lieutenants at Baltimore argued that the delegates who had bolted at Charleston had in fact abdicated their seats and that their places ought to be taken by other more moderate representatives from their respective states. Douglas was resigned to another bolt by most of the returning Southerners his

[103] *Baltimore Patriot* quoted in the *Mobile Daily Advertiser*, June 27, 1860.
[104] *Charleston Mercury*, June 23, 1860.
[105] *Cong. Globe*, 36th Cong., 1st sess., app., p. 313.

men could not ultimately bar from the convention. After the expected bolt had occurred, the Douglas men planned to move at once to the balloting for a candidate. This time only two thirds of the votes *remaining* inside the Front Street Theatre would be needed to nominate. If a deadlock occurred, they were prepared to move that a mere majority suffice. Only after Douglas had been securely nominated would the controversial business of the platform be taken up.

The Douglas men had designed a strategy that guaranteed almost certain victory for their leader, but they probably still hoped that common sense more than the manipulation of the convention machinery would carry the day for the Little Giant. Lincoln had been nominated only a month before by the Republicans,[106] and Democratic unity was vitally necessary in the face of the formidable challenge he posed. With at least some of the South apparently intent on supporting a candidate of its own and most of the East firmly Republican, the 1860 election would be decided in the Northwest and along the Border. The only Democrat who could hope to challenge Lincoln or John Bell[107] in those areas was Stephen Douglas.

The Committee on Credentials labored for three days while the rest of the convention business ground to a halt. On Thursday, June 21, it sent both a Majority and a Minority report to the convention floor.[108] This time the anti-Douglas forces were on the minority side and called simply for the readmission of the seceding Southern delegates.[109] The Majority Report predictably called for seating all of the rival Douglasites who were challenging the Charlestonians

106 The Republicans, meeting in Chicago, nominated Lincoln as their candidate for the presidency on May 18, 1860.

107 On May 10, 1860, the Constitutional Union party, meeting in Baltimore, nominated John Bell of Tennessee and Edward Everett of Massachusetts for President and Vice-President on a vague platform endorsing the Constitution and the preservation of the Union. This party was expected to run well in the Border states.

108 Halstead, *Three against Lincoln*, pp. 211–219.

109 The Minority Report also contained a resolution to admit a delegation from Florida; ibid., p. 215. The Douglas men had argued all along that the state had not seen fit to send any accredited representatives to Baltimore and

in the Louisiana and Alabama delegations, and for dividing the Georgia and Arkansas votes between those who had bolted at Charleston and new delegates sympathetic to Douglas. In return, all of the original bolters from Texas and Mississippi were to be readmitted.[110] Thus of the eight delegations who had stalked out of the South Carolina Institute, only two returned to Baltimore intact. In the end the Majority Report was adopted with only minor changes.

Now began the moment that had become all too familiar in Democratic gatherings. Whereas it was the lower South who had led the bolters at Charleston, at Baltimore the Border states formed the vanguard of disruption. Charles Russell of Virginia rose to announce that his state was leaving the convention. North Carolina, Tennessee, Kentucky, Missouri, and part of Maryland followed suit. Oregon and California joined the walkout, and on the following day part of the Massachusetts delegation was gone, including Chairman Caleb Cushing, who handed his gavel to David Tod of Ohio.[111]

Of the thirty-three states that made up the Union in 1860, only thirteen still had full delegations at Baltimore.[112] Thus did Douglas-the-nationalist prepare to receive his nomination at the hands of a convention that now accurately represented only a little more than a third of all the states and almost none of those that would be safely in the Democratic column in November.

The Democratic party now faced the dilemma it had been avoid-

---

should therefore remain outside the convention; ibid., pp. 196, 203. In the end, Florida, like South Carolina, remained unrepresented at Baltimore.

110 Ibid., pp. 212–214. With an eye toward another bolt, the Majority Report cleverly provided that if part of the divided Arkansas and Georgia delegations should fail to participate in the convention, the entire vote of each state could be cast by its remaining delegates.

111 Part of the Arkansas delegation left on June 23; ibid., p. 248. The Ultra Mississippi and Texas delegations refused to participate further in the convention after having been admitted on June 22. Part of the Georgia delegation remained nominally in the convention, but did not participate in the balloting for a candidate.

112 They were New Hampshire, Vermont, Rhode Island, New York, Alabama, Louisiana, Ohio, Indiana, Illinois, Michigan, Wisconsin, Iowa, and Minnesota.

ing for so long. If it proceeded to nominate Stephen Douglas, its gaping schism would become a permanent feature of the political landscape. But if it now rejected the Little Giant, the split would persist in a different form. Only Douglas' voluntary withdrawal as a candidate at this point might have saved the Democracy for a bit longer. Douglas did in fact send two messages to Baltimore offering to step down in the interests of party unity.[113] He later told an audience in Atlanta that he had been prepared to throw his support at the convention to Alexander Stephens.[114]

The Little Giant's apparent magnanimity should not be taken too seriously. The two messages left the decision to withdraw his candidacy squarely in the hands of Douglas' lieutenants on the floor of the convention, and there was no reason to believe that men who had worked long and tirelessly for the Illinois Senator through two hectic Democratic conventions would be inclined to quit now. A close scrutiny of the Baltimore messages also shows that Douglas' offer to step down was highly conditional. The Little Giant would consent to yield only to "some other reliable, Non-Intervention, and Union loving Democrat."[115] That was a rare breed at Baltimore. The Douglas offer was not made public until after his nomination was secure. In spite of his avowed willingness to accept some other candidate, his followers had done all they could to block a New York move to choose Horatio Seymour, the only other contender upon whom most of the delegates might have been able to agree. If Douglas would not withdraw from the deadlocked Charleston convention, there is no real reason to believe he ever seriously considered stepping down at Baltimore with victory, albeit a Pyrrhic one, almost in his grasp.

Two ballots were taken at Baltimore. On the first, Douglas received 173½ of 191½ votes cast[116]—an overwhelming majority. But the Little Giant's camp was not satisfied. Under the rules adopted at Charleston, two thirds of the original membership of

[113] Johannsen, ed., *Letters of Douglas*, pp. 492–493.

[114] Crenshaw, *Slave States*, p. 84.

[115] Johannsen, ed., *Letters of Douglas*, p. 493.

[116] Halstead, *Three against Lincoln*, pp. 249–250.

the convention was needed to nominate. Since Florida and South Carolina had refused to send delegates to Baltimore, 292 votes were represented there, and 196 were necessary for a clear-cut victory.

Once more the clerk began to call the roll of the states; a loud silence from the absent delegations was the most frequent response. Douglas this time managed 181½ votes out of 194½ cast.[117] This was close, but still not enough for two thirds of the original membership of the convention. Daniel Hoge of Virginia now moved that since Douglas had received two thirds "of all votes given in this Convention," he be declared the Democratic nominee for President of the United States. The resolution carried unanimously by a voice vote.[118]

The Douglas men now began a frenzied and belated effort to reestablish their candidate's credentials as a nationalist and a willing adjuster of sectional differences. The Northwesterners offered the vice-presidency to Benjamin Fitzpatrick of Alabama, an old-line anti-Lecomptonite who had once voted to oust Douglas from his chairmanship in the Senate. There is even some evidence that Douglas informally tendered the second place on the ticket to William Lowndes Yancey himself and that the Little Giant's trusted ally, George Sanders of New York, urged Yancey to accept, using the argument that Douglas would probably be dead within six months after the election anyway.[119] He came within a month of being correct. Fitzpatrick at first accepted the vice-presidential nomination, but later withdrew, yielding to administration and Ultra pressure. His place was taken by Herschel V. Johnson of Georgia, who was chosen after the Baltimore convention had adjourned.

The Douglas group had always maintained that since Baltimore was, in theory at least, merely a continuation of the Charleston convention, the platform chosen earlier should stand unchanged. In the hour of victory, however, they consented to amend the platform by the addition of an explanatory resolution offered by Gov-

117 Ibid., p. 251.

118 Ibid., pp. 251–252.

119 *New York Times*, October 23, 1860; *Richmond Whig*, October 25, 1860.

Benjamin Fitzpatrick of Alabama. Nominated as Douglas' vice-presidential running mate, he later changed his mind and withdrew.

ernor R. C. Wickliffe of Louisiana, who promised that it would "give to Stephen A. Douglas forty thousand votes in two of the Southern states of this Union." The amendment stated that "during the existence of the Territorial Governments the measure of restriction, whatever it may be, imposed by the Federal Constitution on the power of the Territorial Legislature over the subject of the domestic relations, as the same has been or shall hereafter be finally determined by the Supreme Court of the United States, should be respected by all good citizens and enforced with promptness and fidelity by every branch of the General Government."[120]

120 Halstead, *Three against Lincoln*, p. 256.

This change amounted to a resurrection of the rejected second plank of the Charleston Minority Report in language intended to be even more palatable to the South. The Charleston plank had recognized that "differences of opinion exist in the Democratic party as to the nature and extent of the powers of a Territorial Legislature, and as to the powers and duties of Congress, under the Constitution of the United States, over the institution of slavery within the Territories,"[121] and had agreed to abide by decisions of the Supreme Court on such matters. The Baltimore plank made no mention of any doubts as to the powers of Congress and thereby avoided the embarrassing implied Northern challenge to the notion of a slave code. It dealt only with the powers of the territorial legislature and did so in a way intended to suggest that the Douglas men had moved closer to the Southern view that the Dred Scott decision had barred territories from acting against slavery. It was a pathetic final effort at reconciliation. The South recognized it for what it was—a concession to it in form but not in fact—and largely ignored it.

Its business finished, what was left of the Baltimore convention adjourned on the evening of June 23. Douglas had at last won a presidential nomination, but he had had to pay a terrible price. It had taken nine weeks, two national conventions, and fifty-nine ballots to nominate the Little Giant and place him on the kind of platform he would accept. In the end his victory was due to states that the Democrats had no hope of carrying in November. The Baltimore convention, which was meant to restore order and unity to the Democracy, succeeded only in splitting it beyond repair. The Democrats had gone north in the hope of breathing new life into their party, but in the end Baltimore seemed to resemble the formal interment of the body that had already died at Charleston. When the seceders at Baltimore walked out of the Front Street Theatre, they made straight for Market Hall only a few blocks away, where many of the original bolters from Charleston had come after adjourning their own gathering at Richmond earlier in June. Together

121 Ibid., pp. 60–61, 72–73.

they nominated the team of John Breckinridge and Joseph Lane on a platform that substantially embodied the planks of the Majority Report at Charleston.[122]

Ultras and Buchananites were not the only people Douglas had angered at Baltimore. Less prejudiced observers both inside and outside the Democratic party surveyed the political wreckage left in the wake of the Douglas steam roller and were disgusted. Those with an eye for legalisms remembered the cavalier treatment of the two-thirds rule and the unprecedented step of choosing the vice-presidential nominee in the National Committee after the convention itself had adjourned. They began to wonder about the regularity of the Douglas ticket. Reasonable men in the North who had intended to support Douglas in November as the man who could best preserve the Union now viewed the shattered Democracy and decided they had no desire to back a loser. They turned instead to Abraham Lincoln, who was looking more and more like a conservative every day.[123]

Perhaps the real tragedy of that spring was that Douglas, seriously ill again[124] and suddenly looking far older than his forty-seven years,[125] won almost every battle that was joined, yet in the end he was no closer to a major victory. Wherever his enemies had dared to stand and fight, the Little Giant had vanquished them, but by July of 1860 the once glittering prize of the presidency seemed but a pale star on the political horizon.

122 For the Baltimore Seceders' convention, see Halstead, *Three against Lincoln*, pp. 265–278. For their platform, see Commager, ed., *Documents*, p. 366. The platform differed from the Charleston Majority version in using slightly less belligerent language on the subject of the acquisition of Cuba and in omitting any specific reference to the protection of slavery on the high seas. It also explicitly granted a territory the right to decide on slavery at the time of admission to the Union as a state—a right that the Majority version at Charleston had only implied.

123 *St. Paul Pioneer and Democrat* quoted in *New York Times*, November 3, 1860.

124 Johannsen, ed., *Letters of Douglas*, pp. 488–489. Douglas wrote in June, 1860, that he was suffering from a throat condition and might have to have an operation.

125 Robert Taft, "The Appearance and Personality of Stephen A. Douglas," *Kansas Historical Quarterly* 21, no. 1 (spring 1954): 17.

For Stephen Douglas the real campaign of 1860 was over almost before it had begun. The Baltimore convention did not adjourn until the last days of June, and more time was wasted trying to find a vice-presidential candidate after Fitzpatrick reconsidered his acceptance and withdrew from the ticket. It was mid-July before the Little Giant was out on the political hustings, and within a month he was betraying in his more candid moments a grave pessimism toward the outcome of the election.[126]

Yet Stephen Douglas continued to wage what was up to then the most vigorous campaign in American history. For the first time, a candidate for the presidency took to the national stump. Douglas visited almost every section of the country at least once. He spoke two or three times a day, usually in the open air under the burning sun of a midwestern summer or the raw autumn chill of New England, and he overtaxed a constitution that was at best frail and had for too long been called upon for almost superhuman feats of endurance.

The country had never seen anything like it and would not again until the century was almost out and another Midwesterner named William Jennings Bryan took his case to the people. Douglas' unprecedented campaign tactics predictably drew the scorn of critics on both sides of the Mason-Dixon Line. Jefferson Davis denounced the Little Giant as "an itinerant advocate of his own claims." The once friendly *New York Times* was now supporting Lincoln and labeled Douglas' peripatetic campaign "vulgar," although "thoroughly in keeping with his character and political habits."[127] The Little Giant remained undeterred.

Although there were four candidates in the 1860 presidential race, a close study of the campaign suggests that in most areas of the country there was a meaningful struggle between only two men, and upon rare occasions, three. Only in a handful of states, such as New York, New Jersey, and Pennsylvania, was there ever anything approaching a true four-way contest. Indeed, if four

[126] *New York Tribune*, July 20, 1860; *New York Times*, August 10, 1860; Milton, *Eve of Conflict*, p. 492; Allen Johnson, *Stephen A. Douglas*, p. 431.

[127] Rainwater, *Mississippi*, p. 135; *New York Times*, August 16, 1860.

rather closely matched contenders had in fact entered the political lists of each state, Douglas might well have won as a compromise candidate, standing forth as a true moderate and the best man to preserve the Union before a nation that perhaps was beginning to have long overdue second thoughts about the reckless course it had embarked upon.

But in New England and much of the Northwest, Breckinridge and Bell were largely ignored, and the only real contest was between Lincoln and Douglas. Most of the deep South was committed to Breckinridge before the campaign ever got under way. Along the Border, Douglas and Bell vied for the old Whig vote. That there was even a two-way contest in a few parts of New England and the lower South, as well as along the Border, was due to Douglas' taking his campaign bandwagon all the way from the rocky Republican terrain of Augusta, Maine, and Rutland, Vermont, and Concord, New Hampshire, right down to Mobile and New Orleans. Here perhaps is the best justification for Douglas' claim to have been the only really national figure in the 1860 race.

Throughout Douglas' many campaign speeches ran the theme of compromise and moderation. The Little Giant tried to convey an image of conservatism in an age breaking in mad haste for the extremist fringes. He identified himself with the memory of Henry Clay. Above all, he took his case to the people as a national leader. In Bangor, Maine, he told his audience that popular sovereignty alone of the current political creeds could be proclaimed in every section of the Union.[128] But to proclaim a thing is not the same as seeing it accepted. Throughout his wide-ranging campaign, he only once altered the content of his beliefs to suit the changed political latitudes. In the far northern climes of Clifton, Maine, Douglas broke his consistency and announced that under his Freeport Doctrine a territory could not only abolish and regulate slavery, but might exclude it as well.[129]

When he despaired of the existence of any latent feelings of Unionism to which he might appeal, Douglas did the next best

[128] *New York Times*, August 23, 1860; *New York Tribune*, August 31, 1860.
[129] *New York Tribune*, September 18, 1860.

thing and stressed his role as a multisectional candidate—the only one of the four contenders who was a true friend of both the North and the South. With a lapse into the kind of sentimentality that seemed to enter his speeches frequently now, he reminded a New York audience that his father had been born on the free soil of Vermont, his children down in the slave country of North Carolina.[130]

While Douglas continued to campaign in the familiar role of nationalist, his opponents were stealing his thunder. Each of his three rivals detached one facet of Douglas' traditional national appeal, adopted it as his own, and in the end put it to better use than the Little Giant himself. Breckinridge in 1860 made a more convincing friend of the South. The Kentuckian persuaded many of the Southern moderates upon whom Douglas had relied in the past that he was less of a threat to their way of life than the Senator from Illinois. Bell and Everett, on their vague platform endorsing the Union and the Constitution, made a better offering of that kind of benign ambiguity which had often passed for moderation and compromise at the hands of the Little Giant. Abraham Lincoln would portray himself as a more likely proponent of free-soil, and some members of his party in the Northwest during the campaign even began to adopt the notion of popular sovereignty as their own.[131]

Douglas would need 152 of 303 electoral votes to be elected President, but the 73 votes from all of the South below the Border states looked unpromising, as did New England with its 41. The 7 votes from California and Oregon were at best doubtful. In order to win, Douglas would have to carry all of the Border states, all of the Northwest, and at least New York and New Jersey among the Middle Atlantic states. Douglas' best strategy would have been to concentrate his campaign on these three crucial areas. Yet this is precisely what Douglas did not do. He instead focused his efforts on just those states he had little chance of carrying in November. He made repeated visits to New England that summer, particularly to Maine and Vermont. These two states together could muster only

[130] *New York Times*, September 13, 1860.
[131] Henry C. Hubbart, *The Older Middle West*, pp. 142–143.

ten votes, which would almost certainly go for Lincoln anyway. He campaigned in New York City, but largely ignored the important upstate vote. He visited only part of the vital border area, where his campaign had its best opportunity for converting undecided voters. Yet he spent almost three weeks of the campaign in the inhospitable political climate of the lower South.

The only rational explanation for such behavior on the part of an astute and experienced political figure like Stephen Douglas would seem to be that almost from the outset of the campaign he knew that he could not win the presidency. His national ambitions therefore took the more realistic and enlightened form of trying to poll as large a popular vote as possible and to emerge from the political debacle he saw coming as the acknowledged leader of his party. There was also Congress to think about, and a study of Douglas' tours through the East suggests that he spent much of his time in close districts where the Democratic candidates had some hope of victory. Most important of all, in New England and the South, where he spent so much of his time, Douglas faced just those people whose intolerance and recklessness were doing the most to tear a nation in two. He did not come so much seeking their votes as to warn them of their folly. He came less in the role of campaigner and more as the defender of common sense and the Union. Douglas the politician had yielded to Douglas the statesman.

With the Democratic vote split, Bell and Everett in the race, and Lincoln unlikely to get a majority of the popular vote—perhaps not even a majority of the electoral college—the Democrats logically should have tried to patch up their differences and either united upon one candidate or pooled their efforts in such a way as to defeat the Republicans. Two different sets of proposals looking in this direction were in fact put forward.

The so-called fusion movement is perhaps the most misunderstood aspect of the 1860 campaign. Quite simply, it sought to unite anti-Republican voters in a given state on a single slate of electors that roughly reflected the relative strength in that state of all candidates opposing Lincoln. At very least, this strategy hoped to throw the presidential election into the House of Representatives by preventing Lincoln from obtaining a majority in the electoral college almost by default, for if no slate of electors pledged to a single opposition candidate could command a plurality in a state, that state's entire electoral vote would pass to Lincoln. At most, Lincoln might be defeated outright in the electoral college since all fusion electors were, in theory at least, to vote as a unit for the candidate with the best chance of beating the Republican nominee. Since in only a few states was there a genuine four-way contest, the possibilities for fusion were rather limited from the outset. Only in New York, Pennsylvania, Rhode Island, and New Jersey did the fusion movement achieve serious and formal proportions, and only in the last did it result in the choice of any Democratic electors.

Stephen Douglas was predictably hostile to the whole idea of fusion. In July he issued a public manifesto rejecting the whole notion out of hand,[132] although he would later temper his stand by opposing only fusion with "any men or any party who will not enforce the laws, maintain the Constitution, and preserve the Union in all contingencies."[133] Few people failed to guess it was John Breckinridge whom Douglas had in mind. The whole concept of fusion was justified on the negative grounds of defeating Lincoln and had little appeal for the aggressive and dynamic Douglas. Furthermore, it would have meant curbing his campaign efforts in some states and thereby would have compromised his claim to be the only contender who was waging a national campaign.

From a somewhat more practical point of view, Douglas knew that he needed *all* the electoral votes of two key states where the fusion movement had taken hold—New York and New Jersey—and not just part. The Little Giant probably also tended to look upon fusion as essentially an administration ruse to elect Breckinridge. The only states where the scheme was pushed with any persistence were in the North, where Douglas knew he stood a better chance than any other Democrat. The most that could be expected from fusion was that the election would ultimately be thrown into

[132] *New York Herald*, July 19, 1860.
[133] *New York Times*, September 13, 1860.

the House of Representatives where, with each state casting one ballot, Douglas might not receive a single vote.

A negative version of the fusion scheme called for all three non-Republican contenders to withdraw and throw their support behind some compromise candidate. Jefferson Davis took the credit for this plan, but the readiness with which most historians accept him at his word seems quite unwarranted. The only evidence of the proposal consists of a single short paragraph in Davis' own memoirs, published more than twenty years later, in which he alleged that while Bell and Breckinridge consented to the scheme, Douglas refused and maintained that if he withdrew, his Northern supporters would vote for Lincoln.[134] Davis' account is strangely lacking in details. He never tells us if his proposals were submitted in writing, or if a conference actually took place between him and the three candidates. There is no record to suggest that Douglas either met or corresponded with Davis at any time in the summer of 1860. The Little Giant mentioned a proposal to withdraw from the race only twice during the entire campaign and in doing so made no reference to Davis.[135] Douglas and his followers would have distrusted any such scheme. The Jefferson Davis of 1860 was not the Davis of 1861 who led a South with some pretensions to unity. There was no guarantee that he could make good on his promise to withdraw Breckinridge and Bell from the race. Douglas further reasoned that if he withdrew, no Democrat could be elected, but if Breckinridge pulled out, Douglas might still win.[136] Even should Douglas lose, he would be in firm control of the Democratic party. Finally, the most likely compromise candidate would have been Horatio Seymour of New York, whom Douglas had gone to great lengths to block at Baltimore.

By September, Douglas' campaign was half over. He continued to argue and to plead and sometimes to preach, but as the contest entered the homestretch, he most frequently came to warn. He

[134] Jefferson Davis, *The Rise and Fall of the Confederate Government*, I, 52–53.

[135] *New York Times*, September 13, 1860.

[136] Emerson D. Fite, *The Presidential Campaign of 1860*, p. 295.

talked less of slavery now and more about saving the Union. He portrayed Lincoln as the overt candidate of the abolitionists, but the secret favorite of those who wanted an excuse for secession.[137] He was not interested in merely telling people what they wanted to hear. The hour was too late for that. At times he talked like a man who really did not want to win at all. In his attempt to adopt a high national line he made some remarks at Albany that sounded proslavery to Northern ears.[138] Yet down in Raleigh, North Carolina, he announced, "I would hang every man higher than Haman who would attempt by force to resist the execution of any provision of the Constitution which our fathers made and bequeathed to us."[139] He startled a group at his birthplace in Brandon with the announcement that Vermont was a good state to be born in, "provided you emigrate while young."[140]

The campaign had begun to take its toll of the Little Giant. A close study of the photographs made of him during 1860 reveals a shocking change in his physical appearance.[141] By the end of the year, Douglas was an old man. His personal finances, which had always suffered from a lack of liquidity, were now stretched to the breaking point, and it was rumored that he had borrowed several hundred thousand dollars from August Belmont.[142] He was drinking heavily again too. Charles Francis Adams was on the same train with the Illinois Senator on a trip from Chicago to Cleveland that summer, and years later he wrote that when the train paused at Toledo, Douglas burst in upon William Seward, who happened to be asleep in the next car, and exhorted his long-time political enemy to get up and greet the crowd. Adams noted that the Little Giant had a bottle of whiskey with him and concluded that he was

137 *New York Times*, September 7, 1860.

138 Ibid., July 25, 1860.

139 Douglas' complete Raleigh speech is found in Fite, *Campaign of 1860*, Appendix, pp. 276–300.

140 Alvin P. Stauffer, "Douglas in Vermont," *Vermont History* 28, no. 4 (October 1960): 263–264.

141 Taft, "Appearance and Personality of Douglas," p. 17.

142 *Richmond Whig*, June 22, 1860.

"plainly drunk."[143] He was in probably much the same condition when he told a Boston audience, "Won't it be a splendid sight to see Douglas and old Abe all in Washington together—for the next President is to come from Illinois."[144]

The East never became very enthusiastic over anything Douglas had to say that summer and tended to find his repeated references to popular sovereignty boring.[145] Only the strong stand he took in support of the Union later in his campaign elicited something like a warm response from his audiences.[146] He could still rely on help from the *Boston Herald* and the *Providence Post* in New England, and the *Albany Atlas and Argus* together with the *Buffalo Courier* in New York, but the once strongly pro-Douglas *New York Times* had now gone over to Lincoln.[147] The old Douglas lieutenants were beginning to desert too. Forney still protested his fidelity to the Little Giant but was acting more and more like a Republican every day.[148] The enigmatic Fernando Wood provided only a slender reed of support, urging Northern Democrats to vote for Douglas, Southerners for Breckinridge.[149]

There was also trouble along the Border, which for so long had been a traditional bastion of Douglas strength. As early as May, the Little Giant had warned that the Democracy could very well lose the Border states in November.[150] Although Douglas failed to devote the time to this area that a sound strategy demanded, he spent twelve hectic days there in late August and early September. He talked like a new edition of Henry Clay in an obvious move to rally the vital old Whig vote to his standard.[151] At Petersburg he reminded his audience of the historical and commercial ties between

143 Charles Francis Adams, *An Autobiography*, pp. 65–66.

144 *Vicksburg Weekly Sun*, September 10, 1860.

145 *New York Times*, September 29, 1860.

146 Ibid., September 13, 1860.

147 Ibid., July 17, 1860.

148 Halstead, *Three against Lincoln*, pp. 9, 303; *Richmond Examiner*, September 6, 1860.

149 *New York Times*, July 7, 1860.

150 *Cong. Globe*, 36th Cong., 1st sess., p. 2153.

151 *Richmond Examiner*, September 1, 1860.

Virginia and his own Northwest.[152] For a while it looked like Douglas' visit had yielded impressive dividends. A new wave of moderate pro-Union sentiment followed in the wake of his tour, and Douglas' political stock rose along the Border.[153] Governor Letcher of Virginia came out for the Little Giant, as did the influential *Missouri Republican* with its large following in St. Louis.

Yet the Little Giant could never bring the full force of his campaign to bear along the Border. Many influential politicians still resented the fate of its favorite sons at Charleston and vented their anger on Stephen Douglas. Andrew Johnson now threw his weight to Breckinridge.[154] Bell and Everett were cutting heavily into the Whig and pro-Union vote, which had always been Douglas' great source of strength in the Border region. Indeed, Douglas' efforts there seem to have served only to hinder Breckinridge without really helping his own cause. The major beneficiary of his tour would appear to have been ultimately not the Little Giant at all, but John Bell.

Even the Northwest was beginning to look uncertain. Douglas could still count on the support of influential newspapers like the *Cleveland Plain Dealer*, the *Cincinnati Enquirer*, the *Ohio Statesman*, the *Indianapolis Sentinel*, and the *Detroit Free Press*, along with the *Milwaukee Press and News*. There was also the superb Douglas machine, still functioning smoothly after its great victory of 1858. But somehow these were not enough. The Northwest was moving steadily away from Stephen Douglas. It was more strongly free-soil than ever. There was another Westerner in the field now, and the people liked the new Lincoln with his image of quiet moderation and prudence. Friendly editors still stressed Douglas' credentials as a compromiser and his presumably good relations with the Southern people, if not their leaders. The *Peoria Daily Democratic Union* continued to talk of the ties of the Northwest to the South and spoke hopefully of "The Mississippi valley, which may be

152 Crenshaw, *Slave States*, p. 80.

153 *Richmond Examiner*, September 1, 1860; *New York Times*, September 1, 1860.

154 Crenshaw, *Slave States*, p. 179.

called the neutral ground."[155] But the great rivers along which Douglas always ran well were less important now. Those waterways, running from north to south, represented the ties of the Old Northwest to the Old Southwest, and those ties had grown weak. Ideologically the two sections were farther apart than ever. Then too, the Northwest had begun to outstrip its Southern counterpart in the growth of its population and economy so that there was no longer a true community of interests. The great burst of railroad and canal building in the 1850's had not only made the river less important to the Northwesterners as a means of transportation, it had also diverted a large portion of their trade from the South to the East.[156] Douglas still did well along the rivers of the Northwest in 1860, but the dividing line between Republican and Democratic control moved noticeably downstream.

Perhaps most important of all, Douglas in 1860 simply neglected the Northwest, the area that represented his one great base of strength, in favor of far less promising sections of the country. Douglas was on the campaign trail in Iowa when he learned in early October that the Republicans had swept the state elections in Indiana and Pennsylvania. Instead of staying in the Northwest and fighting all the harder to redress the balance, Douglas made plans to go south.[157]

Most members of the Douglas camp had written off the South before the campaign ever got under way, but the Little Giant was strangely optimistic in the early days of the contest. In July he confided to Charles Lanphier that Breckinridge would carry only South Carolina and Mississippi while Missouri, Arkansas, Louisiana, Texas, Alabama, and Georgia would go for Douglas.[158]

It was a curiously naive attitude for a veteran of so many politi-

155 Howard C. Perkins, ed., *Northern Editorials on Secession*, I, 50.

156 The *New York Times*, December 24, 1860, estimated that 90–95% of all the produce of the Northwest that was shipped out of the area went east rather than south.

157 The news of the Pennsylvania and Indiana elections reached Douglas at Cedar Rapids, Iowa, on October 8. By October 19, he was in St. Louis on the start of his Southern tour.

158 Johannsen, ed., *Letters of Douglas*, pp. 497–498.

cal wars. Perhaps Douglas' surprising strength among Southern editors misled him. The *Atlanta Southern Confederacy*, the *Memphis Appeal*, the *Memphis Evening Democrat*, and the *Montgomery Confederation* made an impressive addition to the traditional list of Douglas papers in the South, which included the *Augusta Constitutionalist*, the *New Orleans True Delta*, and, of course, the old reliable *Mobile Register*. At the same time, however, the majority of Southern newspapers, particularly those serving the crucial rural areas, favored either Breckinridge or Bell. Perhaps Douglas also relied too heavily upon the support of a few influential Southern politicians, ranging from the lukewarm Thomas L. Clingman, who announced for Douglas only to desert him for Breckinridge in September,[159] through the somewhat more stable Letcher of Virginia and Toombs of Georgia, to Soulé of Louisiana and little Alexander Stephens, who remained steadfast to Douglas to the very end.

Yet even Alexander Stephens never let his loyalty blind him to political reality. He wrote a friend in July that the only hope he could see for Douglas' candidacy was that the Little Giant might take enough votes away from Lincoln in the North to throw the election into the House. He added, "I am pained and grieved at the folly which thus demanded the sacrifice of such a noble and gallant spirit as I believe Douglas to be."[160] To an astute observer like Stephens, the Little Giant lacked almost every one of the necessary ingredients for victory in the South. With the possible exception of Alabama, he had nothing approaching a political organization in any state below the Mason-Dixon Line. The Ultras and not Douglas were in command of the Democratic party machinery and the forces that helped shape public opinion in the South, and the Ultras would vote for Breckinridge. Most of them knew that he could not be elected in November, but some hoped he would win if the election were thrown into the House. Others simply wanted to defeat Douglas and thought Breckinridge the most likely means to that end. Still others were intent upon secession and actually wanted to

[159] *Richmond Examiner*, September 11, 1860.

[160] Phillips, ed., *Correspondence of Toombs*, p. 485.

see Lincoln elected in order that they might have an excuse to leave the Union. They voted for Breckinridge in order to hurt Douglas, who alone stood any realistic chance of defeating the Republican candidate.

The Douglas who came south in mid-October was a different man from the one who had campaigned along the Border only two months before. When he had crossed the Mason-Dixon Line on August 25 at the beginning of his first Southern campaign tour of 1860, Douglas was still talking and acting like a politician with some pretensions to victory in November. He had limited his twelve-day visit to the Border area, which had always been a prime source of his strength. He had delivered major speeches at Baltimore, Raleigh, Staunton, Richmond, Norfolk and Petersburg, and had made dozens of others, particularly at the little towns in the Shenandoah. For a moment it had seemed like the great days of '58 all over again with banners and floats and torchlight parades and speeches from hotel balconies to thousands of people gathered below. He had recited the famous Douglas catechism of popular sovereignty and national expansion, and had entered a plea for prudence and common sense on the slavery question.[161] He would lash out against secession, but only in response to a question shouted from the audience. He had warned his listeners at Norfolk that Lincoln's election in itself would not be sufficient reason to secede,[162] and farther south, at Raleigh, had flatly announced that he would hang anyone who tried.[163] But for the most part, Douglas had been content to couch his plea for union in terms of an appeal to common memo-

161 For Douglas' key speeches during his trip to the Border see Fite, *Campaign of 1860*, Appendix, pp. 276–300; Crenshaw, *Slave States*, pp. 77–82; J. Jeffery Auer, ed., *Antislavery and Disunion: Studies in the Rhetoric of Compromise and Conflict*, pp. 263–269; Stevens, "Life of Douglas," pp. 623–624; *New York Times*, August 28, 29, 1860, September 1, 5, 7, 1860; *Richmond Examiner*, September 1, 1860.

162 *New York Times*, September 15, 1860; Auer, *Antislavery and Disunion*, p. 264.

163 Fite, *Campaign of 1860*, pp. 282, 294–296. Douglas seems to have found his remarks on hanging embarrassing and tried belatedly to modify them. *Cong. Globe*, 37th Cong., special sess., p. 1443.

ries of 1776 and Andrew Jackson and the historical ties of Virginia to the Old Northwest.[164]

The second Southern tour was much different.[165] Douglas had come south many times before, sometimes on business, more often for political reasons. This time he came to try to save the Union. The Republican victories in the Pennsylvania and Indiana state elections at the beginning of October had confirmed his earlier fears that Abraham Lincoln would be the next President of the United States. As he had done so many times before in his long political career when he sensed a crisis, Douglas turned southward.

This time he no longer limited his visit to the Border region or to that handful of cosmopolitan towns along the great river where he had always been well received and that still held out the promise of some degree of electoral success. Now he took his cause right to the heartland of secession sentiment: to Vicksburg and Montgomery and Nashville, to Macon and Atlanta. There was none of the gaiety and color of his former political processions through the South—no booming cannons or pretty girls or torchlight parades. The times were too serious for that. Only Mrs. Douglas and James Sheridan, his secretary, accompanied him now. Douglas would still plead and reason with the South, but he also warned it bluntly of the folly of secession and demanded its continued allegiance to the Union. On October 19 he announced to an audience at St. Louis, the first major stop on his trip, "I am not here to ask your votes for the Presidency. I am here to make an appeal to you in behalf of the Union and the peace of the country."[166]

He grew steadily bolder and more outspoken as his tiny entourage made its way South. On October 24 he told a large crowd who had come from a half-dozen states to hear him speak at Memphis that Lincoln's election alone would constitute no real threat to the

[164] See Douglas' Norfolk remarks on August 25, 1860, in Auer, *Antislavery and Disunion*, pp. 266–268; Stevens, "Life of Douglas," p. 623; *New York Times*, August 28, 29, 1860, September 15, 1860.

[165] Actually Douglas' third visit below the Mason-Dixon Line in 1860, if one counts his visit to Louisville, Kentucky, at the end of September. Crenshaw, *Slave States*, pp. 82–83.

[166] Milton, *Eve of Conflict*, p. 498.

South's vital interests since that section would still continue to control Congress and the Supreme Court. He charged the Ultras with being secessionists in disguise and Breckinridge with working to elect Lincoln in the Northwest in order to have a convenient excuse to take the South out of the Union. He spoke for more than three hours that bright autumn afternoon and closed with a ringing and, for Douglas, an unusually lyrical appeal for unity: "I travelled yesterday through West Tennessee and looked out upon one of the loveliest countries the eye of man ever beheld—a country bearing the evidence of a kind providence that had smiled upon it and cherished its people, and I reflected what manner of man he must be who would precipitate this Union into Revolution."[167]

He had been tired before he ever came south, and the ceaseless travel and long speeches in the open air only weakened him more. He was frequently hoarse now[168] and a spectator in Atlanta who sat near the platform noticed "a stony glare about Douglas' eyes, particularly the left one."[169] He was worried now too—not for himself, but for Mrs. Douglas. He had received a number of threats upon his life. A mysterious accident beset the *Virginia*, which was bringing him downriver to Mobile, and Douglas had to change to the *Natchez*.[170] The Little Giant felt that at least one attempt was made to wreck his train in the South, although he never made any public reference to the plot.[171]

Douglas turned in the worst performance of his tour when he spoke from the steps of the Capitol at Montgomery on November 2. The Little Giant was obviously suffering from fatigue and appeared confused. For almost three hours he struggled through his speech, stammered, lost his voice, and repeated himself with exasperating frequency. His audience returned his pleas for sanity

[167] Douglas' Memphis speech is in the *Memphis Daily Appeal*, October 25, 1860.

[168] Auer, *Antislavery and Disunion*, p. 271.

[169] *Mobile Daily Advertiser*, November 6, 1860.

[170] Ibid. A guard rail on the upper deck of the *Virginia* broke and forty people, including Senator and Mrs. Douglas, were injured when they fell onto the main deck. See also *New Orleans Picayune*, November 9, 1860.

[171] Milton, *Eve of Conflict*, p. 498; Auer, *Antislavery and Disunion*, p. 271.

and the Union with hoots of derision and an occasional egg or over-ripe tomato.[172]

Douglas made the last speech of his campaign at Mobile on the evening of November 5. The election was the next day. Once more he began with a defense of popular sovereignty, but soon turned to a plea for the Union. He added for the first time that he would not be a candidate for any election that wound up in the House of Representatives.[173] The thousands of people who had come to hear the Little Giant listened quietly, applauded politely, and in the end voted for Breckinridge.

He stayed at the Battle House in Mobile, but spent most of his waking hours down the street at the office of the *Mobile Register*, where he sat with his old ally Forsyth and watched the election returns as they came off the telegraph. Even Douglas, who in retrospect had appeared resigned to defeat as early as the summer, was not prepared for the news that began to make its way with exasperating slowness over the wire. He had scored a clear victory in only one state, Missouri, with its nine electoral votes. His triumph there might have been predicted, for of all the states, Missouri was most closely identified with those two bastions of Douglas strength below the Mason-Dixon Line: the Border and the river. Yet even in Missouri Douglas won by a margin of less than five hundred votes.[174] Douglas' only other victory was in New Jersey, where he picked up three of the seven electoral votes. Lincoln claimed the other four. The *New York Times* saw behind Douglas' strength in the Garden State the sinister hand of the Camden and Amboy Railroad, whose political influence, said the *Times*, made New Jersey "the South Carolina of the North."[175] A more realistic explanation would seem to be that the fusion movement had scored its only triumph there in 1860. The New Jersey victory was far more significant than its three electoral votes might suggest, for it meant that Doug-

172 Douglas, "Montgomery Address," p. 529.

173 Johannsen, "Stephen A. Douglas and the South," p. 48.

174 In Missouri, Douglas received 58,801 votes; Bell, 58,372; Breckinridge, 31,317; Lincoln, 17,028. *The Tribune Almanac and Political Register for 1864*, p. 70.

175 *New York Times*, November 10, 1860.

las was the only one of the four candidates who had been able to win electoral votes in both a slave and a free state. Perhaps the Little Giant was the most truly national candidate after all. He could also take consolation from the news from California, which he lost to Lincoln by only six hundred votes.[176]

The popular vote told a much more heartening story. Douglas ran second only to Lincoln and had polled 1,375,157 votes to the Republican candidate's 1,866,452. His popular strength came within 60,000 votes of surpassing the combined total for Breckinridge and Bell.[177] In the North he ran far ahead of both of them put together, and even the South did not present a picture of a complete rout. Breckinridge carried 72 of the slave states' 120 electoral votes, but the combined total of the Douglas and Bell popular vote in the South alone exceeded his by more than 100,000.[178] Douglas showed surprising strength in Richmond with its hostile press, trailing Breckinridge by only 400 votes.[179] He continued to perform well in those areas that formed the traditional base of his power in the South. He ran well along the river. He polled twice as many votes in that part of Tennessee adjacent to the Mississippi as he did in the other two thirds of the state combined.[180] Douglas on the whole made a good showing in the popular vote along the Border, although the figures confirmed that Bell had indeed been the primary beneficiary of the Little Giant's campaign there.[181]

But it was the electoral vote that determined the outcome of the election, and although the Republicans could muster only about 40 percent of the popular vote, they had 180 votes in the electoral college to Breckinridge's 72, Bell's 39, and the 12 of Stephen Douglas. Abraham Lincoln would be the next President of the United States.

Douglas and his little party left Mobile shortly after the election

[176] *Tribune and Almanac for 1864*, p. 70.

[177] Ibid. Breckinridge received a popular vote of 847,953; Bell, 590,631.

[178] Ibid. Douglas received 163,525 votes in the South; Bell, 515,973. Breckinridge polled 570,871.

[179] *Richmond Enquirer*, November 9, 1860.

[180] Crenshaw, *Slave States*, p. 185 n.

[181] *Tribune Almanac for 1864*, p. 70.

and went by boat to New Orleans.[182] Perhaps it was there that Douglas for the first time noticed that the news of Lincoln's victory was carried in some Southern papers in the black-bordered columns usually reserved for obituaries.[183] Even the loyal and reasonable Forsyth was preparing an editorial in the *Register* calling for a state convention to discuss Alabama's next move. Sheridan later wrote that he had never seen Douglas more despondent.[184]

Douglas stayed six days in New Orleans, delivering impromptu speeches and penning an open letter. He regretted the election of Lincoln as much as any man in America, but warned that it did not by itself constitute a cause for secession. "The President," he said, "can do nothing except what the law authorizes. . . . Four years will soon pass away, when the ballot-box will furnish a peaceful, legal and constitutional remedy for all the evils and grievances with which the country may be afflicted."[185] Perhaps here is the best evidence of all of the nonpolitical nature of Douglas' second Southern tour. He had waited until after the election was over to visit the largest city in the South and the one in which he had the greatest following, choosing to ignore a telegram sent him on November 1 by Pierre Soulé, who pleaded that a visit by Douglas to New Orleans "would be of immense effect and by increasing our majority in the city perhaps enable us to carry the state."[186] Once he had arrived, he preached the same line of high unionism and restraint that had characterized his whole journey.

In times past Douglas would have stayed longer in New Orleans; his overseers would have come down from Mississippi and there would have been business to discuss and time to partake of the good food and drink of the old French city. But there was so little time now. There would soon be real trouble brewing in the land,

[182] The Douglas family went on the *Alabama*. For an account of Douglas' arrival in New Orleans and his warm reception there, see the *New York Times*, November 15, 1860; *New Orleans Picayune*, November 9, 10, 1860.

[183] *Vicksburg Weekly Sun*, November 12, 1860.

[184] Milton, *Eve of Conflict*, p. 500.

[185] Johannsen, ed., *Letters of Douglas*, pp. 500–502.

[186] Telegram of Pierre Soulé and W. C. Templeton to Douglas, New Orleans, November 1, 1860; Douglas MSS.

and whenever Douglas sensed a crisis, he moved. In mid-November of 1860 he turned instinctively toward the political storm center that was Washington. On the fourteenth he, Mrs. Douglas, and the loyal Sheridan boarded the *James Battle* for the trip up the Mississippi.[187] The times were too urgent for the kind of slow ocean voyage by way of New York that he needed so badly.[188] It was the last time he would see the South or travel on the broad river that had so often brought him down to Dixie in happier times and bound him to the people who dwelt along its banks.

Perhaps some who watched Douglas make his way up the gangplank that morning thought they detected that a little of the old bounce had gone out of his step or that the characteristic fire had left his eye.[189] But in their place there was not resignation or defeat, but a grim determination to carry on. The country would need him now more than ever. Douglas had been beaten but was far from broken. He had lost the prize he had coveted for most of his adult life, but the moment of his true greatness had only begun.

[187] Milton, *Eve of Conflict*, p. 502.

[188] The *New York Times*, November 15, 1860, reported Douglas seriously ill.

[189] Ibid.; *Mobile Daily Advertiser*, November 6, 1860.

7. The Union Forever

Stephen Douglas came back to Washington late in 1860 without a role. The little man who stepped down from the cars at the old Baltimore and Ohio station behind the Capitol that cold morning of December 1[1] knew better than any other Northern leader the magnitude of the crisis that was now upon the country and the lateness of the hour.[2] He had never taken Southern threats of secession over the last ten years lightly, and he knew that this time the slave states were in deadly earnest, that even now South Carolina was preparing to leave the Union,[3] and that Mississippi and Alabama, Florida and Georgia were not far behind her. Better than most members of his own party, far better than the scores of new Republican congressmen who would soon be flocking into Washington, the Little Giant realized that it was no "artificial"[4] crisis that now faced the country. He knew that the South would

[1] *Washington Daily National Intelligencer*, December 4, 1860.

[2] Robert W. Johannsen, ed., *The Letters of Stephen A. Douglas*, pp. 503–506.

[3] South Carolina passed its Ordinance of Secession December 20, 1860, at Charleston.

[4] A favorite term of Lincoln's. See John G. Nicolay and John Hay, eds., *Complete Works of Abraham Lincoln*, VI, 125, 130.

not easily be forced or coaxed back from the brink of disunion. Far more clearly than the tall man out in Illinois, who was at that moment closing down his law office and preparing to leave the old yellow-brown house on Eighth Street in Springfield for his new address on Pennsylvania Avenue, Douglas sensed that only quick, decisive action might still somehow hold America together. He doubted privately that even this would succeed.[5]

The country now stood in desperate need of Douglas' great gifts as a nationalist and a shaper of compromise, but thoughtful men must have wondered if these traditional virtues were enough for the seriousness of the times and if his aggressive, pragmatic style of problem-solving would mesh with the sheer size of the crisis that now faced the country. The Douglas of early December, 1860, was still without plan or program or direction. He stood ready to try to lead the American people out of the great dangers to which years of recklessness and folly and pride had brought them, but whether they would follow was very much open to question.

Even more doubtful was the degree of power Douglas could bring to bear on the crisis. Under Illinois law he had not had to give up his Senate seat to run for the presidency. He could look forward to four more years in the upper chamber. He was still a great national figure. He had polled the second largest popular vote in the presidential election. He had been the only candidate to wage a truly national campaign and the only one who in the end had won electoral votes on both sides of the Mason-Dixon Line. His great campaign had helped to tilt the balance in dozens of closely contested races and brought many Democratic congressmen back to Washington. He was still the most powerful Democrat on Capitol Hill and the *de facto* leader of his party. He remained influential in the Border states, which held the key to the national crisis in the days that lay ahead and had to be kept in the Union at almost any cost. Large segments of moderate opinion in both the North and the South still looked to him for guidance.

Yet Stephen Douglas had no illusions about the extent of his

[5] Johannsen, ed., *Letters of Douglas*, p. 503.

political power. He knew that he could expect the deep-seated animosity of the incumbent President and the opposition of the next. He knew he had the wholehearted confidence of neither major party.[6] Although the Republicans would not have an absolute majority in a full Congress, effective control would be theirs unless all Democrats stayed in their seats and sought help from the few Americans in the House.[7] Yet even now shortsighted men in Columbia and Montgomery, in Jackson and Milledgeville, were preparing to withdraw their representatives from Washington.

Douglas' first public statement upon returning to Washington was brief and eloquent. He begged the nation to put aside any thought of former party divisions, any concern for personal and political prejudices: "Let all asperities drop, all ill feeling be buried, and let all real patriots strive to save the Union."[8]

But if the country heard, it did not listen, and the dark storm clouds of civil war continued to gather on the political horizon. Four days later the stock market plunged sharply,[9] and by December 20 Douglas was urging the Senate not to adjourn for the traditional Christmas recess: "I know we do not feel like going abroad and enjoying a holiday. I trust there may be something done to restore peace to the country. This is a good time to do it, and I hope we shall remain in session."[10] And that same day down in Charleston at Institute Hall, where less than a year before the Democrats had assembled to nominate the next President of the United States, the

[6] Howard K. Beale, ed., *Diary of Gideon Welles*, I, 34.

[7] The Congress that assembled on December 3, 1860, was divided as follows: Senate, 38 Democrats, 2 Americans, 25 Republicans; House, 101 Democrats, 23 Americans, 113 Republicans. *Tribune Almanac* for 1860, pp. 17-18. After the elections of November, 1860, it was estimated that the next Congress would be divided: Senate, 29 Republicans, 37 Democrats and Americans; House, 108 Republicans, 129 Democrats and Americans. James F. Rhodes, *History of the United States from the Compromise of 1850*, II, 501 n.

[8] Remarks made by Douglas on the evening of December 1, 1860, to well-wishers who had come to serenade him at his Washington home upon his return to the Capital. *Washington Daily National Intelligencer*, December 4, 1860.

[9] *New York Times*, December 5, 1860.

[10] *Cong. Globe*, 36th Cong., 2nd sess., p. 158.

delegates from all over South Carolina met to sign the Ordinance of Secession.

Douglas now plunged himself into the urgency of the moment with that great energy and ceaseless motion with which he had greeted every major challenge in his long public life. In the hour of crisis the bitterness of the defeat in November was forgotten, and concern for the desperate state of his personal finances shoved aside.[11] He readily agreed to serve on the bipartisan Senate Committee of Thirteen, which had been hastily formed to try to forge a compromise that might yet somehow save the Union. He encouraged former President Tyler in his plans for a peace conference of all the states to be held in Washington,[12] and he tried desperately to keep the other states of the lower South from following South Carolina out of the Union. To the people of Georgia, whose representatives were about to meet in convention to decide the fate of their state, he sent a message: "We have hope. . . . Don't give up the ship; don't despair of the Republic."[13]

On January 3 Douglas rose to deliver his first major address to the Senate since the previous spring. It was one of his longest and most impassioned speeches. It was also one of his worst.

The Senate galleries were packed to overflowing as they always were when Douglas spoke. He could still send a thrill of excitement through the audience with his powerful, rolling oratory, but careful listeners now found difficulty in following the loose thread of his argument and grew exasperated at the apparent contradictions that filled his speech.[14] He cautioned the South that the election of Lincoln was in itself no cause for secession, and then proceeded to denounce the incoming President as a dangerous radical intent on stamping out slavery and stirring up servile insurrection in the South.[15] He blamed all the present troubles on the proponents of congressional intervention, and then shocked his audience with the

[11] Johannsen, ed., *Letters of Douglas*, p. 508.

[12] Ibid., p. 507.

[13] *Cong. Globe*, 36th Cong., 2nd sess., p. 668. Johannsen, ed., *Letters of Douglas*, p. 506.

[14] *New York Times*, January 5, 1861.

[15] *Cong. Globe*, 36th Cong., 2nd sess., app., pp. 38–39.

announcement that "coercion is the vital principle upon which all government rests."[16] He also entered a plea for Senator Crittenden's plan for the resurrection of the Missouri Compromise line and its extension to the Pacific—a move that would have required an unprecedented degree of congressional interference. Furthermore, Douglas was faintly dishonest in criticizing Republican opposition to the Crittenden plan. It was not, as Douglas tried to maintain, an instance of the party that for years had bewailed the repeal of the Missouri Compromise now refusing to reinstate it. The Crittenden scheme called for positive protection of slavery below the 36°30′ line; the original 1820 legislation had only agreed to permit its spread there.[17]

His views on secession appeared immature and strangely provincial. Douglas seemed primarily worried that the South might close the Mississippi River and deprive the Northwest of its outlet to the sea.[18] He ridiculed the feeble, hesitant reaction of Buchanan, yet proceeded to advocate a policy not markedly different from that of the President himself. He poked fun at Buchanan's lame contention that the federal government had no right to coerce a state, yet cautioned against the use of force.[19] Douglas confessed weakly that South Carolina's secession was an accomplished fact: "I agree that it is wrong, unlawful, unconstitutional, criminal. In my opinion, South Carolina had no right to secede; but she has done it."[20]

The country was not impressed by Douglas' realism. The *New York Times* remarked that Douglas "could have given no more conclusive proof that he is not the man for any greater emergencies than those which arise in the ordinary partisan conflicts of the day. . . . He lends strength and courage to the disunion movement by proclaiming its triumphant success before it has struck the first real blow in the tremendous work it has undertaken." The *Times* concluded, "With an opportunity seldom offered to any public man

16 Ibid., app., p. 40.

17 Ibid., app., p. 41. Johannsen, ed., *Letters of Douglas*, pp. 504–505.

18 *Cong. Globe*, 36th Cong., 2nd sess., app., pp. 39–40. Johannsen, ed., *Letters of Douglas*, p. 505.

19 *Cong. Globe*, 36th Cong., 2nd sess., app., pp. 40-41.

20 Ibid., app., p. 39.

to render his country a distinguished and immortal service, he has capitulated at the very first summons of surrender."[21]

But Douglas had not capitulated, nor would he capitulate in the months that lay ahead. He was still largely an undisciplined political force striking out in all directions at once in a desperate effort to prevent disaster. At the first overt act of secession back in December he had swung into motion, but he had not yet begun to act. In early January he was still a man searching for a sound political footing.

Slowly a course of action began to take shape in Douglas' mind. In his January 3 speech he had proposed two ways to deal with secession: by force of arms or by "peaceable adjustment of the matters in controversy."[22] The first alternative Douglas appeared to rule out altogether in the early months of 1861: 'I will not meditate war, nor tolerate the idea, until every effort at peaceful adjustment shall have been exhausted, and the last ray of hope shall have deserted the patriot's heart."[23] Douglas might ridicule the South for leaving the Union because it could not have a slave code,[24] but he never for a moment made the mistake many Northern politicians on both sides of the aisle did in underestimating the resolution of the South or the determination of its people to fight for what they considered their way of life.[25] Douglas' error was of the opposite kind. For too long he discounted the possibility that the North might in the end resort to total war to preserve the Union. In January he predicted that if hostilities ever did in fact break out, they would be brief and the end result would be two separate nations. "Surely," he exclaimed to his Northern colleagues, "you do not expect to exterminate or subjugate ten million people, the entire population of one section, as a means of preserving amiable relations between the two sections!"[26] Three weeks later he spoke with

[21] *New York Times*, January 5, 1860.
[22] *Cong. Globe*, 36th Cong., 2nd sess., app., p. 39.
[23] Ibid.; Johannsen, ed., *Letters of Douglas*, p. 504.
[24] *Cong. Globe*, 36th Cong., 2nd sess., p. 58.
[25] Ibid., app., p. 42.
[26] Ibid.

disdain of "that class of Union men who propose to destroy the Union in order to preserve it; to break it up in order to maintain it."[27]

The second alternative, "the peaceable adjustment"[28] of outstanding differences between the North and the South, meant simply another major compromise, this time in the form of an amendment to the Constitution. Efforts at effecting a formal compromise occupied the majority of Douglas' public pronouncements on the national crisis from the time Congress reconvened in December until the firing on Fort Sumter in April.

Yet perhaps the search for a formal constitutional compromise was not really uppermost in Douglas' mind. Perhaps that search was in fact primarily a means of delay—a means to dissuade hotheads in both the North and the South from making any precipitate move. Douglas also must have seen in his repeated calls for compromise a convenient way to embarrass the incoming President, should he refuse to support such a move, and a means to split Lincoln from the radical members of his party, should he consent.

Douglas-the-politician continued to talk of a compromise, but Douglas-the-statesman in the early weeks of 1861 began to turn his attentions elsewhere—toward a plan for peaceful separation. Despairing of forging any acceptable compromise and unwilling to see the country led into the horrors of civil war, Douglas was for a time willing to devise a scheme under which the dissident Southern states might depart in peace. His was a predisposition more than a policy. He was always careful to point out that he was first of all in favor of reconciliation through a constitutional amendment and would consider separation only as a last resort.[29] After all, in any sectional dispute he now belonged first to the North, and he had grown wary of doing anything that would once more cause him to be labeled an appeaser.[30] Yet his prescription for avoiding war was implicit in almost everything Douglas said and did right up to the eve of Fort Sumter. He went to great lengths not to an-

[27] Ibid., p. 668.

[28] Ibid., app., p. 39.

[29] *Cong. Globe*, 37th Cong., special sess., p. 1460.

[30] Ibid., 36th Cong., 2nd sess., app., p. 41.

tagonize the South. In the early weeks of 1861 he seemed often to blame the North in general and the Republicans in particular, more than the secessionists themselves, for the present crisis.[31] He urged the Senate to stop describing the South's course as one of "insurrection" since, he explained, "It does not do any good to use terms that irritate."[32] In February he urged against trying to carry the United States mail in the South "under the existing difficulties where the carrying of them will lead to collision and perhaps to bloodshed."[33]

Early in the year Douglas seemed to be feeling his way toward advocating acceptance and perhaps recognition in one form or another of the secessionist government of South Carolina: "We are bound," he instructed the Senate, "by the usages of nations, by the laws of civilization, by the uniform practice of our own Government, to acknowledge the existence of a Government *de facto*, so long as it maintains its undivided authority."[34] Right up to the time the first shot of the Civil War was fired, Douglas urged a flexible attitude toward the question of the federal forts in the South: "Whoever holds the States in whose limits those forts are placed is entitled to the forts themselves, unless there is something peculiar in the location of some particular fort that makes it important for us to hold it for the general defense of the whole country."[35] He then at once proceeded to exclude those forts at Charleston and Pensacola, which were currently causing most of the trouble, from the list of installations vital to the national welfare and safety. In the same speech he urged against trying to collect federal revenues in seceded states since "it is morally wrong to collect revenue from a people you do not protect."[36] When the national spotlight began to fall more and more on Fort Sumter, Douglas favored evacuation

31 Ibid., 37th Cong., special sess., pp. 1443, 1461; and 36th Cong., 2nd sess., app., pp. 38–39.

32 Ibid., 36th Cong., 2nd sess., p. 1080.

33 Ibid.

34 Ibid., app., p. 41.

35 Ibid., 37th Cong., special sess., p. 1459.

36 Ibid.

and had little use for Republican plans to reinforce or revictual the garrison.[37]

As he had often done in the past,[38] Douglas, beneath the screen of furious activity he presented to the world, was in fact desperately playing for time—time for tempers to cool in the South, time for the neophyte Republicans to awaken themselves to the realities of governing a nation and to the magnitude of the crisis that now faced it. In the first weeks of 1861 he saw secession by South Carolina as an accomplished fact, albeit an unpleasant one. He hoped to avoid a course that would precipitate other Southern states into joining her and together forming a Southern confederacy.[39] As 1861 wore on and more states left the Union and the Confederacy began to take shape, Douglas still urged prudence and delay on the part of the government in Washington. While accurately assessing the underlying unity of the Southern people, Douglas grasped the fundamental nature of the divisive forces at work in their government —the personal and state jealousies that one day would go far toward hastening its defeat—and he pleaded for patience.[40] In the case of Fort Sumter, Douglas saw a small, relatively unimportant and quite indefensible garrison in the harbor of a Southern city rapidly becoming a symbol—another one of those symbols and abstractions that had done so much to bring America to the present crisis. Thoughtful, well-meaning people in the South who represented the moderate opinion that Douglas always hoped would some day reassert itself below the Mason-Dixon Line wrote to warn that the stubborn attitude on the part of the federal government toward the Charleston forts was playing into the hands of the fire-eaters. "Give up Sumter and Pickens," wrote Douglas' old ally H. W. Miller from Raleigh, "and we can beat the secessionists in this state."[41]

[37] Ibid., p. 1461.

[38] Particularly during the Lecompton controversy, the conventions of 1860, and the presidential campaign of that year.

[39] *Cong. Globe*, 36th Cong., 2nd sess., app., p. 39.

[40] Ibid., p. 1461; Nevins, *The War for the Union*, I, 20.

[41] H. W. Miller to Douglas, Raleigh, N.C., March 31, 1861; Douglas MSS.

Sometime early in 1861 an extraordinary plan began to take shape in Douglas' mind. Ever since his 1853 visit to Europe he had been attracted to the German Zollverein. He now outlined in a lengthy document that came to light after his death a plan for a customs union for all of North America, stretching from "the frozen ocean to the Isthmus of Panama."[42] The scheme would, of course, have included the Confederate States and would have provided a measure of adjustment to the secession crisis until political reunion might one day take place. Douglas' proposal was undated, but it must have been drawn up after the Mississippi River had been effectively closed to Northern commerce sometime in February, since in the course of his exposition Douglas remarked that the people of the Northwest could never recognize the right of the South to "deprive them of all access to the ocean and all communication with the markets and people of the world beyond the great waters."[43] W. H. Russell of the *London Times* states in his diary, in an entry dated April 4, that Douglas mentioned the plan to him at a dinner attended by a large number of members of the new Lincoln cabinet.[44] The most realistic date for the proposal would therefore seem to be sometime in March or late February.[45]

This extraordinary scheme, with its apparent acceptance of political separation by the South for the time being in return for a loose form of economic union, was paradoxically the last flowering of the old-style nationalism of Stephen Douglas—the nationalism based on the ready assumptions of one who had begun his political career almost thirty years before as a confirmed disciple of Andrew Jackson. With his talk about Canada and Latin America, Douglas was making one last effort to restore the old momentum of expansion that had always been central to his concept of the nation. The emphasis on economic ties that dominated the customs

[42] Stephen A. Douglas, *An American Continental Commercial Union or Alliance*, ed. J. Madison Cutts, p. 13.

[43] Ibid., p. 21.

[44] W. H. Russell, *My Diary North and South*, entry for April 4, 1861.

[45] Douglas' first public hint at the customs union proposal was in his Senate speech of February 20, 1861. *Cong. Globe*, 36th Cong., 2nd sess., pp. 1051–1053; also see 37th Cong., special sess., p. 1461.

union scheme was wholly in keeping with Douglas' brand of nationalism, which had always at bottom been materialistic in its expression. Physical growth and prosperity had consistently claimed the major share of the attentions of the Illinois Senator. Dams and tariffs and railroads and harbors and homesteads—these were the things he understood best. There was still a great deal of Jackson and more than a little of the old Whig in Stephen Douglas.

This venerable political recipe might have once more worked its magic a few years earlier. But in the present crisis it seemed to have an anachronistic ring. Given the lateness of the hour, another dose of national expansion and the prospect of increased commerce were simply not enough for the country. And by March of 1861, with seven Southern states now gone from the Union, the American people probably began to feel that the easy, tolerant hand of Douglas, who had always mistrusted the centralization of too much power in Washington, who had always taken a benevolent, indulgent attitude toward sectionalism, and who even now counseled acceptance of secession, no longer suited the needs of the hour. They followed instead those who felt that there might be something worse than the use of force and the civil war that would follow hard upon it.

While Douglas acted like a man who sought some formula for the peaceful separation of the South from the North, he continued to talk as one in desperate search of a formal compromise that might somehow reunite the country. He lent his support to almost every one of the major compromise proposals that filled the overheated political atmosphere of Washington in the early months of 1861, and he was one of the sponsors of the Crittenden Amendment—the most important of them all.[46]

[46] The central part of the Crittenden proposal called for amending the Constitution to extend the 36°30′ line to the Pacific, prohibiting slavery above it, but, unlike the Missouri Compromise, protecting the institution below it. Other passages called for strict enforcement of the Fugitive Slave Law, federal compensation for slaves forcefully taken from their owners, prohibition of the abolition of slavery in the District of Columbia and in federal installations within the slave states. Also included were safeguards against interference with the domes-

But the restless Little Giant was not content merely to support the proposals of others. A few days after Crittenden had introduced his plan, Douglas outlined to the Senate one of his own.[47] It began with the familiar Douglas plea for nonintervention by the federal government in the problems of slavery in the territories: "Congress shall make no [new] law on the subject of slavery in the Territories." Furthermore, the existing status of slavery in any given territory was to remain unchanged until its population reached fifty thousand, at which time it "shall have the right of self-government as to its domestic policy," although it had not yet attained statehood. There were to be no further acquisitions of new territory "except by treaty or the concurrent vote of two-thirds in each House of Congress." In addition, the right to vote and hold public office in territories as well as states was to be limited to white men. The final sections of the Douglas compromise endorsed those parts of the Crittenden proposal that called for a stronger law on fugitive slaves and that forbade the abolition of slavery in the District of Columbia or on federal property within a state.[48]

Douglas' proposal at first glance appeared quite unexceptional. It would not have altered immediately the existing status of slavery in any state or territory. But the willingness with which Douglas, by virtue of his two-thirds requirement for the addition of any new land to the national domain, in effect gave the Republicans a veto over any further projects of territorial acquisition, suggested that he was now willing to surrender his old and cherished goal of continual national expansion.

Something else too had disappeared from the traditional Douglas catechism. By raising the size of the population necessary for a territory to decide on the question of slavery to fifty thousand, Doug-

---

tic slave trade and a call for rigid enforcement of laws against the African slave trade. Finally, there were to be no future amendments changing the status of slavery in America.

[47] Douglas introduced his compromise proposals on December 23, 1860, in the Committee of Thirteen. He outlined them to the Senate itself on January 3, 1861. *Cong. Globe*, 36th Cong., 2nd sess., app., pp. 41–42.

[48] Ibid., p. 41.

las had outwardly severely qualified his concept of popular sovereignty. Of the five existing territories—New Mexico, Utah, Kansas, Nebraska, and Washington—and the three that were about to be organized—Dakota, Colorado, and Nevada—only Kansas and New Mexico had populations in excess of that figure. Kansas was to become a state in only a few weeks.[49] Therefore, under Douglas' proposal, the status of slavery in every territory except New Mexico was to be frozen by Congress for some time to come. Yet the change was more apparent than real. What Douglas had given up was the hard side of popular sovereignty, the inflexible, exclusive, doctrinaire side that had for a long time now lacked relevance to the territorial experience. The soft, practical side—the side that served best as a means to national unity and a fair reflector of political realities—remained basically unchanged. By early 1861 it was more obvious than ever that slavery was not going to gain a permanent foothold in the new lands west of the Mississippi. Western climate was joining hands with the climate of majority public opinion in the nation to force an end to the expansion of the peculiar institution. Only New Mexico of all the territories still provided slavery with a legal welcome, and it too showed signs of turning to free-soil. Douglas' compromise would simply have ratified the existing status of all free-soil territories, while permitting change in the one territory where slavery had a legal, although tenuous, foothold.[50] Where the current status of slavery reflected popular opinion in the territory, there was no need for change; in the one area where it probably did not, there was provision for change.

Douglas was far from alone in recognizing the attractions inherent in the idea of popular sovereignty. The Republicans early in

[49] Kansas became a state on January 29, 1861. New Mexico in 1860 had a population of 93,516. Utah, the next territory in population, had only 40,273 inhabitants in 1860. *Population of the United States in 1860, Compiled from the Original Returns of the Eighth Census*, pp. 573, 575.

[50] New Mexico, organized under the 1850 Compromise without any federal restriction on slavery, passed a territorial slave code in 1859 and repealed it early in 1862. William A. Keleher, *Turmoil in New Mexico, 1846–1868*, p. 165. Allan Nevins, *Emergence of Lincoln*, II, 403, 409. In 1860 there were only 46 Negroes in New Mexico out of a population in excess of 93,000. *Eighth Census*, p. 572. Only about half of these Negroes were slaves.

1861 voted to organize the territories of Colorado, Nevada, and Dakota without any congressional prohibition on slavery and even balked at repealing New Mexico's slave code. Douglas immediately described the move as an abandonment by the Republicans of the heart of the Chicago platform and a major concession to the slave states.[51] But in fact the Republicans had stopped far short of specifically endorsing the hard side of popular sovereignty and had embraced only a specious form of the soft side. They knew that the climate of the Rockies and plains was unsuited to slavery and that these new territories would be free-soil. If the Republican gesture was intended as a concession toward the South in the interest of reaching a detente on slavery, it was too late by several years. Thus, ironically, in the end Douglas himself gave up the hard side of his program, while his political opponents tried to take over the soft side for their own.

From the outset the chances for a constitutional compromise were at best poor. The outlook for a sectional rapprochement had begun to dim a year before when Yancey led his fellow Southerners out of Institute Hall in Charleston; after South Carolina seceded in December, it was very dark indeed. When the Senate Committee of Thirteen failed to produce an acceptable compromise and the Washington Peace Conference called by John Tyler proved an exercise in futility that February, even Stephen Douglas must have felt the quest was hopeless. Perhaps this explains the apparent nonchalance with which he continued to put forward compromise proposals that outwardly overthrew so much that had long been axiomatic to the Douglas creed, while he devoted his most serious efforts to finding a method of peaceful separation.

Throughout the last decade the idea of compromise had been steadily falling from favor, and by 1861 a large portion of Americans north and south distrusted the whole notion. Too often in the past the shapers of a major national compromise had proclaimed their work a final solution to the problems posed by slavery, only

[51] *Cong. Globe*, 36th Cong., 2nd sess., p. 1391.

to see the fragile equilibrium they had engineered disappear and a new wave of unrest and demands for a fresh settlement sweep the land. Most of the important compromise proposals in the months prior to the outbreak of war were put forward by representatives of states close to the border.[52] Neither the lower South nor New England appeared really to want a formal settlement. The South was now under the control of men who seemed to want a war. The North for its part looked back upon the dismal record left by previous compromises and decided that they had been in reality merely a disguise for one capitulation after the other to the demands of the South. Early in the year the *New York Times* remarked that compromises "have been tried over and over again and in each instance the controversy has been broadened and sharpened and made worse instead of better." It called the current negotiations "contests rather than compromises—struggles of the South to secure concessions from the North." The *Times* denounced the South for using negotiations as part of a scheme "by which the fruits of the terror inspired by actual disunion were to be gathered" and for treating compromise "too much like a part of the secession movement."[53]

So much that had aided the settlements of 1850 and 1854 was now missing from the national political picture in 1861. Those earlier compromises were concerned primarily with the future of slavery in the territories. At bottom they dealt with events on the national periphery; neither North nor South thought that the survival of its whole way of life was really involved. The politics of slavery was still considered a game in which the stakes were high but not yet vital. There were more pieces on the national political chessboard in those days—more components that a skilled manipulator like Douglas could juggle and rearrange to the eventual satisfaction of the spokesmen of all the sections. In 1850 the admission of California as a free state could be balanced against a

[52] The important compromise proposals were put forward by John Crittenden of Kentucky, Tom Corwin and John Sherman of Ohio, Henry Winter Davis of Maryland, and Douglas of Illinois, and by the Peace Conference called at the instigation of Virginia.

[53] *New York Times*, January 10, 1861.

stronger fugitive slave law, a smaller Texas against federal financial aid to that state, the restriction of the slave trade in the District of Columbia against stronger guarantees that slavery itself would not be abolished there.

The situation early in 1861 was different. The challenge facing the country was more awesome and immediate, its composition more monolithic. The South had come to feel that the whole future of slavery was at stake and with it the entire way of life below the Mason-Dixon Line. No longer was the central focus of compromise the territorial periphery; secession struck at the foundations of the Union itself. Earlier in the decade just ended there had still been some semblance of equality between the sections, some realistic pretensions to a balance that shrewd politicians like Douglas could help to strike. By 1861 the South was very much a minority section. In April of that year the long awaited census figures were announced.[54] They showed that the South had lagged markedly behind the North and West in growth over the last ten years, and its demands for a dominant voice in national affairs began to seem more and more preposterous.[55]

In past settlements there had been the priceless ingredient of time —time for overheated political tempers to cool, time to break in complex new machinery like the Fugitive Slave Law. Now the South looked at new census results that meant it would soon be losing six more congressmen to the North and West; it looked at the growing industrial power of the North and at the new intransigence of the men who led it, and decided that time was no longer on the side of the slave states.[56] Nor were the newly arrived Republicans, sampling the heady taste of power for the first time, likely to prize patience high among the political virtues.

If the earlier compromises had resolutely dealt with some of the problems facing the country, they had also just as resolutely ig-

54 Ibid., April 2, 1861.

55 The 1860 census showed that in the decade just ended the free states had increased their population by 41.3%, the slave states by only 27.4%. *Tribune Almanac for 1862*, p. 55.

56 *New York Times*, April 2, 1861; *Cong. Globe*, 36th Cong., 2nd sess., p. 1388.

nored others. The legislation of 1850 and 1854 had left in their wake an uncomfortably large number of unanswered questions concerning the powers of Congress and the territories over slavery. Embarrassing differences had been papered over with vague and frequently ambivalent language. It may have been the most practical way out of the difficulty, but the leaders of the North and South in 1861 no longer thought first of practicality. They talked of morals and rights and ways of life, and demanded sharp and clear definition in place of the old benign ambiguity.[57]

The old Whigs, with their emphasis on union and compromise, had disappeared as a political party. Douglas had put together the compromise of 1850 behind the august shield provided by Henry Clay.[58] But Clay was gone now too, and there was no one to take his place in the move toward a compromise—no one to stand as a symbol of national unity above party.

Douglas too had changed. He had just emerged from a bitter presidential campaign, and the mire of partisan politics still clung to him. He had become too controversial and had made too many enemies in recent years to command the immense amount of trust needed to mold a compromise and force it through. He did not have the confidence of the leaders of the South. The West, on which Douglas had based so much of his strength and which he always considered an instrument working toward sectional reconciliation, no longer existed as a separate political force. It too had lost its identity in the madness of the times, and its people had rushed to join the North or the South.

Douglas-the-compromiser no longer seemed to fit the needs of the age. He had always been best at reflecting a consensus and ratifying an existing balance of power in his formal compromises. Now the country needed a more imaginative and revolutionary settlement if it was to continue as one nation. It demanded an architect; Douglas offered the services of an engineer. The Crittenden proposal, which he supported, appeared regressive to many people. With its resurrection and extension of the Missouri Compromise line, it

[57] *Cong. Globe*, 36th Cong., 2nd sess., pp. 661 and 1388.
[58] Holman Hamilton, *Prologue to Conflict*, pp. 133–150.

seemed to offer little more than a dynamic return to the past. Douglas' own plan, with its implied brake on national expansion and on further change in the status of slavery in the territories, would have frozen a status quo that most Americans now found unacceptable. There was also something ludicrously anachronistic in his continued calls for congressional nonintervention in the hour of national crisis.[59]

There were other difficulties as well. The settlements of 1850 and 1854 had taken the form of simple legislation. Douglas now felt that any new compromise should not only be incorporated into the Constitution under the difficult amending process, but made forever irrevocable.[60] In the past, Douglas could carry on his maneuvers toward compromise secure in the knowledge that his party dominated all three branches of the government. Now any settlement had to take into account the large number of Republicans in Congress who could easily block any attempt to obtain the two-thirds majority needed for a Constitutional amendment.

In 1850 and 1854 Douglas had been able to count on the White House for ready support of his efforts at compromise. But Abraham Lincoln was different. His party had been born in opposition to the Kansas-Nebraska Act, and he had spent eight years attacking the repeal of the Missouri Compromise. Lincoln remembered that slavery had been fastened upon the new American nation in the compromises that went into the making of the Constitution and that the institution had been extended by the legislation of 1820, 1850, and 1854. He now saw the proposals for another compromise as merely a thinly disguised Democratic plot.[61] He had been elected President on the Chicago Platform that opposed the further extension of slavery, and now the Democrats and the South were asking him to surrender the essence of that platform before he took office —perhaps even as a precondition for his being able to take the helm

[59] *Cong. Globe*, 36th Cong., 2nd sess., pp. 661, 668, 1081; app., p. 41. Johannsen, ed., *Letters of Douglas*, pp. 504–505.

[60] *Cong. Globe*, 36th Cong., 2nd sess., p. 1388 and app., p. 41.

[61] Nicolay and Hay, eds., *Works of Lincoln*, VI, 77–78, 82.

of a united country at all.[62] The Republicans were new to power and insecure. They feared that any compromise would destroy their fragile political identity.[63] In the weeks following the 1860 election the Republicans set their minds against most of the plans for compromise that were put forward and in the end defeated both the Crittenden and Douglas proposals.[64] Douglas called on Lincoln repeatedly in late February and early March to urge the need for compromise, but all his efforts produced only one noncommittal reference to the whole idea of a formal settlement in the closing paragraphs of the Inaugural Address.[65]

Douglas' relations with the new President were, however, from the outset cordial—far better than those he had enjoyed with Buchanan over the last three and a half years. Shortly after the President-elect arrived in Washington, Douglas called on him at Willard's Hotel and pledged his help and support in the crisis that now faced the republic. It must have been an emotional encounter. Governor Pollock of Pennsylvania was present that day, and he later wrote that tears came to Lincoln's eyes as he seized his old adversary's hand and said simply, "God bless you Douglas."[66]

But the good feeling between the two men should not be exaggerated. Lincoln was still the leader of the rival party. Within a few weeks of assuming office he removed a large number of Douglas' friends from important government posts.[67] Douglas, for his

[62] *New York Times*, January 28, 1861.

[63] Carl Schurz, *The Reminiscences of Carl Schurz*, II, 211–214.

[64] The Crittenden and Douglas proposals were defeated by the Republicans in the Joint Committee of Thirteen late in December, 1860. George F. Milton, *Eve of Conflict*, p. 525; Rhodes, *History of the United States*, III, 151–155. *Cong. Globe*, 36th Cong., 2nd sess., app., p. 41. A subsequent attempt to revive the Crittenden proposals together with part of Douglas' plan before the whole Senate was likewise defeated on January 16, 1861. *Cong. Globe*, 36th Cong., 2nd sess., pp. 237, 409.

[65] Allen Johnson, *Stephen A. Douglas*, p. 464; Louis Howland, *Stephen A. Douglas*, p. 362. The reference in Lincoln's Inaugural Address is found in Henry Steele Commager, ed., *Documents of American History*, p. 388.

[66] See notes of Governor James Pollock in *Journal of the Illinois State Historical Society* 23 (April 1930): 169.

[67] *Washington Daily Morning Chronicle*, October 26, 1864.

part, in the six weeks from the Inauguration to Fort Sumter, continued to treat Lincoln with something approaching indulgence. The man who had dominated the Washington scene for fifteen years could not help looking upon the President-elect as something of a provincial—perhaps even a little naive. In late February Douglas described Lincoln as "eminently a man of the atmosphere which surrounds him. He has not yet got out of Springfield. . . . He does not know that he is President-elect of the United States."[68]

Douglas may have been acting more and more like a statesman every day, but he had not ceased altogether to be a politician. He might hold Lincoln's hat on Inauguration Day and escort Mrs. Lincoln in the grand march at the ball that followed, but he had not for a moment forgotten the hard realities of party politics. Two days after Lincoln had taken the oath as the sixteenth President of the United States, Douglas rose in the Senate to deliver an enthusiastic and, upon closer examination, wholly misleading endorsement of the Inaugural Address. He concluded that Lincoln had given up any plans to resort to war in order to coerce the South back into the Union.[69] He snatched out of context Lincoln's noncommittal references to the possibility of a compromise and announced that the President now clearly favored amending the Constitution.[70] As for Lincoln's policy on Fort Sumter, Douglas stated confidently that if "the withdrawal of the troops would facilitate a peaceful solution, he is pledged to abandon the fort and withdraw the troops."[71]

Douglas knew better. Perhaps he still thought of Lincoln as the newcomer—the provincial, the "man of the atmosphere which surrounds him"—and was simply trying to put words in the President's mouth. Perhaps too he was feeling his way toward the unofficial role of premier and was making his first show of rallying Congress behind the new President. The most likely explanation of Douglas' interpretation of the Inaugural Address would, how-

[68] Johnson, *Stephen A. Douglas*, p. 461.
[69] *Cong. Globe*, 37th Cong., special sess., p. 1437.
[70] Ibid.
[71] Ibid.

ever, seem to be that, far earlier than most people in Washington, the Little Giant had grasped the deep and fundamental cleavage in the Republican party between the moderates and the radicals. By praising Lincoln as a man who sought compromise and had virtually given up plans for using force against the South, Douglas hoped to split the President from hard-liners like Wade, Sumner, and Trumbull. If the Republicans could be divided as the Democrats were divided, Douglas might yet emerge as the holder of the ultimate balance of power in Washington. For a while Douglas' scheme seemed to be working. Only days after the Inauguration the author of the *Diary of a Public Man* confided that many Republican Senators "knew Mr. Douglas to be really uttering the sentiments and sketching the policy of the President"![72]

The politician in Douglas died hard, but he was not the only man in the Capital who knew how to use people for his own ends. Abraham Lincoln understood what a valuable ally Stephen Douglas would make, and from the first moment of the President-elect's arrival in Washington he took the Little Giant into his confidence as he did no other Democrat. He flattered Douglas by reading him some passages from the Inaugural Address he would deliver in a few days. He asked his advice on Sumter and led him to believe that he agreed that the garrison should be evacuated.[73] In the end Lincoln went farther than Douglas in bending his old adversary to his own purposes.

In the Senate Douglas continued to go through the motions of urging his program for a major compromise on the one hand or peaceful separation on the other.[74] But a curious and unusual note of despair seemed to have crept into the Little Giant's public utterances late in March. He appeared less interested in the present crisis and talked more of the past and what might have been. He

[72] F. L. Bullard, ed., *Diary of a Public Man*, p. 95.

[73] Ibid., pp. 69, 91.

[74] *Cong. Globe*, 37th Cong., special sess., pp. 1459–1460, 1501. On March 15, Douglas told the Senate (p. 1459): "We cannot deny that there is a southern confederacy, *de facto*, in existence, with its capital at Montgomery. We may regret it. I regret it most profoundly; but I cannot deny the truth of the fact, painful, mortifying as it is."

filled his speeches with nostalgic references to popular sovereignty and the legislation of 1850 and 1854. Douglas too was beginning to show signs of the strain that the secession crisis had placed on the leaders of the nation. He lost his temper in an exchange with Republican Senators Daniel Clark and Timothy Howe, and in the only public reference he ever made in the Senate chamber to his defeat in the late presidential election, he exclaimed:

> Seven states are out of the Union, civil war is impending over you, commerce is interrupted, confidence destroyed, the country going to pieces, just because I was unable to defeat you. . . . You can boast that you have defeated me, but you have defeated your country with me. You can boast that you have triumphed over me, but you have triumphed over the unity of these States. Your triumph has brought disunion; and God only knows what consequences may grow out of it. . . . If I had succeeded in defeating your party at the presidential election, thereby rendering it certain that the policy of that party was not to be carried into effect, the people of the southern States would have rested in the security that they were safe, and the Union never would have been dissolved.[75]

Douglas was right in part. His election in itself quite probably would have done little to stem the tide of secession, and as President, caught up in the great sweep of events, he might have acted much like Abraham Lincoln. But if the nation could have elected Stephen Douglas President, that decision would have been a sign of the vigor of the underlying forces of moderation that might ultimately have pulled the country back from the brink of civil war. His election would have been more a reflection than a cause of unity, but no less desirable for being so.

During recent months, Douglas had appeared to deviate from the line of high Unionism he had adopted in the course of the 1860 campaign. His frantic efforts at compromise on the one hand and peaceful separation on the other suggested that perhaps his earlier pledges to preserve the Union by force if necessary had been set aside permanently.

[75] Ibid., p. 1503.

It took the news that began to come over the telegraph from Charleston that weekend of April 13–14 to complete the transformation that had begun in Stephen Douglas during the campaign for the presidency, to awaken him fully to the futility of his attempts at conciliation, and to shake him out of his nostalgic preoccupation with an era that he now knew was closed forever. Douglas had a better understanding of the South than almost any other Northern leader. But he was not prepared for the kind of insanity that sent the first shell arching out from Fort Johnson over the calm waters of Charleston Harbor toward Fort Sumter early on the morning of April 12.

On the evening of the Sunday that Washington learned of Sumter's fall, Douglas drove to the White House to call on President Lincoln. He stayed for more than two hours. Once more the President took his old rival into his confidence and showed him the order that he was about to issue calling for 75,000 volunteers. Douglas came back with the suggestion that the figure should be 200,000 and added, "You do not know the dishonest purposes of those men as I do."[76] The reserved and qualified account of that meeting Douglas issued to the press the next day did not tell the full story of that historic evening: "The substance of the conversation was that while Mr. Douglas was unalterably opposed to the administration on all its political issues, he was prepared to sustain the President in the exercises of all his constitutional functions to preserve the Union, and maintain the Government, and defend the Federal Capital."[77] It was a pedantic distinction and Douglas knew it. George Ashmun, who rode back from the White House in the same carriage with him that Sunday and to whom Douglas confided the details of the meeting later wrote: "I venture to say that no two men in the United States parted that night with a more cordial feeling of a united, friendly, and patriotic purpose than Mr. Lincoln and Mr. Douglas."[78]

[76] *Washington Daily Morning Chronicle*, October 26, 1864; John G. Nicolay and John Hay, *Abraham Lincoln: A History*, IV, 79–84.

[77] Johannsen, ed., *Letters of Douglas*, p. 509.

[78] *Washington Daily Morning Chronicle*, October 26, 1864.

Douglas now launched into a frenzy of activity. The man who for so long had closed his eyes to the use of force now called for total victory. The same man who in the past had urged the evacuation of Sumter now demanded that it be retaken at once. That was even more than Lincoln himself counseled. He scoffed at those military advisers who urged the North to adopt a defensive posture, and he called instead for carrying the war to the South. Douglas, who for so long had pleaded for patience toward the South, now replied to a question concerning the fate of the hundreds of Confederate sympathizers still in Washington: "If I were President, I'd convert them or hang them all within forty-eight hours."[79] The Little Giant was among the first to recognize the importance of keeping the Border states uncommitted and the Southern frontier far away from an easily defended natural boundary like the Ohio River. It was Douglas who first pointed out to Lincoln the strategic importance of Maryland and the vital necessity of holding strong points in Virginia like Fortress Monroe, Old Point Comfort, and Harpers Ferry.[80] A rumor began to circulate through Washington that the President had offered Douglas a brigadier generalship. Lincoln later disclaimed any knowledge of such a plan, but conceded diplomatically that Douglas did indeed have a firm grasp of military strategy.[81] Douglas quite probably would not have accepted a generalship if it had been tendered him. He had never been attracted to military life, and his only criticism of Lincoln's Inauguration was that the large number of troops in the parade up Pennsylvania Avenue had made the whole affair "too militaristic."[82] Yet one cannot help speculating on the influence the restless, energetic, imaginative Douglas would have exercised as a field commander upon the Northern armies which moved with such exasperating slowness in the first months of the war. He would never have lacked for mobility.

[79] Anonymous article in *Atlantic Monthly* 8 (August 1861): 212.
[80] *Washington Daily Morning Chronicle*, October 26, 1864.
[81] *Atlantic Monthly* 8: 212.
[82] Bullard, *Diary of a Public Man*, p. 79.

The change that Fort Sumter worked in the relationship between Lincoln and Douglas was an important turning point in the life of the Little Giant and in the history of the country, but it must not be removed from its larger historical setting and inflated out of all proportion. Ever since the 1858 campaign Lincoln and Douglas had been drawing closer together in their views on a wide variety of subjects, while the skies began to darken on the national horizon. Nor was Stephen Douglas the only Democrat to rally to the President in the hour of crisis. Even James Buchanan threw what remained of his power and prestige behind Lincoln after Sumter. It is in fact difficult to see how Douglas could have acted otherwise than he did.

A great change took place after the first shots of war had been fired, but it occurred more within the personality of Douglas himself than in his behavior, which had been undergoing a slow but perceptible transformation ever since the campaign of 1860. The forces that had in the past been at war within his spirit, the contradictions that had clouded his popular image and hindered his effectiveness at almost every turn, were now laid to rest. The old talk of compromise, which had come to have about it a hollow and hopeless ring, could now be forgotten. The old Douglas nationalism, which for too many years had relied on the sheer momentum of national expansion and prosperity to override all the problems of the country, and which had in the end been unable to cope with the sectionalism it so readily accepted, now passed into Unionism. Douglas did not cease to be a Jacksonian, but in the last letter he ever wrote he remembered another Jackson—the Jackson who had dealt swiftly and firmly with the Nullifiers.[83] In his country's most awesome crisis Douglas had at last found the role for which he had so long been searching. The man who had once talked like a Nationalist and acted as a Federalist had now become a Unionist. The man who had so often seemed unable to catch up with the times now, in his own words, "spoke of the present and the future, without reference to the past."[84]

[83] Johannsen, ed., *Letters of Douglas*, p. 513.
[84] Ibid., p. 510.

The old struggle between the politician and the statesman in Douglas was over. "A man," he wrote in that last letter, "cannot be a true Democrat unless he is a loyal patriot."[85] The old need to repress any references to the moral dimension of politics—that need which for too long had made Douglas' pronouncements seem somehow two-dimensional to those who liked him and downright cynical, if not immoral, to those who did not—was gone now. Morality and policy had converged, and Douglas could speak unashamedly of the "imperative duty of every Union man—every friend of Constitutional liberty to rally to the support of our common country, its government and Flag. . . ."[86]

On April 21 Stephen Douglas left Washington for the last time and began one of the most misunderstood episodes of his long political career. Civil War scholars and biographers alike, perhaps in a hurry to finish with their work and end the Little Giant's story with a grand and dramatic flourish, almost invariably show Douglas, alarmed over rumors of disunion sentiment in Egypt, leaving the Capital in a burst of patriotic fury to return to his people and rally Illinois to the Union.[87] The scene is often embellished with a sketch of one of those White House encounters that have about them more of the work of the dramatist than of the serious historian: a highly agitated Douglas rushes into Lincoln's office waving a telegram testifying to secessionist sentiment in lower Illinois and begs the President for advice. Upon Lincoln's suggestion that he return home at once to stem the tide of disunion, Douglas, as the story goes, announces that he will leave for Illinois the next day.[88] One version has it that Douglas was in fact on a secret presidential mission to organize a huge Northwestern army to sweep the enemy

[85] Ibid., p. 513.

[86] Ibid., p. 512.

[87] Milton, *Eve of Conflict*, p. 564; Allan Nevins, *The War for the Union*, I, 148–149; Henry P. Willis, *Stephen A. Douglas*, p. 345; Johannsen, ed., *Letters of Douglas*, p. 511n.; J. G. Randall, *Lincoln the President*, I, 367ff.

[88] Willis, *Stephen A. Douglas*, p. 345n.; William H. Herndon, *Life of Lincoln*, p. 434n.

from the entire Mississippi Valley, thus anticipating Ulysses S. Grant by several years.[89]

There is almost no evidence to support this melodramatic and rather naive explanation of Douglas' last journey. Once more the stubborn tendency to portray Douglas as essentially a failure and a tragic hero has gotten the best of historical objectivity: Douglas who could not be President could at least be the loyal servant of one; Douglas who could not preserve the Union could at least hold Illinois together. In a moment of pity, the historian generously grants Douglas a meager taste of the heroic in his final moments.

Douglas himself does not appear to have seen anything particularly urgent about his trip out to Illinois. He and Mrs. Douglas proceeded by easy stages, stopping for at least two speeches in Ohio and not reaching Springfield until April 25. Only upon arriving in Illinois did Douglas begin to appreciate the existence of disunion sentiment. On the twenty-ninth he wrote Lincoln: "I found the state of feeling here and in some parts of our State much less satisfactory than I could have desired or expected when I arrived."[90]

The degree of pro-secession, anti-Union feeling in Egypt in the early spring of 1861 is easily exaggerated. The Copperheads, who were later to play such a large part in Illinois politics during the Civil War, had not begun to emerge as an identifiable force in these early days of the conflict. When they finally did take on coherent form, their base of power was not Egypt at all, but Chicago—at the opposite end of the state. Lower Illinois was eventually to provide a higher proportion of Union soldiers relative to its population than any other area of America.[91] Douglas himself never even visited Egypt on this trip, delivering his major address in Springfield[92] before a legislature that was now heavily Republican in both houses and hardly needed to be converted to Lincoln's policy! The contention that only Douglas' timely intervention prevented civil war in

[89] Johnson, *Stephen A. Douglas*, p. 479.

[90] Johannsen, ed., *Letters of Douglas*, p. 511.

[91] Clark E. Carr, *Stephen A. Douglas*, p. 133.

[92] Douglas made another important speech at Chicago on May 1, 1861. *New York Tribune*, June 13, 1861.

Illinois[93] is refuted by the words of Douglas himself. Four days after arriving in Springfield he confidently wrote Lincoln, "There will be no outbrake[*sic*] however and in a few days I hope for entire unanimity in the support of the government and the Union."[94]

One must look deeper for the true reason behind Douglas' last trip back to Illinois. The best explanation would seem to be that the Little Giant felt somewhat awkward and uncomfortable in Washington and was still without an outlet for his great political skill and restless energy. In the preservation of the Union he had, after Sumter, found a goal once more worthy of himself, but in late April of 1861 he was still without a clear-cut role to play. Congress, which for so long had been his natural political home, had by now adjourned.[95] The unofficial role of premier, toward which Douglas had been moving, perhaps unconsciously, still eluded him. The War Democrats, of whom Douglas would eventually have been the natural leader, had yet to take shape as a real political force on the national scene. He was a welcome visitor at the White House now, but hardly a political intimate of the President.

As he had done so often before in his long public career, upon reaching a political impasse, Douglas moved. If there was much that was new in the Stephen Douglas of April, 1861, there was much that was old as well. He preached the new Unionism, but much of what he had to say had a familiar ring. He talked of the vital strategic importance of the Border and of the need to keep the great river systems of the Northwest, particularly his beloved Mississippi, open to the sea.[96]

There were practical as well as sentimental reasons behind this last journey by Stephen Douglas. He was sure of the justice of his

93 E. L. Kimball, "Richard Yates," *Journal of the Illinois State Historical Society* 23 (April 1930): 38.

94 Johannsen, ed., *Letters of Douglas*, p. 511.

95 The special session of the Senate, 37th Congress, adjourned March 28, 1861; *Cong. Globe*, 37th Cong., special sess., p. 1526. The House, which did not go into special session, adjourned March 2, 1861; ibid., 36th Cong., 2nd sess., p. 1433. Both houses would reassemble on July 4.

96 Johnson, *Stephen A. Douglas*, p. 481; *Cong. Globe*, 37th Cong., 1st sess., p. 35.

course in supporting Lincoln wholeheartedly in the war effort, but he had reservations about its political wisdom.[97] Old supporters were puzzled at the sudden switch from the man who had been the proponent of compromise to the man who now threw all of his weight behind Abraham Lincoln.[98] Douglas was anxious to explain to the people in Illinois who had sent him back to the Senate two and a half years before that one could be a good Unionist without ceasing to be a good Democrat. In the last letter he ever wrote, Douglas announced, "I am neither the supporter of the partizan [*sic*] policy nor the apologist for the errors of the Administration. My previous relations to them remain unchanged. But I trust the time will never come when I shall not be willing to make any needful sacrifice of personal feeling and party policy for the honor and integrity of my country."[99]

On April 25 Douglas delivered one of the great speeches of his life before a joint session of the Illinois Legislature at Springfield.[100] He began in a way wholly out of keeping with the usually bumptious style of the Little Giant: he confessed to an error. He had, he said, in his long search for compromise and reconciliation been guilty of "leaning too far to the southern section of the Union against my own,"[101] and now he acknowledged his mistake. The man who for so long had sought a pacific adjustment of differences and had earlier in the year devoted most of his efforts to plans for a peaceful separation, now announced unequivocally that "the shortest way to peace is the most stupendous and unanimous preparation for war."[102] But he vowed that the North did not seek to

[97] Thus Douglas' frequent and labored distinction between his support of the administration to preserve the Union and his refusal to aid it "politically." Johannsen, ed., *Letters of Douglas*, pp. 509–514.

[98] Johannsen, ed., *Letters of Douglas*, pp. 511–513; 513 n–514 n.

[99] Ibid., p. 512.

[100] The speech may be found in the *New York Tribune*, May 1, 1861, and in pamphlet form: *Speech of Senator Douglas before the Legislature of Illinois, April 25, 1861* (n.p., n.d.).

[101] Ibid.

[102] *New York Tribune*, May 1, 1861; Douglas' Springfield speech of April 25, 1861.

subjugate the South or make war on its rights. Douglas had often in the past sacrificed perspective in his haste to deal with whatever crisis happened to be at hand. Now he appeared to transcend the immediate questions posed by a nation in the throes of mobilization. He reminded his listeners of the higher duty they owed not only to themselves, but to the generations that would follow and to the cause of self-government.[103]

Douglas spoke for two hours that night. When he finished, the heavily Republican legislature gave him a standing ovation. The telegraph tapped out his speech onto the front page of almost every major newspaper north of the Mason-Dixon Line.

Douglas spoke again at Chicago on May 1.[104] There in the Wigwam, where Lincoln had received his party's nomination almost one year ago to the date, Stephen Douglas, who for so long had instinctively sought the middle ground of compromise and moderation, announced flatly to the thousands who had come to listen that now every man must be either for the Union or against it: "There can be no neutrals in this war; only patriots and traitors."[105] All attempts at compromise had been doomed from the start. The leaders of the South, he said, had been planning to break up the Union from the time they had lost the fight over Lecompton. But he did not counsel a vindictive attitude: "The innocent must not suffer, nor women and children be the victims."[106] Perhaps he was thinking of the two Southern girls he had married and of his sons and of the infant daughter who lay buried down in Dixie.[107]

He had been unwell ever since the Springfield speech and his wife and close friends now urged a brief rest at the Tremont House he had always loved. A few days of leisure and he would once more be strong enough to continue his arduous journey through Illinois.

[103] Ibid.
[104] *New York Tribune*, June 13, 1861.
[105] Ibid.
[106] Ibid.
[107] Stevens, "Life of Douglas," p. 637.

But Douglas did not seem to get any better. On May 10 he wrote to Virgil Hickox, beginning his letter with an apology for not being able to write in his own hand because he had lost the use of his arms through "a severe attack of rheumatism."[108] By the fifteenth all future public appearances by the Little Giant were canceled until further notice. On the twenty-seventh Douglas' personal physician arrived from Washington.[109] The eminent doctors[110] who hurried in and out of the Tremont House were baffled as to the exact nature of the illness.

Shortly after 9 o'clock on the morning of June 3 Stephen Douglas died. At that same hour, out in the mountain country of western Virginia at the little town of Philippi, Union troops were handing the Confederate forces their first defeat of the war.

It is said that shortly before death came, Douglas awakened from his coma and his mind grew suddenly clear. Turning to those who had taken up the deathwatch around his bed, he said, "Tell my children to obey the laws and uphold the Constitution."

The story has about it the unmistakable ring of apocrypha. On the other hand, Douglas had in fact uttered almost the identical phrase in the course of his Springfield speech only a few weeks before.[111] His hardheaded, unsentimental colleagues who later rose in Congress to eulogize their fallen comrade readily accepted the legend.[112] So do most of his biographers.[113]

A quarrel at once arose over just what Douglas had meant in his last injunction. Republicans and most Northern Democrats were quite sure that he had issued a final call to all Americans to rally behind Lincoln in defense of the Union. But old Southern friends

[108] Johannsen, ed., *Letters of Douglas*, p. 511.

[109] Dr. Thomas Miller; Milton, *Eve of Conflict*, p. 567.

[110] Doctors Miller, McVickar, and Hay attended Douglas during his last illness. Stevens, "Life of Douglas," p. 633n.

[111] *New York Tribune*, May 1, 1861.

[112] *Cong. Globe*, 37th Cong., 1st sess., pp. 33, 36, 39.

[113] Milton, *Eve of Conflict*, pp. 568–569; Johnson, *Stephen A. Douglas*, p. 488; Frank E. Stevens, "Life of Stephen Arnold Douglas," *Journal of the Illinois State Historical Society*, 16: 633.

GENERAL ORDERS, No. 29.

WAR DEPARTMENT,
ADJUTANT GENERAL'S OFFICE,
Washington, June 4, 1861.

The following order has been received from the War Department and is published for the information of the Army:

WAR DEPARTMENT, *June* 4, 1861.

The death of a great statesman, in this hour of peril, cannot be regarded otherwise than as a national calamity. Stephen A. Douglas expired in the commercial capital of Illinois yesterday morning at 9 o'clock. A representative of the overpowering sentiment enlisted in the cause in which we are engaged. A man who nobly discarded party for his country. A Senator who forgot all prejudices in an earnest desire to serve the republic. A Statesman who lately received for the Chief Magistracy of the Union a vote second only to that by which the President was elected, and who had every reason to look forward to a long career of usefulness and honor.

A patriot, who defended with equal zeal and ability the constitution as it came to us from our fathers, and whose last mission upon earth was that of rallying the people of his own State of Illinois, as one man, around the glorious flag of our Union, has been called from the scene of life and the field of his labor.

This Department recognising in the loss one common to the whole country, and profoundly sensible of the grief it will excite among millions of men, hereby advises the Colonels of the different regiments to have this order read to-morrow to their respective commands, and suggests that the colors of the republic be craped in mourning in honor of the illustrious dead.

SIMON CAMERON,
Secretary of War.

BY ORDER:

L. THOMAS,
Adjutant General.

OFFICIAL:

Assistant Adjutant General.

Mr. Lincoln's army learns of Douglas' death. Original handbill in author's collection.

like Alexander Stephens were just as sure that Douglas had handed down an indictment against Lincoln's whole policy of the use of force against the seceding states.[114] Such was the sickness of the times. But Douglas now knew what he meant and that was what really mattered.

[114] Alexander H. Stephens, *A Constitutional View of the Late War between the States*, II, 419–420.

8. The Summing Up

Stephen Douglas died at forty-eight, an age when most statesmen are only beginning their greatest work. His death was unexpected and untimely, but was it really unfortunate? Had not the man's greatness reached its peak long before—during the hard, bitter fight against Lecompton or in the long campaign against Lincoln a year later—and had not his career been on a slow but steady decline ever since? Had he not perhaps outlived his usefulness to both himself and his people? And had not the fates that preside over the destinies of nations and the men who lead them, in a rare moment of benevolence summarily removed Douglas from the national political stage rather than see him linger on, a pathetic and anachronistic figure who neither belonged to the present age nor really understood it?

Many of the works dealing with Douglas and the coming of the Civil War seem to support this interpretation of his last years. In doing so they fall prey to the tendency in American historiography to portray Douglas as an essentially tragic character. Douglas' story is almost always told in the shadow cast by the outsized figure of Abraham Lincoln. The godlike national hero, the embodiment of good, the martyr who was destroyed by evil is placed beside the smaller figure of the Illinois Senator, the less-than-perfect man who destroyed himself.[1]

It is not a new error; Douglas' contemporaries usually made the same mistake. As early as 1854 a newspaper in Missouri was comparing the Little Giant to Samson, destroying his party in the ill-considered move to ram through the Kansas-Nebraska Act.[2] Four years later during the joint debates Lincoln was praised for his astuteness in forcing Douglas to destroy himself politically by his answer to the Freeport Question. In the presidential campaign of 1860 Greeley's *Tribune* pronounced Douglas "a consummate actor in the higher walks of tragedy,"[3] and his failure in his great bid for the presidency served only to reinforce the popular image. Carl Schurz saw in Douglas' exposition of popular sovereignty an instance of a political tragedy of great dramatic content. In his view Douglas had become a victim of his own devices and was now hopelessly entangled in the intricacies of the very doctrine he had created.[4]

Observers steeped in the teachings of Freudian psychology might be intrigued by Douglas' heavy drinking, the perennially desperate state of his finances, and his personal carelessness that grew steadily more serious at the end of his life.[5] They might wonder at some of his unusual remarks and actions during the 1860 campaign and conclude that here was a man who not only expected defeat but at times seemed to court it. They might even go a step farther and point out that Douglas' many serious illnesses always seemed to follow hard on the heels of some major political setback or dis-

1 James F. Rhodes, *History of the United States from the Compromise of 1850*, I, 492–493, II, 343, III, 414–415; Louis Howland, *Stephen A. Douglas*, pp. 210–221, and 371; Pieter Geyl, *Debates with Historians*, p. 254; William G. Brown, *Stephen A. Douglas*, pp. 140–141; Edgar Lee Masters, "Stephen A. Douglas," *The American Mercury* 22 (January 1931): 23.

2 Allan Nevins, *Ordeal of the Union*, II, 141–142.

3 *New York Tribune*, August 31, 1860.

4 Carl Schurz, *The Reminiscences of Carl Schurz*, II, 84.

5 Charles Francis Adams, *An Autobiography*, pp. 65–66; Henry P. Willis, *Stephen A. Douglas*, pp. 348–349; Allan Nevins, *Emergence of Lincoln*, I, 351, 384; George F. Milton, *Eve of Conflict*, p. 567; Robert W. Johannsen, ed., *The Letters of Stephen A. Douglas*, p. 508.

appointment.[6] They would then take careful note of the unusual circumstances of Douglas' death, coming as it did at a relatively early age and so soon after the completion of a vigorous tour through Illinois. Perhaps they would be driven to the conclusion that Douglas himself, somehow realizing that his great days were over and that there was nothing more to live for, had unconsciously moved to meet the benevolent hand of fate.

Interpretations like these speak well for the writer of drama but not of history. Douglas' shortcomings were in the last analysis political more than psychological. His basic error was one of timing. He continued to preach the virtues of compromise to an age which had largely become disillusioned with the concept. He sought to hold and occupy the rapidly diminishing supply of political middle ground when most of his countrymen were breaking in mad haste for the extremist fringes. He remained fundamentally a conservative in what was in retrospect the beginning of the liberal age in Anglo-Saxon politics. He continued on his old course of pragmatism and benign ambiguity when the country cried out for doctrine and definition. When he finally succumbed to the clamor around him and proclaimed his popular sovereignty to the world, he had in fact created a principle that often seemed to objective observers to be no principle at all. He had more than his share of charisma, but the people in his later years never quite trusted him nor the professed neutrality with which he seemed to greet each new national crisis. His studiously amoral pronouncements were more and more taken for immorality. He was the strongest and most consummate politician of his era, but the people seemed inclined to entrust their national destiny to weaklings on the one hand and would-be gods on the other.

Douglas was first of all a nationalist, but the kind of nationalism he preached during the years before the Civil War seemed to grow steadily more irrelevant. Douglas belonged to the high national pe-

[6] For example, Douglas' illnesses of March, 1858, November, 1859, and June, 1860; see also Douglas' "Autobiographical Sketch" in Johannsen, ed., *Letters of Douglas*, p. 60.

riod of American history. His political outlook was fundamentally Jacksonian. He had been born in the first full year of the War of 1812. He had reached his majority when Andrew Jackson was President. The first political speech the young Douglas ever delivered was a ringing defense of Old Hickory.[7] So were his first major address in Congress[8] and the last letter he ever wrote.[9]

Like the Jacksonians', Douglas' nationalism was basically multisectional, amoral, and materialistic. Like theirs, his sympathies lay with the West, but he knew that his political future depended upon the continued support of the South. Like the Jacksonians, he would have preferred to avoid all discussion of slavery and to concentrate on work in behalf of national expansion and prosperity. For Douglas, as for Jackson, the bonds of nationality were best strengthened by an appeal to narrow economic and sectional self-interest, coupled with an occasional resort to a display of federal power.

But as the 1850's wore on, most Americans may have come to feel that if they were to deal with the challenge to the nation posed by the continued existence of slavery, they were going to need something more than the blunt, crude, materialistic nationalism of Jackson and Douglas. The people now heard the voices of the Lincolns and the Sewards and the Sumners who talked of more subtle yet stronger bonds of unity—of morality and higher law and national purpose—and slowly they began to listen.

Douglas, during the decade prior to the Civil War, grew steadily more out of step with his times. The roots of his political behavior lay in an era that by 1848 was ending forever—an era when discussion of slavery could either be ignored or carried on without any reference to morality, an era when the problems associated with the peculiar institution could still be solved by easy compromise on the one hand or another dose of national expansion on the other.

Douglas' intense involvement in the politics of the 1850's easily obscures his lack of awareness of the changing moral climate

7 Ibid., pp. 112–115.

8 *Cong. Globe*, 28th Cong., 1st sess., pp. 43ff. and app., pp. 112–115.

9 Johannsen, ed., *Letters of Douglas*, pp. 512–513.

around him. His words suggested an acceptance, even a willingness, to change, but too often his actions seemed designed to support the moral status quo of the years prior to the end of the Mexican War. His occasionally spectacular departures from the niceties of custom and tradition, such as the break with Buchanan in 1857 and the unprecedented stump campaign of 1860, tended to disguise a deeper predisposition to move slowly and deliberately, if at all. Although Douglas responded to any new problem with a furious burst of energy, in the end he seemed often to confuse mere motion with significant change. The kind of changes Douglas advocated in the years before the Civil War were often more apparent than real. During much of the last part of his life, Douglas' reluctance to change with his age in a meaningful fashion placed him in danger of becoming a political relic while still a young man.

But a year before his death a transformation began to take place in Stephen Douglas. The man who, in spite of all his apparent involvement, had remained for too long somehow detached from the political world around him began to stir. Now he not only moved, he began to act. The transformation was gradual, not sudden. If there was a turning point, it probably occurred that October day in 1860 when Douglas squarely faced the fact that Abraham Lincoln would be the next President of the United States and turned south to try to dissuade the secessionists from the reckless course upon which they were about to embark. His efforts were at first fumbling and halting, like some great giant who had slumbered long and had not yet fully awakened. When he came back to Washington that December he still went through the old motions of compromise and spoke the language of conciliation. But there was a difference now: once the South resorted to force, Douglas was prepared to answer in kind.

And there was another change too. The old diffuse nationalism of Douglas had begun to transform itself into the more specific stuff of Unionism. It did not happen overnight; but by the time Beauregard's men had fired the first shot over the calm waters of Charleston Harbor into Fort Sumter, Douglas had found in the preservation of the Union a cause worthy of his outsized talents and energy.

He must have taken a great deal of pleasure in watching the newly arrived Republicans set aside their concern for morals and higher laws and irrepressible conflicts in favor of dealing with the awesome tasks posed by secession, mobilization, and civil war. Here were the concrete problems Douglas understood. Here was the kind of work he knew how to do best.

Stephen Douglas left Washington for the last time in April of 1861 as a man who had been lost and then had found himself. He was still a bit uncertain about the exact nature of his role and the next step he was to take and the degree of power he could command, but with his total commitment to the preservation of the Union and his support of President Lincoln, he was now on the right course. After a few weeks in his beloved Northwest, out on the political hustings among the people from whom he always seemed to draw new strength, he would have returned to the seat of the government that needed him so desperately and played out his finest moments.

The greatest chapter in Douglas' life remained unwritten. He would never have completely forsaken his party, but he would have been the natural leader of the loyal opposition and of the War Democrats who were about to emerge as a clear political force.[10] With his strong public support of President Lincoln and his great prestige in Congress, Douglas would have been a more likely candidate for the unofficial role of premier than Seward, who coveted it. His characteristic aggressiveness would have infused the entire early war effort with a sorely needed sense of vitality and would have been a valuable counterweight to the counsel of more timid spirits like McClellan and Cameron. Douglas would have be-

[10] In his last letter Douglas wrote, "I know of no mode by which a loyal citizen may so well demonstrate his devotion to his country as by sustaining the Flag, The Constitution, and the Union, under all circumstances and under every Administration regardless of party politics against all assailants at home and abroad." He praised "the great leaders of the opposition sinking the partizan in the Patriot," and concluded, "If we hope to regain and perpetuate the ascendancy of our party we should never forget that a man cannot be a true Democrat unless he is a loyal patriot." Johannsen, ed., *Letters of Douglas*, pp. 512–513; Nicolay and Hay, *Lincoln*, IV, 83.

come the unchallenged spokesman for the Northwest, and with his great love for the Mississippi and his understanding of its importance he would probably have pushed for the opening of a second front in the West and the concentration of the war effort there long before Lincoln himself. His great strength along the Border and among moderate Southerners might have helped to shorten the Civil War by encouraging the growth of an effective peace party in the Confederate States. The deep affection he still held for the Southern people would have worked to mitigate the agonies of Reconstruction.

There was a tragedy about Douglas' death, but it was not his. It was America's. Representative Samuel Cox of Ohio summed it all up and spoke for the nation when he said simply to the hushed House that had assembled to pay tribute to the Senator from Illinois, "Who is left to take his place?"[11]

Stephen Douglas is buried in a white marble tomb on the south side of Chicago, not far from the university he helped to found. There is an iron railing around the monument and a caretaker in attendance. He says quite a few people still stop by these days. A few yards away the trains roar down to New Orleans over the rails of the Illinois Central Douglas helped to push south. A little farther on, an eight-lane expressway pulls the heavy morning traffic toward the heart of the city he built and called home. And beyond that is Lake Michigan.

A granite shaft rises skyward from the tomb, and on top there is a bronze statue of the Little Giant. The monument rests firmly on the good soil of Illinois, but Douglas himself is looking eastward across the waters of the lake—toward Washington.

[11] *Cong. Globe*, 37th Cong., 1st sess., p. 36.

CRITICAL ESSAY ON SOURCES

A complete bibliography of all major sources consulted may be found at the end of this study. Discussed below are only those which are either of exceptional historical merit, necessary to an understanding of the last years of Douglas' career, or of a controversial nature.

Manuscripts

With the publication of *The Letters of Stephen A. Douglas*, edited by Robert W. Johannsen (Urbana, 1961), almost all known Douglas letters were made available to scholars in convenient, carefully annotated form. Correspondingly, the scholar's best opportunity for uncovering new and useful material now lies in a study of letters to and about Douglas rather than by him.

The Douglas Papers at the University of Chicago proved to be the most useful single manuscript source for the purposes of this work. The collection comprises some fifteen to twenty thousand letters to Douglas, written largely during the period with which this study is concerned. It is only now in the process of being catalogued and researchers must cut their way through much that is of a routine, unexceptional nature. Yet it is time well spent, for nowhere else can the scholar, with diligence and patience, uncover so much that is vital to an understanding of Douglas and his times.

Useful and illuminating references to Douglas are to be found in the Jeremiah Black Papers, the Hamilton Fish Papers, the Reverdy Johnson Papers, the Horatio King Papers, and the Logan Family Papers in the Library of Congress. The Henry E. Huntington Library in San Marino contains valuable Douglas material in the Brock, Lamon, and Lieber Collections.

Published Sources

The single most valuable published source for Douglas' political career is the *Congressional Globe*. A thorough reading of all of Douglas' speeches and remarks in the Senate, as well as a survey of his colleagues' references to him, are indispensable for an accurate interpretation of his policy, strategy, tactics, and political personality. Yet the *Globe* has been curiously neglected by even Douglas' best biographers.

Newspapers

The *New York Times* provides both the fairest journalistic view of Douglas and the best guide to the events that shaped his political environment from day to day. The *New York Tribune* is also useful for the latter purpose, but the student must always allow for its deep-seated hostility to Douglas. In the Capital, the *Washington Union* and, after its demise in 1859, the *Washington Constitution*, are useful as the mouthpieces of the Buchanan administration. The *Washington Daily National Intelligencer* is fairer in its treatment of Douglas and particularly useful for obtaining glimpses of his personal and social life as well as of his movements in and out of the Capital. The *Chicago Times* is valuable as an unofficial spokesman for the Douglas cause up to mid-1860, when it was taken over by Cyrus McCormick, who was hostile to Douglas. In the South, the *Memphis Daily Appeal*, the *Mobile Daily Register*, and the *New Orleans True Delta* are the most useful pro-Douglas organs. The *Charleston Courier*, the *Charleston Daily Mercury*, the *New Orleans Daily Picayune*, the *Richmond Examiner*, the *Richmond Enquirer*, and the *Vicksburg Weekly Sun*, although differing in the degree of their hostility, provide a useful guide to anti-Douglas feeling below the Mason-Dixon Line. The Kansas papers have generally been overlooked by Douglas scholars. The *Atchison Weekly Champion*, the *Lawrence Herald of Freedom*, the *Lawrence Republican*, the *Lecompton National Democrat*, the *Topeka State Record*, and the *Weekly Leavenworth Union* all proved valuable for understanding Douglas' image on the frontier.

Books

LETTERS AND SPEECHES

The Letters of Stephen A. Douglas (Urbana, 1961), edited by Robert W. Johannsen, is an indispensable source for Douglas scholars. There is a great need for the publication of Douglas' collected speeches, but only the Lincoln-Douglas Debates and Douglas' 1859 Ohio speeches are available in book form. *Created Equal? The Complete Lincoln-Douglas Debates of 1858* (Chicago, 1958), edited by Paul M. Angle, is the most recent edition of the debates, although Edwin Erle Sparks, ed., *The Lincoln-Douglas Debates of 1858* (Springfield, 1908), is more useful for an understanding of the setting of the debates, their color, and their impact. *In the Name of the People: Speeches and Writings of Lincoln and Douglas in the Ohio Campaign of 1859* (Columbus, 1959), edited by Harry V. Jaffa and Robert W. Johannsen, reprints Douglas' speeches at Columbus, Cincinnati, and Wooster, as well as his famous article in the September, 1859, edition of *Harper's*, and Jeremiah Black's rebuttal to that article on behalf of the Buchanan administration.

The Works of James Buchanan (12 vols., Philadelphia, 1908–1911), edited by John Bassett Moore, while marred by some glaring omissions, is necessary for an understanding of the Buchanan-Douglas feud. The fifth volume of James D. Richardson, ed., *Messages and Papers of the Presidents* (10 vols., New York, 1904), contains the key speeches and writings of Franklin Pierce and James Buchanan during their terms as President. Richard K. Cralle, ed., *The Works of John C. Calhoun* (6 vols., New York, 1888), is useful for an understanding of the Southern Ultra position on the doctrine of popular sovereignty and the question of slavery in the territories. The fourth and fifth volumes of Dunbar Rowland, ed., *Jefferson Davis, Constitutionalist: His Letters, Papers and Speeches* (10 vols., Jackson, Mississippi, 1923), contain some useful references to Douglas and his doctrines by the future President of the Confederacy. Although *The Collected Works of Abraham Lincoln* (8 vols. and index, New Brunswick, New Jersey, 1953–1955), edited by Roy P. Basler, is a newer work, it does not seem to be a particular improvement over the older *Complete Works of Abraham Lincoln* (12 vols., New York, 1894), edited by John A. Nicolay and John Hay, with its excellent index and convenient format. The *Lincoln Papers* (2 vols., New York, 1948), edited by David C. Mearns, draws upon the Robert Todd Lincoln Collection and has an occasional illuminating reference to Douglas. Ulrich B. Phillips, ed., *The Correspondence of Robert Toombs, Alexander H. Stephens, and Howell Cobb* in the *Annual Report of the American Historical Association for 1911*, vol. 2 (Washington, 1913), yields some useful insights into the views of Southerners, both moderates and Ultras, toward Douglas.

DIARIES, MEMOIRS, REMINISCENCES, AND AUTOBIOGRAPHIES

Useful sources for an understanding of the Illinois political scene include Isaac N. Arnold, *Reminiscences of the Illinois Bar Forty Years Ago* (Springfield, 1881); *The Diary of Orville Hickman Browning* (2 vols., Springfield, 1925–1933), edited by T. C. Pease and J. G. Randall; and Usher F. Linder, *The Early Bench and Bar of Illinois* (Chicago, 1879). Henry Villard, *Memoirs* (2 vols., New York, 1904), and Carl

Schurz, *Reminiscences* (3 vols., New York, 1908), are valuable for a study of the Lincoln-Douglas Debates of 1858.

For Douglas' career in Washington, James G. Blaine, *Twenty Years in Congress* (2 vols., Norwich, Connecticut, 1884–1886), contains some interesting and fair appraisals of the Little Giant by a member of the Republican party. George W. Julian, *Political Recollections, 1840–1872* (Chicago, 1884), and John Sherman, *Recollections of Forty Years in the House, Senate, and Cabinet* (2 vols., New York, 1895), present the views of two of the leading Republicans from the Northwest. Charles Francis Adams, *An Autobiography* (New York, 1916), is predictably hostile to Douglas but has some valuable comments on his private life. Sara Agnes Pryor, *Reminiscences of Peace and War* (New York, 1905), contains pleasant sketches of the Douglas family and revealing comments on James Buchanan. *The Diary of James K. Polk* (4 vols., Chicago, 1910), edited by Milo M. Quaife, helps to illuminate the dark corners of James Buchanan's personality.

For Southern views of Douglas, the best sources are Jefferson Davis, *The Rise and Fall of the Confederate Government* (2 vols., New York, 1881); Henry S. Foote, *War of the Rebellion or Scylla and Charybdis* (New York, 1866); and Alexander H. Stephens, *A Constitutional View of the Late War between the States* (2 vols., Philadelphia, 1868–1870), which is perhaps the fairest appraisal of Douglas by any contemporary, North or South.

For Douglas' course during the hectic first months of 1861, three works are of considerable value: W. H. Russell, the American correspondent of the London *Times*, *My Diary North and South* (Boston, 1863); the anonymous *Diary of a Public Man* (Chicago, 1945), edited by F. L. Bullard; and the first volume of *The Diary of Gideon Welles* (3 vols., New York, 1960), edited by Howard K. Beale.

BIOGRAPHIES

Of the Douglas biographies from the last century, only James W. Sheahan, *The Life of Stephen A. Douglas* (New York, 1860), has real value to the historian. Although his book suffers from the obvious limitations of a campaign biography, Sheahan probably knew Douglas better than anyone outside of his immediate family.

One of the earliest Douglas biographies from this century is still in many ways the best. Allen Johnson, *Stephen A. Douglas: A Study in American Politics* (New York, 1908), takes an analytical approach to Douglas' personality and policies. Its author possessed deeper insight into Douglas' political character than any other biographer. The full title of George Fort Milton's *The Eve of Conflict: Stephen A. Douglas and the Needless War* (Boston, 1934), suggests the theme of the most exhaustive Douglas biography. Although the book is indispensable for Douglas scholars, its central contention that Douglas could almost alone have averted civil war is difficult to accept in its entirety. Frank E. Stevens, "Life of Stephen A. Douglas," in the *Journal of the Illinois State Historical Society* 16 (1923), is particularly useful for an understanding of Douglas' early life in Illinois. Although Stevens' work contains much unduplicated material, its value to historians has been largely lost through indifferent documentation. William Garrott Brown, *Stephen A. Douglas* (Cambridge, 1902), illuminates Douglas' restless, pragmatic approach to political problems. Louis Howland, *Stephen A. Douglas* (New York, 1920), is a fair appraisal of Douglas' strengths and weaknesses. Clark E. Carr, *Stephen A. Douglas* (Chicago, 1909), benefits from the author's personal recollections of Douglas. William Gardner, *Life of Stephen A. Douglas* (Boston, 1905), and Henry Parker Willis, *Stephen A. Douglas* (Philadelphia, 1910), contain little new. The most recent Douglas biography is Gerald M. Capers, *Stephen A. Douglas: Defender of the Union* (Boston, 1950), a brief, readable, and balanced appraisal of the Little Giant. Robert W. Johannsen is nearing completion of the first major biography of Douglas in more than thirty-five years. If this book lives up to the high standards of scholarship set by Johannsen in his earlier works, it will be a valuable contribution to American historiography.

There is a profusion of biographies on the other leading political figures of these years. The following is a survey of only those works that have proved especially helpful to a study of Douglas.

There is no great biography of James Buchanan. George Ticknor Curtis, *The Life of James Buchanan* (2 vols., New York, 1883), never particularly satisfactory, is long out of date. Philip Shriver Klein, *President James Buchanan* (University Park, Pennsylvania, 1962), is essentially an apologia. Its author has made the best of a difficult job.

The biographies of John C. Calhoun are many and, in general, quite good. Calhoun is of interest to this study primarily for purposes of tracing the development of the states' rights doctrine and gaining an understanding of Southern opposition to popular sovereignty in the territories. To this end, Charles M. Wiltse, *John C. Calhoun, Nullifier, 1829–1839* (New York, 1949), and *John C. Calhoun, Sectionalist, 1840–1850* (New York, 1951), proved quite useful. Gerald M. Capers, *John C. Calhoun—Opportunist* (Gainesville, 1960); Richard N. Current, *John C. Calhoun* (New York, 1963); William M. Meigs, *The Life of*

John Caldwell Calhoun (New York, 1917); and August O. Spain, *The Political Theory of John C. Calhoun* (New York, 1951), all add to the picture of this inscrutable figure.

Lewis Cass's career is important primarily in tracing the development of the doctrine of popular sovereignty. While Frank B. Woodford, *Lewis Cass: The Last Jeffersonian* (New Brunswick, New Jersey, 1950), is a much more recent study, Andrew C. McLaughlin, *Lewis Cass* (New York, 1891), proved better suited to this purpose.

Biographies of Jefferson Davis are plentiful, but frequently mediocre. Hudson Strode, *Jefferson Davis: American Patriot, 1808–1861* (New York, 1955), and *Jefferson Davis: Confederate President* (New York, 1959), tend to adopt the standard Southern view of Douglas, but their author is fairer to the Little Giant than his subject ever was.

An investigation of Horace Greeley's career is helpful in gaining an understanding of the attitude of Northern antislavery men toward Douglas. Harlan Hoyt Horner, *Lincoln and Greeley* (Urbana, 1953), argues that the doctrine of popular sovereignty was a grave handicap to Douglas in New England and the Middle Atlantic States. J. A. Isely, *Horace Greeley and the Republican Party, 1853–1861* (Princeton, 1947); Ralph R. Fahrney, *Horace Greeley and the Tribune in the Civil War* (Cedar Rapids, Iowa, 1936); and Glyndon G. Van Deusen, *Horace Greeley: Nineteenth Century Crusader* (New York, 1953), are valuable in helping to unravel the tangled story of Greeley's tentative support of Douglas in the 1858 campaign following the Little Giant's strong stand against Lecompton.

The great Lincoln biographers are almost uniformly just in their appraisal of Stephen Douglas. Albert J. Beveridge, *Abraham Lincoln* (2 vols., Boston, 1928), devotes a larger proportion of its text to a study of Douglas than does any other major Lincoln work. Although the author's death prevented him from carrying his study beyond the Lincoln-Douglas Debates, Beveridge's keen analyses of Douglas' personality and policies make these two volumes indispensable for an understanding of Lincoln's great rival. While Beveridge's style is fundamentally analytical, Carl Sandburg's is basically narrative. His *Abraham Lincoln: The Prairie Years* (2 vols., New York, 1926), evokes the flavor and color of political life in Illinois as does no other work on either Lincoln or Douglas. J. G. Randall, *Lincoln the Liberal Statesman* (New York, 1947), and volume I of *Lincoln the President: Springfield to Gettysburg* (2 vols., New York, 1946), are especially useful for their observations on the Lincoln-Douglas Debates and the principle of popular sovereignty. John G. Nicolay and John Hay, *Abraham Lincoln: A History* (10 vols., New York, 1890), proved appropriate for gaining an understanding of Douglas' relationship with Lincoln during the secession crisis of 1861. William H. Herndon and Jesse W. Weik, *Life of Lincoln* (New York, 1949), is not always reliable, but it contains much material not available elsewhere. Don E. Fehrenbacher, *Prelude to Greatness: Lincoln in the 1850's* (Stanford, 1962), is valuable for its observations on the strategy and issues in the Lincoln-Douglas Debates.

There is need for a modern, full-length biography of John Slidell. Until it is written, Louis M. Sears, *John Slidell* (Durham, 1925), will have to suffice.

Alexander Stephens was Douglas' most influential admirer south of the Mason-Dixon Line. Henry Cleveland, *Alexander H. Stephens* (Philadelphia, 1866), and E. Ramsay Richardson, *Little Aleck: A Life of Alexander H. Stephens* (New York, 1932), are particularly useful in explaining the attitude of a moderate Southerner toward Douglas in general and his doctrine of popular sovereignty in particular.

Conversely, William Lowndes Yancey was Douglas' most implacable enemy in the South. John W. Dubose, *The Life and Times of William Lowndes Yancey* (2 vols., New York, 1942), while not a great biography, is the only full-length study of the Alabama fire-eater.

GENERAL HISTORIES

For many years, James Ford Rhodes, *History of the United States from the Compromise of 1850* (8 vols., New York, 1907–1919), was the standard work on the Civil War era. Its first three volumes are still required reading for any serious student of Douglas' age, but the strong personal prejudice of the author against the Little Giant detracts from the historical value of the set.

For providing an understanding of the various party conventions of 1860, nothing can rival Allan Nevins' six-volume *Ordeal of the Union: Ordeal of the Union* (2 vols., New York, 1947); *The Emergence of Lincoln* (2 vols., New York, 1950); *The War for the Union* (2 vols., New York, 1959–1960). Nevins does not attempt to disguise his basic dislike for Douglas, and his treatment of the Little Giant is at times hostile and uneven.

The best political history of the period under consideration is Roy F. Nichols, *The Disruption of American Democracy* (New York, 1967). Nichols is especially useful for understanding the intricacies of the Lecompton struggle and the causes of the split in the Democratic party. His treatment of Douglas is balanced and fair.

Avery O. Craven, *The Growth of Southern Nationalism, 1848–1861* (Baton Rouge, 1953), places the blame for the Civil War on an exaggerated concern for moral issues and a preoccupation with those same pernicious abstractions that Douglas so greatly feared.

J. G. Randall and David Donald, *The Civil War and Reconstruction* (Boston, 1961), contributes little new to the Douglas story, portraying the Illinois Senator as well-intentioned but occasionally blundering.

SPECIAL HISTORIES

Although an extensive study of the Kansas-Nebraska Act falls outside the scope of this work, a knowledge of Douglas' motives in passing the 1854 legislation is necessary for a fuller understanding of the doctrine of popular sovereignty and Douglas' attitude toward the Lecompton Constitution. Three works proved especially useful for this purpose. P. Orman Ray, *The Repeal of the Missouri Compromise* (Cleveland, 1909), argues that Douglas was motivated by a desire to placate Senator David Atchison of Missouri, who is described as the real moving force behind the act, and, to a lesser extent, by a need to improve his own standing in the South, with an eye toward the presidential nomination. James C. Malin, *The Nebraska Question, 1852–1854* (Lawrence, Kansas, 1953), sees behind Douglas' sponsorship of the Kansas-Nebraska Act an overriding urge to get on with the larger work of national expansion in general and a Pacific railroad in particular. Reconciling the quarreling factions of the Democracy was regarded by Douglas primarily as a means to this larger goal, Malin argues. He also sees the Little Giant as a statesman waging a heroic battle for local self-government in an age of relentless centralization of authority. Robert R. Russel, *Improvement of Communication with the Pacific Coast as an Issue in American Politics, 1783–1864* (Cedar Rapids, Iowa, 1948), stresses the role of Douglas' interest in the construction of a Pacific railroad.

For a study of events in Kansas following the passage of the 1854 legislation, William F. Zornow, *Kansas* (Norman, Oklahoma, 1957), is valuable as a general history of Kansas. Two older works, Leverett W. Spring, *Kansas: The Prelude to the War for the Union* (Boston, 1885), and Eli Thayer, *A History of the Kansas Crusade* (New York, 1889), help to clarify the tangled story of the conflict between pro- and antislavery forces during the territorial period.

For the Buchanan-Douglas feud, three monographic works proved to be of exceptional use. Philip G. Auchampaugh, *James Buchanan and His Cabinet on the Eve of Secession* (Boston, 1965), is a favorable treatment of Buchanan. George D. Harmon, "President James Buchanan's Betrayal of Governor Robert J. Walker of Kansas," in *Aspects of Slavery and Expansion, 1848–1860*, Lehigh University Publications, vol. III, no. 7, (Bethlehem, Pennsylvania, 1929), portrays Buchanan as a pawn of the Southern Ultras. Vincent C. Hopkins, *Dred Scott's Case* (New York, 1951), is a scholarly study of the decision that precipitated much of the trouble between the two men.

For a grasp of the political situation in Illinois, Arthur Charles Cole, *The Era of the Civil War, 1848–1870* (Springfield, 1919), is an indispensable source. It contains much information not readily available elsewhere and some excellent election maps. T. C. Pease, *The Story of Illinois* (Chicago, 1949), devotes less space to the years under consideration, but is nonetheless a useful work. Henry Clyde Hubbart, *The Older Middle West, 1840–1880* (New York, 1936), has some interesting observations on attitudes in Illinois toward slavery. Bessie Louise Pierce, *A History of Chicago* (3 vols., New York, 1940–1957), has, in its second volume, important information on Douglas' financial interests.

On the Lincoln-Douglas Debates, the leading monographic study is Harry V. Jaffa, *Crisis of the House Divided* (Garden City, New York, 1959). This is an ambitious attempt to analyze in depth the issues explicit and implicit in the 1858 campaign. Although required reading for all Douglas scholars, it is a rather ponderous work. Richard Allen Heckman, *Lincoln vs Douglas: The Great Debates Campaign* (Washington, 1967), is essentially a narrative treatment composed of summaries of the candidates' speeches and entertaining glimpses of local color. *The Illinois Political Campaign of 1858* (Washington, 1958), edited by David C. Mearns, is a facsimile of the scrapbook Lincoln kept from newspaper clippings of the debates.

For an understanding of the various party conventions of 1860, one work stands out above all others. Murat Halstead's on-the-scene reports of the conventions are now available in a modern edition: *Three Against Lincoln: Murat Halstead Reports the Caucuses of 1860* (Baton Rouge, 1960), edited by William B. Hesseltine. Robert W. Johannsen's essay, "Douglas at Charleston," in *Politics and the Crisis of 1860* (Urbana, 1961), edited by Norman A. Graebner, supports the thesis that the Douglas men underestimated the lengths to which the Southern Ultras at Charleston would go to have their way. Percy Lee Rainwater, *Mississippi: Storm Center of Secession, 1856–1861* (Baton Rouge, 1938), contains an able discussion of Douglas' strength and weakness in the South during 1860.

The best accounts of the campaign of 1860 are those dealing with the struggle below the Mason-Dixon Line. Ollinger Crenshaw, *The Slave States in the Presidential Election of 1860*, Johns Hopkins University Studies in Historical and Political Science, series LXIII, no. 3,

(Baltimore, 1945), contains a wealth of information not easily available elsewhere. Lionel Crocker, "The Campaign of Stephen A. Douglas in the South," in *Antislavery and Disunion: 1858–1861* (New York, 1963), is valuable for an understanding of the strategy, tactics, and results of Douglas' campaign in the slave states. Emerson D. Fite, *The Presidential Campaign of 1860* (New York, 1911), discusses the contest in the North as well as the South. Although a less detailed study than either Crenshaw's or Crocker's, it is well worth reading as a narrative of those crucial months of 1860. Reinhard H. Luthin, *The First Lincoln Campaign* (Cambridge, 1944), presents the story of the 1860 campaign from Lincoln's standpoint. Its author argues that Lincoln and Douglas were both essentially moderate candidates and that the Democrats lost the election more than the Republicans won it.

Although the Compromise of 1850 does not properly fall within the period covered by this work, a study of the role Douglas played in its passage is important for an understanding of his later career. Holman Hamilton, *Prologue to Conflict* (Lexington, Kentucky, 1964), analyzes Douglas' motives and strategy and gives him much of the credit for forcing the compromise through Congress. George D. Harmon, "Douglas and the Compromise of 1850," in *Aspects of Slavery and Expansion, 1848–1860*, Lehigh University Publications, vol. III, no. 7, (Bethlehem, Pennsylvania, 1929), is particularly useful as a guide to Douglas' early relationship with the doctrine of popular sovereignty.

Jesse T. Carpenter, *The South as a Conscious Minority, 1789–1861: A Study in Political Thought* (Gloucester, Massachusetts, 1963), is a brilliant analysis of the South's changing ideological defense of its sectional interests. This book goes far toward explaining why Douglas' popular sovereignty was never warmly received in the South during the 1850's. Cora M. Gettys, "The Nationalism of Stephen A. Douglas" (Master's thesis, University of Chicago, 1915), is useful for gaining an understanding of the materialistic bias inherent in Douglas' view of the nation and its welfare during most of his career.

Journal Articles

Allan Nevins, "Stephen A. Douglas: His Weaknesses and His Greatness," *Journal of the Illinois State Historical Society* 42 (December 1949), is a brilliant and incisive assessment of Douglas' political character. The picture of Douglas contained in this article is much more even and consistent than the one that can be extracted from the author's *Ordeal of the Union* series. George Fort Milton, "Douglas' Place in American History," *Journal of the Illinois State Historical Society*

26 (January 1934), is basically an abstract of the themes running through the author's full-length biography, *The Eve of Conflict*. Milton portrays Douglas as a nationalist battling against the folly of sectionalism, a realist whose faith in the application of intelligence to political problems placed him at odds with an age preoccupied with emotion-charged abstractions. The author argues that Lincoln's policies led to the Civil War, while the successful implementation of Douglas' views would have prevented it. George Murray McConnel, "Recollections of Stephen A. Douglas," in *Transactions of the Illinois State Historical Society for 1900* (Springfield, 1901), is particularly valuable for its account of an interview in 1854 during which Douglas revealed to the author his personal antipathy toward the institution of slavery. Robert Taft, "The Appearance and Personality of Stephen A. Douglas," *Kansas Historical Quarterly* 21 (Spring 1954), contains the largest collection of photographs of Douglas compiled under one cover. It is especially valuable for revealing Douglas' shocking physical deterioration during the last year of his life.

There are a number of outstanding articles on the doctrine of popular sovereignty. Allen Johnson, "The Genesis of Popular Sovereignty," *Iowa Journal of History and Politics* 3 (January 1905), is still the most sophisticated analysis of the development of that principle. James B. Ranck, "Lewis Cass and Squatter Sovereignty," *Michigan History Magazine* 14 (Winter 1930), is a study of the views of the most important exponent of popular sovereignty for the territories during the period before 1850. For understanding Douglas' relationship to the doctrine, two articles are of unusual importance. Robert W. Johannsen, "Stephen A. Douglas, Popular Sovereignty, and the Territories," *The Historian* 22 (August 1960), argues that there was more principle and less expediency in Douglas' espousal of popular sovereignty than his detractors would care to admit. Edward McMahon, "Stephen A. Douglas: A Study of the Attempt to Settle the Question of Slavery in the Territories by the Application of Popular Sovereignty, 1850–1860," *Washington Historical Quarterly* 2 (April–July 1908), is a convenient summary of the development of the doctrine at the hands of the Little Giant. Charles W. Ramsdell, "The Natural Limits of Slavery Expansion," *Mississippi Valley Historical Review* 16 (September 1929), is a classic work of American historiography. It not only supports Douglas' view that the primary dynamic behind the spread of slavery was economic rather than political, but adds weight to the contention that a just application of Douglas' popular sovereignty would have ultimately been as effective a barrier to the westward expansion of slavery as Lincoln's positive prohibition by Congress. Robert R. Russel, "What

Was the Compromise of 1850?" *Journal of Southern History* 22 (August 1956), is valuable for its efforts to clear up the appalling confusion that has surrounded the meaning of the territorial clauses of the 1850 Compromise. The author, however, seems to feel that the Utah and New Mexico Acts were more positive and explicit in permitting territorial control over slavery than they in fact were.

For a study of the Kansas-Nebraska Act, Roy F. Nichols, "The Kansas-Nebraska Act: A Century of Historiography," *Mississippi Valley Historical Review* 43 (September 1956), is an indispensable survey of the many interpretations of the 1854 legislation. Most explanations of Douglas' motives in sponsoring the Kansas-Nebraska Bill tend to be somewhat unrealistically monistic. Frank H. Hodder, "The Railroad Background of the Kansas-Nebraska Act," *Mississippi Valley Historical Review* 12 (June 1925), sees Douglas motivated primarily by a desire to open the way for the construction of not one but two Pacific railroads. James C. Malin, "The Motives of Stephen A. Douglas in the Organization of Nebraska Territory: A Letter Dated December 17, 1853," *Kansas Historical Quarterly* 19 (November 1951), stresses Douglas' overriding devotion to national expansion and to the development of the Mississippi Valley and the West.

There are five articles that are important for understanding the Buchanan-Douglas feud. Philip C. Auchampaugh, "The Buchanan-Douglas Feud," *Journal of the Illinois State Historical Society* 25 (April 1932), blames Douglas for the disruption of the Democratic party. O. M. Dickerson, "Stephen A. Douglas and the Split in the Democratic Party," *Proceedings of the Mississippi Valley Historical Association* 7 (1913–1914), is less harsh in its judgments, but maintains that political expediency more than principle was at the bottom of Douglas' stand against Lecompton. At the same time, Dickerson rejects the notion that Douglas' reply to Lincoln's Freeport Question must assume the major share of responsibility for the split in the Democratic party. Reinhard H. Luthin, "The Democratic Split During Buchanan's Administration," *Pennsylvania History* 11 (January 1944), argues that agitation over Kansas was more the product of the struggle between the Buchanan and Douglas factions of the Democracy than it was the result of Southern pressure for slavery expansion. Richard Stenberg, "An Unnoted Factor in the Buchanan-Douglas Feud," *Journal of the Illinois State Historical Society* 25 (January 1933), maintains that much of the ill feeling between the two men can be traced to Buchanan's secret desire to seek a second term as President. The best study of the English Bill is found in Frank H. Hodder, "Some Aspects of the English Bill for the Admission of Kansas," *Annual Re-*

port of the American Historical Association for 1906 1. This study is particularly useful for refuting the usual assumption that the terms under which a virtual plebiscite on the Lecompton Constitution was held in Kansas were heavily weighted in favor of acceptance.

Allan Nevins and Willard L. King, "The Constitution and Declaration of Independence as Issues in the Lincoln-Douglas Debates," *Journal of the Illinois State Historical Society* 52 (Spring 1959), is an able exposition of some of the more subtle questions raised in the course of the 1858 campaign.

George Fort Milton, "Stephen A. Douglas' Efforts for Peace," *Journal of Southern History* 1 (August 1935), argues that if Douglas had opposed Lincoln in a straight two-party race in 1860, Douglas would have been elected easily and there would have been no secession and no civil war. Milton also implies that even after Lincoln's election, the adoption of either Douglas' compromise plan for the territories or his customs union scheme would have prevented the war. The article is provocative, but not always convincing.

Robert W. Johannsen, "Stephen A. Douglas and the South," *Journal of Southern History* 33 (February 1967), is an able account of Douglas' long, and ultimately unsuccessful, attempt to persuade the South that he represented no threat to its true interests. Johannsen's article points up the impossible goal Douglas set for himself in seeking to remain a nationalist in a sectional age and a moderate in an era of extremism.

BIBLIOGRAPHY

Unpublished Materials

Manuscript Collections

The Jeremiah S. Black Papers, *Manuscript Division, Library of Congress*

The Brock Collection, *Henry E. Huntington Library*

The Papers of Caleb Cushing, *Manuscript Division, Library of Congress*

The Papers of Stephen A. Douglas, *University of Chicago Library*

The Hamilton Fish Papers, *Manuscript Division, Library of Congress*

The Reverdy Johnson Papers, *Manuscript Division, Library of Congress*

The Horatio King Papers, *Manuscript Division, Library of Congress*

The Lamon Collection, *Henry E. Huntington Library*

The Lieber Collection, *Henry E. Huntington Library*

The Logan Family Papers, *Manuscript Division, Library of Congress*

Theses and Dissertations

Fretz, Barbara Catharine. "The Changing View in History, with Special Reference to the History of Stephen A. Douglas." Ph.D. dissertation, Cornell University, 1938.

Gettys, Cora M. "The Nationalism of Stephen A. Douglas." Master's thesis, University of Chicago, 1915.

Heckman, Richard Allen. "The Lincoln-Douglas Debate, Freeport, Illinois, August 27, 1858." Master's thesis, Indiana University, 1956.

Published Materials

The Congressional Globe

Newspapers

Atchison (Kansas) *Weekly Champion*

Charleston Courier

Charleston Daily Mercury
Chicago Daily Times
Chicago Tribune
Habana (Cuba) *Crónica de La Marina*
Lawrence (Kansas) *Herald of Freedom*
Lawrence (Kansas) *Republican*
Lecompton (Kansas Territory) *National Democrat*
Memphis Daily Appeal
Mobile Daily Advertiser
Mobile Daily Register
New Orleans Daily Picayune
New Orleans True Delta (daily and weekly editions)
New York Herald
New York Times
New York Tribune
Richmond Enquirer
Richmond Examiner (daily and semiweekly editions)
Richmond Whig
Topeka State Record
Vermilion County (Illinois) *Press*
Vicksburg Weekly Sun
Washington Constitution
Washington Daily Morning Chronicle
Washington Daily National Intelligencer
Washington Daily Union
Weekly Leavenworth Herald

Books

Adams, Charles Francis. *Charles Francis Adams: An Autobiography*. New York: Houghton Mifflin, 1916.

Adams, Henry. *The United States in 1800*. Ithaca, N.Y.: Cornell University Press, 1955.

The American Almanac for 1859. Vol. XXX. Boston, 1859.

Angle, Paul M., ed. *Created Equal: The Complete Lincoln-Douglas Debates of 1858*. Chicago: University of Chicago Press, 1958.

———. *Lincoln 1854–1861*. Springfield: Abraham Lincoln Association, 1933.

Arnold, Isaac N. *Reminiscences of the Illinois Bar Forty Years Ago*. Springfield, 1881.

Auchampaugh, Philip G. *James Buchanan and His Cabinet on the Eve of Secession*. Boston: J. S. Canner, 1965.

Auer, J. Jeffrey, ed. *Antislavery and Disunion: 1858–1861*. New York: Harper, 1963.

Baringer, William. *Lincoln's Rise to Power*. Boston: Little, Brown, 1937.

Barton, William E. *Lincoln and Douglas in Charleston*. Charleston, Ill.: The Charleston *Daily Courier*, 1922.

Basler, Roy P., ed. See Lincoln, Abraham. *The Collected Works of Abraham Lincoln*.

Beale, Howard K., ed. See Welles, Gideon. *The Diary of Gideon Welles*.

Becker, Carl L. *The Declaration of Independence: A Study in the History of Political Ideas*. New York: Knopf, 1960.

Berwanger, Eugene H. *The Frontier against Slavery: Western Anti-Negro Prejudice and the Slavery Extension Controversy*. Urbana: University of Illinois Press, 1967.

Beveridge, Albert J. *Abraham Lincoln*. 2 vols. Cambridge: Houghton Mifflin, 1928.

Blaine, James G. *Twenty Years of Congress*. 2 vols. Norwich, Conn., 1884–1886.

Boney, F. N. *John Letcher of Virginia: The Story of Virginia's Civil War Governor*. University, Ala.: University of Alabama Press, 1966.

Brown, William Garrott. *Stephen A. Douglas*. Cambridge: Houghton Mifflin, 1902.

Browning, Orville H. *The Diary of Orville Hickman Browning*. Edited with introduction and notes by T. C. Pease and James G. Randall. 2 vols. Springfield: Illinois State Historical Library, 1925–1933.

Buchanan, James. *The Works of James Buchanan*. Edited by John Bassett Moore. 12 vols. Philadelphia: Lippincott, 1908–1911.

Bullard, F. L., ed. *The Diary of a Public Man*. Chicago: Abraham Lincoln Book Shop, 1945.

Burton, William L. *Descriptive Bibliography of Civil War Manuscripts in Illinois*. Evanston, Ill. Northwestern University Press, 1966.

Calhoun, John C. *The Works of John C. Calhoun*. Edited by Richard K. Cralle. 6 vols. New York, 1888.

Capers, Gerald M. *John C. Calhoun—Opportunist*. Gainsville: University of Florida Press, 1960.

———. *Stephen A. Douglas: Defender of the Union*. Boston: Little, Brown, 1959.

Carpenter, Jesse T. *The South as a Conscious Minority, 1789–1861: A Study in Political Thought*. Gloucester, Mass.: Peter Smith, 1963.

Carr, Clark E. *Stephen A. Douglas*. Chicago: McClurg, 1909.

Chambers, William N. *Old Bullion Benton.* Boston: Little, Brown, 1956.

Cleveland, Henry. *Alexander H. Stephens.* Philadelphia, 1866.

Cole, Arthur C. *The Era of the Civil War, 1848–1870.* Springfield: Illinois Centennial Commission, 1919.

———. *The Irrepressible Conflict, 1850–1865.* New York: Macmillan, 1934.

———. *Lincoln's "House Divided" Speech.* Chicago: University of Chicago Press, 1923.

Commager, Henry Steele, ed. *Documents of American History.* 7th ed. New York: Appleton, Century, Crofts, 1963.

Cralle, Richard K., ed. See Calhoun, John C. *The Works of John C. Calhoun.*

Craven, Avery. *The Growth of Southern Nationalism, 1848–1861.* Baton Rouge: Louisiana State University Press, 1953.

Crenshaw, Ollinger. *The Slave States in the Presidential Election of 1860.* Johns Hopkins University Studies in Historical and Political Science. Series 63, no. 3. Baltimore: Johns Hopkins University Press, 1945.

Crocker, Lionel G. *An Analysis of Lincoln and Douglas as Public Speakers and Debaters.* Springfield: Charles C Thomas, 1968.

Croly, Herbert. *The Promise of American Life.* Edited by Arthur M. Schlesinger, Jr. Cambridge: Harvard University Press, 1965.

Current, Richard N. *John C. Calhoun.* New York: Washington Square Press, 1963.

Curtis, George Ticknor. *The Just Supremacy of Congress Over the Territories.* Boston, 1859.

———. *The Life of James Buchanan.* 2 vols. New York, 1883.

Cutts, J. Madison. *A Brief Treatise upon Constitutional and Party Questions and the History of Political Parties.* New York, 1866.

Davis, Jefferson. *Jefferson Davis, Constitutionalist: His Letters, Papers, and Speeches.* Edited by Dunbar Rowland. 10 vols. Jackson: Mississippi Department of Archives and History, 1923.

———. *Jefferson Davis: Private Letters, 1823–1889.* Edited by Hudson Strode. New York: Harcourt, Brace & World, 1966.

———. *The Rise and Fall of the Confederate Government.* 2 vols. New York, 1881.

Dickinson, Daniel S. *Speech at Cooper Institute, New York, July 18, 1860.* Washington, D.C., 1860.

Dodd, William E. *Statesmen of the Old South.* New York: Macmillan, 1921.

Donald, David H. *Lincoln's Herndon.* New York: Knopf, 1948.

Douglas, Stephen A. *An American Continental Commercial Union or Alliance.* Edited by J. Madison Cutts. Washington, D.C., 1889.

———. *The Letters of Stephen A. Douglas.* Edited by Robert W. Johannsen. Urbana: University of Illinois Press, 1961.

Dubose, John W. *The Life and Times of William Lowndes Yancey.* 2 vols. New York: Peter Smith, 1942.

Dumond, Dwight Lowell, ed. *Southern Editorials on Secession.* New York: Century, 1931.

Fahrney, Ralph R. *Horace Greeley and the Tribune in the Civil War.* Cedar Rapids, Iowa: Torch Press, 1936.

Fehrenbacher, Don E. *Prelude to Greatness: Lincoln in the 1850's.* Stanford: Stanford University Press, 1962.

Filler, Louis. *The Crusade against Slavery, 1830–1860.* New York: Harper, 1960.

Fite, Emerson D. *The Presidential Campaign of 1860.* New York: Macmillan, 1911.

Flint, Henry Martyn. *Life of Stephen A. Douglas.* New York, 1860.

Foner, Eric. *Free Soil, Free Labor, Free Men: The Ideology of the Republican Party before the Civil War.* New York: Oxford University Press, 1970.

Foote, Henry S. *War of the Rebellion or Scylla and Charybdis.* New York, 1866.

Ford, Thomas. *A History of Illinois.* Chicago, 1854.

Gardner, William. *Life of Stephen A. Douglas.* Boston: Roxburgh, 1905.

Gates, Paul W. *Fifty Million Acres: Conflicts over Kansas Land Policy, 1854–1890.* Ithaca, N.Y.: Cornell University Press, 1954.

Geyl, Pieter. *Debates with Historians.* Rev. ed. New York: Meridian Books, 1958.

Graebner, Norman A., ed. *Politics and the Crises of 1860.* Urbana: University of Illinois Press, 1961.

Greeley, Horace. *Recollections of a Busy Life.* New York, 1868.

———, and Cleveland, John F., eds. *A Political Text-Book for 1860.* New York, 1860.

Halstead, Murat. *Three against Lincoln: Murat Halstead Reports the Caucuses of 1860.* Edited by William B. Hesseltine. Baton Rouge: Louisiana State University Press, 1960.

Hamilton, Holman. *Prologue to Conflict: The Crisis and Compromise of 1850.* Lexington: University of Kentucky Press, 1964.

Harmon, George D. *Aspects of Slavery and Expansion, 1848–1860.* Lehigh University Publications. Vol. 3, no. 7. Bethlehem, Pa. Lehigh University, 1929.

Heckman, Richard Allen. *Lincoln vs Douglas: The Great Debates Campaign*. Washington, D.C.: Public Affairs Press, 1967.

Hendrickson, James E. *Joe Lane of Oregon: Machine Politics and the Sectional Crisis, 1849–1861*. New Haven: Yale University Press, 1967.

Herndon, William H., and Weik, Jesse W. *Life of Lincoln*. Introduction and notes by Paul M. Angle. New York: World, 1949.

Hesseltine, William B. *Sections and Politics: Selected Essays by William B. Hesseltine*. Edited by Richard N. Current. Madison: State Historical Society of Wisconsin, 1968.

Hofstadter, Richard. *The American Political Tradition*. New York: Knopf, 1948.

Hopkins, Vincent C. *Dred Scott's Case*. New York: McMullen, 1951.

Horner, Harlan H. *Lincoln and Greeley*. Urbana: University of Illinois Press, 1953.

Howland, Louis. *Stephen A. Douglas*. New York: Scribner, 1920.

Hubbart, Henry Clyde. *The Older Middle West, 1840–1880*. New York: Appleton-Century, 1935.

Isely, J. A. *Horace Greeley and the Republican Party, 1853–1861*. Princeton: Princeton University Press, 1947.

Jaffa, Harry V. *Crisis of the House Divided: An Interpretation of the Issues in the Lincoln-Douglas Debates*. Garden City, N.Y.: Doubleday, 1959.

———. *Equality and Liberty: Theory and Practice in American Politics*. New York: Oxford University Press, 1965.

——— and Johannsen, Robert W., eds. *In the Name of the People: Speeches and Writings of Lincoln and Douglas in the Ohio Campaign of 1859*. Columbus: Ohio State University Press, 1959.

Johannsen, Robert W., ed. See Douglas, Stephen A. *The Letters of Stephen A. Douglas*.

———, ed. *The Lincoln-Douglas Debates of 1858*. New York: Oxford University Press, 1965.

Johnson, Allen, ed. *Readings in American Constitutional History*. New York: Houghton Mifflin, 1912.

———. *Stephen A. Douglas: A Study in American Politics*. New York: Macmillan, 1908.

Jones, James P. *"Black Jack": John A. Logan and Southern Illinois in the Civil War*. Tallahassee: Florida State University Press, 1967.

Jones, W. T., ed. *Machiavelli to Bentham*. Vol. 2 of Masters of Political *Thought*. Edited by Edward McChesney Sait. 3 vols. London: Harrap, 1942–1959.

Julian, George W. *Political Recollections, 1840–1872*. Chicago, 1884.

Katz, Irving. *August Belmont: A Political Biography*. New York: Columbia University Press, 1968.

Keleher, William A. *Turmoil in New Mexico, 1846–1868*. Santa Fe: Rydal, 1952.

Kirwan, Albert D. *John J. Crittenden: The Struggle for The Union*. Lexington: University of Kentucky Press, 1962.

Klein, Philip Shriver. *President James Buchanan*. University Park, Pa.: Pennsylvania State University Press, 1962.

Knoles, George Harmon, ed. *The Crisis of the Union, 1860–1861*. Baton Rouge: Louisiana State University Press, 1965.

Krug, Mark M. *Lyman Trumbull: Conservative Radical*. New York: A. S. Barnes, 1965.

Lincoln, Abraham. *The Collected Works of Abraham Lincoln*. Edited by Roy P. Basler. 8 vols. and Index. New Brunswick, N.J.: Rutgers University Press, 1953.

———. *Complete Works of Abraham Lincoln*. Edited by John G. Nicolay and John Hay. 12 vols. New York, 1894.

———. *The Lincoln Papers*. Edited by David C. Mearns. 2 vols. New York: Doubleday, 1948.

Linder, Usher F. *The Early Bench and Bar of Illinois*. Chicago, 1879.

Locke, John. *Second Treatise on Civil Government*. In *John Locke on Politics and Education*. Edited by Howard R. Penniman. New York: Van Nostrand, 1947.

Luthin, Reinhard H. *The First Lincoln Campaign*. Cambridge: Harvard University Press, 1944.

Magdol, Edward. *Owen Lovejoy: Abolitionist in Congress*. New Brunswick, N.J.: Rutgers University Press, 1967.

Malin, James C. *The Nebraska Question, 1852–1854*. Lawrence, Kans.: Malin, 1953.

Masters, Edgar Lee. *Children of the Market Place*. New York: Macmillan, 1922.

McConnel, George Murray. *Presidential Campaigns*. New York: Rand, 1908.

McLaughlin, Andrew C. *Lewis Cass*. New York, 1891.

Mearns, David C., ed. See Lincoln, Abraham. *The Lincoln Papers*.

Meigs, William M. *The Life of John Caldwell Calhoun*. New York: Neale, 1917.

Merk, Frederick. *Manifest Destiny and Mission in American History*. New York: Knopf, 1963.

Milton, George Fort. *The Eve of Conflict: Stephen A. Douglas and the Needless War*. Boston: Houghton Mifflin, 1934.

Moore, Glover. *The Missouri Controversy, 1819–1821.* Lexington: University of Kentucky Press, 1953.

Moore, John Bassett, ed. See Buchanan, James. *The Works of James Buchanan.*

Morison, Samuel Eliot. *The Oxford History of the American People.* New York: Oxford University Press, 1965.

Morrison, Chaplain W. *Democratic Politics and Sectionalism: The Wilmot Proviso Controversy.* Chapel Hill: University of North Carolina Press, 1967.

Nagel, Paul C. *One Nation Indivisible: The Union in American Thought, 1776–1861.* New York: Oxford University Press, 1964.

Nevins, Allan. *The Emergence of Lincoln.* 2 vols. New York: Scribner, 1950.

———. *Ordeal of the Union.* 2 vols. New York: Scribner, 1947.

———. *The War for the Union.* 2 vols. New York: Scribner, 1959–1960.

Nichols, Roy F. *The Disruption of American Democracy.* New York: Free Press, 1967.

Nicolay, John G., and Hay, John. *Abraham Lincoln: A History.* 10 vols. New York, 1890.

———, eds. See Lincoln, Abraham. *Complete Works of Abraham Lincoln.*

Ogden, Rollo, ed. *Life and Letters of Edwin Lawrence Godkin.* 2 vols. New York: Macmillan, 1907.

Oldroyd, Osborn H. *Lincoln's Campaign.* Chicago, 1896.

Olmsted, Frederick Law. *The Cotton Kingdom.* Edited by Arthur M. Schlesinger. New York: Knopf, 1962.

Orth, Samuel P. *Five American Politicians.* Cleveland: Burrows, 1906.

Pease, T. C. *The Story of Illinois.* Rev. ed. Chicago: University of Chicago Press, 1950.

——— and Randall, James G., eds. See Browning, Orville H. *The Diary of Orville Hickman Browning.*

Perkins, Howard C., ed. *Northern Editorials on Secession.* 2 vols. New York: Appleton-Century, 1942.

Petersen, William F. *Lincoln-Douglas: The Weather as Destiny.* Springfield: Charles C Thomas, 1943.

Peterson, Merril D. *The Jefferson Image in the American Mind.* New York: Oxford University Press, 1960.

Phillips, Ulrich B., ed. *The Correspondence of Robert Toombs, Alexander H. Stephens, and Howell Cobb. Annual Report of the American Historical Association for 1911*, Vol. II. Washington, D.C.: Government Printing Office, 1913.

Pierce, Bessie Louise. *A History of Chicago.* 3 vols. New York: Knopf, 1940–1957.

Polk, James K. *The Diary of James K. Polk.* Edited by Milo M. Quaife. 4 vols. Chicago: McClurg, 1910.

Pressly, Thomas J. *Americans Interpret Their Civil War.* Princeton: Princeton University Press, 1954.

Pryor, Sara Agnes. *Reminiscences of Peace and War.* New York: Macmillan, 1905.

Quaife, Milo M., ed. See Polk, James K. *The Diary of James K. Polk.*

Rainwater, Percy Lee. *Mississippi: Storm Center of Secession, 1856–1861.* Baton Rouge: Claitor, 1938.

Randall, J. G. *Lincoln the Liberal Statesman.* New York: Dodd, Mead, 1947.

———. *Lincoln the President: Springfield to Gettysburg.* 2 vols. New York: Dodd, Mead, 1946.

——— and Donald, David H. *The Civil War and Reconstruction.* 2d ed. Boston: Heath, 1961.

Rawleigh, W. T., ed. *Freeport's Lincoln.* Freeport, Ill.: W. T. Rawleigh, 1930.

Ray, P. Orman. *The Repeal of the Missouri Compromise.* Cleveland: A. H. Clark, 1909.

Rhodes, James Ford. *History of the United States from the Compromise of 1850.* 8 vols. New York: Macmillan, 1907–1919.

Richardson, Eudora Ramsey. *Little Aleck: A Life of Alexander H. Stephens.* New York: Bobbs, 1932.

Richardson, James D., ed. *A Compilation of the Messages and Papers of the Presidents, 1789–1902.* 10 vols. New York: Bureau of National Literature and Art, 1904.

Rousseau, Jean Jacques. *The Social Contract.* Edited by G. D. H. Cole. London: Dent, 1913.

Rowland, Dunbar, ed. See Davis, Jefferson. *Jefferson Davis, Constitutionalist: His Letters, Papers, and Speeches.*

Russel, Robert R. *Improvement of Communication with the Pacific Coast as an Issue in American Politics, 1783–1864.* Cedar Rapids, Iowa: Torch Press, 1948.

Russell, W. H. *My Diary North and South.* Boston, 1863.

Sandburg, Carl. *Abraham Lincoln: The Prairie Years.* 2 vols. New York: Harcourt, 1926.

Schlesinger, Arthur M. *New Viewpoints in American History.* New York: Macmillan, 1922.

Schurz, Carl. *The Reminiscences of Carl Schurz.* 3 vols. Garden City, N.Y.: Doubleday, 1913.

Scrugham, Mary. *The Peaceable Americans of 1860–1861.* New York: Longmans, 1921.

Sears, L. M. *John Slidell.* Durham, N.C.: Duke University Press, 1925.

Seifert, Shirley. *The Senator's Lady.* Philadelphia: Lippincott, 1967.

Sheahan, James W. *The Life of Stephen A. Douglas.* New York, 1860.

Sherman, John. *Recollections of Forty Years in the House, Senate, and Cabinet.* 2 vols. New York, 1895.

Smith, Elbert B. *The Death of Slavery: The United States, 1837–1865.* Chicago: University of Chicago Press, 1967.

Smith, Theodore Clark. *Parties and Slavery, 1850–1859.* New York: Harper, 1906.

Spain, August O. *The Political Theory of John C. Calhoun.* New York: Bookman Associates, 1951.

Sparks, Edwin Erle, ed. *The Lincoln-Douglas Debates of 1858.* Springfield: Illinois State Historical Library, 1908.

Spring, Leverett W. *Kansas: The Prelude to the War for the Union.* Boston, 1885.

Stephens, Alexander H. *A Constitutional View of the Late War between the States.* 2 vols. Philadelphia, 1868–1870.

Stephenson, Nathaniel W. *Abraham Lincoln and the Union.* New Haven: Yale University Press, 1918.

Strode, Hudson. *Jefferson Davis: American Patriot, 1808–1861.* New York: Harcourt, Brace, 1955.

———. *Jefferson Davis: Confederate President.* New York: Harcourt, Brace, 1959.

———, ed. See Davis, Jefferson. *Jefferson Davis: Private Letters, 1823–1889.*

Taylor, Richard. *Destruction and Reconstruction.* New York, 1879.

Thayer, Eli. *A History of the Kansas Crusade.* New York, 1889.

Thompson, William Y. *Robert Toombs of Georgia.* Baton Rouge: Louisiana State University Press, 1966.

Tocqueville, Alexis de. *Democracy in America.* Edited by Phillips Bradley. 2 vols. New York: Knopf, 1963.

The Tribune Almanac and Political Register, 1859–1871. New York, 1859–1871.

Van Deusen, Glyndon G. *Horace Greeley: Nineteenth Century Crusader.* Philadelphia: University of Pennsylvania Press, 1953.

———. *William Henry Seward.* New York: Oxford University Press, 1967.

Villard, Henry. *Memoirs of Henry Villard.* 2 vols. Boston: Houghton Mifflin, 1904.

Voegeli, V. Jacque. *Free but Not Equal: The Midwest and the Negro during the Civil War.* Chicago: University of Chicago Press, 1967.

Weinberg, Albert K. *Manifest Destiny.* Baltimore: Johns Hopkins University Press, 1935.

Weiss, John. *Life and Correspondence of Theodore Parker.* 2 vols. New York, 1864.

Welles, Gideon. *The Diary of Gideon Welles.* Edited by Howard K. Beale. 3 vols. New York: Norton, 1960.

Wellman, Paul I. *The House Divides: The Age of Jackson and Lincoln from the War of 1812 to the Civil War.* New York: Doubleday, 1966.

Wheare, K. C. *Abraham Lincoln and the United States.* New York: Macmillan, 1949.

Williams, W., ed. *Appleton's New and Complete United States Guide Book for Travellers.* New York, 1854.

Willis, Henry Parker. *Stephen A. Douglas.* Philadelphia: Jacobs, 1910.

Wilson, Edmund. *Eight Essays.* New York: Doubleday, 1954.

Wiltse, Charles M. *John C. Calhoun, Nullifier, 1829–1839.* New York: Bobbs-Merrill, 1949.

———. *John C. Calhoun, Sectionalist, 1840–1850.* New York: Bobbs-Merrill, 1951.

Woodford, Frank B. *Lewis Cass: The Last Jeffersonian.* New Brunswick, N.J.: Rutgers University Press, 1950.

Zornow, William F. *Kansas: A History of the Jayhawk State.* Norman, Oklahoma: University of Oklahoma Press, 1957.

Articles

Anderson, James W. "The Real Issue: An Analysis of the Final Lincoln-Douglas Debate." *Lincoln Herald* 69 (spring 1967): 27–39.

Armstrong, W. D. "Lincoln-Douglas Debates." *Journal of the Illinois State Historical Society* 22 (January 1930): 607–614.

Auchampaugh, Philip G. "The Buchanan-Douglas Feud." *Journal of the Illinois State Historical Society* 25 (April 1932): 5–48.

Baringer, William E. "Campaign Techniques in Illinois—1860." *Transactions of the Illinois State Historical Society for 1932*, pp. 203–281.

Barnhart, John D. "The Southern Element in the Leadership of the Old Northwest." *Journal of Southern History* 1 (May 1935): 186–197.

Bauer, Marvin G. "The Influence of Lincoln's Audience on His

Speeches." *Quarterly Journal of Speech Education* 11 (June 1925): 225–229.

———. "Persuasive Methods in the Lincoln-Douglas Debates." *Quarterly Journal of Speech Education* 13 (February 1927): 29–39.

Beall, Edmond. "Recollections of the Lincoln-Douglas Debate Held in Alton, Illinois, October 15, 1858." *Journal of the Illinois State Historical Society* 5 (January 1913): 486–487.

Bean, W. G. "Anti-Jeffersonianism in the Ante-Bellum South." *North Carolina Historical Review* 12 (April 1935): 103–124.

Billington, Ray A. "The Historians of the Northwest Ordinance." *Journal of the Illinois State Historical Society* 40 (December 1947): 397–413.

Brown, William Garrott. "Lincoln's Rival." *Atlantic Monthly* 89 (February 1902): 226–236.

Clinton, J. W. "Polo [Illinois] in War Time." *Journal of the Illinois State Historical Society* 4 (July 1911): 201–211.

Cross, Jasper W. "The Civil War Comes to Egypt." *Journal of the Illinois State Historical Society* 44 (summer 1951): 160–169.

Dickerson, O. M. "Stephen A. Douglas and the Split in the Democratic Party." *Proceedings of the Mississippi Valley Historical Association* 7 (1913–1914): 196–211.

Dodd, William E. "The Fight for the Northwest." *American Historical Review* 16 (July 1911): 774–788.

Douglas, Stephen A. "The Montgomery Address of Stephen A. Douglas." Edited by David R. Barbee and Milledge L. Bonham, Jr., *Journal of Southern History* 5 (November 1939): 527–552.

Doyle, Cornelius J. "Address of Cornelius J. Doyle at Winchester, Illinois, July 5, 1930." *Journal of the Illinois State Historical Society* 23 (October 1930): 439–458.

Dunne, Edward F. "Abraham Lincoln." *Journal of the Illinois State Historical Society* 9 (April 1916): 7–22.

Ellis, Lewis E. "A History of the Chicago Delegation in Congress, 1843–1925." *Transactions of the Illinois State Historical Society for 1930*, pp. 52–149.

Evans, Joseph F. "Lincoln at Galesburg." *Journal of the Illinois State Historical Society* 8 (January 1916): 559–568.

Frisch, Morton J. "The Lincoln-Douglas Debates and History." *Lincoln Herald* 57 (Winter 1956): 17–19.

Gay, William H. "Reminiscences of Abraham Lincoln, Quincy, and the Civil War." *Journal of the Illinois State Historical Society* 7 (October 1914): 248–261.

Gertz, Elmer. "Joe Medill's War." *Lincoln Herald* 47 (December 1945): 2–12.

Greeley, Horace. "Greeley's Estimate of Lincoln." *Century Magazine* 42 (July 1891): 371–382.

Gridley, J. N. "The Husted or Jacksonville Raid." *Journal of the Illinois State Historical Society* 5 (July 1912): 207–211.

Goodspeed, Thomas Wakefield. "Lincoln and Douglas." *Journal of the Illinois State Historical Society* 26 (October 1933): 183–201.

Harper, Robert S. "New Light from a Lincoln Letter on the Story of the Publication of the Lincoln-Douglas Debates." *Ohio Historical Quarterly* 68 (April 1959): 177–187.

Heckman, Richard Allen. "Out-of-State Influences and the Lincoln-Douglas Campaign of 1858." *Journal of the Illinois State Historical Society* 59 (Spring 1966): 30–47.

Heinl, Frank J. "Newspapers and Periodicals in the Lincoln-Douglas Country, 1832." *Journal of the Illinois State Historical Society* 23 (October 1930): 371–438.

Hendrickson, James E. "The Rupture of the Democratic Party in Oregon, 1858." *Pacific Northwest Quarterly* 58 (April 1967): 65–73.

Herriott, F. I. "Senator Stephen A. Douglas and the Germans in 1854." *Transactions of the Illinois State Historical Society for 1912*, pp. 142–158.

Hodder, Frank H. "The Railroad Background of the Kansas-Nebraska Act." *Mississippi Valley Historical Review* 12 (June 1925): 3–22.

———. "Some Aspects of the English Bill for the Admission of Kansas." *Annual Report of the American Historical Association for 1906* 1: 201–210.

———. "Stephen A. Douglas." Introduction by James C. Malin. *Kansas Historical Quarterly* 8 (August 1939): 227–237.

Horner, Harlan H. "Lincoln Rebukes a Senator." *Journal of the Illinois State Historical Society* 44 (Summer 1951): 103–119.

———. "The Substance of the Lincoln-Douglas Debates." *Lincoln Herald* 63 (Summer and Fall 1961): 89–98, 139–149.

James, D. D. "The Lincoln-Douglas Debate—Charleston." *Journal of the Illinois State Historical Society* 8 (January 1916): 569–571.

Jeffrey, Kirk, Jr. "Stephen Arnold Douglas in American Historical Writing." *Journal of the Illinois State Historical Society* 61 (Autumn 1968): 248–268.

Johannsen, Robert W. "Stephen A. Douglas and the South." *Journal of Southern History* 33 (February 1967): 26–50.

———. "Stephen A. Douglas, 'Harper's Magazine,' and Popular

Sovereignty." *Mississippi Valley Historical Review* 45 (March 1959): 606–631.

———. "Stephen A. Douglas, Popular Sovereignty, and the Territories." *The Historian* 22 (August 1960): 378–395.

———. "The Douglas Democracy and the Crisis of Disunion." *Civil War History* 9 (September 1963): 229–247.

Johnson, Allen. "The Genesis of Popular Sovereignty." *Iowa Journal of History and Politics* 3 (January 1905): 3–19.

———. "Illinois in the Democratic Movement of the Century." *Journal of the Illinois State Historical Society* 11 (April 1918): 1–13.

Kimball, E. L. "Richard Yates." *Journal of the Illinois State Historical Society* 23 (April 1930): 1–83.

Kooker, Arthur R. "Abraham Lincoln: Spokesman for Democracy." *Journal of the West* 4 (April 1965): 260–271.

Krout, John. "The Maine Law in New York Politics." *New York History* 17 (July 1936): 260–272.

Luthin, Reinhard H. "The Democratic Split during Buchanan's Administration." *Pennsylvania History* 11 (January 1944): 13–35.

———. "Lincoln the Politician." *Lincoln Herald* 48 (February 1946): 2–11, 41.

Lynch, William O. "The Convergence of Lincoln and Douglas." *Transactions of the Illinois State Historical Society for 1925*, pp. 155–173.

Malin, James C. "The Motives of Stephen A. Douglas in the Organization of Nebraska Territory: A Letter Dated December 17, 1853." *Kansas Historical Quarterly* 19 (November 1951): 321–353.

Masters, Edgar Lee. "Stephen A. Douglas." *The American Mercury* 22 (January 1931): 11–23.

Matheny, James H. "A Modern Knight Errant—Edward Dickinson Baker." *Journal of the Illinois State Historical Society* 9 (April 1916): 23–42.

McConnel, George Murray. "Recollections of Stephen A. Douglas." *Transactions of the Illinois State Historical Society for 1900*, pp. 40–50.

McMahon, Edward. "Stephen A. Douglas: A Study of the Attempt to Settle the Question of Slavery in the Territories by the Application of Popular Sovereignty, 1850–1860," *Washington Historical Quarterly* 2 (April and July 1908): 209–232, 309–332.

McMurty, Gerald. "The Different Editions of the Debates of Lincoln and Douglas," *Journal of the Illinois State Historical Society* 27 (April 1934): 95–107.

Milton, George Fort. "Douglas' Place in American History." *Journal of the Illinois State Historical Society* 26 (January 1934): 323–348.

———. "Stephen A. Douglas' Efforts for Peace." *Journal of Southern History* 1 (August 1935): 261–275.

Mitgang, Herbert. "Echoes of Mr. Lincoln and Mr. Douglas." *New York Times Magazine*, February 9, 1958, pp. 17, 32, 34, 36, 39.

Nevins, Allan. "Stephen A. Douglas: His Weaknesses and His Greatness." *Journal of the Illinois State Historical Society* 42 (December 1949): 385–410.

———, and King, Willard L. "The Constitution and Declaration of Independence as Issues in the Lincoln-Douglas Debates." *Journal of the Illinois State Historical Society* 52 (Spring 1959); 7–32.

Nichols, Roy F. "A Hundred Years Later: Perspectives on the Civil War." *Journal of Southern History* 33 (May 1967): 153–162.

———. "The Kansas-Nebraska Act: A Century of Historiography." *Mississippi Valley Historical Review* 43 (September 1956): 187–212.

Pollock, Governor James. "Douglas the Loyal." Introduction by Esther Cowles Cushman. *Journal of the Illinois State Historical Society* 23 (April 1930): 163–170.

Ramsdell, Charles W. "The Natural Limits of Slavery Expansion." *Mississippi Valley Historical Review* 16 (September 1929): 151–171.

Ranck, James B. "Lewis Cass and Squatter Sovereignty." *Michigan History Magazine* 14 (Winter, 1930): 28–37.

"Reminiscences of Stephen A. Douglas," *Atlantic Monthly* 8 (August 1861): 205–213.

Richardson, William A., Jr. "Pen Pictures of the Central Part of the City of Quincy as It Was When Douglas and Lincoln Met in Debate." *Journal of the Illinois State Historical Society* 18 (July 1925): 393–406.

Roberts, Percy. "Mr. Douglas' Article on Popular Sovereignty." *De Bow's Review* 27 (December 1859): 625–647.

Russel, Robert R. "The Pacific Railway Issue in Politics Prior to the Civil War." *Mississippi Valley Historical Review* 12 (September 1925): 187–201.

———. "What Was the Compromise of 1850?" *Journal of Southern History* 22 (August 1956): 292–309.

Ryan, Daniel J. "Lincoln and Ohio." Introduction by C. B. Galbreath. *Ohio Archaeological and Historical Quarterly* 32 (January 1923): 1–281.

Sanborn, John Bell. "Some Political Aspects of Homestead Legislation." *American Historical Review* 6 (October 1900): 19–37.

Sanger, Donald B. "The Authorship of General Orders Number 29." *Transactions of the Illinois State Historical Society for 1933*, pp. 67–79.

Schafer, Joseph. "Who Elected Lincoln?" *American Historical Review* 47 (October 1941): 51–63.

Schapsmeier, Edward L., and Frederick H. "Lincoln and Douglas: Their Versions of the West," *Journal of the West* 7 (October 1968): 542–552.

Simon, John Y. "Union County in 1858 and the Lincoln-Douglas Debate." *Journal of the Illinois State Historical Society* 62 (Autumn 1969): 267–292.

Smith, Donnal V. "The Influence of the Foreign-Born of the Northwest in the Election of 1860." *Mississippi Valley Historical Review* 19 (September 1932): 192–204.

"A Southerner's Estimate of the Life and Character of Stephen A. Douglas." *National Quarterly Review* 40 (January 1880): 173–193.

Stauffer, Alvin P. "Douglas in Vermont." *Vermont History* 28 (October 1960): 256–267.

Stenberg, Richard. "An Unnoted Factor in the Buchanan-Douglas Feud." *Journal of the Illinois State Historical Society* 25 (January 1933): 271–284.

Stevens, Frank E. "Life of Stephen Arnold Douglas." *Journal of the Illinois State Historical Society* 16 (October 1923 and January 1924): 247–673.

Stevenson, Adlai. "Stephen A. Douglas." *Transactions of the Illinois State Historical Society for 1908*, pp. 48–73.

Taft, Robert. "The Appearance and Personality of Stephen A. Douglas." *Kansas Historical Quarterly* 21 (Spring 1954): 8–33.

Taylor, Hannis. "The Lincoln-Douglas Debates and Their Application to Present Problems." *North American Review* 189 (February 1909): 161–173.

Turner, Frederick Jackson. "Western State-Making in the Revolutionary Era." *American Historical Review* 1 (October 1895 and January 1896): 70–87, 251–269.

Venable, Austin L. "The Conflict between the Douglas and Yancey Forces in the Charleston Convention." *Journal of Southern History* 8 (May 1942): 226–241.

Villard, Henry. "Recollections of Lincoln." *Atlantic Monthly* 93 (February 1904): 165–174.

Vinson, Colonel John W. "Personal Reminiscences of Mr. Lincoln." *Journal of the Illinois State Historical Society* 8 (January 1916): 572–580.

Wallace, Joseph. "Stephen A. Douglas: Some Old Letters by, and Relating to, the Distinguished Statesman." *Transactions of the Illinois State Historical Society for 1901*, pp. 111–116.

Washburne, E. M. "Abraham Lincoln in Illinois." *North American Review* 141 (October and November 1885): 307–319, 454–463.

White, Horace. "Abraham Lincoln in 1854." *Transactions of the Illinois State Historical Society for 1908*, pp. 25–47.

Wright, Quincy. "Stephen A. Douglas and the Campaign of 1860." *Vermont History* 28 (October 1960): 250–255.

Yates, Richard. "Address at the Jacksonville Centennial: October 6, 1925." *Journal of the Illinois State Historical Society* 18 (October 1925): 575–635.

Zane, Charles S. "Lincoln as I Knew Him." *Journal of the Illinois State Historical Society* 14 (April 1921): 74–84.

INDEX